COLORADO

Trading Post *by Harold Von Schmidt*
depicts Bent's Fort on the Arkansas
River in southeastern Colorado, the
region's commercial hub during the
1830s and 1840s. A replica of the
original was built on the same site
and is now a living history museum.
Courtesy, The Anschutz Collection

American Historical Press
Sun Valley, California

COLORADO

AN ILLUSTRATED HISTORY OF
THE HIGHEST STATE

Thomas J. Noel and Debra B. Faulkner

© 2006 American Historical Press
All Rights Reserved
Published 2006
Printed in South Korea

Library of Congress Catalogue Card Number: 2006931593
ISBN 13: 978-1-892724-52-6
ISBN 10: 1-892724-52-9
Bibliography: p. 386
Includes Index

CONTENTS

ACKNOWLEDGMENTS

Many archivists, librarians, colleagues, students, friends, family and other scholars helped us with this book. Thanks to everyone, including those not mentioned here. A tip of the hat to the Denver Public Library's Western History Department, especially Phil Panum, Bruce Hanson, Kay Wisnia, Coi Drummond Gehrig, Joan Harms, John Irwin, James Jeffery, Colleen Nunn, Janice Prater, Trina Purcell, Ellen Zazzarino and Jim Kroll.

At the Colorado Historical Society Library, we are indebted to Rebecca Lintz, Barbara Dey, Debra Neiswonger and Ruba Sadi as well as Historical Society staff Thomas Carr, Steve Grinstead, Ben Fogelberg, Moya Hansen, Modupe Labode, Eric Paddock, Keith Schrum and David Wetzel. At the Auraria Library archives Frank Tapp and Mike Gryglewicz assisted us. Joanne West Dodds of the Pueblo Library District has been of help on this and other related projects, as have Terry Ketelsen and his staff at the Colorado State Archives.

The Museum of Western Colorado in Grand Junction, especially Judy Prosser and David Bailey, shared information and materials.

Darlene Dueck, curator of the Anschutz Collection, the finest Western U.S. art collection in private hands, not only facilitated use of those priceless images here but also gave us a personal tour of the treasures in that collection.

Our colleagues, students and former students at the University of Colorado at Denver have also contributed, especially history chair Myra Rich, Owen Chariton, Bill Convery, Mike Ducey, Jay Fell, Mark Foster, Marcia Goldstein, Rebecca and Geoff Hunt, Paul Malkoski, Kara Miyagishima, Judy Morley, Jim Walsh, Jim Whiteside, and Amy Zimmer. At American Historical Press, we appreciate the assistance of Carolyn Martin.

Thanks to the individuals and organizations that supported this project and added their own stories to the final chapter of this book. We apologize for the many people, places and things not included.

Lastly we would like to thank our patient, neglected spouses, James Faulkner and Vi Noel, and pets, Tootsie the dog and Max the cat.

Thomas J. Noel and Debra B. Faulkner

Opposite page top
Utes retreated from the advancing White railroad culture, only to have the Denver & Rio Grande build this depot at Ignacio on the Southern Ute Reservation as shown in this 1900 painting, Ignacio Train Depot, *by Oscar E. Berninghaus. Courtesy, The Anschutz Collection*

Opposite page bottom
Frederic Remington captured Rocky Mountain cowboy life in art, such as this 1904 painting, A Cold Morning on the Range. *Courtesy, The Anschutz Collection*

Like many Colorado communities returning to their urban cores, Fort Collins has restored its original Old Town, shown her circa 1940s, as a pedestrian-friendly historic district and retail area. Courtesy, Tom Noel Collection

9

1

COLORFUL COLORADO AND ITS PALEO INDIANS

Red rocks, like these at Colorado National Monument in the Colorado River Valley near Grand Junction, gave the state its name. Photo by Tom Noel

The history of Colorado reflects people's changing relationship to the land and their ever-evolving creative adaptations. From the earliest hunter-foragers 12,000 years ago through the increasingly urbanized cultures of the twenty-first century, Colorado's physical environment has shaped its inhabitants and their lifestyles as surely as they have shaped the land.

Iron-rich stones and soils throughout much of the state inspired the Spanish to give Colorado its name, a Spanish word meaning "reddish." Francisco Vásquez de Coronado on his 1540 expedition gave that name to its major river. Three centuries later, the state that had been born around the Colorado River's headwaters took the same name.

A roughly rectangular state in the central western U.S., Colorado is largely defined by a dry, high-altitude climate. Its topographic features are oversized, vast, towering and extreme. Besides saddling North America's highest mountain ranges, the state encompasses a wide variety of other eco-regions—from short grass prairie to southwestern desert, from dusty canyon lands to verdant mountain valleys.

Nearly two-fifths of Colorado—the eastern portion—is covered by high plains. The land looks flat, but actually slopes gently upwards toward the Rocky Mountains, rising from around 3,300 feet above sea level at the Kansas border to the mile-high elevation of today's Front Range cities. Prairies once occupied by great numbers of bison, antelope, deer and prairie dogs have become grazing lands for cattle, sheep and other livestock. Prairie grasses have been plowed under to plant fields of alfalfa, corn, hay, sunflowers and wheat.

RIVERS

Majestic mountains comprise the most dramatic and well-known two-fifths of Colorado's geography. Along their spine, the Continental Divide directs run-off in opposite directions, spawning five major river systems. The North Platte, South Platte, Rio Grande and Arkansas flow eastward toward the Atlantic Ocean; the Colorado River runs west to the Pacific.

Especially precious because of its scarcity in Colorado, water has always determined patterns of

Colorado rivers flow out of the mountains through steep, rocky canyons, such as this spectacular stretch of Big Thompson River between Estes Park and Loveland. Courtesy, Tom Noel Collection

Opposite page below
The Rio Grande flows from its headwaters in the San Juan Mountains through Colorado's San Luis Valley, where Hispanics established the state's first permanent towns during the 1850s. Photo by Tom Noel

Buffalo thrived on the plains and in the mountain parks of Colorado as depicted in this painting, The Gathering of the Herds, 1866, by William Jacob Hays. Courtesy, The Anschutz Collection

migration and settlement. Nomadic hunters pursued the animals that followed the streams. Waterways became pathways through the wilderness for Indians, explorers and trappers. Creeks washed traces of gold from the mountainsides, and hopeful prospectors followed the streams back up into the mountains, looking for mineral mother lodes. As increasingly complex irrigation systems diverted water to where it was needed, farming and ranching expanded into what explorer Major Stephen H. Long labeled in 1820 "The Great American Desert." Long concluded that the lack of water resources made the land unfit for farming. Boosters later repackaged "The Great American Desert" as the "Garden of Eden" to attract settlers. Yet today's dead and dying towns, along with the struggling farmers and ranchers of eastern Colorado, suggest that Long was not entirely wrong.

Left
Sunflowers have become a major crop cultivated on Colorado's eastern plains. Photo by Tom Noel

THE FOURTEENERS

Of the fifty-four Colorado mountains measuring 14,000 feet or higher, Pikes Peak is the best known, having given its name to the gold rush that brought 100,000 fortune seekers to an isolated, sparsely populated area. Pikes Peak is America's most famous mountain and easy to identify, a striking sentinel overlooking the eastern plains.

Native Americans probably climbed Pikes Peak before EuroAmericans came to Colorado, but the first recorded ascent was by Dr. Edwin James, a member of the Long expedition, who ascended the peak with some companions in 1820.

Longs Peak, the second most famous Colorado peak, was first scaled in 1868 by a party that included William N. Byers, the founding editor of the *Rocky Mountain News*, and Major John Wesley Powell, the illustrious, one-armed explorer. The last Fourteener to be climbed was Crestone Peak, which was conquered by Albert R. Ellingwood and Eleanor S. Davis in 1916.

The highest Fourteener is Mount Elbert, at 14,433 feet, and the lowest is Sunshine, at 14,001. Mount Massive is more eyecatching than neighboring Mount Elbert, inspiring its fans to contemplate construction of a thirteen foot rock pile on top to make it the highest peak.

Colorado's mountains have "grown" and "shrunk" over the years with measurements and re-measurements. In recent years Grizzly Peak was demoted from Fourteener status. Mount Ellingwood, which some consider a Fourteener, is officially considered a part of Mount Blanca. Many mountains come close to 14,000 feet, and more than 600 Colorado peaks soar over 13,000 feet. To the chagrin of Coloradans, one peak in California is higher than Mt. Elbert. That is 14,495-foot Mount Whitney, which lost its title as the nation's highest when Alaska, with 20,300-foot Mount McKinley, became the fiftieth state.

As the Highest State, Colorado has 14,000-foot high mountains such as the San Juan Range shown here, that catch clouds and wring out moisture, giving birth to the Arkansas, Colorado, Platte and Rio Grande rivers. Photo by Tom Noel

The eastern third of Colorado is relatively flat and treeless. On that high, dry plain, early settlers often built sod houses, such as this one. Courtesy, Colorado Historical Society

THE HIGHEST STATE

Colorado's mean elevation is 6,800 feet above sea level, legitimizing its claim as the "Highest State." That average altitude is boosted considerably by its five major mountain ranges.

The rugged mountains and their severe weather have always complicated travel and settlement. Yet the Rockies have consistently tempted the adventurous with treasures and dared them to take risks on the chance of big payoffs. Ancient hunters sought warm and durable bighorn sheep hides, trappers came for furs and miners sought out metals.

The eighth largest state, Colorado measures 276 miles north to south and 387 miles east to west. The state's 104,247 square miles form an imperfect rectangle. This is due to the curvature of the earth's surface and several boundary surveying errors. Locals boast that Colorado would be the larg-est state in addition to being the highest state, if only it could be flattened out.

The plateau, which makes up the western part of the state, is outlined by deeply carved canyons, flat-topped mesas and unusual rock formations, fashioned by eons of wind and water erosion. Tucked beneath protective arches etched into canyon walls, some of the earliest architecture in North America survives at Mesa Verde. Colorado's Western Slope has long been a place of mysteries and discoveries, from dinosaur fossils to fossil fuels.

San Luis Valley in the south, framed by the Sangre de Cristo peaks on the east and the San Juans on the west, is the largest of Colorado's mountain parks. This high, dry valley's huge underground aquifer feeds shallow lakes, wetlands, artesian wells and the headwaters of the Rio Grande River. Spanish place names still reflect the Mexican colonists who settled here a generation before Euro-American gold seekers arrived.

Colorado's "Front Range," a piedmont running parallel to the mountains and strategically located where the eastern foothills meet the plains, has been a natural north-south corridor for as long as people have inhabited the landscape. The relatively

Above
Canyons and mesas typify western Colorado as shown in Colorado Canyon *painted by Samuel Colman. (1870/after) Courtesy, The Anschutz Colletion*

Below
Native Americans, such as these Ute snake dancers, camped in the green, sheltered river and creek bottoms that also attracted White settlers. Courtesy, Colorado Historical Society

benign weather of tree-shaded Front Range creek and river valleys attracted Native Americans, who camped there in winter. Later, White settlers sought out the same grassy, tree-shaded, well-watered valleys to build trading posts, towns and eventually the largest urban areas of the state.

PALEO-INDIANS

The first people to venture into this formidable landscape moved with the seasons and the game. They wintered along the Front Range, hunted during spring on the high plains, then followed the game to the cooler high country in late summer and autumn.

Paleo-Indian camps were the original mobile home parks. Just as the flora and fauna changed with the seasons, so did the habitations of the people dependent upon them. Winters might be spent in rock shelters or cottonwood groves along the Front Range streams, where fresh water was always available and the weather was generally less extreme than in the mountains or on the high plains. In early spring the natives set out for the high plains, where plant shoots and root foods were abundant. Waterfowl and small game—as well as bison, elk, deer and antelope—were all drawn to the plains during the spring and early summer. Later in summer human migration followed waterways up to the mountain valleys to hunt bighorn sheep, deer, elk and buffalo.

At autumn's first chill, preparations began for winter. Wild game was cut into strips, then smoked, dried, jerked or pounded into pemmican. Bones were split and the nutritious marrow removed. Later, fragments could be boiled and the fat skimmed for bone grease. Packed into tightly woven baskets lined with pitch or hide containers, the food supplies were transported down to the winter camp, and the cycle began all over again.

To kill game, the Indians fashioned sharp spear points and knives by painstakingly flaking away chips of stone. Pursuing, killing and butchering the hulking beasts with such simple tools was dangerous and difficult.

Projectile points of these peripatetic peoples have been uncovered at hundreds of sites around Colorado. They have been found amid bones of

Big Horn Sheep, Colorado's state mammal, were admired by the Utes for their dexterity in negotiating the toughest mountain terrain. Courtesy, Tom Noel Collection

Elk, which once populated the plains as well as the high country, were hunted by Indians and remain a favorite target for modern outdoorsmen. Courtesy, Tom Noel Collection

long-extinct bison and mammoths, proving that humans roamed this landscape more than 12,000 years ago.

FOLSOM PEOPLE

In the 1920s Black cowboy George McJunkin rode the range near Folsom, New Mexico, a few miles south of the Colorado border, keeping one eye open for stray cattle and the other for bones. Although uneducated, he was a great bone collector. When he saw giant skeletons protruding from the washed-out wall of an arroyo one day, he quickly dismounted and started digging. McJunkin collected many of these bones, which he stored back at the ranch bunkhouse. Although he was always talking about these oversized bones no one paid much attention until 1925. That year, Dr. Jesse Figgins, director of the Denver Museum of Natural History, paid a visit along with a team of archaeologists. They marveled at McJunkin's discovery, pronouncing the bones remains of giant, extinct bison: *Bison antiquus figginsi*.

Teams from the Denver Museum of Natural History spent the next three summers excavating the Folsom site. They recovered numerous bison bones. More importantly, they discovered among the bones nineteen hand-carved projectile points. Delicate fluting on both sides distinguished these as the now-famous Folsom points. Before this discovery, scholars thought that the human race, *Homo sapiens*, had been in the New World for only a few thousand years. Folsom points, dated at around 11,000 to 9,000 B.C., proved that human beings had occupied Colorado and the American Southwest for at least 11,000 years.

Archaeological analysis revealed that these Paleo-Indians ingeniously leveraged the terrain to their advantage. A river of bones in an ancient arroyo at the Olsen-Chubbuck bison kill site in the Arkansas River valley represents the "surround and drive" method of hunting that stampeded entire herds of bison off high cliffs into narrow, steep-sided canyons where they died of injuries and suffocation, deeply piled one on top of another. The remains represent nearly 200 animals, including bulls, cows and calves.

Distinctively fluted Folsom points found amid the skeletons of Bison antiquus figginsi *during the 1920s revealed that* Homo sapiens *had occupied Colorado some 12,000 years ago. Courtesy, Denver Museum of Nature and Science*

Even a large group of people could butcher and cook only part of the animals before the carcasses began to rot and the stench became unbearable. At the Olsen-Chubbuck site, bones reveal that about 74 percent of the animals had been heavily butchered, and another 16 percent lightly butchered. Some meat was preserved as pemmican—dried and mixed with marrowfat, tallow and wild berries—and transported by dog-drawn *travois* as the group moved on.

Other Paleo-Indian game drive sites in the mountain parklands and at high altitudes around the Continental Divide include the remnants of long, converging walls used to funnel panicked game into basins, where they could be more easily trapped and slaughtered. Rock cairns and hunting blinds were strategically constructed throughout the drive systems. Thus, even the earliest Coloradans employed the topography and natural materials in their struggle for survival.

The Roberts Buffalo Jump site is on the north fork of the Cache la Poudre River, twenty-five miles northwest of Fort Collins. The Roberts family and several archaeologists have found hundreds of buffalo bones in the riverbed and tools suggesting that various tribes used this site over thousands of years. The natives drove bison herds over this sixty-foot high cliff to their deaths and harvested the meet along the river bank at one of Colorado's best known prehistoric kill sites. Photo by Tom Noel

Native American rock art, like these Ute petroglyphs near Dove Creek in Mesa County, have long intrigued modern Coloradans. This lady is studying the bear claws typical of Ute artists. Courtesy, Tom Noel Collection

The Paleo-Indian culture evolved into what archaeologists call the Archaic Period, from roughly 5800 B.C. to A.D. 150. During this period temporary shelters, like small *tipis* and *wickiups*, were replaced at some annual campsites by semi-permanent pit houses with food storage cists beneath the floors and outdoor work areas. Bows and arrows represented a tremendous technological leap. Using artifact and rock art evidence, archaeologists place their Colorado introduction in the period from A.D. 100–400. Not only were bows and arrows lightweight and easily portable, but they also vastly improved speed, strength and accuracy of hunters.

The inner spiritual life of prehistoric peoples centered on "vision quests." The personal pilgrimage followed prescribed paths to higher spiritual life. Supplicants sought healing powers, prowess as warriors, success in personal endeavors or communication with guardian spirits. At ritual stops along the route, prayers were chanted, offerings were made, pipes were smoked and meditations undertaken. Petroglyphs and pictographs found at sacred places showed the animals and the rain for which Indians prayed. Rock outcroppings on the tops of mountains were natural lightning rods and places of primordial energy transmission between the earth and

Wickiups were tipi-shaped brush shelters made with juniper, pinon or lodgepole pine and covered with animal hides. They provided shelter for the Utes, and probably prehistoric people like the Folsom. Courtesy, Tom Noel Collection

the heavens. The Old Man Mountain site outside Estes Park is believed to have been a sacred vision quest site for at least 3,000 years.

With increased cultural stability and more reliable food sources came corresponding population increases throughout prehistoric societies. Families and crops grew together. As fewer community members were devoted to full-time food acquisition, creativity and invention also thrived.

Late prehistoric sites are found throughout Colorado. Farmers plowing fields, developers constructing residential subdivisions and shopping malls, and road builders all turn up evidence of ancient habitation. Prior to the erection of Denver International Airport in the 1990s, an archaeological survey team, part of a legally mandated environmental impact study, identified the Monaghan Camp—eight hearths, spear points, stone implements and plant remains dating to about 3000 B.C.—on a low knoll between the present-day Concourse A and Concourse B.

2

MESA VERDE

Mesa Verde National Park provides scenic insight into the lives of the early Coloradans who lived there. Of the many cliff dwellings, Cliff Palace is the largest. Photo by Tom Noel.

The first Coloradans remain elusive, but thanks to some remarkable Colorado women, the world does know about the prehistoric Indians who built cliff dwellings in what is now Mesa Verde National Park. Those preservation-minded women and many others became acquainted with Mesa Verde through the work of pioneer photographer William Henry Jackson. He toured Colorado with the Hayden Survey in 1874, when a prospector led him to the ruins. Jackson exhibited his photographs of the abandoned cliff dwellings at the 1876 Philadelphia and 1893 Chicago World's Fairs.

Mesa Verde was also well known to the Wetherill family who grazed cattle there. While rounding up stray cattle in 1888, Richard Wetherill discovered Cliff Palace. The Wetherills, besieged by scholars and tourists, led expeditions to the haunted canyons and mesa tops. Tourists looked for the most macabre mummies as well as the best preserved baskets and pots to take home as trophies. The Wetherills sold their own Mesa Verde collection in 1889 for $3,000 to the Colorado Historical Society, where it is prominently exhibited to this day.

When the Swedish archaeologist Gustaf Nordenskiöld loaded up a Denver & Rio Grande boxcar in Durango with prized artifacts bound for Scandinavia, even nonchalant westerners began to scratch their heads. Fortunately, some farsighted ladies realized that Mesa Verde would soon be a thoroughly looted shambles unless it received protection.

Virginia McClurg had fallen in love with the mysterious ruins when she first visited as a *New York Graphic* reporter. Concerned by vandalism and looting, McClurg made preserving Mesa Verde her lifelong crusade. She lectured and circulated petitions for the protection of the area and its artifacts. In 1897 she convinced the Colorado Federation of Women's Clubs to join her Cliff Dwellings Association crusade.

Although some men scoffed, women's clubs were a powerful force for reform at the turn of the last century. They had been active in making Colorado the first state in the nation where men voted to give women equal suffrage. After getting the vote in 1893, the ladies of Colorado used it to champion progressive causes such as national parks.

Seeing archaeological treasures from Mesa Verde placed on the train at this station in Durango to be shipped to Scandinavia alerted Coloradans to the need to preserve what remained of the ancient Indian cities. Photo by Tom Noel

Thousands of clubwomen joined McClurg in writing to representatives, senators and presidents—and to their wives. The ladies finally found attentive men in Colorado Congressman John F. Shafroth, Colorado U.S. Senator Thomas M. Patterson and President Theodore Roosevelt. In 1906 Mesa Verde was designated a national park, the first such park to focus primarily on preserving the artifacts of Native Americans.

While Virginia McClurg had argued that Mesa Verde should be made a local park controlled by her Cliff Dwellings Association, her chief assistant in the women's club campaign, Lucy Peabody, maintained that federal designation as a national park was the best way to preserve the ruins. McClurg split with Peabody after losing this debate.

As a rival attraction, McClurg spearheaded construction of replica cliff dwellings in a natural red sandstone bluff at Manitou Springs. She decorated her newly fabricated ruins with materials from Mesa Verde and elsewhere. While Mesa Verde National Park lay in a remote site unreachable by any rail line, the new cliff dwellings at Manitou were conveniently located on the Denver & Rio Grande railroad, just a few miles west of Colorado Springs.

The Manitou Cliff Dwellings opened in 1907 and have been operating ever since. Next to the dwellings, a Pueblo Revival structure houses a four-story gift shop, snack bar and exhibits. Employees include Native Americans who dance, make pottery and beadwork, talk with tourists and pose for photos.

Women persuaded the federal government not only to create Mesa Verde National Park in 1906, but also to pass the National Antiquities Act that same year. This law targeted looters pilfering artifacts from Mesa Verde and other Native American ruins throughout the United States. The Antiquities Act made it a federal crime to remove or destroy prehistoric or historic buildings or objects on federally owned land.

International attention came to Mesa Verde in 1978 when the United Nations Educational, Scientific and Cultural Organization (UNESCO) designated the park as the first World Heritage Site in the United States. People from around the world were astonished at the Mesa Verde ruins. There, a culture without written language, without the wheel, without metallurgy or even horses, had built elaborate stone cities.

Manitou Cliff Dwellings, constructed at Manitou Springs between 1904 and 1906, provided tourists with a more accessible site than the real thing at Mesa Verde. Courtesy, Tom Noel Collection

The Federation of Colorado Women's Clubs, led by Virginia McClurg and Lucy Peabody, spearheaded the campaign to designate Mesa Verde, a much looted and vandalized site, a National Park. Courtesy, Tom Noel Collection

THE FIRST MESA VERDEANS

The cities were built by a people who had been long known as the "Anasazi," a Hopi word meaning "ancient ones" or "ancient enemies." In recent years, the term has been replaced by Ancient Puebloan or Proto-Puebloan to avoid the negative "enemy" connotations sometimes associated with Anasazi. This was done in deference to, and after consultation with, modern-day Puebloans thought to have descended from Mesa Verdeans.

Regardless of their name, the first inhabitants of Mesa Verde initially settled there around A.D. 1. Prior to that time, these ancient people had lived temporarily in caves or rock shelters among the mesas of Colorado's southwestern desert canyons. Then they began experimenting with horticulture, probably borrowing seeds, ideas and methods from bands they

Jesse Fewkes began archeological excavation and restoration at Mesa Verde two years after President Theodore Roosevelt made it a national park in 1906. Courtesy, Denver Public Library

encountered who had connections to Mexico, which excelled at corn cultivation. The Colorado mesa tops were fertile and the rainfall usually sufficient. But farming required putting down roots in order to plant, to water, to cultivate, and to protect and harvest the crops. So Ancient Puebloans settled down in substantial pithouses built near their cornfields. They dug excavations about three feet deep and added wooden walls that rose another three to five feet above ground. They used logs, sticks, brush and dirt to make flat roofs. These dwellings had indoor cooking hearths and food storage compartments. A single hole in the ceiling provided both smoke ventilation and entrance to the structure via a ladder.

BASKETMAKERS

Hot summers in the piñon-juniper zone made clothing optional, but cold and snowy winters were a different story. Strips of animal hide and fur were sewn together using bone awls and sinews to make warm robes. Sandals and cords were made of woven yucca fibers. The Ancient Puebloans raised weaving to a fine art, often producing decorated fabrics with elaborate designs and patterns in contrasting colors. They also used yucca leaves to make baskets that led archaeologists to call them the "Basketmaker" culture.

The Basketmakers also developed an *atlatl*, or spear thrower, that made it possible to kill game with longer, stronger and more accurate thrusts. Even though corn had become a staple, hunting and foraging remained a main means of food acquisition. The land supplied a variety of berries, nuts and seeds, as well as rabbit, deer and other animals. In times of famine, the Indians ate cactus fruit and even tree bark.

These Native Americans made stone *manos* and *metates* for grinding seeds, corn and piñon nuts into meal. They also made wooden planting sticks and toolkits of assorted knives and scrapers. They created pipes, whistles and flexible cradleboards made of woven reeds, and fashioned necklaces and other personal ornaments from bones, seeds and stones. In rock crevices or beneath cave floors, they buried their dead with offerings of tools and trinkets for their loved ones to use in the afterlife.

Around A.D. 450-750 the Basketmakers added beans and squash to the diet of corn, wild game, berries, nuts and plants. Their discovery and the development of ceramics also improved the lives of Ancient Puebloans. At first they made coiled pots by spiraling ropes of clay upward from a circular base around baskets. When the baskets were burned they discovered the clay hardened and transformed.

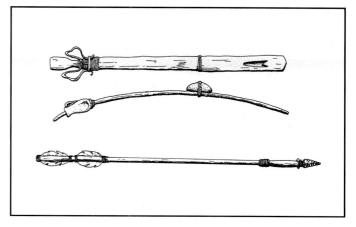

The Ancient Puebloans living in cliff dwellings and pithouses of the American southwest developed the atlatl *(spear thrower). As the most feared weapon of the day, it greatly increased the speed, accuracy and force of spears hurled at hunted animals or human enemies. Drawings by Bill Tate, Courtesy, Tom Noel Collection*

Someone got the idea to forego the baskets and simply fire the pots and ceramics were born. Later potters developed both utilitarian and decorative refinements.

Colorado's earliest water engineers, the prehistoric Indians at Mesa Verde developed water storage and diversion systems to sustain their crops during sparse and sporadic rainfall. Stone walls along slopes controlled runoff, and creeks were dammed to create reservoirs. Irrigation ditches routed water to thirsty fields. Along with irrigation technology, the natives developed elaborate dances and prayers to coax the heavens into showering them with rain.

Between A.D. 750-1100, the Ancient Puebloan villages evolved from clustered single-family pithouses into connected multi-family units called *pueblos*. Earlier crude post-and-adobe construction evolved to more permanent and substantial stone structures of two and three stories. Many such housing complexes were grouped around central plazas, with their living rooms facing circular underground chambers or *kivas*, which apparently served both ceremonial and recreational functions. As large as twelve to fourteen feet in diameter and seven or eight feet deep, *kivas* resembled the earlier pithouses in being mostly underground, with holes in the center of their flat roofs that served as both chimneys and entrances. Inside, a vertical shaft on one side provided ventilation for the fire, and dressed stone faced the curved walls. A small opening incorporated into the floor of most *kivas* connected the residents with Mother Earth.

SIPAPU

Sipapu is the Hopi word for the tiny symbolic hole in the center of a *kiva*, the round ceremonial chamber of both the ancient and modern Pueblo Indians. But, the *sipapu* is not just a hole in the ground; it is the embodiment of the Indians' creation myth. The *sipapu* represented a passageway from the underworld from whence, according to Puebloan creation myth, the first human beings emerged into the world. After Mother Earth and Father Sun mated, the Ancient Puebloans were born inside Mother Earth. Confined to dark, damp, subterranean regions, the first people prayed to Father Sun and Mother Earth for deliverance. The

Mesa Verde Pottery includes distinctive black on white vessels with geometric patterns. Courtesy, Mesa Verde Museum Association

This floor plan for Cliff Palace at Mesa Verde National Park shows the circular kivas, or ceremonial chambers. There, these Paleo-Indians may have gathered to pray for rain, a good corn crop and successful hunting. Courtesy, Tom Noel Collection

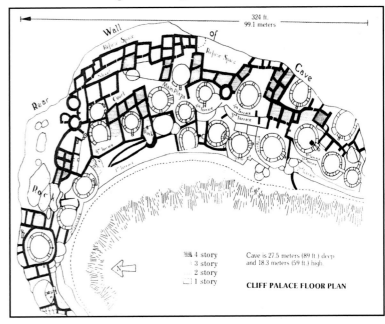

Great Spirit heard and led the good people into a better world. First they climbed to another cave where there was a little more light—the world of twilight. From twilight, the people climbed out to another cave with still more light—the world of dawn.

Sipapus were built into the dirt floors of Basketmakers' pithouses and, later, into the *kivas* of the cliff dwellers. *Kivas*, like pithouses, were covered over with dirt so that they looked like a womb in Mother Earth. When people died, their spirits could live on by going back through the *sipapu* to Mother Earth.

PREHISTORIC TRADE

Artifacts associated with the Ancient Puebloans provide evidence of widespread trading. Cotton was not grown in the vicinity of Mesa Verde, yet woven cotton cloth has been found among their possessions. Likewise, seashells and turquoise could only have been acquired through trade or distant travel.

At the same time Mesa Verde flourished, a sister civilization arose in New Mexico. There, Chaco Canyon became the likely locus of an extensive web of exchange between prehistoric cultures of the American southwest. A network of Chacoan "Great Houses" spread across southwestern North America, and the tradition's appearance in Colorado is evidenced by examples at the Escalante ruins, the Yucca House and Mud Spring ruins and the Chimney Rock Pueblo west of Pagosa Springs. The proliferation of Great Houses heralded the dawning of Mesa Verde's Great or Classic Pueblo Period, A.D. 1100-1300. Chacoan influence had a strong impact on structural design and masonry style. Ancient Puebloan architecture of this period reached its apex, mirroring the Chaco Canyon complexes on a slightly smaller scale. Multi-unit dwellings and round towers reached several stories in height.

CLIFF DWELLINGS

Ancient Puebloans gradually moved from scattered villages to high-density housing complexes and proto-cities. But the most significant and intriguing development of the Classic Pueblo Period was the migration from mesa-top pithouses and pueblos to

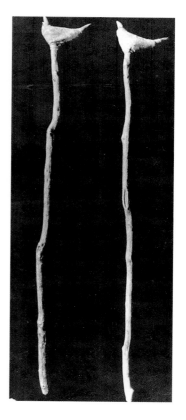

Among the artifacts found in Mesa Verde's cliff dwellings were these crutches. They suggest that this Indian culture had the time and the resources to care for the elderly and the disabled. Courtesy, Colorado Historical Society

residences sheltered in cliff-face alcoves high above the canyon floors.

Mesa Verdeans constructed an estimated 600 to 800 cliff dwellings. By the 1200s, people descended *en masse* to inhabit these architectural phenomena. Why did they choose to build on such inaccessible—albeit dramatic—real estate? The erosion-carved niches provided excellent protection from the elements, as well as year-round solar heating. Rainwater that percolated through the porous sandstone caps accumulated in "seep holes" at the backs of the alcoves. But the most obvious advantage was strategic. After centuries of living peacefully in exposed mesa-top homes without even defensive walls, the Indians now had easily-defended cliff dwellings.

Human beings could reach the cliff dwellings only by precarious descent from the mesa tops using ladders and shallow toe and hand holds etched into the cliff faces, or by arduous hikes up from the canyon floors.

The largest Mesa Verde complex, Cliff Palace, contains more than 200 rooms and twenty-three *kivas*. The multi-storied buildings rest on terraces within the sandstone alcove. T-shaped doorways lead to rooms with interior walls that still retain remnants of original plastering and paint, sometimes decorated with geometric designs.

AN ANCIENT ENIGMA

Today the windows of these stone cities stare blankly out across Mesa Verde. Within just a few decades after the completion of the last great cliff dwelling, the Ancient Puebloans disappeared from Mesa Verde. Theories have abounded about their sudden exodus ever since the ruins were first detected by Spanish explorers during the 1700s.

Most archaeologists believe that environmental exhaustion played a major role in the demise of the

Above
Dioramas, such as this one at the Mesa Verde National Park Museum, depict the 1200s when Ancient Puebloan people occupied the cliff dwellings. Courtesy, Tom Noel Collection

Opposite page top
Kiva ceremonial chambers, corn dances and rain dances at modern pueblos, as in this scene at Zuni, have been traced to traditions established at Mesa Verde. Photo by W. H. Jackson, courtesy, Tom Noel Collection

Opposite page bottom
The Ancient Puebloan village hidden beneath Chimney Rock near Pagosa Springs has been excavated and preserved as the northernmost outpost of the Ancient Puebloan people. Today the National Forest Service offers guided tours of the site, which also features occasional dances by modern day Taos Indians, who claim the site as an ancestral home. Photo by Tom Noel

Mesa Verde culture. Centuries of agriculture depleted the once fertile soil, and generations of ever-more-efficient hunters and foragers depleted the native plants and wildlife. Water shortage, too, may have become a critical problem for the last Ancient Puebloans to live in the Mancos River canyons. Dendrochronological evidence, gathered from tree rings, whose width indicates wet and dry years, records a severe drought lasting from 1276–1299. These were a people accustomed to surviving in arid lands, but there were many more of them—and many more crops dependent upon irrigation—than ever before.

Environmental stress may well have created social stress as crucial resources became more and more difficult to acquire. The relatively sudden shift to defensible citadels in the cliffs suggests the incursion of a previously unknown and substantial threat. Might the danger have come from outsiders desperate for food and water? Might different

Natives at Taos, shown here, as well as many archaeologists, claim that today's Pueblo Indians are descendants of the Ancient Puebloan people who left Mesa Verde in the late 1200s. Photo by Tom Noel

Indian rock art, such as this petroglyph near Del Norte in the Rio Grande Valley, tells their story in stone. Courtesy, Denver Public Library

extended-family factions have clashed over scarce resources to the point of civil warfare?

One controversial theory suggests that the Ancient Puebloans of Mesa Verde practiced cannibalism. Bashed-in skulls, projectile punctures, human bones cooked in ceramic ware and coprolites (feces) containing traces of digested human flesh present disturbing possibilities. A 1973 University of Colorado excavation uncovered, in addition to four intact burials, the scattered and broken, burned, cut, or crushed bones of twenty-nine other individuals—mostly young adults and children.

ROCK ART

Ancient Puebloan rock art at sites like Petroglyph Point in Mesa Verde offer graphic impressions of this enigmatic culture. Anthropomorphic figures float amongst antlered deer, elk and simple abstractions in artwork signed with handprints. Humanized lizards dance across the rock face to the music of Kokopelli, the most recognizable figure in the Puebloan petroglyphic pantheon.

Enchanting representations of this hunch-backed flutist, traditionally associated with rain and fertility, appeared throughout the arid southwest after A.D. 1000. A little less supplication for fertility and a lot more for rain might have extended the cliff dwellers' Colorado stay. Instead, only ruins remain, played by the canyon winds for hundreds of years in a ghostly song.

At Mesa Verde, the National Park Service has constructed interpretive facilities, such as this observation porch overlooking Spruce Tree House, in a style echoing the stone and viga (log) construction of the cliff dwellings. Photo by Tom Noel

Mesa Verde's Far View Visitors Center is designed in the circular shape of an Ancient Puebloan kiva. From here, sightseers can see 100 miles into Arizona and New Mexico, where the vertical stones of Ship Rock Mountain sail amid the mesas. Photo by Tom Noel

THE RE-GREENING OF MESA VERDE

Lightning started large wildfires at Mesa Verde National Park in 1996 and 2002. The damage remains evident to visitors at Far View Visitor Center and nearby Far View Lodge. From the highest spot at Mesa Verde—the Sipapu Lounge atop Far View Lodge—you can see a huge 5,000-acre black scar. The fire crossed the only road in the park and came to within 100 yards of the Far View Lodge and Visitor's Center, forcing the park to close.

On August 17, 1996 thunderstorms left double rainbows over the mesa. Lightning continued into the night, leaving one tree smoldering in Soda Canyon. Fanned by the next day's hot breezes, it burst into flames. Tongues of fire as high as 100 feet raced through dry Utah juniper, gambel oak and piñon pine. The wildfire damaged 387 archaeological sites but also uncovered some new ruins. The 2002 fires burned even more park acres and exposed many more archaeological clues previously hidden in the underbrush.

Both infernos closed the entire park. Wet springs have since pushed larkspur, lupine and bright yellow flowers galore up through the blackened soil. By July the park is ablaze with the pinky-purple fireweed.

Wildfires eight centuries ago might explain one of the many mysteries of Mesa Verde: Why the Ancient Puebloans left their pueblos for cliff dwellings. Perhaps fires and drought forced these prehistoric Indians to leave the scorched mesa top for cool, fireproof cliff houses.

One female ranger interviewed in the Sipapu Lounge offered another theory. "I think it was the women. They got tired of carrying those big water pots on their heads up to the mesa top from the seeps in the cliff overhangs. 'Look, guys,' they said, 'if you want us to keep fetching the water you need to build us new houses in the cliffs where the water is.'" Men may have seen the wisdom of these women and also realized that cliff houses would enable them to better defend the waterholes.

The Sipapu Bar, a modern-day watering hole, tops the Far View Lodge, a handsome Neo-Pueblo-revival edifice. You climb to the bar through a circular tower from the dining room and gift shop below. From the bar's outdoor deck, you see why the place is called Far View. Silvery, snow-capped La Plata Mountains decorate the eastern horizon, while Ship Rock Mountain rises to the south. To the north lie the of towns and farms and ranches of the Mancos Valley. Sleeping Ute Mountain dominates the western horizon, threatening to awaken anytime and chase off palefaces and liberate the Utes from their southwest Colorado reservations. Because this giant guardian lay down and went to sleep, the Utes believe, Spanish and then Anglo-Americans invaded Colorado, their centuries-old homeland.

3

HISPANICS

Franciscan priests Francisco Atanasio Dominguez and Silvestre Vélez de Esclante set out with a small expedition in 1776 to find an overland route between Santa Fe and Monterey. They explored the upper Rio Grande, Dolores and Colorado rivers, but never reached California. Courtesy, Tom Noel Collection

In the same month and year that the founding fathers declared the United States independent from the British Empire, two Franciscan friars launched a 2,000-mile expedition from Santa Fe into the mysterious landscape of Colorado. On a mission sanctioned by both the church and the governor of New Mexico, they sought to chart an overland route from Sante Fe to Monterey, the capital of Spanish California. Atanasio Dominguez and Silvestre Vélez de Escalante shared a love of adventure and a commitment to saving the souls of the region's heathen aboriginals.

With God and government on their side, Spanish missionaries ranged far and wide across what is now the United States, from Florida to Texas to California. Father Francisco Garcés explored California and the Hopi villages in what would become Arizona. He sent Dominguez and Escalante a letter persuading them to seek a more northerly route to avoid the Grand Canyon and "hostile Indians."

When the 1776 Dominguez-Escalante expedition encountered their first *Yuta* (or "Ute") near present-day Montrose, they flattered him with gifts and he agreed to guide them. Christened "Anastasio" by Father Dominguez, this Ute led the party to Grand Mesa, a lush and bountiful hunting ground. In gratitude, the devout friars introduced the Indians to the Gospels. The crossed sticks symbol that the Christians revered was familiar to the Utes, who often used the cross as a design in their pictographs, beadwork, and weaving. Out of courtesy to the strangers, the Indians agreed to accept Christianity. To sweeten that decision, the padres also reputedly used chocolate to convert even the most hardened heathens. The Utes' own traditional hospitality required the Spaniards to smoke the peace pipe and share a meal in their *tipis*. Anastasio, who had an injured hand ("*manco*"), for whom the Spanish named the Mancos River, left them in the hands of a friendly Laguna Pueblo guide. He took them all the way to the Great Salt Lake.

Fathers Dominguez and Escalante never did find a route to California. Encountering formidable winter blizzards in what would become Utah, the friars sought divine guidance and cast lots. Heavenly oversight arranged the lots to order the friars to return to Santa Fe, thus avoiding the winter perils of the Wasatch and Sierra Nevada mountains.

Padres Dominguez and Escalante's 1776 exploration of western Colorado resulted in a diary, a page of which is seen here. This published report from Father Escalante first described and mapped much of what would become the state of Colorado. Courtesy, Colorado Historical Society

Don Juan de Oñate led the first Spanish expedition up the Rio Grande in 1598, as depicted in this diorama at the Colorado History Museum in Denver. Courtesy, Tom Noel Collection

Nevertheless, their expedition through western Colorado provided the first map and report on what had been *terra incognita*.

EARLY SPANISH EXPEDITIONS AND NATIVE AMERICANS

Even before the Dominguez-Escalante expedition, earlier Spanish explorers had scouted out the American Southwest. As far back as 1549, seductive tales of golden cities lured the conquistador, Don Francisco Vasquez de Coronado, northwards on a quest for the Seven Cities of Cibola. His failure to find the fabled treasures dampened Spanish interest in the northern fringes of New Mexico. Far richer gold and silver lay in Mexico and Central and South America and other parts of the global Spanish empire.

Spanish explorers ventured into various parts of southern Colorado throughout the 1600s and 1700s

The Spanish claimed Colorado's Rio Grande Valley in the 1700s. When Lieutenant Zebulon Pike showed up there in 1807 with U.S. Army troops, he was arrested as an alien invader. The Fort where he was captured has been reconstructed by the Colorado Historical Society, as shown here. Photo by Perry Eberhart, courtesy, Tom Noel Collection

The Spanish were the first Europeans to explore, write about, map and settle Colorado. Yet, as this caricature by Frederick Remmington may suggest, Anglo-Americans showed little respect for Spanish conquistadors and their claims. Courtesy, Denver Public Library

for glory, gold and God. More often than not, they also sought to retaliate against the indigenous peoples who raided Spanish settlements to steal horses and youngsters, whom they prized. Even these punitive parties looked for potential farmlands and evidence of gold or silver deposits. They labeled the local flora and fauna and sprinkled the landscape with sonorous Spanish names. Antonito, Conejos, Durango, Guadalupe, Las Animas, Pueblo, Purgatoire, San Luis, Sangre de Cristo and Trinidad endure as evidence that the Spanish were the first Euro-Americans to explore, map, claim and christen Colorado.

After years of exploitation and cruelty at the hands of the Spanish intruders, various Pueblos joined Taos in the Pueblo Revolt of 1680. Savagely, the usually peaceful Pueblo tribes attacked the presidios of Taos and Santa Fe and most of northern New Mexico, killing more than 400 Spaniards.

The natives did not remain free for long. Twelve years after the Taos Revolt, Spanish rule was ruthlessly restored in New Mexico by Don Diego de Vargas. Although he murdered or chopped off limbs of the Pueblo Indians as a cruel lesson, de Vargas reached out more kindly to the Utes. On a trip up the Rio Grande, de Vargas encountered a Ute band in the San Luis Valley of Colorado. He persuaded them to accompany him back to Santa Fe, initiating a period of renewed interaction between the cultures.

During the 1700s the Utes used horses to increase their range and expand their power. Ute raids on Pueblo villages became more frequent, and some arrogant bands even dared to pillage small Spanish settlements. The Utes considered their attacks upon these interlopers who dared encroach upon their territory entirely justified. The Utes seldom killed in the course of these attacks, but New Mexican villages were plagued by these hit-and-run raiders who eluded retribution by disappearing into the mountains they knew so well.

In the early 1700s New Mexico's first provincial governor, Juan de Oñate, brought Spanish pioneers into the northernmost reaches of the American Spanish Empire. With the establishment of Albuquerque (1706) and Santa Fe (1709), Spain began settlement of the Rio Grande Valley. Oñate personally led a well-equipped expedition across Colorado's southeastern corner in 1601. Subsequent Spanish excursions included Juan de Archuleta's 1664 exploration of El Cuartelejo, a settlement on the Arkansas River east of present-day Trinidad.

Above
The oldest church still in use in Colorado opened in 1858 in the San Luis Valley town of Conejos. This 1874 photo of Our Lady of Guadalupe Church by Timothy O'Sullivan of the U.S. Geological Survey shows the original adobe structure. After a 1926 fire, it was rebuilt with the brick exterior and completed twin towers. Courtesy, Tom Noel Collection

Right
Hispanic architecture and art add color to Colorado as evidenced by this painting of Denver's St. Cajetan's Church by Carlos Fresquez. Courtesy, Tom Noel Collection

In 1706, in a colorful religious ceremony, General Juan de Ulibarri formally took possession of the upper Rio Grande Valley for the Spanish Crown, dubbing it the province of San Luis. Thus, Spain unfurled the first European flag on Colorado soil seventy years before the United States was born on the eastern shore of the American continent.

FRENCH COLORADO

The Spanish were not, however, the only Europeans making contact and inciting conflict in the American Southwest in the 1600s and 1700s. In 1682 French explorer Robert Cavelier de La Salle appropriated all of the territory drained by the Mississippi basin, which included the eastern slope of present-day Colorado. When New Mexico Governor Antonio Valverde returned from chasing Comanche raiders all the way to the South Platte

River, he reported spotting French encampments. The Comanche and Pawnee tribes, newly empowered and emboldened by their acquisition of horses and firearms, aligned themselves with Spain's Old World rival and New World nemesis. With French encouragement and equipment, they raided both Indian Pueblos and Spanish settlements throughout the southeastern plains. After Pawnee, armed with French weapons, massacred all but ten of

French explorers named the river Plat, the French word for shallow (Anglo-Americans later changed the spelling to Platte). They found Arapaho and Cheyenne camped there as shown in this painting, Encampment on the Platte River *(1866), by Thomas Worthington Whittredge. Courtesy, The Anschutz Collection*

Kayakers riding the South Platte River through downtown Denver follow the route of French trappers. Courtesy, Tom Noel Collection

and the date were found carved in a cottonwood trunk at the mouth of the Uncompahgre. Encouraged by Rivera's reports that the Rockies contained gold and silver, the New Mexican governor sponsored more expeditions into the region.

A GOOD GOVERNOR

Don Juan Bautista de Anza, Governor of New Mexico from 1777–1788, deserves to be remembered for the daring and unusual way he dealt with the Comanches who plundered both Spanish settlements and Pueblo villages. The Mouache Ute band and the Jicarilla Apache joined Governor de Anza to defeat the Comanches with a combined force of more than 1,000. They slew many of their important chiefs, including the formidable Cuerno Verde (Green Horn). Those not killed were taken prisoner.

Having gained the Indians' respect through conquest, Governor de Anza strove to end the destructive cycle of retribution which had damaged both sides for so long. His efforts led to peace not only between the Indians and the Spaniards, but also between habitually warring tribes such as the Utes and Comanches. De Anza was the first governor determined to help the Comanches rather than punishing, executing, or enslaving them. In 1787 he attempted to make agriculturalists of these nomadic natives of the Southwest. Provided with land along the Arkansas as well as seed, farming implements, grazing flocks, and teachers to help them learn agricultural techniques and build a new village, the Indians seemed poised to succeed.

Less than a year after San Carlos' establishment, the Comanches abandoned this agrarian experiment. The strange death of an Indian woman was taken as a bad omen, and de Anza's return to his home in Sonora left the Indians fearful that his successors might not offer the same guarantees of cooperation and protection. They recognized that de Anza was unique in his willingness to share the land and its resources with the native inhabitants and to deal with them fairly and honorably. Had more of the first Euro-Americans shared his approach to relationship-building with the indigenous populations, the story of intercultural interactions in early Colorado and the American West might have unfolded quite differently.

Pedro de Villasur's forty-two soldiers in June 1720, Plains Indians traded with the French for the next thirty years without Spanish interference.

In 1739 two French trappers, brothers Paul and Pierre Mallet, traveled a tributary of the Missouri River westward on a pioneer trek from French Illinois to Spanish Santa Fe. They named it Plat, the French word for "flat," "shallow," "dull" or "spiritless." French trappers also named the mountains that gave birth to the Platte—"Les Montagnes Rocheuses"—the Rocky Mountains.

Rumors of gold and silver in the Rocky Mountains to the north attracted a Spanish explorer, Juan Maria de Rivera, in 1765. Rivera led a prospecting party into the San Juan and Sangre de Cristo Mountains of future Colorado in search of precious metals. After crossing the La Plata ("silver" in Spanish) Mountains, Rivera followed the Dolores River all the way to the Gunnison River. His name

EUROPEANS & INDIGENOUS PEOPLES

Encounters between the native peoples of Colorado and the first Europeans to arrive in the American West impacted Indian cultures dramatically. Although Spanish law forbade selling or trading horses to the Indians, the natives soon obtained the prized animals through raiding or illegal barter. Mounted hunters and warriors commanded expansive ranges, and entire Indian nations ebbed and flowed across the landscape of Colorado's prairies and western plateau in dynamic contests for territory and resources.

By the early 1500s the Athabascan speaking Navajo and Apache people had migrated from the western side of the Rocky Mountains to northwestern New Mexico and the Eastern Plains of Colorado, respectively. Ute Indians ranged throughout the western slope, the southern valleys and the mountains of the future state. Comanches broke away from the Shoshone tribe and leveraged their horsepower to muscle onto the eastern plains. Utes allied with the Cheyenne in the late 1700s to push out the Kiowa and Comanche, who in turn allied with the Utes to push the Apaches south into New Mexico by 1810. The Arapaho and Cheyenne moved from the Black Hills onto the Colorado high plains after 1800.

Alliances between Indians and Spaniards were as mercurial as the ever-shifting inter-tribal alliances throughout the early period of contact. In the case of the Utes, cooperation with the Europeans was generally regarded as mutually beneficial. Periodic military expeditions into Ute territories sent by New Mexican governors in the early seventeenth century proved unsuccessful and expensive and were finally curtailed in 1641, when the governor realized neither side would prevail. These first confrontations left an indelible impression on the Utes, who recognized the superiority of Spanish weapons and tactics. Unable to beat them, the Utes joined them by making a peace which, with the exception of occasional aberrant episodes, essentially ended Ute hostilities toward the Spanish.

Protestant Coloradans looked down on the Catholicism of Hispanics, who had settled the state before they arrived. Among the criticisms was the contention that Hispanics were Pentitentes, who practiced radical forms of penance such as the reenactments of the crucifixion, show here. Courtesy, Colorado Historical Society

The adobe homes of Hispanic Coloradans, like the Weld County residence shown in this 1938 photo by Jack Allison, were condemned by many English-speaking observers as mud huts. Not until the 1900s would gringos discover the aesthetic and functional merits of adobe construction. Courtesy, Library of Congress

TRADE FAIRS

Ute contact with the peddlers and padres from New Mexico was limited. The Utes mostly kept to themselves in river valleys and the remote high-altitude parks—San Luis Valley, South Park, Middle Park, and North Park—in what they called the "Shining Mountains." Annually, they took part in trade fairs sponsored by the governor near Taos. Utes brought the tanned hides, furs and buffalo skins prized by the Spanish to trade for knives, utensils, axes, bridles, beads and trinkets. Navajo at these fairs bartered with distinctive "chief blankets" valued by both the Utes and the Spaniards. During these years, the Utes did not weave, but made baskets which the Navajo had stopped producing, so the two tribes, usually enemies, filled each others'

needs. All Indians participated in the fairs on condition of truce throughout the event.

Five tanned hides might be equitably bartered for one buffalo robe or one mare. Some of the most lucrative trade was in captives and children sold into slavery. The illegality of these transactions only served to inflate the prices. A captive woman could be purchased for thirteen buckskins, eight horses or thirty pesos—roughly the equivalent of two months' salary for a Spanish soldier. Slaves were usually put to work on Spanish farms. As Spanish slaves, many Utes learned how to care for horses, a knowledge shared with their people when they escaped or were liberated.

After the Utes obtained horses from the Spanish, they greatly expanded their range throughout Colorado. Hostile Utes kept Spanish settlers out of the San Luis Valley until the 1850s. Courtesy, Colorado Historical Society

PERIPHERAL PIONEERING

The general outcome of early Spanish forays into Colorado might be characterized as pioneering, yet peripheral; they came, they saw, but they never really conquered. With insufficient military support from the distant viceroyalty in Mexico City, sparsely populated provincial settlements proved too difficult to defend. Despite Spain's official claims, the northernmost lands of New Mexico remained under Indian control throughout the "Spanish Colonial" era that began with Oñate's 1598 trip up the Rio Grande and ended with Mexican Independence in 1821. Still, inroads made by those original European explorers began a profound and lasting Spanish influence upon the state.

THE MEXICAN COLONIAL PERIOD

The Adams-Onís Treaty of 1819 established the border between the United States and Mexico. In Colorado, the Arkansas River defined the boundary, leaving everything south and west of that river—two-thirds of the future state—in Spanish territory. Governor Don Luis de Onís recruited Catholic farmers, fur trappers and artisans from Mexico, the United States, allied European nations and even Napoleonic exiles from France. All were welcomed to settle on free, tax-exempt tracts of land to safeguard the new borderland as naturalized Mexican citizens.

Even after Mexico gained its independence in the revolution of 1821, many of the Onís policies regarding frontier settlement continued to be followed. Mexican land grants induced intrepid and pious pioneers into the southern part of Colorado to plow, to pasture, to prospect or to proselytize. The Colonization Law of 1824 gave preference to Mexican citizens and made special provisions for soldiers. Mexican law, like the previous Spanish law, permitted land grants to certain foreigners, including contractors bringing in settlers at their own expense.

The Treaty of Guadalupe-Hidalgo, which ended the Mexican-American War in 1848, stipulated that land grant recipients in the regions of the southwest ceded to the United States would retain title to their lands, whether or not they chose to

Mexican land grants in Southern Colorado remain contested to this day. Not until 2004 did the Colorado Supreme Court reverse previous decisions and honor traditional Mexican communal land use as authorized in documents such as the Sangre de Cristo Land Grant. This upset the scheme of a Texas land magnate who had bought 77,000 acres in Costilla County and fenced out traditional community use for grazing, wood gathering, hunting, fishing and piñon pine nut collecting. In one of the poorest counties in the state, these centuries-old practices had been crucial to the well being of the people of San Luis— the county seat and oldest town in Colorado. The adobe ruins seen here at the edge of San Luis, overlooking the Texas land grab, epitomize the ongoing struggle of pioneer Hispanic clans to regain their land rights. 1992 Photo by Tom Noel

become U.S. citizens. The redrawing of maps to transfer to the United States, California, Arizona, Nevada, Utah, New Mexico, part of Wyoming and much of Colorado, transforming the northern half of Mexico. Regions which had been part of New Spain/Mexico for centuries were absorbed into the United States. As Anglos began to arrive on the scene, the territorial rights of indigenous Indian tribes were disregarded and the validity of Spanish and Mexican land grants often became contested in U.S. courts. Some of the claims remained in litigation for generations.

Post-Columbian contact with imperialistic European cultures disrupted indigenous cultures throughout the Americas. In the lands that would eventually comprise Colorado, tribes allied with the Spanish clashed with those friendly to the French. The introduction of horses, firearms and new religious beliefs changed the dynamics of Indian life and death. Contact between the peoples of the Old World and the New were rarely cooperative as they vied for survival and success in the American Southwest. No lives changed so radically as those of the Native Americans, who once had Colorado to themselves.

Above
Although the largest ethnic minority in Colorado, Hispanics did not gain much political power until the 1970s. Federico Peña, show here, served as one of Denver's most successful mayors from 1981 to 1993. In addition to spearheading construction of Denver International Airport, Peña helped capture a Denver National League baseball team and restored many of the city's schools, libraries and other public buildings. Following Peña's success, other Hispanics rose to political prominence. In 2005 brothers John and Ken Salazar became the first Hispanic Coloradans elected to, repectively, the U.S. House and the U.S. Senate. Courtesy, Tom Noel Collection

Left
After seeing other groups demand equal rights, Hispanics began protesting for equal rights during the 1970s. These demonstrators marched on Denver's main Post Office and Federal Building. Courtesy, Denver Public Library

4

NATIVE AMERICANS

In the beginning, there was nothing but sky and clouds, sunshine and rain. The Great Spirit lived alone in the middle of the sky. To amuse himself, he poked a hole in the heavens and poured dirt and water through it to make the mountains. Then he came down to earth and touched it with his magic stick. Where he touched the earth, flowers and bushes and trees grew. When leaves turned bright colors and fell off the trees, he gathered them up. He took the prettiest leaves into his hand and blew on them. They grew feathers and became birds.

The Great Spirit made antelope, buffalo, prairie dogs, bighorn sheep, mountain goats, rabbits, squirrels and coyotes. They lived happily until coyote began stealing things and causing fights. The Great Spirit became disgusted with his fighting creatures. So he decided to make one big, wise, fierce animal to rule the rest—the grizzly bear.

No people lived on earth until the Great Spirit cut sticks and put them in a bag. Coyote waited until the Great Spirit left and then pawed the bag to see what was inside. Many, many people came running out, running in every direction and speaking many different languages. The Great Spirit became angry, very angry. He had planned to give each group its own place on the earth so they would not fight. Their fighting, and that of the animals, stained the land and the Colorado river red with blood. The Great Spirit grabbed the bag and saw that only one people remained. He set them down high in the Red Rock mountains and said: These people will be very brave and very strong and special. They will be called Ute.

—Ute Creation Myth

PROTO-UTES

For at least 200 years after the Ancient Puebloans deserted Mesa Verde—probably for the Rio Grande Valley—Colorado's southwest apparently remained uninhabited. In the northwest corner of the future state, however, Fremont people had settled by around A.D. 400 and stayed until around A.D. 1200. This culture is named for the Fremont River of east-central Utah, where distinctive ruins were first found in the 1920s. Fremont people created ceramic pottery, practiced some horticulture and left distinctive rock art.

The Fremont people, who occupied western Colorado around A.D. 800 to A.D. 1150, drew these Carrot Men pictographs near the town of Rangely. Photo by Rick Athearn, courtesy, Bureau of Land Management

Around 1200 the Fremont people evolved into, or were replaced by historic tribes—the Utes, Paiutes and Shoshones. These proto-historic Ute Indians followed a lifestyle that varied little from the Fremont culture, migrating in seasonal cycles as hunter-foragers in the mountains, on the western plateaus and in the San Luis Valley. They built *wickiups*, shelters braced by many inward-leaning poles joined at the apex and covered with smaller branches, brush, bark or animal skins. Because everything they used in their daily lives was biodegradable, little of their material culture survived. Tree scars left by bark stripping, scatters of rock flakes from tool and point making, or charred fire pit stones might be all that remain to indicate a long-ago campsite. Fortunately for archaeologists, the Utes relied on and refined pictographic rock art to depict a changing way of life.

After acquiring horses from the Spanish, Ute Indians began depicting them in their rock art. This early attempt at portraying horses is in Dominguez Canyon, a tributary of the Gunnison River near Delta, Colorado. Photo by Tom Noel

THE UTES

The Utes came to control much of Colorado. They are the states's oldest continuous residents. The mountain tribe has been in the area since at least the 1400s, when they moved in from Utah, which is named for them.

Utes are physically shorter, darker and stockier than the Plains Indians. They also differ from the Plains tribes in belonging to the Shoshonean linguistic family, centered in California, Nevada and Utah. Seven different Ute bands—the Capote, Grand River, Mohuache, Uncompahgre, Uintah, Yampa and Weminuche—occupied central and western Colorado and eastern Utah. After acquiring the horse, the Utes also ranged into New Mexico and Arizona, raiding Pueblo Indian and Hispanic settlements.

Utes were first recorded by the 1776 Domínguez Escalante expedition led by two Spanish Franscican priests. In his journal, Father Escalante describes the Utes, who guided the Spanish, as "all of good

Horses were unknown in the New World until Columbus' arrival in the Americas. The dissemination of the horse throughout the indigenous populations of the southwest and the Great Plains may have begun with Ute slaves who escaped from the Spanish and seized the magnificent animals for themselves.
The horse empowered tribes of the American West to range over greater distances than they had ever dreamt of, expanding their hunting grounds and enabling them to pursue and herd game with awesome efficiency. Horses could carry many times the burden of the dogs they had relied upon before and allowed them to move with larger groups. The landscape became less delimiting as they traveled farther, faster and more fearlessly into new territories. Courtesy, Tom Noel Collection

features and very friendly." The Utes led the Spanish party through the Western Colorado Plateau and gave them deer meat jerky and dried berries. Yankees were less kind to the Utes. Frederick C. Chapin expressed a typical view in his *Land of the Cliff Dwellers* (1890) where he called the Utes "a wild tribe" who "do not wish to be civilized."

After the U.S. Army built Fort Garland in the San Luis Valley in the 1850s, the U.S. began to fight with, and make treaties with the Utes. By the 1863 Treaty of Conejos, the tribe agreed to a reservation consisting of the western third of Colorado. After Whites found silver and gold on that reservation, the Utes signed the 1873 Brunot Agreement opening up the San Juan Mountains to prospectors.

In 1879 a rebellious band of Utes slaughtered White River Indian Agent Nathan Meeker and eight other agency employees. The Utes had become hostile after Meeker asked Major Thomas Tipton Thornburgh to bring 200 soldiers onto the reservation. The Utes ambushed Thornburgh and killed him and eleven of his men at Milk Creek. When the public learned that Meeker's sixty-four year old widow and teenage daughter had been kidnapped and raped by the Utes, many wanted to exterminate the tribe or at least shove them out of Colorado. Bloody repercussions were avoided partly through the peacekeeping efforts of the diplomatic Ute Chief Ouray. Although the Uintah, Uncompahgre, Grand River and Yampa bands of northwest Colorado were moved to the Uintah Reservation in northeastern Utah, the Weminuche, Capote and Mouache bands remain on the Southern Ute and Mountain Ute reservations in southwest Colorado.

COLORADO PLAINS TRIBES

The Utes had faced an invasion of plains Indians a century before White encroachment. The Apache, the Pawnee and the Comanche all appeared on the Colorado plains after they obtained horses. Before becoming horseback hunters, the Apache had farmed in the Arkansas River Valley, raising corn, squash, beans, melons and sunflowers. After acquiring horses, they became hunters and expanded their territory south and west. The Spanish retaliated

Chief Ouray of the Utes, is depicted in a painting by Robert Lindneux in the Ute Indian Museum, maintained by the Colorado Historical Society in Montrose. Ouray was a steadfast advocate of peace between his people and the government. Courtesy, Colorado Historical Society

On the Plains, Cache La Poudre River *(1865),* *painted by Thomas Worthington Whittredge.* *Courtesy, The Anschutz Collection*

against the Apache in 1779 when New Mexico governor Juan Bautista de Anza and his troops defeated a band and killed their leader, Cuerno Verde (Green Horn), along what is now Greenhorn Creek, flowing near the city of Pueblo.

As EuroAmerican settlement pushed eastern tribes west, the Apache, the Comanche and the Pawnee were pushed out of Colorado and replaced by the Arapaho and the Cheyenne, allied tribes who moved into Colorado during the early 1800s.

ARAPAHO

The name "Arapaho" may be derived from the Pawnee word meaning "buyer" or "trader." The Arapaho called themselves "bison path people" or "our people." This small tribe of Plains Indians with

After confining Native Americans to reservations, Whites tried to "civilize" and "Christianize" their children at Indian schools. Among the faces of these Arapaho youngsters, there is not a single smiling student. Courtesy, Denver Public Library

their light skin and prominent noses, were also known as the "Tattooed People." After scratching their breasts with a yucca leaf needle, they rubbed wood ashes into the wound to make an indelible chest tattoo.

The Arapaho, part of the Algonquin family, once lived in the Great Lakes area. After crossing the Missouri River, the tribe split into bands led by chiefs, such as Little Raven, Niwot and Friday, during the 1840s and 1850s. As many as 5,000

Arapaho occupied eastern Colorado, camping along the South Platte and its tributaries. The Utes resisted Arapaho expeditions into the high country. So it was in eastern Colorado that the Southern Arapaho would make their last stand.

As one of the smaller plains tribes, the Arapaho found it wise to befriend rather than to fight larger tribes such as the Sioux and the Cheyenne. They also tried to befriend the Whites, whom they called "spider people." Too late the Arapaho realized the significance of the web of roads, survey lines and fences with which palefaces were measuring and seizing the land. At first, the Indians welcomed the gold seekers trespassing on what the federal government recognized as Arapaho land in the 1851 Fort Laramie Treaty. That treaty promised to the Arapaho and the Southern Cheyenne the territory between the Platte and the Arkansas rivers at the

Native American women, like these Cheyenne portrayed in a diorama at the Colorado Historical Society, designed, created, erected and took down tipis. They could pack and unpack their homes in a few hours and could regulate the temperature inside by manipulating the flaps. Courtesy, Tom Noel Collection

eastern base of the Rockies. Seven years later that treaty's promises were undone by the discovery of gold in the sands of Cherry Creek and the South Platte River.

Little Raven, the main Southern Arapaho chief, and Niwot (Left Hand), chief in the Boulder area, initially welcomed Whites. When thousands settled along rivers and creeks that had been Arapaho campsites, however, hostilities arose. As 100,000 Whites poured into Colorado with the gold rush, some of the Indians pondered moving east, reckoning that it must be empty after the mass westward migration of palefaces. Arapaho remained in Colorado until the 1869 Medicine Lodge Treaty. Little Raven and other Southern Arapaho signed this agreement consigning them to a reservation in Oklahoma. Northern Arapaho were confined to the Wind River Reservation in Wyoming.

THE CHEYENNE

The Cheyenne call themselves the "Tsistsistas" (Called Out People). The word Cheyenne is thought to have come from a Sioux word meaning "people who speak a strange language" or from the French *chien* (dog), based on the Cheyenne Dog Soldiers, the tribe's warrior society, or perhaps on the use of dogs to pull Cheyenne travois before they acquired the horse.

The Called Out People were once fisherman along the Great Lakes, where they also cultivated beans, corn, squash, sunflower, wild rice and other plants. When the White men came, the Cheyenne were pushed west by eastern tribes who had acquired guns. Gun toting tribes pushed the Cheyenne all the way to the banks of the Red River—the boundary between Minnesota and the Dakotas—before an old Cheyenne woman played a trick on raiding Assiniboins. She was preparing a meal in her lodge one night by torch light. Most of her tribe were out on a hunt. Suddenly her wolf-dog started howling and growling at the darkness. She peaked outside. Assiniboine warriors had surrounded the deserted camp and were preparing to plunder it.

The woman thought quickly. She grabbed her torch and ran toward the steep cliff overhanging the Red River, shouting and waving the flame to attract the enemy. Reaching the edge of the cliff, she threw her torch over it. In the darkness she lowered herself into a small hole in the cliff. She waited there while the Assiniboine rushed after the torch, thinking she was

CHIEF LITTLE RAVEN

Before Denver began, Arapaho Indians settled along Cherry Creek, which they named for the wild chokecherries they harvested along its banks. The Arapaho also traded with French trappers.

The Arapaho fondness for Cherry Creek led the St. Louis fur trader, Auguste P. Chouteau, to host a trading camp on the creek in 1815. Chouteau traded with the Arapaho and other tribes for buffalo robes, beaver pelts and wild horses. Chouteau found as many as 1,500 Arapaho camped on the future site of Denver.

Arapaho friendliness to the argonauts flooding into Denver after the 1858 gold strike is well-illustrated by the saga of the Blue brothers. The Blues, and a few others, made the mistake of leaving the South Platte River road for a shortcut into Denver. When Daniel Blue and his two brothers ran out of food and water, he survived only by eating their corpses. An Arapaho found Daniel and nursed the lost, starving goldseeker back to physical and mental health. The Arapaho then took Blue to Denver, where he reported in his statement of May 12, 1859:

> Alexander, my eldest brother, died, and at his own last request, we used a portion of his body as food on the spot, and with the balance resumed our journey towards the gold regions. We succeeded in traveling but ten miles, when my younger brother, Charles, gave out, and we were obliged to stop. For ten days we subsisted on what remained of our brother's body, when Charles expired from the same cause as the others. I also consumed the greater portion of his remains, when I was found by an Arapahoe Indian, and carried to his lodge, treated with great kindness, and a day and a half thereafter brought to . . . Denver City.

Arapaho hospitality was poorly repaid in 1864 at the Battle of Sand Creek. The Whites tried to exterminate the Arapaho, even their women and children. After massacring the Southern Cheyenne and a few Arapaho, Colonel John M. Chivington spent another week chasing Little Raven and his Arapaho band, who seemed to vanish into the land. Later, the surviving Arapaho were forced out of Colorado

Little Raven, head chief of the Southern Arapaho, welcomed palefaced prospectors and settlers to his camp at the confluence of Cherry Creek and the South Platte River. After generously sharing the land, water, grass and trees along Cherry Creek and the South Platte, he was poorly repaid by Whites who massacred Southern Arapaho, along with the Cheyenne, at Sand Creek. Courtesy, Tom Noel Collection

and onto reservations in Wyoming and Oklahoma.

Little Raven lamented: "It will be a very hard thing to leave the country that God gave us. ... That fool band of soldiers cleared out our lodges, and killed our women and children at Sand Creek. Left Hand, White Antelope and many chiefs lie there, and our horses were taken from us there. ... Our friends are buried there, and we hate to leave these grounds."

In 1994 Denver opened Little Raven Street, stretching from 15th Street and Elitch Gardens up to 20th Street and the Flour Mill Lofts. Cheyenne/Arapaho Park was dedicated on June 7, 1996 at 9300 East Iowa Avenue in Aurora. Wildflowers frame a ceremonial Indian circle, red sandstone slabs inscribed with Indian memories and an abstracted lodge pole and I-beam sculpture by an Indian artist. Belatedly, Denver is celebrating the Arapaho camp in which the city was born.

still carrying it. The women heard the death cries and moans of the Assiniboine as they ran over the bluff to their deaths.

When the rest of the Cheyenne returned the next morning, they found the dead bodies and their guns at the foot of the cliff. From that time on, the Cheyenne had guns. Thus armed, they lived in the Red River and Missouri river valleys. Not until the 1740s did they cross the Missouri River to live in the Black Hills. They moved west partly because terrible epidemics of smallpox and measles devastated the tribe back in the Midwest.

In the Black Hills, the Cheyenne continued to raise crops and live in earth lodge villages. Then the Called Out People met the Arapaho and Sioux, with whom they formed alliances. From these tribes, the Cheyenne acquired horses and learned to ride and to hunt buffalo. Out on the plains, the Cheyenne abandoned their earthen lodges and took to living in *tipis*, shelters made from buffalo skins stretched over a conical framework of poles. These light, mobile homes were transported, along with other gear, on *travois*, horse draws fashioned from lodge poles.

White settlers dismissed Native American technology as hopelessly primitive, certain they could learn nothing from it. Yet the most remarkable, efficient and popular structure built in modern day Colorado—Denver International Airport—was inspired by tipis. The translucent, Teflon-coated fiberglass tents of the DIA terminal allow in the light and solar energy that make it bright and energy efficient. Courtesy, Tom Noel Collection

Like the Arapaho, the Cheyenne became buffalo Indians. On the high plains, they found bison herds that sometimes covered 200 square miles during the summer mating season. The Cheyenne lived in, slept on, wore, ate, traded, played with, and fashioned weapons from various parts of the buffalo, for which they had twenty-seven different words.

In the early 1800s the Arapaho and Cheyenne tribes split up. The Southern Cheyenne and Southern Arapaho moved southwest to the land between the Platte and the Arkansas rivers in search of

buffalo. The northern Arapaho and Cheyenne headed into Nebraska and Wyoming.

Native Americans grew more aggressive during the 1990s. This mass rally organized by the American Indian Movement protested the Denver Columbus Day parade, claiming that Christopher Columbus exterminated Native Americans. Photo by Jim Havey

PALEFACES

Initially, the Arapaho and the Cheyenne were friendly to Whites. Both tribes traded at Forts Jackson, Lupton, St. Vrain and Vasquez as well as Bent's Fort, where William Bent married a Cheyenne named Owl Woman. Following the Minnesota Sioux uprising of 1862, warfare swept across the Great Plains. Colorado, where gold seekers sought to dispossess Native Americans of their lands, did not escape the conflict.

After scattered conflicts during the 1860s, Plains Indians were forced to renegotiate the 1851 Treaty of Fort Laramie. In 1861 the Southern Arapaho and Southern Cheyenne, or their alleged representatives, agreed to the Treaty of Fort Wise. It gave them a much smaller reservation in a dry, bleak southeastern Colorado. The only water flowing there, an intermittent stream named the Big Sandy, has become infamous under the misnomer of Sand Creek, as in Sand Creek Massacre.

Many Native Americans did not sign the treaties and resisted White advances. The U.S. government did not keep promises that it made in the Fort Laramie and Fort Wise treaties. Increasingly hostile incidents culminated in the 1864 Sand Creek Massacre, where about 165 Cheyenne and Arapaho—mostly children, women, and old men—were slaughtered. In retaliation, Native Americans raided and burned Julesburg in 1865, but were defeated at Summit Springs in 1869, the last Colorado battle for the Plains Indians.

NATIVE AMERICANS TODAY

Colorado Territory contained 6,000 Indians in 1860, according to the U.S. Census, and approximately 30,000 American Indians in 2000. Colorado's Native American population declined until the 1940s, at which point it began increasing because of improving situations on the reservations and the migration of many Indians into Denver. In 2000 Indians comprised 0.9 percent of Colorado's population. Far from being a vanished race extant only in a museum, Native Americans are a growing, evolving community. In 1993 one Coloradan of Native American ancestry, Ben Nighthorse Campbell, became the first Indian to sit in the U.S. Senate.

Around 19,000 American Indians and Alaska Natives now live in the six-county metro Denver region. Denver County alone has more than 5,300 Native Americans. Colorado's urban Indian population has been growing since the 1950s, when the U.S. government initiated its American Indian Relocation Program. The goal was to bring Indians from reservations to several designated cities, including Denver, where they would be given work and assistance in relocating. Since reservations offered few jobs, many Indians sought out the urban world and its opportunities. Although the program was voluntary, Native Americans were in fact pressed not too subtly into trying a city lifestyle for which they were totally unprepared. Routine tasks such as paying electric bills or using public transit were completely foreign to the reservation-reared people. The friends and family who had been their support at home were replaced by indifferent urban strangers.

American Indians in Colorado have enjoyed a cultural renaissance since the 1980s, reflected in an increasing number of Indian Pow Wows held throughout the state. Indian dancing, music, art, culture and food are showcased at these festivals, which generally welcome non-Indians. Denver's annual January Indian Market has become a major trade show, celebrating Indian art and crafts. Some 2,000 Utes on the Ute Mountain Reservation and another 1,600 on the Southern Ute Reservation welcome visitors to their museums, cultural centers, casinos and guided tours.

Colorado's Native American community, spearheaded by Senator Campbell, celebrated another cultural victory in 2000 with the designation of the Sand Creek Massacre location as a National Historic Site. Not only the wretched past treatment of Indians, but also their often unfortunate current status, is being brought to the public attention in hopes of improving the lives of Colorado's Native Americans.

Ben Nighthorse Campbell became the first Native American elected to the U.S. Senate. Among his achievements were helping to establish the National Museum of the American Indian in Washington, D.C. Courtesy, Tom Noel Collection

5

EXPLORERS, TRAPPERS AND TRADERS

A Trapper Crossing the Mountains, *by William Tylee Ranney, circa 1853. Courtesy, The Anschutz Collection*

In mid-November 1806, Lieutenant Zebulon Montgomery Pike halted halfway up the Colorado peak that would bear his name. Winded and exhausted, he declared that its lofty summit would never be conquered. Less than fifteen years later botanist Edwin James would prove him wrong. Thirty-seven years later Julia Holmes, the first woman to climb the 14,110-foot summit, followed a well-traveled trail to the top. Marveling at the view from the pinnacle soon thereafter, Katherine Lee Bates drew inspiration for a song she called "America The Beautiful."

Pikes Peak, rising majestically from the plains of southern Colorado, had been "discovered" hundreds of years earlier by the Utes, the Spanish explorers and trappers of various nationalities. Pike, however, first officially documented its existence for the U.S. government. The mountain became U.S. property as a part of the 1803 Louisiana Purchase. With that $15 million purchase from French Emperor Napoleon Bonaparte, President Thomas Jefferson doubled the size of the United States. The vast geographic addition, which included most of eastern Colorado, was *terra incognita* to Americans. Soon after Lewis and Clark returned from exploring the northern boundary of the purchase, Lieutenant Pike and a small group of soldiers set out to probe the southern reaches of the virgin territory. The loosely defined southern border of Louisiana followed the Red and then the Arkansas River, both of which Pike was instructed to explore to their headwaters.

Pike confused the rivers, following the Arkansas rather than the Red, and never located the source of either waterway. After being daunted by the Royal Gorge of the Arkansas, Pike headed north to the South Platte then south to cross the Sangre de Cristo Mountains into the Rio Grande Valley. There, near the confluence of the Conejos River and the Rio Grande, Pike erected a stockade, complete with U.S. flag, in Spanish territory. Spanish troops captured this invading army and marched it under guard to Santa Fe for interrogation. From Santa Fe the Yankee invaders were escorted another 500 miles to Chihuahua in Mexico. After taking testimony and confiscating many of Pike's papers and maps, Spanish officials turned him and his men loose to find their way back home.

Pike, the "lost pathfinder," was arrested upon his return to the U.S. under suspicion of negotiating with the Spanish and being part of the Aaron Burr conspiracy. Whether unappreciated explorer or secret spy, Pike tried to prove his loyalty by serving in the War of 1812. There he lost his life in the invasion of Yorkville (now Toronto). Though his exploration of the southern boundary of the Louisiana Purchase rivals that of Lewis and Clark on the northern boundary, Pike has received far less recognition. Yet his expedition produced a valuable report that would guide development in the future state of Colorado.

THE LONG EXPEDITION

Despite Pike's report on the southwestern portion of the Louisiana Purchase, the region received little attention until 1819. That year, President James Monroe authorized the expedition of Major Stephen H. Long, a mathematics instructor from West Point. Long headed this scientific expedition of nineteen, including two map-making topographical engineers, a zoologist and two landscape painters. Long's party followed the South Platte River into Colorado in July of 1820. At the foot of the mountains, the Long Expedition Report noted that the river "is 25 yards wide, having an average depth of three feet, its water clear and cool, and its current rapid. Its valley is narrow and serpentine, bounded by steep and elevated hills, embosoming innumerable little lawns of semi-circular form." Dr. Edwin James, the party botanist and surgeon, delighted in the discovery of large, delicious raspberries as well as cottonwood trees, the only native tree on the semi-arid high plains.

Unable to squeeze through the rugged South Platte River Canyon as it flowed out of the Front Range near what is now Littleton, the Long party headed south to Pikes Peak. On the way, artist Samuel Seymour painted what he, perhaps craving sweets, called "Poundcake Rock," now renamed Castle Rock.

Dr. James talked two of the crew into trying to climb Pikes Peak with him. After bushwhacking through aspen, evergreens and slippery granite, they camped on ground so steep they had to secure themselves with poles and sticks to keep from rolling

Above
Lieutenant Zebulon Pike was sent to explore the southern boundary of the Louisiana Purchase in 1806 by President Thomas Jefferson. Pike, the "lost pathfinder," failed to find the headwaters of the Arkansas River, which separated the Louisiana Purchase from New Spain, but did provide a valuable report on much of what in now Colorado. Courtesy, Denver Public Library

Opposite page top
Major Stephen H. Long conducted the first official U.S. survey of the upper South Platte River in 1820. He reported that its valley was a desert and suggested leaving that land (present day northeastern Colorado) to the Indians and the buffalo. Courtesy, Colorado Historical Society

downhill. The next day they slogged past weather-stunted trees at the timberline into what Dr. James called "a region of astonishing beauty . . . low but brilliant flowering alpine plants." After reaching the summit and admiring the view for an hour, they raced darkness back to the timber.

When he was not scaling mountains, James meticulously described and illustrated Colorado's flora. Near the ponderosa forested divide separating the Platte and the Arkansas valleys (around present-day Palmer Lake), he documented a previously unclassified delicate blue wildflower with striking spurs. What James called *Aquilegia canaderais* is now

The Long expedition, sent west to find the source of the South Platte River, got as far as Waterton Canyon, shown here in the expedition report painting by Samuel Seymour. Baffled by this canyon just southwest of today's Denver, Major Stephen H. Long and his party never did reach the river's headwaters up in South Park. Courtesy, Tom Noel Collection

Dr. Edwin James, the Long expedition botanist, admired Colorado wildflowers such as the pin cushion cacti and the columbine, which later became the state flower. Courtesy, Tom Noel Collection

commonly known as the columbine, Colorado's state flower.

On expedition maps, Long labeled Colorado's Eastern Plains the "Great American Desert" and expressed his doubt that the region would ever support agriculture or extensive settlement. High mountains and deserts, Long concluded, would make Colorado more of a barrier than a goal.

THE SANTA FE TRAIL

Although Long urged that the land be left to the Native Americans, Euro-American fur traders followed his route west to do business with Native Americans and Mexicans. Spain had not allowed trade with the U.S. during the Spanish Colonial period, but when Mexico gained its independence in 1821, all that changed. William Becknell, a Missouri merchant, undertook the first successful trading expedition between Mexico and the U.S., establishing the Santa Fe Trail in the process. This legendary route into the American Southwest began in Independence, Missouri, then followed the Arkansas River through Kansas and southeastern Colorado. The Mountain Branch of the trail followed the Animas River to Trinidad then crossed Raton Pass and headed south to Santa Fe, New Mexico. The journey covered nearly 900 miles and took about eight weeks by ox-drawn wagon. Travelers faced blizzards, hail storms, thunderstorms, drought, hordes of insects, rattlesnakes, accidents and the threat of hostile Indian attacks. But many still considered the Mountain Branch preferable to the alternative: the Cimarron Cutoff. Though shorter and more direct, this southern branch of the trail took its name and its danger from the Cimarron Desert it traversed—a fifty-mile stretch with nary a waterhole to be found. Teamsters driving ox-drawn wagons that averaged only about ten miles a day faced the better part of a week without any place to replenish their water supplies.

Becknell and those who followed along the Santa Fe Trail proved that the trip could be undertaken by wagon trains—wagons laden with dry goods and hardware that returned to Missouri bearing Mexican gold and silver. Despite the known hardships and dangers, Americans' pioneering spirit and capitalistic zeal sparked many to brave the hazards.

THE FUR TRADE

Fashion can shape history. The fad for soft, silky beaver-pelt top hats led fur traders and trappers into the wilds of America's Rocky Mountains during the early 1800s. They sought the pelts highly prized by fashionable Europeans and Americans along the east coast. The regions surrounding both Pikes and Longs Peaks were home to the industrious critters whose soft furs were in such demand. A single beaver pelt could bring as much as eight dollars back east. Trappers also found an abundance of bear, elk, deer, bighorn sheep and bison—all sources of sustenance and income.

Traders and trappers became "mountain men," living off the land and in cooperation with the various Indian tribes. They learned from each other and benefited from each other's traditions, techniques and technologies. Like the indigenous peoples, mountain men dressed in fringed buckskins and warm buffalo robes or bear skins.

Many of them took Indian wives, cementing alliances through marriage and obtaining helpmates skilled in processing skins and hides in the bargain. Without an Indian partner to prepare the animal

Bent's Old Fort on the Arkansas River, the boundary between the U.S. and Mexico until 1848, was the commercial center for the Southern Rockies. Yankee, French, Hispanic, Native Americans and even the Bent's African American cook, Charlotte, gathered here. Reconstructed as a National Historic Site and living history museum by the National Park Service, it includes this fur trading room specializing in beaver pelts and buffalo hides. Courtesy, Tom Noel Collection

hides for market, mountain men rarely succeeded.

At first, fur trade companies established an annual *rendezvous* system where fur trappers and traders gathered to sell their wares to the big outfits such as John Jacob Astor's American Fur Company, the country's first big business and prototype monopoly until the rise of Manuel Lisa's Rocky Mountain Fur Trade Company. The *rendezvous* was a trade fair held in a central, temporary location, such as Taos, New Mexico; Brown's Hole, Colorado; or Jackson, Wyoming. There, Indians and Euro-American entrepreneurs convened for business and pleasure each summer. Manufactured goods were bartered for animal skins and Indian handcrafts. Those gathered smoked pipes, drank whiskey, gambled, held contests and collected payment for a year's worth of furs—and sometimes proceeded to spend it in a few riotous days of dissipation.

Before long, these lively annual swap meets were replaced by permanent trading posts established at strategic junctions of rivers or trails. On the southeastern Colorado plains along the Arkansas River and the Santa Fe Trail, the Bent brothers, George and William, and their partner, Ceran St. Vrain, erected Bent's Fort in 1832. It soon became the hub of commerce and cultural exchange for traders, trappers, hunters, freighters and travelers of many nationalities.

The most popular trade items were priced dearly. A woolen blanket cost about $20, a plug of tobacco went for $5, gunpowder was $4 per pound and sugar was priced at $3 per pound. A hatchet was worth about $6, and whiskey of questionable quality went for $5 per pint. Rifles, flints, knives, coffee and traps cost ten times what they cost in St. Louis. Candles, cookware, yard goods, sewing items, medicines, spices, playing cards and even children's toys were available for barter or outright purchase at Bent's Fort and other early trading posts.

THE FRENCH CONNECTION

The French contribution to the history of Colorado and the West is often overlooked. During the exploratory era French mountain men helped lead westward explorers such as Lewis and Clark and Long, who hired three French-Canadian guides. These *courieurs du bois* were among the most expe-

Louis Vasquez, a Franco-Hispano fur trader and trapper, established Fort Vasquez on the South Platte River at what is today Platteville, Colorado. His adobe fort has been reconstructed as a museum operated by the Colorado Historical Society. Courtesy, Tom Noel Collection

rienced and efficient trappers of the era. Ceran St. Vrain was only one of the Frenchmen who left his name on the Colorado landscape—the St. Vrain River and Fort St. Vrain, his trading post which evolved into a town in northeastern Colorado. The Cache la Poudre River, flowing through present Rocky Mountain National Park and Fort Collins, was so-dubbed by French fur traders who hid their gun powder in its canyon.

On Colorado's Western Slope, Frenchman Antoine Robidoux found his way into the Green River country in the 1820s. More than twenty trappers worked for him when he erected Fort Robidoux, a trading post on the Gunnison River near its junction with the Uncompahgre River (now the town of Delta). When the gold rush brought in thousands of Anglos, most of the French left the area.

Even remote northwestern Colorado attracted enough mountain men to briefly support Fort Davy Crockett in Brown's Hole. But its trading heyday was short-lived, and the outpost offered so little else to attract anyone that it earned the nickname of Fort Misery. Like other Colorado trading posts, the fort had been built to cash in on the most lucrative years of the beaver trade. By 1840, however, the demand for the pelts had dropped sharply, as fickle fashion switched to silk top hats.

THE FRÉMONT EXPEDITIONS

After two decades the fur trade began to decline. But mountain men found new roles in guiding Americans west to tantalizing prospects in California and Oregon territory. To officially survey routes west, the U.S. commissioned John Charles Frémont. Starting in 1842 he led five expeditions in search of possible railroad routes across Colorado. As a guide, Frémont enlisted Kit Carson, a scout well acquainted with the Rocky Mountains due to his long experience as a trapper and trader. Carson guided Frémont's third expedition in 1845 up the Arkansas River from Bent's Fort. They successfully crossed Colorado's lofty Continental Divide, and went on to California—just in time to play a role in the long-anticipated Mexican War.

WAR WITH MEXICO

When the United States eventually provoked Mexico into hostility, Colonel Stephen W. Kearney and the American Army of the West left Bent's Fort in order to take Santa Fe. The U.S. appointed Charles Bent as governor of the province.

Mexican retribution came, however, in 1847 with the uprising at Taos Pueblo. The rebellion was

Kit Carson, a short, slight, modest man, became the best known of the Mountain Men and served as a guide for explorers such as John C. Frémont. Carson also served as commandant at Fort Garland in Colorado's San Luis Valley, (shown in the sketch on the following page) made shortly after its 1851 opening. The officer, shown here with his family, lived in the officer's quarters at Fort Garland. Courtesy, Denver Public Library and Colorado Historical Society

Since 1945 the Colorado Historical Society has operated the adobe outpost of Fort Garland built in the 1850s, as a museum. Courtesy, Denver Public Library and Colorado Historical Society

put down by U.S. troops, but Bent and several others were killed in the battle. The 1848 Treaty of Guadalupe Hidalgo ended the war with Mexico. It also transferred to the U.S. Mexico's northern half—California, Arizona, Nevada, Utah, New Mexico and the southern and western half of Colorado.

This giant new acquisition brought a renewed push for a transcontinental railroad route. St. Louis businessmen financed Frémont's fourth expedition toward this end. He decided to undertake the journey in mid-winter—despite dire warnings—to demonstrate the year-round feasibility of his route. The party made its way over the Sangre de Cristo range, but ran into trouble as they attempted to cross the San Juan Mountains. Extreme winter weather and abortive reconnaissance forays ultimately cost Frémont eleven of his thirty-three men, all of his mules and most of his equipment.

JOHN W. GUNNISON

Frémont's failure did not dampen hopes for a railroad route across the mountains. The discovery of gold in California in 1849 spawned redoubled efforts. In 1853 Congress funded John Gunnison and the Topographical Corps to explore the Central Rockies with a team of thirty scientists and engineers, a large military escort and twenty mule-drawn wagons. Gunnison's party found a more practical way out of the San Luis Valley than Frémont's ill-fated expedition had taken. They traveled over Cochetopa Pass and down the Gunnison River to the Colorado River, following part of the trail blazed by Padres Dominguez and Escalante seventy-five years earlier. But the terrain was so imposing and the journey so difficult that Gunnison concluded it would require an extensive series of tunnels. Gunnison never got the chance to deliver his report in person. When his entourage followed the Colorado River into Utah, Paiute warriors attacked and killed him.

Though numerous transcontinental surveys were completed, planned western railroads went nowhere until after 1865. Issues of slavery and territorial boundaries which exploded into the coming Civil War disrupted and divided the West. Future Colorado was split into four territories: Utah on the west,

Longs Peak, a 14,255-foot flat-topped mountain named for explorer Stephen Long, is the centerpiece of today's Rocky Mountain National Park. Visible from Denver and much of the Front Range, it is second in fame only to Pikes Peak. Courtesy, Tom Noel Collection

New Mexico in the south, and Kansas and Nebraska northeast of the Arkansas River.

Native peoples who lived and hunted in these regions found themselves subjected to increasing emigrant hordes following western trails to Santa Fe, Salt Lake City and California. Still, prior to 1858, Colorado was viewed by Americans as a place to travel *through* rather than *to*. But a discovery at the confluence of two Front Range waterways would transform the mountain and desert barrier into a destination for 100,000 fortune seekers.

FORGOTTEN HISPANIC TRADER: MARIANO MEDINA

Among Colorado's forgotten Hispanic heroes, one of the most fascinating was Mariano Medina, whose pioneer settlement preceded the city of Loveland. Born in Taos, New Mexico in 1812, Medina explored the streams of Colorado as early as the 1830s, looking for beaver pelts. Western explorers and soldiers, such as John C. Frémont, used Medina as a guide. They described him as a reliable, daring fellow, skilled in wilderness survival with an incomparable knowledge of the Colorado Rockies.

Like other successful mountain men, Medina depended heavily on an Indian wife, Tacanecy, who was skilled in preparing beaver pelts and buffalo robes. In 1858 Medina, Tacanecy and their children settled on the Big Thompson River near the razor-edged hogback known as Devil's Backbone. The Medinas soon had company as friends settled in with them along the river bank. Mariano's Crossing, according to the March 7, 1860 *Rocky Mountain News*, was "a new town recently laid out at the crossing of Thompson River, on the Laramie road 40 miles north of this city. Several houses are already underway." Mariano's Crossing, also known as Miraville or Big Thompson, and later as Namaqua, became one of Northeastern Colorado's first sizeable communities. The 1860 census taker found forty-five families residing there.

Mariano's Crossing became a notable stop on the route from Denver to Wyoming after Medina built a toll bridge over the Big Thompson River. Mariano used wood planks and log piers strong enough to support horse teams and wagons. Each end of the bridge was closed with a locked gate. One dollar, paid to Mariano Medina, opened the gates.

Business boomed with the 1859 Colorado Gold Rush. In addition to the bridge, Medina and his Mexican employees erected a corral and stable, a store, a saloon, overnight housing for travelers and a livery stable for the Wells Fargo stage line. These log-and-adobe buildings were whitewashed and placed around a central plaza in the Mexican style. For his family, Medina constructed a two-story log home, whose fine furniture and other luxuries astonished visitors. Perhaps the best dressed man in early Colorado, Medina regularly wore boiled, ironed white shirts, blue trousers with red trim, a

Right
Mariano Medina poses at his home/inn/trading post on the Big Thompson River where Mariano's Crossing has evolved into the town of Loveland.

Opposite page
Medina, one of the most successful and long-lived mountain men, owned this rifle case, powder horn, shot pouch and bullet, and other tools of the fur trade, which are now in the Colorado History Museum in Denver. Courtesy, Colorado Historical Society

fur trimmed coat and exquisite, beaded moccasins made by Tacanecy.

In his adobe store, Medina sold everything from potatoes to salted meats, from whiskey to Tacanecy's deerskin clothing and braided leather bridles. Like many other frontier women, Tacanecy also raised chickens, garden produce and fruit, which she sold at the Medinas' store.

Mariano's neatly whitewashed buildings organized around a plaza presented a prettier picture than the usual ramshackle collection of dirt, canvas and log cabins that passed for a town in Colorado's puppy days. A post office opened there in 1868 and the first postmaster renamed Mariano's Crossing. He called it Namaqua, suppos-edly an Indian name meaning "by the water."

Among the visitors to Namaqua were Generals Grant, Sheridan and Sherman. By 1874 the settlement had reached a population large enough that Medina erected a log schoolhouse for all the children, including his sons Louis, Antonio, Martin and Rafaelito, and daughters Rosita and Marcellina.

Medina owned "all the land I can see from here," including Mariano Lake and Mariano Butte, with its view of Pikes Peak. His large house had such luxuries as mirrors, a bookcase, a china closet, two lamps, a clock and a rocking chair. Mariano dressed neatly in Mexican clothing, drank moderately and put up many famous friends at Namaqua, including Kit Carson, Louis Vasquez, James Beckwourth, Antoine Janis, Jim Baker and Father Joseph Machebeuf. Father Machebeuf, the French missionary who in 1868 became Colorado's first bishop, said Mass in Mariano's house for the Medinas and others, including Protestants and heathens, who were astonished to hear Gregorian Chant sung in the wilderness.

Namaqua remained a post office town until 1879, when it was eclipsed by its neighbor three miles to the east, the booming railroad town of Loveland. Medina did not live to see his town become a ghost. He died in 1878 and was taken to the Namaqua Cemetery, a quarter mile south of his crossing. There the Medina family plot was surrounded by a low wall and white gate decorated with a blue cross. At his request, Mariano was buried in his covered wagon with his two grey horses, a tomahawk, some candles and a jug of whiskey to take into the next world.

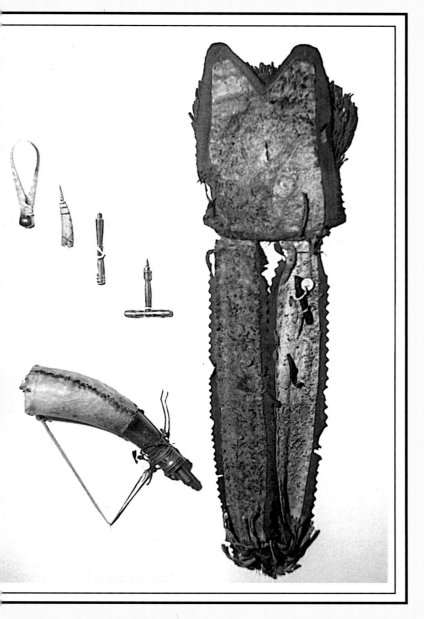

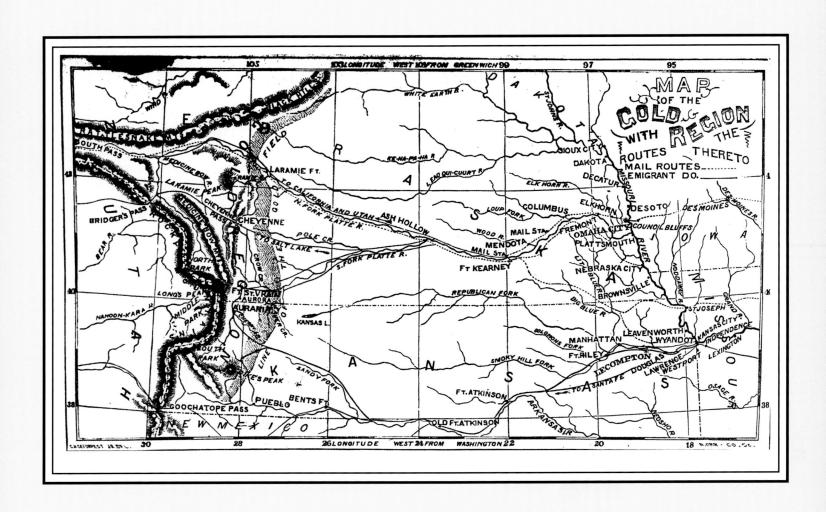

6

GOLD

The Russells' July 1858 gold strike at Cherry Creek and the South Platte River triggered one of the great mass migrations in U.S. history. As estimated 100,000 fortune seekers headed for the Colorado gold fields, using maps such as this one in a guidebook published by William N. Byers. Courtesy, Tom Noel Collection

Like thousands of other '49ers, William Green Russell passed through Colorado on his way to the California gold fields. When his party camped a few days along the Front Range, Russell took a good look around. An experienced miner with an eye for the rock formations and streambed gravels likely to bear "color," Russell made a mental note. The place had potential.

His observation wasn't enough to waylay the prospecting party hell-bent on California's purported riches. But a few years later, when Russell and his friends had returned to Auraria, Georgia, it was enough to launch yet another expedition westward in early spring 1858—this time to prospect Colorado's Rocky Mountain region in earnest. Starting with eight intrepid argonauts, the party grew as it approached its goal, attracting dreamers like a magnet. By the time they reached the confluence of Cherry Creek and the South Platte River, their entourage numbered more than a hundred.

Twenty days of unsuccessful panning sent most of them packing. Those who kept the faith continued digging in sediments at the mouth of Dry Creek in early July 1858. There it was at last—gold! Russell's persistent party extracted about $200 worth of the precious metal in the next few weeks before depleting the pocket. Something less than a bonanza, the promising find nonetheless launched the Pikes Peak Goldrush of 1859.

Timing and publicity were everything. The panic of 1857 and the resultant economic depression had exacted a grim toll from retailers and consumers alike. Merchants in towns along the Missouri embraced the boon of a new gold rush with rapacious zeal, eager to outfit the optimistic prospectors for their journeys west. Kansas City, Leavenworth, Atchison, Omaha and St. Louis all touted themselves as the natural jumping-off-point for gold seekers heading into the territory that would become Colorado.

Two routes into the new land of gold were already well established by 1859. The Platte River route, which also led to Utah, California and Oregon, was the most traveled road, but tracked north of the new discoveries. The Santa Fe (Arkansas River) Trail veered off to the south. Two river routes running between the Platte and the Arkansas offered alternatives: the Smoky Hill and the Republican trails. Each claimed to be the most direct, shortest and safest route. More than twenty-five guidebooks to the goldfields appeared in 1859 to recommend various routes. Bestsellers in a society parched for opportunity, these guides promised the moon. Gold, if you believed them, lay everywhere just for the grabbing.

DENVER CITY

The 1858 Russell strike and several other smaller discoveries led town promoters to anticipate a rush the following spring. These speculators on Colorado's golden future hurried in to plan settlements and hawk real estate. The St. Charles Town Company staked the first claim on the future site of Denver, but made the mistake of leaving the claim during the winter.

Across Cherry Creek from St. Charles, the Russells established the Auraria Town Company on November 1, 1858. Another more experienced town promoter from Leavenworth, William Larimer, jumped the abandoned St. Charles claim on the east side of Cherry Creek. Larimer's group had arrived with official commissions signed by Kansas Territorial Governor James Denver to establish Arapahoe County, Kansas Territory, stretching all the way from the Kansas border to the mountains. At the November 22, 1858 founding ceremony, Larimer named his town Denver City in hopes of currying additional favors from Governor Denver.

Larimer's Denver City ultimately absorbed Auraria in 1860 after the Russells left to look for mother lodes in the mountains. They uncovered a rich gold lode in Russell Gulch near Central City. When the Civil War started, however, the Russells gave up Colorado gold altogether to go fight for the Confederacy. Yankees took over the Russells' Colorado claims and, in yet another reminder that history is written by the victors, the city that arose on the Russells' gold discovery bears no memory—not even a street name—to honor the Georgians who started it all.

Experienced gold miners, such as William Green Russell, panned placer gold out of streams, but realized it had washed down from mother lodes upstream in the Rockies. These volcanic mountains had been enriched by molten solutions that extruded gold into fissures and cracks. Erosion had worn away the mountains and washed some of the precious yellow metal downstream to tease prospectors. Courtesy, Colorado Historical Society

WILLIAM BYERS:
COLORADO'S SPOKESMAN

The virtues of Denver City and Colorado were trumpeted by William Byers, an opportunistic newspaperman who founded the *Rocky Mountain News* on April 23, 1859. Byers used the *News* to boost the baby city and the Pikes Peak Region. In early issues aimed at Omaha, St. Louis and other cities filled with potential immigrants and investors, Byers even declared Denver the steamboat hub of the Rockies. On September 10, 1859 the *News* launched a "Boat Departures" column: *"Ute* and *Cheyenne* for mouth of the Platte. Scow *Arapahoe* for New Orleans. All laden with passengers and freight." Subsequent announcements for the benefit of eastern investors and the national press proclaimed ships sailing from Denver to major port cities. Although the rest of the country might be fooled, some locals, well aware that the South Platte was not navigable, dubbed the *News* the "Rocky Mountain Liar."

Yet people poured into Colorado, even when discoveries fizzled. Hopeful '59ers headed west by the thousands that spring. They set out from supply towns along the Missouri River on horseback and in covered wagons pulled by oxen or mules. Others came on foot, pushing handcarts or wheelbarrows. One imaginative entrepreneur offered passage on his "Wind Wagon," a wheeled vehicle with a giant sail intended to cut travel time by sailing on the prairie breezes. Its maiden voyage was cut short, however, soon after its departure, when it was blown into a gully from which it never emerged.

Probably only about half of those who embarked on the journey actually made it to the Pikes Peak country. Many changed their minds along the way; others succumbed to disease, hunger, dehydration or Indian attack. Those who survived the trip quickly discovered that the guidebooks had lied. The creek beds were not lined with gold for the taking, and the so-called "cities" were comprised of slapped-together planks lining dusty streets. Hearts sank. Hopes fell. Embittered "go backs" abandoned the false Eldorado as quickly as they had flocked to it, warning those they encountered coming west to reconsider and cut their losses.

William N. Byers became Colorado's prime promoter after starting the Rocky Mountain News *in 1859 to publicize Colorado's prospects. The* News, *which is still going strong, puffed Colorado's climate, scenery, farming, ranching and tourism, as well as mining. Courtesy, Tom Noel Collection*

Although Byers' newspaper and his guidebook to the gold fields were popular, he never quite succeeded in selling his wife Elizabeth on the frontier's charms. "Had I known of the hardships and experiences which lay before me in this pioneer country," Elizabeth said, "all the gold in the mountains could not have induced me to come." Courtesy, Denver Public Library

MAJOR STRIKES

Fortunately for Colorado's future, the Russell brothers weren't the only prospectors poking around the territory. By the summer of 1859, news of other major gold finds renewed the faith of the persistent. In the winter of 1858, Captain Tom Aikins and his sons had found "color" while panning Boulder Creek and established Boulder City. David Horsfel and Matthew McCaslin struck pay dirt about eight miles up Boulder Canyon on January 16, 1859 and created the camp of Gold Hill. They established Colorado's first mining district that spring—Mountain District No. 1—to regulate subsequent mining claims and impose a bit of law and order. The Gold Hill Laws of 1859 favored working miners over outside speculators, requiring owners to work their claim at least one day out of ten or forfeit it. Still another district tried to resolve squabbles by banning attorneys.

That same winter, near present-day Idaho Springs, gold rush veteran George A. Jackson made Colorado's first major gold strike. After thawing a promising spot on icy Clear Creek, he began digging in the frozen ground. Jackson reported in his diary that he eventually found "fine color" and one gold nugget. Jackson sat on his secret until his return the following spring. News of his strike prompted thousands of others to also head for the hills.

Below
Of 100,000 hopefuls setting out for Colorado, some painted "Pikes Peak or Bust" on their wagons. Many got both. They saw the peak, but busted as gold seekers and went back home. The 1860 census showed that only about a third of those setting out for the Pikes Peak diggings got there and stayed.
Courtesy, Tom Noel Collection

Above and Below
Of all the tragedies involved in Colorado's gold mining era, the most bizarre befell five argonauts who hired Alfred Packer to lead them into the gold country around Breckenridge. After foolishly attempting to head into the high Rockies in winter, the five perished. Only Packer survived—by feasting on his companions. The Colorado cannibal was condemned to life in prison after judge and jury became convinced that he murdered his meals.
Courtesy, Tom Noel Collection

CENTRAL CITY

The gold strike that solidified Colorado's bonanza reputation came on May 6, 1859 when John H. Gregory of Georgia uncovered the region's first great mother lode. He found an underground vein which produced far more gold than the fragments that had been washed downstream as placer gold. Gregory Gulch soon gave rise to the nearby boomtowns of Apex, American City, Bald Mountain, Black Hawk, Central City, Eureka, Gold Dirt, Missouri City, Mountain City, Nevadaville, Nugget, Russell Gulch and Tip Top.

In the Central City region, the town of Black Hawk emerged as the smelting center. The white frame Presbyterian Church on the hill, seen in this 1864 photo by George D. Wakely, survives to this day. Courtesy, Tom Noel Collection.

Gold veins that would be worked for the next hundred years gave Central City and surrounding Gilpin County towns the nickname "The Richest Square Mile on Earth." That claim was never true, but it helped attract investors and miners. And when Central City and Black Hawk would adopt casino gambling in the 1990s, the "richest" claim helped, once again, to attract fortune seekers.

Thanks to the fame of Central City and an influx of '59ers, mining camps sprouted up all over the Pikes Peak country. Some became towns. Most became ghosts, when mining played out after a year or two or three. At Jackson's find on Clear Creek, the town of Idaho Springs sprang up with a mineral hot springs to help it flourish. In South Park on the headwaters of the South Platte, Alma, Buckskin Joe, Fairplay, Hamilton and Tarryall popped into being. Cañon City and Colorado City were platted along the base of the southern Rockies. West of Denver, Golden City was founded where Clear Creek emerges from its Front Range canyon, a strategic location that made Golden a supply base for the mountain mining settlements and briefly made it the territorial capital.

PLACER GOLD

Colorado's gold came in two types. Placer gold was found in streambeds and along creek banks, both in the mountains and along the Front Range. It came in many shapes: dust, nuggets, shot, wire, scale and grains. Like cash, placer gold was easy to carry and ready to spend, with no refinement required. The only equipment needed to prospect for this type of gold was a pan. Household versions would do, but professional models for those who could invest a bit were specially made of sheet iron with sloping sides and often copper bottoms.

The equipment was simple, but the work was not. Prospectors squatted for hours beside streams, filling their pans with debris from the bed, then agitating the contents just below the water's surface to wash away dirt, sand and lighter rocks. Gold flecks, being heavier, would remain in the bottom of the pan. Some pieces might be large enough to extract with forceps. But the best method for removing the small bits of gold involved the use of mercury, which attracted the metal, creating an amalgam. When heated, this amalgam separated out into the mercury, which could be reused, and the gold left as residue.

Placer gold panning was labor intensive and inefficient. Impatient prospectors soon put devices such as rockers and sluice boxes to work for them, winnowing much more silt or gravel in the same amount of time. Hydraulic mining was a more invasive, aggressive method. From a dammed source upstream, pressurized water was shot through a hose and nozzle with enough force to blast away entire hillsides. Since all these methods required the use of constantly running water, work came to a halt whenever the streams froze.

LODE GOLD

The second type of Colorado gold was lode gold. Found in veins within rock formations, lode gold was the stuff of big strikes. Extracting it was complex, difficult and often dangerous. Many of the '59ers were California veterans who helped those less experienced to master the art and science of hard rock prospecting. Gold diggers learned that certain types of rocks or rock formations were known to be associated with lode gold. Out-croppings of quartz were generally good places to sink a pick and shovel and start digging. Veins of gold ore could be mere inches or several feet thick. They might peter out quickly or run for miles into the earth. In the best of all possible scenarios, they led to the "Mother Lode," a substantial deposit of the precious ore.

Following a vein of gold through solid rock required backbreaking labor and heavy equipment. As the tantalizing trail descended, mine shafts and tunnels had to be dug and shored up. Blast holes were filled with powder to blow the rock to bits. Hired miners were easy to come by, and safety was not a priority for most mine owners and managers. Accidents happened; people were killed or disabled. But there were always others to take their places, and there was always a chance that the Mother Lode lay waiting just a few feet deeper.

Unlike placer gold, lode gold was neither easily transported nor in pure form. It was part of the rock, and extracting it from the surrounding quartz and other material was a major undertaking. Whims and windlasses brought chunks of ore from deep in the

mines to the surface by the ton. By 1860 most major lode mining camps in Colorado had their own stamp mills, which crushed the raw ore with heavy weights in a series of steps producing finer and finer particles. From that point, the process resembled placer extraction, washing and agitating the sediment, then treating it chemically to separate the precious metal.

Hard-rock mining was not a poor man's game. The massive equipment, labor, transportation and processing costs represented substantial investments. But the potential returns from lode mining more than offset the capital expenditures for those who succeeded in Colorado's mountain camps. Most of the thousands who came to Pikes Peak country with little or no money did not fare as well. Once their luck and their resources ran out, they sought work in the mines for about one to three dollars per ten- or twelve-hour day. If board were thrown into the compensation package, they might even manage to put away enough to try their hand once again as self-employed prospectors.

Ruins of the Vindicator Mine ore sorting house linger as a century-old reminder of the time when Cripple Creek shone as "The World's Greatest Gold Camp." Photo by Tom Noel

MINING THE MINERS

The Pikes Peak country attracted more than miners, speculators, investors and town builders. Many who came had no intention of squatting by streams or picking at rocks. These pioneers knew that where there were people, there too were needs. Merchants arrived to set up hardware, dry goods, saloons and grocery stores. Lawyers and bankers arrived to handle claims and manage funds. Freighters came, left, and came back again and again, transporting supplies from the east at exorbitant rates. Gamblers and swindlers came to relieve the unwary of their gold dust or hard-rock profits. Reputable women provided services from laundry to home cooking, while women of another sort offered less wholesome comforts for a price. All positioned themselves to "mine" the miners in one way or another.

CRIPPLE CREEK GOLD

Ironically, the Pikes Peak gold rush bypassed the greatest discovery of all. Just southwest of Pikes Peak, on a scrawny, stony trickle called Cripple Creek, a bowl of gold far richer than all the other Colorado discoveries combined lay hidden underground. Cowboy Bob Womack, who kept his eye open for "float gold" while herding cattle, found what he was looking for in 1890. Within a decade

Right
As mines sank deeper into the earth, miners used powerful drills to blast out the Gold Standard Mine near Cripple Creek. Once they excavated gold ore, miners hoisted it to the surface in large metal buckets big enough to carry a man. Photos by Harry Buckwalter, Courtesy, Colorado Historical Society

Below
As mine owners grew richer and miners grew poorer, miners formed unions to fight for better hours, pay and working conditions. The State of Colorado usually sided with mine owners and sent in the National Guard to protect mines worked by non-union labor, as in this 1896 view of Leadville's Emmett Mine. Courtesy, Colorado Historical Society

some 10,000 people had flocked to what became the largest and last major Colorado gold strike.

Ultimately Cripple Creek, unlike Central City, did become the world's richest gold district, out producing mining districts in Australia, Canada, Russia and South Africa by 1900. That year Cripple Creek District mines enabled Colorado gold production to reach an all time high of $28,762,036. Labor wars in subsequent years eroded profits as miners struck for the right to unionize and campaigned for safer conditions, a minimum wage of three dollars an hour and an eight-hour work day. Mine owners crushed the strike, but the industry never fully recovered from these bitter confrontations between the owners and their workers.

GOLD MINING IN THE TWENTY-FIRST CENTURY

Some traces remain of the golden era that gave birth to Colorado. All but one gold mine have closed and the smelters that once dominated the state's industry are silent and smokeless. A gold domed State Capitol and a United States Mint may remind Coloradans of their golden origins. Up in the hills, old mine shafts, tailings and mill skeletons still scar mountains in the gold belt that ran from Boulder County southwest to San Miguel County.

Although far less visible, gold still glitters in Colorado. Newmont Gold of Denver, after merging with Normandy Mining Ltd. of Australia, emerged during the early 2000s as the world's largest gold mining company. AngloGold, a Johannesburg, South Africa-based firm second in size only to Newmont, began operating in Colorado as the Cripple Creek and Victor Gold Mining

Above and page opposite
Just above the defunct Vindicator, the Cresson reopened in the mid 1990s as a huge pit mine and cyanide heap leaching operation. Colorado's only active gold mine is worked seven days a week, twenty-four hours a day by a crew of over 300 and a fleet of eighty-five ton trucks. Photos by Tom Noel

Company. CC&V reopened the old Cresson Mine as a cyanide heap leaching operation in 1994. CC&V is yielding $2–$3 million a day from old mine dumps and mill waste. While miners a century ago recovered less than half the gold due to primitive ore processing methods, CC&V today recovers more than 90 percent of the precious metal.

Charlene Wilson, Human Resources Director for Anglo Gold Ashanti North America Inc., the majority owner of CC&V, told the July 2, 2005 *Rocky Mountain News* that CC&V's Cripple Creek mine employs 315 and is desperately looking for more skilled miners. The mine is processing 150 tons of ore for each ounce of gold recovered. In 2004 CC&V's Cresson Mine yielded a record 329,029 ounces. This required removing some 50 million tons of ore from a vast pit and trucking it

to heap leach pads. There the ore is soaked with cyanide to precipitate out the gold for recovery. The three-mile wide pit has consumed hundreds of old-time mines, as well as the ghost towns of Altman, Elkton, Independence, Midway and Winfield in a frantic, gigantic, modern-day gold grab.

Besides Anglo Gold and Newmont, other Colorado gold mining firms include AMAX, Gold Fields Exploration, Gold Seek, Mount Royal Ventures, Phelps Dodge, Royal Gold, Sovereign Gold and U.S. Gold. As coal, natural gas and oil mining also boomed during the early 2000s, wages of $40,000 to $80,000 a year once again sparked excitement. New mining prospects and high wages spawned a new case of gold fever, but nothing like the get-rich-quick epidemic that gave birth to Colorado Territory in 1861 and to the State of Colorado in 1876.

GAMBLING ON GOLD & OTHER THINGS

In a state founded on a gamble on gold, Coloradans have long been risk takers. Native Americans fancied gambling. They carved bones and stones with notches that have led anthropologists to bet they were gambling devices. Historic tribes also wagered on games such as Hand and Double Ball, as well as on horse races. The two tribes with Colorado reservations today, the Southern Utes and the Ute Mountain Utes, both opened casinos during the 1990s.

Gambling became a major amusement for miners swarming into Colorado with the 1859 gold rush. Gambling saloons galore offered such card games as Monte, Rouge et Noir, Over and Under 7, Chuck-a-Luck, Poker and Blackjack, as well as Dice and Roulette. Colorado Territory and most local governments outlawed gambling and used fines on gambling as a source of income. Whenever government funds ran low, officials raided gambling joints and fined those involved to fill the town treasury.

Poker Alice, Edward Chase, Vaso Chucovitch, Doc Holliday, Bat Masterson, Jefferson Randolph "Soapy" Smith and other noted gamblers operated in Colorado. Gambling remained illegal until 1982, when the state, after a favorable 1980 vote, established a lottery with 50 percent of the revenues going for prizes and 40 percent to Greater Outdoors Colorado to fund ranch and farm preservation easements, parks, recreation and open space acquisition programs.

In 1990 voters approved another constitutional amendment legalizing limited gambling in the old gold mining towns of Black Hawk, Central City and Cripple Creek beginning October 1, 1991. Gaming tax income was awarded 50 percent to the Colorado General Fund, 28 percent to the State Historical Fund for preservation projects, 10 percent to the three gaming communities, and 12 percent to the involved counties—Gilpin and Teller.

This time, gambling paid unusual dividends, generating some $200 million in taxes for restoring landmark buildings in all sixty-four Colorado counties. The State Historical Fund, which is

After the 1990 vote, when Coloradans approved limited stakes gaming for the withering gold mining towns of Black Hawk, Central City and Cripple Creek, a new bonanza began. Old abandoned mines, such as this one in Black Hawk, suddenly became multi-million dollar casino sites. Photo by Tom Noel

administered by the Colorado Historical Society, has contributed financing and expertise to almost 2,000 preservation projects undertaken by Colorado communities.

Thanks to these preservation grants, even the smallest, poorest towns have been able to restore their old, cherished landmarks—one-room schools, Carnegie Libraries and railroad depots. Core city churches have been given firm new foundations, leak-proof roofs and protective glass for their stained glass windows. Elegant old hotels approaching ruin have been restored, often as low-income housing for the disabled and elderly. From the State Capitol to the prehistoric ruins at Mesa Verde, historic places have been preserved for future generations. And the once ghostly, now reinvigorated golden cities of Black Hawk, Central City and Cripple Creek once again attract fortune seekers with the cry that there really is "gold in them thar hills."

The old Glory Hole Saloon in Central City reopened in 1992 as a deluxe casino, bar and restaurant, complete with a master chef. Photo by Tom Noel

7

SETTLERS

Horace Greeley, editor of the leading U.S. newspaper, the *New York Tribune*, went west in the summer of 1859 to personally verify extravagant tales of Colorado's golden riches. His stagecoach was hailed a half-mile outside of Denver by Count Henri Murat, a mounted, well-dressed gentleman who invited Greeley to accompany him to the El Dorado, the finest—and only—hotel in the baby town. The grandly named establishment turned out to be a seventeen-by-twenty-foot shack of cotton-wood planks, with a mud-and-stick chimney and dirt floors. When the proprietor, Count Murat, charged Greeley an exorbitant one dollar for a hair-cut, and his wife, Katrina, presented a bill of three dollars for doing his laundry, the famous editor grudgingly acknowledged that "the country harbored at least one man determined to make the best of his opportunities."

The Murats were among the first Denver pioneers, arriving in early November, 1858. They wasted not a moment looking for gold themselves, but instead set to work preparing to relieve others of whatever dust or nuggets they were lucky enough to find. Though their claim to aristocratic title was dubious, there was no doubt that Henry and Kate—as they were generally known in the West—epitomized a great many early Colorado settlers. Henry Murat headed for the Pikes Peak country with no fixed purpose other than to make a fast buck. He pursued a variety of occupations—barber, dentist, innkeeper and gambler—making and losing several fortunes in the course of his lifetime.

His wife, on the other hand, represented the stabilizing influence of women in the fledgling territory. Throughout her husband's fiscal fiascos and extravagances, she sustained a steady income by providing various domestic services to the overwhelmingly male population. Her apple strudels and pies brought two dollars each from homesick young men who missed fresh baked goods even more than they missed their mothers. Usually paid in gold dust, Katrina often stitched that currency into her waistbands and petticoats for safekeeping. It was said that she once had so much of the heavy metal upon her stout person that it took four teamsters to hoist her up onto her wagon seat. Another legend has the Countess single-handedly holding off rampaging Indians with a shotgun while barricaded behind sacks of flour.

Settlers crossing the High Plains hoped to strike it rich and build new homes in Colorado. Courtesy, Tom Noel Collection

The Count and Countess Henri Murat opened Denver's first hotel—the El Dorado—depicted here. The Murats made a tidy profit selling apple strudels and haircuts. Courtesy, Denver Public Library

Countess Murat is best known as the "Betsy Ross of Colorado" for crafting the future state's first U.S. flag. The most likely of many versions of this story has Old Glory originally flying from the El Dorado's fifty-foot flagpole to greet the first overland stage arriving in Denver City on May 1, 1859. With no yard goods available in the rough new settlement, Katrina reputably fashioned the star-spangled banner from her own red, white and blue French lingerie. This memorable sight, flapping in the breeze, provided a short-lived spectacle. The patriotic creation was stolen after just four days—little wonder in a town where males comprised more than 95 percent of the population.

Hardworking and resourceful women like Katrina Murat saw to it that the slapped-together boomtowns of Colorado cleaned up and made something of themselves. Men may have forged the trails and platted the towns, but women established homes and communities in the primitive and often wretched conditions.

White women were a rarity in gold rush Colorado. The majority of '59ers were bachelors or left their wives and children back home, intending to send for them as soon as they had scooped up an easy fortune. Only a few women accompanied their husbands, fathers or brothers west on their quest for a new life, however ill-considered or foolhardy that pursuit might prove. They did their best to put down roots in the dry and rocky foreign soil.

WOMEN'S GOLD

Margaret Crawford left behind her relatives, her friends, her home and her church to follow her husband to Colorado. She packed as many of her worldly belongings as possible into a prairie schooner and shepherded her three small children on the thirty-four-day wagon train journey from Missouri to Denver. Disappointed with Cherry Creek, her husband pressed on into the mountains, following rugged trails over the Continental Divide. They settled at last in a remote area of northwest Colorado that would one day become the town of Steamboat Springs.

Despite hardships and the threat of Indian raids, Margaret set up housekeeping. She planted the Harison rose bush cutting she had brought from

Missouri and kept alive with her meager water ration throughout their odyssey. The flowers lent a touch of home and hope to their log cabin. Margaret gave cuttings from these new bushes to other women she encountered on the frontier, and they in turn shared cuttings with their acquaintances. Soon the bright yellow blooms graced mining camps throughout the Rockies and earned the nickname of "Women's Gold." The roses came to symbolize the collective positive influence of pioneer women and their determination to bring beauty to their new homes.

Isabella Bird, a spunky English world traveler and writer, described 1870s Colorado as a raw land, tough on women and children, in her classic A Lady's Life in the Rockies. *Courtesy, Denver Public Library*

Above
Behind every successful man is a woman. Hard working Augusta Tabor was the key to Horace Tabor's success as Colorado's richest silver tycoon. Their Leadville home, now a museum, was left behind for a Denver mansion. Courtesy, Colorado Historical Society

Below
Photo by Tom Noel

AUGUSTA TABOR

Little did Augusta Pierce Tabor imagine when she married one of the stonemasons at her father's quarry that devotion to her spouse would take her from her beloved Maine to the wilds of the Pikes Peak country. But ambitious Horace Tabor was a risk taker, and Augusta followed him faithfully— first to the Kansas prairie to homestead in a rattler-infested sod house, then to Colorado to prospect in 1859. After untold ordeals on steep and nearly impassable mountain trails, theirs was the first wagon to get through to the promising diggings at Idaho Springs. Augusta's restless husband kept uprooting the family just as she got settled. The Tabors moved from Idaho Springs to Buckskin Joe to California Gulch to Denver. As the first white woman in many of these mining camps, Augusta was known for her kindness and strength of spirit. Miners, impressed with her industry and gumption, built her a log cabin and treated her with the greatest respect and deference.

While Horace prospected, Augusta not only kept house and raised their son, but also made a steady income taking in laundry and boarders. Although Horace usually failed to find pay dirt, Augusta ran her business and prudently put money aside. Finally, after eighteen years of boomtowns, she had saved enough to open a general store in Oro City (now Leadville). The Tabors lived in rooms at the back and also served as the settlement's first postmasters. Augusta's mercantile business, made possible by her years of toil and thrift, eventually led to Horace Tabor's long-dreamt-of fortune. With prospecting tools grubstaked from the Tabor store, two indigent miners discovered the Little Pittsburgh in Leadville. As the grubstakers, the Tabors got a third of the mine and ultimately bought out the two prospectors to gain sole control of a fabulously rich silver mine.

AUNT CLARA BROWN

Even more adventuresome than women who came West with their male relatives were those few who ventured into the virgin territory on their own. Former slave Clara Brown worked her way to Pikes Peak country as the cook for the men of a sixty-wagon train out of Leavenworth. Rather than gold, Clara sought her long-lost husband and children, who had been sold off to other masters and separated from her years before. Among the thousands of immigrants heading for the hills of Colorado, she hoped to find at least one of them. Instead, Clara found opportunity in Central City, opening the camp's first laundry, while also working as a cook and midwife. Although she was sixty years old, she was accustomed to long hours and hard work. Clara saved her earnings and invested in promising claims. Within a few years, she had amassed a small fortune and owned real estate not only in Central City, but also Denver, Georgetown, Boulder and Idaho Springs. Some of her money went to bring friends west; some was loaned to busted miners to get them back on their feet. Grateful beneficiaries of her kindness and generosity affectionately called her "Aunt Clara."

A devout Christian, Clara Brown had been one of the original members of Jacob Adriance's Union Sunday School in Auraria and helped Adriance and fellow missionary William H. Goode establish Denver's first Methodist congregation. In Central City, Aunt Clara donated some $35,000 to help build what is now the oldest Protestant church in Colorado, St. James Methodist.

In a real-life happy ending, Clara finally located her daughter, Eliza Jane, and was reunited with her and a granddugher in her final years.

SETTLING IN

Churches heralded the arrival of civilization in hellish mining camps. Episcopalians named their first Denver church St. John in the Wilderness. Baptists, Jews, Presbyterians and others also started congregations. The Santa Fe Catholic diocese sent

Women especially hungered for churches to help civilize raw, saloon-filled western towns. They struggled to establish churches and schools like St. Mary's School, shown here, the first private school in Denver. Courtesy, Kirkland Museum.

St. Mary's, still dominates the skyline in Central City, as it did in this 1931 watercolor by Vance Kirkland. Courtesy, Kirkland Museum.

Boulder, the home of the University of Colorado's main campus, also erected Colorado's first public school. Abner Brown, a carpenter as well as a school teacher, built the school with a shingle roof in 1860. Townsfolk contributed glass from their picture frames for windows, only to have Arapaho Indians peer through the panes and distract students. Courtesy, Tom Noel Collection

Father Joseph Machebeuf to build a Denver church, completed just in time to celebrate Mass on Christmas Day 1860. Machebeuf also founded churches in Colorado's mining towns. In Central City, he held mass in various saloons amidst tobacco, booze and commotion. Finally, he grew impatient one day and locked the saloon hall doors, refusing to let anyone out until they contributed gold dust, cash or at least pledges to built St. Mary of the Assumption Church—a landmark to this day.

Schools, too, signaled the coming of social stability. Boulder proudly claimed to be the first community to build a public school in 1860. "Professor" Owen Goldrick opened Denver's first school in a rented log building in Auraria, where he welcomed white, Mexican and Indian children—anyone who could pay the three dollars a month tuition. The residents of many mining camps agreed to set aside one claim per lode to subsidize the establishment of local public schools.

Women hungered for the churches, schools, comfortable homes and orderly neighborhoods they had known back east. They urged men to replace tents and shacks and caves with decent homes. Yearning for respectability, women had many a log cabin sheathed in clapboard that could be painted white. White paint also helped churches and schools stand out as evidence that a community was fit for women and children. As families arrived, sawmills appeared, and frame houses with wooden siding and stores with false fronts sprang up.

Further respectability came with brick and stone buildings that lent stability and elegance to Colorado's hastily built towns.

FLOOD AND FIRE

Local newspapers were the key to establishing a new community's identity and promoting its goods and services. Among the original pioneers to arrive in Colorado was newspaper editor William Byers. He published the first edition of the *Rocky Mountain News* on April 23, 1859. The *News*, like other boomtown papers, carried advertisements for local merchants, professional services, mail order merchandise and even cemetery plots. Not wishing to ally his business exclusively with either Denver City or Auraria in the days before their merger, Byers built his newspaper office on the dividing line between the two—the bed of Cherry Creek—disregarding warnings from the local Arapahoe Indians. The devastating flood of May 20, 1864 swept away the *News* building, printing press and all. Editor Byers quickly reestablished the *News* itself on the higher, drier Denver side of the mischievous creek where it remains to this day.

Floods were unusual in Colorado. The greater threat to early mining camps was fire. The hasty assemblages of frame buildings were virtual tinder-

boxes in the arid climate. The April 19, 1863 fire that destroyed most of Denver's lower downtown prompted city officials to require that all structures constructed thenceforth be made of brick or stone. After an 1873 fire left much of Central City in ashes, that town rebuilt in handsome stone and brick buildings. Many of the new structures, wearing 1874 building dates carved into their facades, adorn what is now the Central City—Black Hawk National Historic Landmark District.

Dario Gallegos operated Colorado's longest lived general store, which remained in the family from 1857 until the 1990s. When his daughter, Genoveva, married his business partner, A.A. Salazar, the store's future as a hub of the settlement of San Luis was assured. Doña Genoveva Salazar y Gallegos became a devoted mother and a noted curandera, or folk healer, who traveled around the San Luis Valley providing herbal remedies, as well as selling medicines in the Salazar Store. She became the matriarch of one of the state's most distinguished Hispanic pioneer families. Opened in 1857, the store still stands on Main Street, although it now has a second story and a stucco surface. Courtesy, Colorado Historical Society

COMMERCE

Supplies were shipped to the new territory from Illinois, Iowa, Missouri, New Mexico or Utah by ox-drawn wagons. The Pikes Peak settlements were more than 600 miles from Missouri River supply bases, and oxen traveled slowly. Freighters plodding across the plains risked Indian attacks, robbers and extreme weather to deliver everything from hardware to groceries, from dry goods to boozy wet goods. Demand far exceeded supply and prices were steep. Toll roads built into the mountains in the 1860s added even more to shipping costs.

New Colorado supply towns emerged along the Front Range to compete with Denver. Golden City, strategically sited where Clear Creek emerges from its gold rich canyons, as well as Colorado City on Fountain Creek and Pueblo on the Arkansas River, all competed to become the territorial capital and commercial hub. Realizing they could not afford to compete with each other as well as these rivals, Denver City and Auraria merged in April 1860. While the territorial capital had been captured by Colorado City and then by Golden, Denver prevailed, becoming the permanent capital in 1868.

The difficulty of transporting people and goods remained a major problem throughout Colorado's early years. The stage line of Russell, Majors and Waddell out of St. Joseph, Missouri was already making regular runs to army outposts in the West when the '59 gold rush began. They introduced the Leavenworth & Pikes Peak Express, with daily service for up to eight passengers able to pay one-way fares of $100 to $125. The Kansas-to-Cherry Creek journey took twelve days along the Republican River Trail. Switching to the South Platte route cut the total time to about a week. Short stops at relay stations along the way provided travelers with food, water, rest and the rudiments of personal hygiene, sometimes including communal hair and toothbrushes, which were tied to a string so that everyone could use them and no one would carry them off.

THE IRON HORSE

Colorado's isolation and high transportation costs kept the territory struggling during the 1860s, when the Civil War and Indians wars also curtailed settlement. Between 1870 and 1893, however, Colorado boomed with its most explosive growth ever. While the population had only grown from 34,277 in 1860 to 39,864 in 1870, it soared to 194,327 in 1880 and reached 539,700 by 1900.

While mining bonanzas and the post-Civil War era of peace and prosperity came into play, railroads were the prime movers behind the mushrooming growth. After the transcontinental railroad bypassed the highest state for the gentler hills of Wyoming, Coloradans began moving to that territory in large numbers. Without a railroad, as the *Cheyenne Daily Leader* put it, Denver and other Colorado towns would be "too dead to bury."

Since the railroad would not build to Colorado, Coloradans decided they must build to the railroad. *Rocky Mountain News* editor William Byers, former territorial governor John Evans and other movers and shakers formed the Denver Pacific Railroad to build a line to Cheyenne and the new transcontinental main line.

Citizens donated labor to help grade the tracks. They even cut trees and made railroad ties for the 106-mile line. Coloradans celebrated the arrival of the Denver Pacific on June 24, 1870. At last, Colorado lay on the nation's railroad maps. Once the Denver Pacific arrived, other railroads followed. After various iron horses galloped into Colorado during the 1870s, gold, silver, coal and other pay dirt began to pay off. Denver became the hub of a spider web of rails that reached nearly every sizeable or promising settlement.

After finishing the Denver Pacific, John Evans presided over the Denver, South Park and Pacific (DSP&P). This narrow gauge line, incorporated in 1872, followed the South Platte River into the Rockies. The DSP&P first stopped at Morrison, a scenic town located in the red sandstone foothills.

The Denver & Rio Grande Railroad's narrow gauge line from Alamosa to Durango has been partially restored as a summer tourist treat—the Cumbres & Toltec Scenic Railroad. As America's highest and longest steam excursion train, it slithers through spectacular mountain scenery in Southern Colorado and Northern New Mexico. Courtesy, Tom Noel Collection

The South Park line crawled up South Platte Canyon and over Kenosha Pass to tap South Park's goldfields. A spur line climbed over Boreas Pass to reach Breckenridge and Summit County's mineral riches. The main line ran through Fairplay and down Trout Creek Pass to the Arkansas River. From the Arkansas, a branch headed north to tap Leadville and what would become its million dollar silver mines. The main line resumed its quest for the Pacific with construction of the Alpine Tunnel, the first transportation bore under the Continental Divide. In 1883 the DSP&P ran out of steam in a mountain valley near Gunnison, 200 miles southwest of Denver. Like the Denver Pacific and all of Colorado's other "Pacific" railroads, the DSP&P never came within a thousand miles of that ocean. When gold and silver were discovered in the San Juan Mountains of Southwestern Colorado, the Denver & Rio Grande quickly built a line through the San Luis Valley and the San Juans to Durango and Silverton. The Durango to Silverton line still operates and another section, from Antonito, Colo-

Above and opposite page.
The Cumbres & Toltec Scenic Rairlroad takes on
water and coal at Antonito where conductor Ray
Martinez boards passengers. The train climbs
10,015 foot high Cumbres Pass. Photos by Tom Noel

rado to Chama, New Mexico, was restored in 1970 for a spectacular summer rail excursion.

David Moffat, one of John Evans' partners in many railroads, beginning with the Denver Pacific, created his own Moffat Road to construct a line to northwest Colorado. This standard gauge railroad ran from Denver to Moffat County in the northwest corner of Colorado. That line helped to bring prosperity to the towns of Fraser, Hot Sulphur Springs, Oak Creek, Steamboat Springs, Hayden and Craig. The old Moffat Railroad, now the Union Pacific, runs to this day, carrying northwest Colorado coal to power plants in eastern Colorado and Texas. These trains of more than 100 coal cars are impressive reminders that steam engines and coal fueled Colorado's first great boom between the arrival of the iron horse in 1870 and the 1893 silver crash.

Railroads began arriving in Colorado during the 1870s. Within the next fifty years, rail lines were built to, or created, hundreds of Colorado towns, many of which sprang up around railroad stations. As these smiling faces on the Moffat Line in northwestern Colorado suggest, railroads often brought prosperity as well as fast, inexpensive connection to the outside world. Courtesy, Colorado Historical Society

STREET RAILWAYS

Railroads fed Colorado's population boom, and street railways enabled cities such as Denver and Colorado Springs to expand outward onto the surrounding prairies. Street railways, later called streetcars and trolleys, began operating in Denver in 1871. Soon streetcar systems also served Aspen, Boulder, Cripple Creek, Durango, Fort Collins, Grand Junction, Greeley and Pueblo. Coloradans settled along these streetcar lines in the larger cities or along the railroad tracks in smaller towns and rural areas. Thanks to railroads and street railroads, 100,000 newcomers called Colorado home by 1900.

While railroads brought 100,000 new settlers to Colorado by 1900, street railways, such as this Cherrelyn Horse Car operating on the Broadway line between Englewood and Denver, enabled Coloradans to settle in streetcar suburbs. The horse pulled the car uphill then climbed aboard for the ride down. Courtesy, Tom Noel collection

8

RANCHING

In the Sagebrush, *by Carl Rungius, early 1900s.*
Courtesy, The Anschutz Collection

Colorado's first cowboys, as well as their cattle, sheep, hogs, burros, horses and other livestock, came north from Mexico. Their tiny adobe villages, founded as early as 1851 in the San Luis Valley along the upper Rio Grande, gave birth to the state's rich ranching heritage.

VAQUEROS

The Hispano *vaquero* was the model for the American cowboy, who borrowed clothing, equipment and herding practices from early Hispanic ranching traditions. Even the word "ranch" is an Anglicized version of the Spanish term *rancho*, meaning a grant of land for the purpose of raising livestock.

Don Juan de Oñate trailed cattle on his pioneer trip up the Rio Grande in 1598. In early Hispanic settlements along that river and its tributaries, cattle provided milk and meat. Like the Indians who used every part of the buffalo, the Spanish used much of the cattle they slaughtered. The tallow made candles while cowhide made leather for clothing, shoes, ropes, saddles and household furnishings.

FEEDING THE GOLD RUSHERS

Hispanic ranchers alone could not feed the thousands of fortune seekers pouring into Colorado after the 1859 gold rush. Soon *gringos* also ventured into the livestock business. That idea dawned on emigrants in wagons pulled by teams of oxen with the family cow following behind. When gold mining did not pan out, some decided that there might be more money in raising livestock.

Pikes Peak guidebooks lured settlers not only with promises of mineral bonanzas but also with descriptions of verdant grasslands suitable for grazing. Jack Henderson, an 1858 gold rusher, was one of the first to abandon mining for ranching. Henderson arrived in Denver with an ox team and a wagonload of supplies. He soon sold the goods, but could not find a place to quarter his cattle. So he took them to an island in the South Platte River and turned them loose. To his surprise, they thrived on native grasses, showing up sleek and fat in the spring. He quickly found a market for them in Denver and the mountain mining towns. This inspired

Before 1900 Colorado ran on horse power and, as this scene in the mining town of Alma documents, burro power. The Colorado livestock industry not only fed, but also transported Coloradans. Business in horses, mules, oxen and burros was as brisk then as it is today in motor vehicles. Courtesy, Colorado Historical Society

Part rodeo and part fiesta, with mariachi bands and swirling senoritas, the Mexican Rodeo Extravaganza attracts a full house to the Denver Coliseum during the National Western Stock Show. Gerald "Gerry" Diaz and his horse Grano de Oro perform here in this celebration of the Hispanic roots of the ranching industry. Photo by Glenn Cuerden

Henderson to set up a ranch on what was then Henderson's Island in the South Platte River. The island is gone today, but Henderson, Colorado, hosts the Adams County Fairgrounds.

JOHN WESLEY ILIFF: KING OF THE CATTLE BARONS

John Wesley Iliff was bitten by the gold bug at age eighteen. His father offered him a $7,500 interest in the family farm back in Ohio, but young Johnny replied, "No, just give me $500 and let me go west."

Quickly sensing that mining was a long shot, the Ohioan opened a general store on Blake Street in Denver. There, Iliff exchanged groceries, clothing and supplies for livestock from cash-strapped immigrants. He rested and fattened the animals on the open range and then sold their beef. With the proceeds, he began buying land along the South Platte in northeastern Colorado.

Iliff began capturing large contracts to provide beef. In 1868 Iliff began supplying meat to the Union Pacific crews constructing the transcontinental railroad through Wyoming. To fulfill this very large order, Iliff bought many of the Longhorns that Charles Goodnight brought up from Texas along the Goodnight-Loving Trail. Soon Iliff was supplying not only the Union Pacific construction crews but also Indian reservations. His cattle fed the Denver Pacific construction crew, building a line from Cheyenne to Denver. Iliff, who received $6.90 per hundred pounds of beef delivered, also fed crews constructing the Colorado Central Railroad from Golden up Clear Creek to the mining towns of Black Hawk, Central City and Georgetown.

By 1878 Iliff owned a ranching empire of 35,000 cattle and 15,558 acres along the northwest side of the South Platte between Greeley and Julesburg. His control of the river and its tributaries gave him a virtual monopoly on the drylands beyond, as well. There, his cattle grazed on an estimated 650,000 acres of public domain.

Every year Iliff bought 10,000 to 15,000 Texas Longhorns, paying ten to fifteen dollars a head for cattle weighing 600 to 800 pounds. He fattened them on grass for a year or two until they reached 1,000 to 1,200 pounds and then sold them for thirty to fifty dollars each.

After Iliff died in 1878, his widow, Elizabeth Sarah Fraser Iliff, took over his vast spread. Elizabeth had come to Denver from Chicago as the Singer Sewing Machine's sales manager for the western region. She had a store in Denver and also sold sewing machines out of a buckboard. Once, when her buckboard broke down out on the plains, she was rescued by the tall, handsome, brown-haired, blue-eyed J.W. Iliff. He had no interest in sewing, but liked her spunk and fell in love with her. She gave up selling sewing machines to marry Colorado's most affluent and eligible bachelor, who had lost his wife to a fatal illness.

Elizabeth soon had her late husband's cattle empire humming as smoothly as one of her sewing machines. She ultimately gave $100,000 to endow the Iliff School of Theology at the University of Denver in honor of her husband.

JOHN WESLEY PROWERS

John Wesley Prowers came to Colorado as a teenager, hauling goods on the Santa Fe Trail to Bent's Fort on the Arkansas River. In 1861 Prowers married Amache, the daughter of a prominent Cheyenne. That same year Prowers bought 100 Missouri cattle and began acquiring prime land along the Purgatoire and Arkansas rivers. He, like Iliff, acquired riverside and creekside lands that gave him control of adjacent waterless uplands.

Prowers did much to improve cattle breeding in Colorado, where he introduced some of the first Herefords in 1871. By 1881 he owned 80,000 acres along forty miles of river frontage and controlled 400,000 acres of rangeland and 10,000 head of cattle. At his death in 1884 Prowers had become Colorado's second millionaire rancher. Prowers County in southeastern Colorado bears his name.

THE BEEF BOOM

Cattle and sheep ranches provided meat for Indians on reservations, soldiers on military posts, railroad construction crews, mining camps and new towns. After railroads arrived in the 1870s, Colorado beef was also shipped to markets back East, including Kansas City and Chicago. By 1880 Colorado produced more beef than any state but

Texas, and more sheep and wool than any state but New Mexico.

Between 1870 and 1880 the number of cattle in Colorado had climbed from 291,000 to 809,000. Ranchers grazed their cattle for free on public lands and paid cowboys less than a dollar a day. Profits as high as 40 percent a year enticed many investors. This cattle boom led to overstocking the American West with more than seven million cattle by 1885.

After cattle exhausted the prairies' buffalo and blue grama grasses, they were replaced by sagebrush, salt brush, Russian thistle and other less nutritious plants, if not by dusty wastes of bare soil. Overgrazing left the animals weakened and malnourished when the blizzards struck. Beginning with a snow storm in November, the winter of 1885-86 gripped the high plains for five months. Howling winds and bitter cold temperatures as low as minus forty-six degrees Fahrenheit kept ranchers and cowboys confined to their houses and bunkhouses while blizzards wiped out their cattle. That winter proved

Above
San Luis, the oldest town in Colorado, retains the communal grazing land seen here between the town and the Sangre de Cristo Mountains. On this vega (Spanish for "grassland"), all town residents can graze their livestock. Established in 1851, San Luis supplied meat and flour to northern Colorado mining towns. Photo by Tom Noel

Opposite page
As gold and silver mining dwindled in the early 1900s, the livestock industry boomed. Encouraged by posters such as this, agriculturalists began gathering in Denver every January for what has evolved into the National Western Stock Show. Courtesy, Colorado Historical Society

to be the first of several disastrous ones. A million or more cattle starved or froze to death. Texas Longhorns, with their thin hides, lack of body fat and light hair which reflected rather than absorbed sunshine, proved especially vulnerable.

SECOND ANNUAL CONVENTION

NATIONAL LIVE STOCK ASSOCIATION

AND NATIONAL EXHIBITION OF RANGE CATTLE

DENVER, COLO., JAN. 24-25-26-27, 1899.

LOW RATES ON ALL RAILROADS.

WOOLIES

Troubles in the cattle industry opened the door for sheep ranchers who were moving north from Colorado's San Luis Valley and New Mexico. Demand for wool to make Civil War uniforms had sparked a Southern Colorado sheep-raising boom in the early 1860s. Sheep required less water than cattle and fed on plants that cattle shunned.

Cattlemen fought the sheep invasion out of the belief that sheep ruined grazing land. Range wars led to violence as thousands of sheep were driven over cliffs and sheep herders' camps and wagons were attacked. Colorado's cattle-sheep wars were as murderous as those of the Johnson County, Wyoming and Lincoln County, New Mexico conflicts. Despite cowboys slaughtering whole flocks and terrorizing or murdering their keepers, the sheep industry grew. By 1900 Colorado boasted 2 million sheep with the count rising to 3 million by 1914. Sheep, in fact, were more numerous than cattle in Colorado between 1900 and 1950.

END OF THE OPEN RANGE

As cattle ranching grew, so did the open range system. On the boundless prairies, cattle traveled in search of grass and water. Allowing cattle to roam free across the range scattered them, but the annual spring and fall roundups gathered most of them back into the herds.

The open range system, however, was doomed by an invention of Joseph F. Glidden. To keep his wife's chickens from escaping their farm in De Kalb, Illinois, Glidden devised a fence by twisting together two strands of wire with pointed barbs at short intervals. After that invention kept his chickens in and his neighbors' livestock out, Glidden patented barbwire in 1874. He rented a small factory in De Kalb and began making the wire. Within a few months Glidden's Barb Fence Company installed steam-powered machinery to increase production to five tons a day. Eager buyers in the treeless prairies bought wire for eighteen cents a pound as fast as he could make it.

Even the most ferocious Longhorns backed off after being cut by the new-fangled fence. Soon other entrepreneurs jumped into the barbwire busi-

Between 1900 and 1950 sheep were more numerous than cattle in Colorado. At nearly every county fair, sheep, such as these Columbias raised by the Esplin family, have competed for blue ribbons. Courtesy, Tom Noel collection

ness. In Pueblo, Colorado, the giant Colorado Fuel and Iron Company began producing barbwire that kept the plant booming. Ranchers began fencing in their herds with barbwire, while farmers used it to keep livestock out of their crops.

Farmers and others objected to livestock owners who fenced off an estimated 2.5 million acres of public land in Colorado alone. Their protests led President Grover Cleveland to sign an 1885 bill outlawing the common ranching practice of appropriating the public domain.

GREELEY: COLORADO'S GREAT AGRICULTURAL COLONY

Farmers, lured by the Homestead Act's 160-acre-per-family allowance, began claiming their own parcels of the open range. They plowed up and fenced much of Colorado's high plains, then dug ditches to irrigate crops. The most successful early experiment at farming the Colorado high plains

came when *New York Tribune* editor Horace Greeley and his agricultural editor, Nathan Meeker, established the Union Colony at Greeley in northeast Colorado along the South Platte River. This agrarian utopia used the collective efforts of its members to build irrigation canals and to fence the colony. Some said the Greeley "saints" did this to keep out other, less godly Coloradans. But colony founder Nathan Meeker explained that "fences would promote order and decency, for our town and colony will be disgraced by cattle running at large through our streets."

The Colorado State Fair has been held in Pueblo every summer since 1887. Attractions include rodeo acts, such as calf roping and trick riding, where this young lady thrilled the crowd. Courtesy, Denver Public Library

PIG PROBLEMS

Sheep and cattle were not the only kinds of livestock raised in Colorado. One Missouri entrepreneur brought a herd of 250 swine to Denver in 1861. Pigs caused problems, according to the August 6, 1863 *Denver Commonwealth:* "People buy hogs, pasture them in the streets and grow rich out of the proceeds, but every housekeeper is daily pestered with them. Nothing but a sentry at the door keeps them out of the house [and] anything left for a moment out of doors is rooted up and eaten up."

From pigs to sheep to cattle, livestock became the most profitable part of Colorado agriculture, with a higher dollar value than all crops combined. By 1900 livestock had become a $40 million industry and as economically important to Colorado as mining.

Above and opposite page
Denver's Stockyards, shown here in 1925, emerged as a major American livestock market and meat processing center. Cattle, sheep and hogs from throughout the Rocky Mountain region rode the rails into stockyards, which are now mostly empty except during the National Western Stock Show, held every January since 1906. Courtesy, Colorado Railroad Museum

VANISHING RANCHES

During Colorado's 1870 to 1893 population boom many ranches, farms and dairies surrounding Denver, Pueblo and other cities were developed. John Brisben Walker converted his northwest Denver alfalfa farm into the town of Berkeley. In northeast Denver, two German barons transformed their horse and cattle farms into suburban developments. Baron Eugene A. von Winkler planned Park Hill, while his friend Baron Walter von Richthofen developed Montclair. During the 1880s real estate boom other cities spread onto what had been ranch land. In the 1890s Cripple Creek sprouted up overnight on what had been cow pasture.

In Denver, Edwin and Louise Harman converted their homestead into the town of Harman, better known today as the fashionable Cherry Creek neighborhood. Rufus "Potato" Clark's vast potato farm evolved into two residential neighborhoods—Washington Park and University Park. On the west side of Denver, Thomas Sloan converted his farm and lake into another residential area, Sloan's Lake, to accommodate the rapidly growing city. By 1902 nearly all of these streetcar suburbs had been annexed by the City and County of Denver.

During the 1900s automobile suburbs further transformed agricultural land on the outskirts of cities and towns into other uses. Hayden Ranch, on West Sixth Avenue in what is now Lakewood, became a federal weapons plant during World War II and later the Denver Federal Center. That huge complex employs thousand of people in hundreds of federal agencies, inspiring Coloradans to boast having a "Little Washington" on what had been a cattle ranch and turkey farm. Likewise, the

Martin Marietta Corporation (now Lockheed Martin Space Systems) transformed the C. K. Verdos Ranch, southwest of Littleton in Jefferson County, into a huge manufacturing complex for missiles, rockets, satellites and other aerospace devices.

Between Denver and Boulder, portions of the Church and Zang ranches became the City of Broomfield. Once a sleepy community of farmers raising broom corn, Broomfield grew so rapidly during the 1990s that it was restructured as Colorado's sixty-fourth county in 2001. Broomfield County, with its huge Flatirons Crossing shopping haven, big box stores, high-rise hotels and office buildings, offers few clues that it was largely agricultural until the 1990s when the fields of broom corn vanished.

Douglas County, mostly ranchland until the 1960s, became the fastest growing county in the United States, mushrooming from 8,407 in 1970 to 175,766 in 2000. Highlands Ranch, a 21,000-acre working cattle ranch in 1970, became Colorado's most populous former ranch. Highlands Ranch originated during the early 1900s as John Springer, like other large ranchers whose money came primarily from non-agricultural activities, took advantage of down markets to buy out small ranchers and farmers at distress sale prices or by acquiring acreage at tax sales. The Phipps family, one of Colorado's wealthiest clans, later acquired Springer's ranch and expanded it into Highlands Ranch. Descendants of Lawrence C. Phipps, Jr., cashed out, selling Highlands Ranch for development of what is now the largest city in Douglas County.

Jefferson County's population has also soared, from 371,753 in 1980 to 527,056 in 2000. The high tide of suburbanization lapped into the foothills when the Ken-Caryl Ranch was acquired by the Johns-Manville Corporation in 1971 and turned into a corporate headquarters, a research and development park, and housing for 13,000 people.

Since 1980 Colorado has been losing about 100,000 acres of agricultural land a year to developers. The Highest State, according to the U.S. Department of Agriculture's Census of Agriculture, is losing rural land faster than any states except Texas and New Mexico. Many ranchers sell all or part of their land to gain financial security for their

Scrawny, half-wild Texas Longhorns were gradually replaced by purebred cattle such as these Herefords, a beefy British breed. The San Isabel Ranch, shown here, was established in Westcliffe in 1874 by the Kettle clan of English immigrants. Photo by Tom Noel

families or to get out of what has often been a risky, marginal business.

The loss of scenic agricultural landscapes has inspired state and local governments, along with various private conservation agencies, to offer conservation easements. By this device, ranchers and farmers are given a tax credit for agreeing not to develop their land. Thanks to increasing protections for agricultural lands as buffers between fast growing cities and towns, Coloradans can still see barns, cows, horses and other barnyard creatures that were once familiar, everyday sights.

COLORADO CATTLE QUEENS

Cowboys and cattlemen get the attention, but women often ran—and still run—Colorado's ranches. John Wesley Iliff's widow Elizabeth oversaw the largest ranch ever to exist in Colorado—15,558 acres and 35,000 cattle. Mrs. Iliff, according to the April 11, 1882 *Cheyenne Daily Leader*, "was the wealthiest woman in Colorado . . . there is no better business woman." The press added that "of the 800 stockwomen now doing business in Colorado, all are well and favorably known . . . of all the failures in stock raising in this Western Country, not one has been made by women. They have got the clearest heads and the best judgments as regarding stock."

More recently, cattlewomen such as Tweet Kimball of the Cherokee Ranch near Sedalia, Bet Kettle of the San Isabel Ranch near Westcliffe, and Mildred Janowitz of the Horse Patch Farms near Parker have made history. In Colorado's famed Anschutz clan, Sue Anschutz-Rodgers has outdone her father and her brother Philip as a rancher, developing one of the state's largest and best run spreads, the Crystal River Ranch in Garfield and Pitkin counties.

Sue Anschutz-Rodgers grew up in Kansas, where her great grandfather, Christian Anschutz, had settled along with other Germans from Russia. These Germans, known as some of the world's best farmers, had been brought to Russia by Tzarina Catherine the Great to farm the Volga Valley.

The Crystal River Ranch with Mt. Sopris in the background (below) is named for the Crystal River which waters the ranch through the Sweet Jessup Ditch (right). Courtesy, Tom Noel Collection

When later czars no longer allowed them to keep their German language, religion, culture and draft exempt status, many of them came to America. They brought with them Russian wheat, a winter crop that transformed the high plains into America's bread basket.

"I grew up with a love of the open land and a love of horses," Anschutz-Rodgers recalls. "I started riding at age three. My mother avoided horses after one stepped on her and she let out the only swear words of her entire life." Sue, like her mother, taught school and began spending summers with her family in Colorado.

She loved the ranch her father had purchased in 1966—the Crystal River Ranch on a mesa overlooking Mount Sopris. Her father and brother Phil spent much of their time with Circle A Oil, the

Anschutz Drilling Company, real estate and other investments. "My father," Sue recalled in 2004, "had a real knack for picking ranchland that had oil on it. As a girl, I would go out with him to check on oil wells and sit there on the wellhead with him, waiting hopefully for it to come in."

"I acquired my father and brother's interests in the Crystal River Ranch in 1987. To learn operations, I shadowed the foreman everywhere. From one bull and about thirty-three cows, we have grown to 1,700 head. We actually have an exact count, including each new calf the day it is born because, while ranchers traditionally keep their records in a little notebook in their shirt pockets, we have computerized our cow-calf operation and also our hay production, where we usually get two crops a year."

9

SODBUSTERS

From the 1920s to the 1950s sugar beets were Colorado's top crop. Photo by Tom Noel

Stephen H. Long examined the tough prairie sod on his 1820 expedition and branded Colorado "The Great American Desert." In his official U.S. government report, he judged it "almost wholly unfit for cultivation and of course uninhabitable by a people depending upon agriculture for their sustenance." Long had no way of knowing that prehistoric Indians in Southwestern Colorado had developed irrigation systems and thrived on raising corn, squash and beans for hundreds of years. Their ability to farm the "desert" resulted in one of North America's greatest and most populous cultures whose spectacular achievements are commemorated at Mesa Verde National Park.

Out on the eastern plains that failed to impress Long, the Apache had likewise grown corn successfully in the Arkansas River Valley. Over thousands of years other tribes cultivated or at least harvested edible plants. Only after they acquired horses did they abandon an agricultural way of life to become buffalo hunters.

Hispanic settlers in the San Luis Valley introduced many crops to Colorado, notably wheat, lettuce, potatoes, onions, peas and other vegetables and fruits that could tolerate Colorado's notorious late and early frosts, hail storms and hot, dry summers. As early as 1856 José Jacques built a water-powered mill on the Conejos River to grind wheat and corn into flour and meal. Such skillful Southern Colorado farmers supplied many of the mining communities in northern and central Colorado during the 1860s and 1870s.

As thousands of people poured into Colorado, the need to develop domestic agriculture became crucial. As long as settlers had to pay high freight charges for expensive food brought in from Southern Colorado, Utah, California and the Midwest, the area would stagnate, if not starve.

The Great American Desert had to be turned into a Garden of Eden. Fortunately, the Mormons in the Utah Desert had shown this could be done. From that even drier territory, fresh fruits and vegetables, butter and eggs, and grains rolling into Colorado proved that the desert could be made productive. Editor William Byers of the *Rocky Mountain News* urged Coloradans to try farming and experimented himself with various crops, including a vineyard and orchard in South Denver. In the

windows of the *News* office as well as in its pages, he puffed locally grown fruits, vegetables and other horticultural triumphs.

One of Byers' sweetest exhibits was the first honeycomb made from Colorado blossoms. It was the proud possession of Isaac McBroom, who brought the first colony of bees across the plains by ox team in 1862. He settled near Littleton, where his cabin is on exhibit at the Littleton Historical Museum. While Whites feasted on home grown honey, Indians complained about stings from the "white man's flies."

Potatoes sustained many of the pioneers. They generally brought spuds along in their wagons and tried to save one or two as seed potatoes to plant when they reached Colorado. "Potatoes are thus far the great staple," noted the April 13, 1864 *Rocky Mountain News*, adding that they were "the easiest crop transported and kept for winter use."

Rufus H. "Potato" Clark, the most prominent pioneer potato planter, raised thousands of spuds in the sandy soil along the South Platte River in what is now South Denver. Clark thrived by supplying not only Denver, but also Central City, Georgetown and other mining towns with tons of his pet product.

Isaac McBroom's 1860s cabin has been relocated and restored on the living history farm at the Littleton Historical Museum. Courtesy, Littleton Historical Museum

Greeley became Colorado's spud city. Record-setting harvests such as this one—18,100 pounds of potatoes in 143 sacks—inspired the northern Colorado community to make Potato Day its town festival. Courtesy, Tom Noel Collection

By the 1880s Colorado was exporting potatoes to other states. Greeley displaced Denver as Colorado's potato capital and touted the size, taste and shapeliness of its potatoes. The *Greeley Tribune* even urged, on April 1, 1874, that "It would be profitable to have a college devoted to teaching the best method for growing potatoes, having potato professors and potato students." Colorado looked like it might become the potato state until the Colorado potato beetle began devastating crops. The San Luis Valley in Southern Colorado continued, however, to be a major potato producing region, making Colorado to this day a rival of Idaho in spuds.

IRRIGATED FARMING

Settlers from wetter regions generally felt that farming would be impossible in Colorado without irrigation. David K. Wall of Golden dug one of the first irrigation ditches in northern Colorado. Wall, who had learned irrigated farming techniques in California, arrived in Colorado in May of 1859 with farming tools, garden seeds and seed potatoes. He called on Editor Byers at the *News* and left some seed packages with him. "All ye who wish fresh

vegetables," Byers advertised in next day's *News*, "walk in and select your packages at twenty-five cents each." In Golden, Wall grubstaked John H. Gregory's gold discovery, helped lay out the town, dug the pioneer irrigation ditch and began supplying crops to hordes of hungry miners.

The Union Colony at Greeley introduced irrigated farming on a much larger scale during the 1870s. Some 600 Union Colonists, each of whom had invested $600 and taken a pledge of temperance and good behavior, worked together to dig canals diverting water from the Cache la Poudre River. These canals ranged from two to five feet in depth, from fifteen to twenty-two feet in width, and from ten to twenty-two miles in length. Each farmer could use the water one day a week to water his or her Greeley acreage. Within fifty years, town founder Nathan Meeker prophesied in the *Greeley Tribune*, "beautiful trees will adorn the scene, fruits of almost every kind will abound, noble mansions, the homes of happy farmers, will extend for miles." Greeley did thrive, becoming second only to Salt Lake City as a prosperous irrigated farming colony.

Another successful agricultural settlement arose around the abandoned army post at Fort Collins, located twenty-five miles up the Cache la Poudre from its confluence with the South Platte at Greeley. Settlers of "good character" could buy memberships for $50, $150 or $250, entitling them to town lots and surrounding irrigated farmland.

To secure the State Agricultural College, Fort Collins residents donated a 240-acre campus site on the south side of town. When the state balked at funding higher education, the Fort Collins Town Company raised money for the college by selling lots. In 1879 the Colorado State Agricultural College finally opened Old Main to students. A fourteen by twenty-eight foot potting shed on the grounds was alternatively used as a bachelors' hall, as a chemical laboratory and as home for the

president and his family of seven. Renamed Colorado State University in 1945, the old aggie college is now a full-blown university with more than 20,000 students. Yet CSU remains best known for advancing horticulture through research and training students in various agricultural sciences.

DRY LAND FARMING

The Agricultural College joined railroads to encourage immigration to Colorado and promote dry land farming. The railroads convinced settlers to

Winter wheat is sometimes called "Russian wheat" because the Volga Deutsch, who are famous for cultivating it, are Germans of Russian ancestry. The wheat is planted in late summer or fall and harvested in early summer, as shown here. It not only collects winter moisture, but also helps to keep bare soil from eroding and blowing away. Courtesy, Tom Noel Collection

sell some of their vast land grant acreage in order to create trackside towns and farms that would generate rail business. The dry land farming campaign encouraged use of drought-resistant crops that could survive without irrigation.

As early as the 1870s the Kansas Pacific Railroad set up agricultural experiment stations on its eastern Colorado line. Agents planted winter wheat in the fall to be nourished by winter snows and harvested in late spring before the hot dry summer arrived. Other happy experiments included raising corn to feed livestock, grazing grasses, and getting some trees to grow, including Chinese elms, Lombardy poplars, Russian olives and evergreens. Kansas Pacific agents reported that "Except to soak some of the seeds or to puddle the roots . . . not one drop of water was applied by human agency." The settler, the railroad concluded, "may adorn his home with trees, may grow fruits and timber, may raise grains and other vegetable food for his family and livestock without resorting to expensive processes of artificial watering."

Grain elevators are the tallest and largest structures in many agricultural towns. They conserve wheat, corn, barley and other grains until the markets and the railroads are ready to take them to processing centers. These concrete giants dominate the tiny hamlet of Amherst in the northeastern corner of Colorado. Photo by Tom Noel

With its promotional campaign, the Kansas Pacific and its successor, the Union Pacific, lured sodbusters to the Great American Desert. Research and education begun by the railroads to market the high plains was continued by the Colorado Agricultural College, which established its own agricultural experiment and educational stations. The CSU station at Cheyenne Wells, for instance, issued bulletins telling people how to survive on the high, dry plains. First of all, they could build their own houses on the treeless prairies out of the native sod, which would keep their families warm in winter and cool in summer. Prospective farmers were instructed to simply dig sod bricks four-inches wide, one-inch thick and sixteen to eighteen inches long and pile them upside down on top of each other, using lumber or stones to frame door and windows openings. Sticks or brush could be used to frame the roof, which should also be covered with sod. Less ambitious farmers might dig a home out of a hillside. For fuel, settlers were instructed to use buffalo or cow chips or corn and sunflower stalks.

Thousands of such low-budget homes were built, but few survive. Dry land farming proved more difficult than the railroads or CSU brochures might have suggested. Drought years—such as those of the 1890s, 1930s and 1950s, 1970s and early 2000s—drove out many farmers and left the eastern Colo-

Right
Colorado's only African American colony, the town of Dearfield in Weld County, recruited members with this poster. Like so many agricultural towns founded with high hopes, Dearfield succumbed to the hot, dry, windy summers and blizzard-blasted winters on the high plains. Courtesy, Denver Public Library

Below
Today, these ruins of the town café mark the Dearfield site. 1996 Photo by Tom Noel

BUILDING THE TOWN OF DEARFIELD

Dearfield Townsite and Settlement

LOCATION.

Two miles south of the Union Pacific Railroad, Masters Station. Seventy-two miles northeast of Denver in Weld County, Colorado. Elevation 3,800 feet above sea level. Population in the farming settlement of Dearfield, 500.

O. T. JACKSON, Founder

We are selling lots and tracts of land in the town of Dearfield on easy payments. Lots $25.00 and up. Tracts $250.00 and up according to their location to the center of the town.

OFFICES:

Dearfield, Masters, Colo. P. O.   Dearfield Agency, Denver, Colorado.

NEGROES FARMING IN EASTERN COLORADO.

Fifteen years ago farming was discussed among leading Negroes in Colorado as a new avenue for employment and self-help. May 5th, 1910 a settlement was started upon Government land in Weld County where 20,000 acres in one body was open for homesteading. One settler filed on 320 acres as a desert claim, and one filed on 160 acres as a homestead claim. These men talked with their friends and got others interested in the plan. Now there are sixty families occupying 15,000 acres of the 20,000 acres. The other 5,000 acres has since been taken up by a good class of white settlers. Within a radius of twenty miles around Dearfield Settlement there are as many more colored families and farmers. There are now in eastern Colorado five hundred colored families on farms and two thousand Negro farmers and farm hands. Just now there is a demand for 500 farmers and farm hands.

The Dearfield Settlement has a Townsite platted on state land consisting of 480 acres. There are eight blocks of town lots for business and residence, and unplatted blocks of 5 or 10 acres (less

rado plains littered with abandoned buildings, tattered windmills and withered dreams.

OTHER AGRICULTURAL COLONIES

Irrigated farming communities such as Longmont, founded in 1871 in Boulder County by the Chicago Colorado Colony, fared better. That town thrived by digging ditches and raising, among other things, pumpkins and turkeys. Mormons from Utah established horticultural hamlets in the San Luis Valley, including Bountiful, La Jara and Sanford.

Nucla, Colorado's only experiment with socialism, was founded by the Colorado Cooperative Company in western Colorado's Montrose County. This utopian organization established its town on the San Miguel River in 1893 with the philosophy that "equality and service rather than greed and competition should be the basis of conduct." Although the town has survived, its founding socialistic philosophy has not.

Another unique colony was Oliver T. Jackson's African American farming colony, established in 1910 east of Greeley. Some sixty Black families settled in Dearfield, but the town, like so many agricultural settlements opened with high hopes, failed within a few decades, leaving only ruins along U.S. Highway 34.

GRASSHOPPERS

Towns such as Dearfield faced myriad ordeals in cultivating the dusty, dry, wind-blasted high plains. Obstacles such as grasshopper plagues retarded Colorado's efforts to become agriculturally self sufficient for decades. Grasshoppers, or Rocky Mountain locusts (*Melanoplus spretus*), became a problem of Biblical proportions.

When Colorado talk turns to these insect pests, the great hopper plague of 1875 cannot be forgotten. Grasshoppers smothered the state, even derailing trains after pulverized hoppers greased the tracks. The high-hopping bugs consumed everything green, then began munching clothes hanging out to dry. On August 2, 1875 the *Rocky Mountain News* reported, "At noon they looked like snowflakes in the sky, filling the air thickly as far as the eye could reach. In the evening they literally covered walls, fences and pavements. Corn was stripped to the bare stalk. The trees were loaded with them. All kinds of garden vegetables were devoured rapidly and lawns and grass plats suffered visibly."

No one dared walk outside for fear of being smothered by hoppers. The *Central City Register* reported that even in that mountain mining town "it seemed as if the whole universe was one vast

Grasshopper invasions began devastating farms in the 1870s, when the state was trying to become agriculturally self-sufficient. Hordes of hoppers, technically know as "Rocky Mountain locusts," even infested cities, as this Colorado Springs storeowner discovered. After the federal government allocated funds to fight grasshopper plagues, one Coloradan celebrated in verse: "Uncle Sam, it appears, has consented at last/To scatter a few of his coppers/Among those cleaned out by the hoppers." Courtesy, Pikes Peak Library District

moving tide of grasshoppers and that universal destruction of vegetation marked their tracks."

Locusts caused billions in property loss, wiping out hundreds of farmers. The hoppers first showed up in destructive hordes in 1864 and sporadically invaded parts of Colorado in subsequent summers. "Colorado," reported the June 12, 1875 *News*, "has millions and millions of these little mowing machines in operation . . . in numerous instances they have colonized and become staid and sober citizens. Each morning they refresh their stomachs with the night's growth of herbage in the vicinity, and they lay around in the sun during the day, kicking up their heels in exultant game, telling grasshopper stories." At least, the press added, "One sweet solemn thought comes to us o'er and o'er again—they cannot eat up our mines."

The 1875 invasion triggered a war. The U.S. Secretary of War offered a $138,000 "grasshopper appropriation" to Colorado and other western states devastated by the locusts. Colorado Governor John L.

Around 200 failed farming communities became ghost towns in Colorado. Go-backers leaving abandoned farmsteads, like this one, sometimes tacked explanations to their shacks, such as: "Eaten out by hoppers. Gone back east to the wife's folks." Photo by Tom Noel

Routt advocated a state appropriation to study the problem and sponsored statutes protecting insectivorous birds. Washington established a federal grasshopper commission that dished out advice such as:

1) Plow under the grasshopper eggs at hatching time,

2) Use kerosene to kill the critters,

3) Flood fields to drown or discourage the hoppers and

4) Use chickens, turkeys, hogs and birds to swallow the problem.

Various inventors came up with grasshopper killers, including a tractor-sized vacuum cleaner that chewed up the bugs and spit them out as fertilizer. But nothing seemed to really work. Grasshoppers thrive to this day and have devastated Colorado as recently as the 1930s, 1950s and 1970s.

During the 1930s, when hoppers compounded Great Depression era problems of drought and the dust bowl, the federal government provided a "government poison" of sawdust, molasses and sodium arsenite, lethal to the insidious insects. Rural roads were darkened by twin tracks of squashed hoppers. Service stations sold hopper guards to put in front of radiator grills so their smashed masses would not shut off air intake and cause automobile engines to overheat.

In July of 1978 the locusts came back by the billions. They marched across eastern Colorado, blotting out the sun and de-greening fields. Governor Richard D. Lamm visited Prowers and Baca County in southeastern Colorado, the hardest hit area. He walked through the infested fields, managing to squish a few of the critters, but thousands more rose up at the sound of his footsteps and buzzed away. The governor called a special session of the legislature to deal with the crisis. At first, Republicans refused to come, saying Lamm invented the crisis to help him win rural votes in the fall elections. They suggested the governor eat grasshoppers.

After Democrats brought boxes of hoppers to the State Capitol to hum away in the house and the senate, the legislature appropriated $2 million for a spraying program. Malathion was applied to rangelands and Sevin to croplands, according to the July 8, 1978 *Denver Post*. Lamm was reelected that fall with the help of thankful farmers, but his sterling reputation as an environmentalist was tarnished by criticism from the Environmental Protection Agency and other bug lovers.

THE WESTERN SLOPE

The Western Slope—all of Colorado west of the Continental Divide—attracted agriculturalists. Moist mountain valleys proved ideal for growing hay, which has long been one of the state's top crops. The Western Slope, however, is best known for its peaches and, to a lesser extent, its pears, apples and cherries.

This peachy phenomenon began after the 1884 construction of the Grand River Ditch, a thirty-five-foot-wide canal, running twenty-four miles from Palisade to Fruita. After Grand River Ditch and other canals began carrying Colorado River water to orchards, Palisade, Grand Junction, Delta, Fruita, Cedaredge, Paonia and other Mesa and Delta County towns flourished. Since the 1990s the same area has also produced Colorado's latest agricultural bonanza. Although a few small, isolated vineyards had opened earlier on an experimental basis, the Grand Valley wine boom put Colorado on the map as a grape growing and wine making state. From four miniscule vineyards in 1990, the industry has grown to more than forty official wineries.

Wine, however, has never been as important to Colorado as beer. The Coors Brewery in Golden claims to be the largest single site brewery in the world. As the nation's number three suds seller in 2005, it merged with the Molson Brewery of Montreal to become more of an international competitor. Anheuser-Busch, the world's largest brewery, opened a mammoth plant north of Fort Collins in 1988. Besides these two giants, Colorado boasts around a hundred brew pubs and micro breweries. All told, the state leads the country in the amount of beer produced per capita, and Colorado farmers provide much of the hops and barley.

On the Western Slope, the town of Olathe has emerged as a major regional producer of sweet corn. This yellow and white maize is now marketed widely, but has not yet become as celebrated as Colorado's most famous single crop: the honeydew melons from the Rocky Ford area.

SUGAR BEETS

While ranking second nationally in melons and lettuce, Colorado led the country by the 1920s in sugar beet production and continued to do so until the industry soured in the 1960s. After the first major sugar beet factory opened in Grand Junction in 1899, the Great Western Sugar Beet Company, as well as three smaller companies, opened some twenty plants in Colorado towns. Beet sugar production encouraged the rise of candy makers such as Jolly Rancher in Wheat Ridge, Enstrom's in Grand Junction, Rocky Mountain Chocolates in Durango, Stephany's in Arvada, and Russell Stover, which moved from Denver to Montrose in 1973.

SODBUSTERS BUSTED

Hundreds of thousands have tried the agricultural life in Colorado. The majority of farmers failed. Many lost their homesteads, either because they could not originally qualify with a five year residency or because of later bank foreclosures. Breaking up the hard, dry sod often proved to be a mistake as the wind carried away the bare top soil.

Indeed, the federal government has wisely returned farmland to native vegetation or preserved prairie with the Pawnee and Comanche National Grasslands. Although many farms and farm towns failed, a few determined, skillful farmers have hung on. Along with large-scale industrial agriculture, they have made at least parts of the Great American Desert productive.

At Rocky Ford in southeastern Colorado's Arkansas River valley, George W. Swink began experimenting with cantaloupe and watermelons in 1875. By the 1890s his delicious melons and cantaloupe were being shipped to grocers and restaurants throughout the nation and as far away as London. Since September of 1878 Coloradans have celebrated Rocky Ford's annual Melon Days, where these before and after photos were taken around 1938. Courtesy, Library of Congress

FLOUR POWER

John Kernan Mullen, king of the Rocky Mountain Grain growers, came to America from Ireland and eventually to Colorado. After working in the San Luis Valley mills and Richard Little's Rough and Ready Mill in Littleton, Mullins helped establish the flour industry. This poor immigrant put together a vast milling empire, stretching from Oregon to Texas, from Missouri to California. Today, Mullen's empire is a part of the global giant Con-Agra, but Mullen's name is still remembered in Colorado because of his philanthropies, including the Mullen Home for the Aged and the Mullen School for Boys.

Employing the tough business practices of other robber barons of the era, Mullen crushed and then bought out competitors to create a near monopoly on grain. Farmers and bakeries alike came to despise the man whose vast grain elevators and mills left them at his mercy in the marketplace.

Shaking hands with J.K. Mullen was unforgettable. After working in flour mills since the age of fourteen, his hands were imbedded with millstone shards.

Never forgetting his Irish birth and upbringing, Mullen did much to employ and uplift Colorado's Irish community. Yet, while giving millions to the Catholic Church and to Irish immigrants, he also donated to Protestant causes and to Denver Mayor Robert W. Speer's City Beautiful crusade to transform Denver from a dusty, drab town into "a Paris on the Platte." His philanthropy, much of it anonymous, helped build Immaculate Conception Cathedral, Mt. Olivet Cemetery, St. Joseph Hospital, St. Cajetan's Church and many other institutions. His five daughters and their descendants also got into the business of charity, leaving Mullen better remembered today for his giving than his taking.

John Kernan Mullen, born into poverty in 1847 in County Connaught, Ireland, died a multi-millionaire in Denver in 1929. Mullen built a grain mill and elevator empire and once strove to make Denver the "Minneapolis of the Rockies". Courtesy, Denver Public Library

10

SILVER CITIES

As the Civil War drew to a close, the bang that had begun Colorado's gold rush became more of a whimper. At first, placer gold had been easy to extract from streams or the earth's surface. Even the least experienced prospector could find the heavy metal with a pick or a pan. By 1864, however, placer gold seemed to be played out. Instead, the gold was being unearthed in hard-to-process rock that required complex chemical techniques. Many an inventor tried to come up with the best, most cost efficient and practical method of smelting Colorado's difficult gold ores. Nathaniel P. Hill succeeded.

Hill, a chemistry professor at Brown University in Providence, Rhode Island, was sent to Colorado by Boston capitalists who had invested heavily in the city of Golden and in Clear Creek mining. Hill opened the first Colorado smelter at Black Hawk to process ores from the Gilpin County mines of Central City and its surrounding camps. During its first years, Hill's plant shipped ore all the way to smelters in Swansea, Wales for the final extraction of pure gold from concentrated ores. Hill visited Swansea and studied the ore processing there, then built a similar plant in Black Hawk in 1868. The prototype smelter solved the problem of refractory ores, making Hill a rich man and a Colorado hero. The mining boom returned.

Gold was not the only precious metal tucked inside the Colorado Rockies. In 1864 Georgetown became the first camp to begin mining silver. Mine operators and owners also needed cheap, fast transportation to get equipment and supplies into their remote sites and to take ore out to be processed. Mule and ox team-pulled wagon trains were almost as slow as they were expensive. Another type of train was called for—the "Iron Horse."

RAILROADS

While other railroad builders' visions had focused on constructing east-to-west, former Civil War General William Jackson Palmer had been gazing south. His Denver & Rio Grande (D&RG) line aimed to bisect Colorado Territory with a north-south spine of feeder lines from mining and agricultural centers on the way to Texas, connecting with Mexican rail routes. Palmer, a town builder as well as a railroad builder, purchased real estate and platted new communities all along his planned routes. Whenever a new mining rush began, as in Leadville, Aspen and the San Juans, Palmer's railroad chugged off in that direction.

General Palmer founded his first and proudest community, Colorado Springs, in 1871. While surveying roadbeds for the D&RG, General Palmer had stopped in Colorado City at the base of Pikes Peak. He liked its mild climate and spectacular scenic beauty. But he did not like the gold rush supply town's myriad saloons and the riff raff they attracted. So he platted a genteel resort town just a few miles to the east that was dry in two senses of the word; not only was it alcohol-free, it didn't even have the natural springs its name implied. Those existed in another nearby community, Manitou Springs, with its many mineral springs. As "taking the waters" was all the rage with the upscale society that Palmer wished to attract to his "Newport in the Rockies," he took some liberty with the naming rights.

The D&RG's greatest innovation was using narrow gauge track and rolling stock, so-called because its tracks were three feet wide instead of the standard U.S. gauge of four feet, eight and one-half

Nathaniel P. Hill, a chemistry professor turned smelting magnate, rose to the top in Colorado, becoming a U.S. Senator and publisher of the Denver Republican *newspaper. Courtesy, Tom Noel Collection*

Georgetown emerged during the 1860s as Colorado's first great silver city. The "Silver Queen," shown here in the 1860s and again in the 1940s, is one of the best preserved mining towns. Courtesy, Denver Public Library (below) and Tom Noel Collection (right)

William J. Palmer, a Civil War hero and general, founded the Denver & Rio Grande Railroad and the town of Colorado Springs shown above. Courtesy, Denver Public Library and Tom Noel Collection

inches. Narrow gauge was easier and cheaper to build as well as more efficient in maneuvering narrow canyons, steep grades, and sharp mountain curves. Throughout the 1870s the D&RG continued to build across Colorado. The Denver to Pueblo route positioned Palmer to win the rail race up the Arkansas River to Leadville. The D&RG line south of Pueblo fed a line over LaVeta Pass into the San Luis Valley and on to the San Juan Mountains, one of many silver bonanzas to lure fortune seekers westward.

LEADVILLE

Oro City, a has-been gold camp perched more than two miles high in California Gulch, was fading fast in 1876 until assayers found silver locked in the local lead carbonate ore. By 1880 two-year-old Leadville was the second largest city in the state, with a population of 14,820. This instant city spread for three-and-a-half miles up and down California Gulch on the Arkansas River headwaters. It was not pretty. Dark, acrid smelter smoke polluted the thin, high-altitude air. The mountain solitude drowned in the eternal racket of ore-processing plants. Surrounding hillsides were denuded for lumber to fuel the smelters melting silver ores. Prospecting holes pockmarked the landscape.

Many people came to supply the mines and miners. Leadville soon had hardware stores, groceries, restaurants and banks, as well as saloons, gambling houses and brothels galore.

The Little Pittsburgh Mine on Fryer's Hill was one of Leadville's first great success stories.

Leadville, whose Harrison Avenue main street is shown here in 1879, sprang up almost overnight amid a spruce forest to become the highest, wildest and largest of America's silver cities. Courtesy, Colorado Historical Society

Prospectors August Rische and George Hook traded shopkeeper Horace Tabor a grubstake of his supplies for equal shares in the venture that soon produced nearly $10,000 a day. Having moved from nearby Oro City with his wife, Augusta, to Leadville in 1877, H.A.W. Tabor became a leading citizen, town promoter and Leadville's first mayor. Luck probably played a larger role than shrewdness in Tabor's fortunate speculations. Among the other lucky success stories produced by Leadville's boom days were Charles Boettcher, David May, Meyer Guggenhiem, Samuel Newhouse and Colorado governors John Routt, James B. Grant and Alva Adams.

Total mining production in Leadville and surrounding Lake County grew from $2 million in 1878 to $9 million the following year, and kept ballooning. Tremendous growth led to tremendous problems. Lack of proper sanitation facilities spread diseases like cholera, typhoid, smallpox and tuberculosis. Ultimately, citizen volunteers built a city waterworks to handle sewage.

Bunco artists, footpads, murderers and robbers plagued the baby city. Vigilantes tried to bring order. On its opening night in 1879, Tabor's Opera House on Harrison Avenue lost much of its audience to a dramatic double lynching down the street.

Leadville's first marshal lasted less than a week. The second was shot and killed only twenty-three days after pinning on his star. Desperate, Mayor Horace Tabor called on a fearless Irishman from County Limerick. Martin Duggan soon proved his mettle. When a blood-thirsty mob of 200 surrounded the jail to lynch a Negro accused of murder, Marshal Duggan single-handedly stared them down. "I managed to make them realize," he said later, "that some of them were sure to be killed if they persisted in interfering with the law."

Duggan even came to the rescue of Leadville's "brides of the multitude," women who offered their companionship for a price. They had been swindled by a slick salesman of fake jewelry. Duggan arrested the "jeweler" and brought him at gunpoint back to the brothel/dance hall. He had each lady lay out her new treasures and forced the swindler to pay back her hard-earned dollars. Duggan then let the crook go, provided he buy drinks for everyone in the sporting house, including his victims and the marshal.

Ten years after his appointment, Marshal Duggan left the Texas House Saloon one night shortly after 4:00 a.m. A shot exploded. Duggan was found in a pool of his own blood, felled by a pistol shot fired at close range just behind his ear. The assassin was never caught.

Gradually, the forces of civilization sought to smooth some of Leadville's rough edges. Churches, schools and hospitals arose; fraternal organizations built recreation halls and provided dignified funerals. Real estate inflated at astounding rates. A lot bought for $25 could be sold six months later for $500. Those who owned rental properties, too, saw tremendous profits, as did

freight lines and the purveyors of goods and services.

Trouble began when miners decided that they too should share in the wealth. They organized a union and struck Tabor's Chrysolite Mine, launching Colorado's first major labor dispute in 1880. Organized as the Miners' Cooperative Union and chartered by the Knights of Labor, Leadville's disgruntled workers demanded wages of three dollars per day and improved working conditions. The management at the Chrysolite had further provoked miners by prohibiting talking on the job. Some speculate that this was an intentional tactic to provoke a strike that would mask the declining profits of the mine. Mine owners hired strikebreak-

Leadville became Colorado's richest mining hub during the 1880s with silver being produced by the ton—make that sixty-five tons of silver bullion—in this Leadville scene. Courtesy, Colorado Historical Society

ers, tensions increased and violence threatened. After three weeks, Governor Frederick Pitkin sent in state troops at the request of mine owners to protect their mines and scab labor. The presence of armed militia broke the strike in its fourth week. Most miners went back to work at the same rate of pay. This coalition of the mine owners with state government, and the military crushing strikes, set the precedent for armed intervention on behalf of the mine owners in future Colorado mining labor disputes.

Production in Leadville and surrounding Lake County mines came to include lead, copper, zinc and even gold. The Little Johnny mine, one of Leadville's richest gold mines, gave rise to the fortune of mine supervisor John J. Brown and his later-famous wife, Margaret, known as the "Unsinkable Molly" Brown after she survived the sinking of the *Titanic.*

Creede sprouted up quickly as a silver camp in a narrow canyon carved by Willow Creek, near its confluence with the upper Rio Grande. Courtesy, Colorado Historical Society

THE WESTERN SLOPE

Meanwhile, on the Western Slope, promising silver discoveries gave rise to the town of Aspen in 1879. By 1890 Aspen had mushroomed into the largest Colorado community west of the Divide. Silver strikes also gave birth to bonanza towns in the San Juan Mountains of southwestern Colorado. Rich ores in the "Silvery San Juans" fed the boomtowns of Ouray, Telluride, Silverton and Creede. George Crawford's company town platted a choice western slope location at the confluence of the Colorado and Gunnison rivers as Grand Junction. After the Grand Ditch was constructed, irrigated farmlands around the new urban center flourished and the Denver & Rio Grande arrived in 1882. Grand Junction ultimately became the most populous town on the Western Slope of Colorado. In 1886, the Teller Institute and Indian School was established there to teach Utes and other native peoples practical trades to help them adapt to new urban white ways.

Gold mining prospered and proliferated in the San Juan Mountain towns such as Ouray. That town, in its breathtaking location surrounded by steep mountains, mined tourists as well as minerals with the help of its famous hot springs pool. Telluride's Sheridan Mine produced not only silver but also gold, zinc, copper and iron, while the nearby Tomboy Mine became one of the world's foremost gold producers. The arrival of the D&RG in July 1882 rescued Silverton from its splendid isolation on the headwaters of the Animas River. Further down the line, Durango arose as a business, smelting and supply center for the San Juan mining district. Creede, the last of Colorado's silver boomtowns, arose in 1890 and enjoyed a brief bonanza before everything changed in 1893.

THE SILVER CRASH OF 1893

By the 1880s Colorado mines were producing so much silver that supply began to exceed demand and prices dropped. Henry Teller and other Western congressmen pushed the federal government to subsidize silver with the Sherman Silver Purchase Act. It required the federal government to buy huge quantities of silver each year. As a result, silver soon flooded the Treasury Department and the Act was repealed in 1893.

The impact on Colorado's economy was immediate and devastating. Thousands employed in the silver mining industry or related businesses were thrown out of work. Men who had ridden the crest of the silver wave to wealth and prominence were laid low just as quickly as they had been elevated. The state faced years of massive unemployment, financial depression and a dwindling population.

Many silver mining camps became ghost towns almost overnight. Others managed to survive by concentrating their efforts on mining gold, coal, molybdenum or other valuables. Georgetown, Leadville, Aspen, Silverton, Creede and other once-bright silver cities quickly lost their luster. Most would never shine so brightly again.

THE TABOR TRIANGLE: A SILVER AGE SAGA

The most famous soap opera in Colorado history began at a New England quarry in 1857 when young stonecutter Horace Tabor married the boss's daughter, Augusta Pierce. The adventurous newlyweds set out for Kansas Territory to try their hand at homesteading. For two years, Augusta battled many hardships. She may have been relieved when news of the Pikes Peak gold rush sent them off to Colorado in search of pay dirt.

In one mining camp after another, as Horace prospected, Augusta not only managed a household and the raising of their son, but also did laundry and took in boarders to support the family. Somehow she managed to put aside cash at every opportunity. By the time the Tabors moved to Oro City in the late 1860s, she had saved enough to start a general store and post office. The successful enterprise grew even more prosperous when the Tabors joined the rush to the nearby silver boomtown of Leadville in 1877.

The fateful day that Horace grubstaked two miners with supplies in exchange for one-third interest in their mining venture changed the course of the Tabors' lives forever. The Little Pittsburgh bonanza made Horace a millionaire "Silver King" by 1878. His political ambitions grew along with his fortune. Lieutenant Governor was a start, but

Horace dreamed of a Republican seat in the U.S. Senate. He could buy nearly anything else he dreamed of, and like so many of the Leadville *noveau riche*, he purchased an ostentatious mansion on Denver's prestigious Capitol Hill.

Augusta was uncomfortable with their newfound wealth and status. She had been happiest working hard and making sacrifices for the future in the earlier years of their marriage. Flaunting one's money was vulgar and foolhardy, she believed in her practical New Englander's heart, and she refused to do so in decorating and furnishing their new show home. Instead, she dismissed the servants her husband hired and took in boarders, as she had always done. Horace was not pleased. Why could she not enjoy their good fortune and splurge a little? The thrifty wife whose efforts had brought him this far was not, he realized, the woman to share his extravagant lifestyle.

That woman appeared in Leadville in 1880. Tabor's friend and business associate William "Billy" Bush introduced him to a bewitching blonde young enough to be his daughter. Horace cared not that she was divorced from her first husband, nor that gossips would have a field day with their affair. The angelic features, heavenly figure and fun-loving spirit of Elizabeth "Baby" Doe captured his heart and robbed him of his common sense. Tabor kept his paramour first at Leadville's Clarendon Hotel, and then, after he became Colorado Lieutenant Governor, in a luxurious suite in Denver's Windsor Hotel. Had he been content to leave the arrangement as it was, the public might have continued to look the other way and tolerate his midlife indulgence. But Horace wanted Baby for his trophy wife and filed for divorce from Augusta.

Augusta resisted the dissolution of their marriage as long as she could, but tearfully acquiesced in January 1883. Horace and Baby Doe had already been secretly married in St. Louis, but now they were free to celebrate their union openly. Because Horace had been appointed to serve out the remainder of Henry Teller's term in the U.S. Senate, the lovebirds planned an extravagant Washington wedding. Baby's gown, a brocaded satin trimmed in marabou stork feathers, was imported from Paris at a cost of $7,000. President Chester Arthur attended

Horace Austin Warner Tabor, Colorado silver king of mythic dimensions, rose to the top only to crash like the silver industry, dying bankrupt in the Windsor Hotel on Denver's Larimer Street. Courtesy, Colorado Historical Society

the nuptial in March 1883, as did several legislators—but not one was accompanied by his wife. Women in the nation's capital had heard the story of the couple's romance and reacted exactly as Denver women had—by siding righteously with the forsaken first wife.

Nevertheless, Horace Tabor and wife number two seemed poised to live happily ever after in the Denver mansion of their dreams, with peacocks and a scandalous nude statue on its lawn. They spent money as fast as it poured out of their Leadville silver mines. Their first daughter, Elizabeth Bonduel Lillie Tabor, was born in July 1884 with the proverbial silver spoon in her mouth. Second daughter Rose Mary Echo Silver Dollar Tabor, born five years later, wore diaper pins studded with diamonds.

The halcyon days came to an abrupt end with the silver crash of 1893. Tabor's mining properties became essentially worthless. Creditors foreclosed on the his mansion, his Tabor Grand Opera House, Tabor Block and other assets. The glamorous and wealthy pair quickly fell on hard times. Those who predicted that a gold-digging Baby Doe would desert Horace as soon as the money ran out were

For thirty-six years after Horace's death, the faithful Baby Doe hung on to his Matchless Mine in Leadville, where she was found frozen to death in 1935. The couple now lie in a connubial grave at Mount Olivet Cemetery in the Denver suburb of Wheat Ridge. Photo by Tom Noel

Fairplay, once the booming Park County seat, remains the sleepy town depicted in this 1970 painting by Muriel Sibell Wolle, author-illustrator of the classic Colorado ghost town guidebook Stampede to Timberline. *Fairplay and other Park County mining communities produced both gold and silver. Courtesy, Denver Public Library*

proven wrong. She remained steadfastly devoted to him through the difficult years following the 1893 silver crash. The family survived on the meager salary Horace made as Denver postmaster until he died in 1899.

Baby Doe and her daughters lived for the next several years in rented rooms in Denver and Leadville. Teenaged Lillie grew increasingly intolerant of her mother and their diminished circumstance and ran away to live with Baby Doe's family. For the rest of her life, she would claim that the famous Horace and Baby Doe were merely her aunt and uncle, not her parents. Silver remained devoted to her mother until she went off to Chicago where she hoped to make her name as a writer or an actress. Her young life ended in a scalding accident in a squalid tenement house.

A heartbroken and destitute Baby Doe lived the last thirty years of her life in the mine shack above the Matchless, the only mine that Tabor still owned. On occasional trips into Denver, dressed

The vintage mining town of Crested Butte, captured in this 1966 watercolor by Muriel Sibell Wolle, was then a semi-ghost town before its re-emergence in recent decades as a booming ski and summer resort. Unlike silver cities which shriveled after the 1893 silver panic, Crested Butte, a coal town, produced its "black gold" well into the 1900s. Courtesy, Denver Public Library

in rags or miner's clothes, she attempted to persuade investors to revive operations at the Matchless, convinced that it still held a fortune in silver. Compassionate Leadville merchants accepted her worthless I.O.U.s for food and supplies.

On February 21, 1935 Elizabeth Tabor was found frozen to death in her drafty shack at the Matchless Mine. No one knew how long the eighty-year old widow had been dead. Scraps of paper stuffed into cracks of the walls with scribbled descriptions of the torturous dreams and visions that haunted her later years left little doubt that she had gone slowly insane.

Augusta Tabor died a wealthy woman in Pasadena, California in 1895 at the age of sixty-one. She had invested her substantial divorce settlement wisely, but she had also been a generous benefactor to both Denver's Unitarian Church and Colorado's Ladies Aid Society.

The Tabor saga resonates throughout Colorado history, partly because of its scandal, drama and tragedy. But its rags-to-riches-to-rags story is also representative of the boom and bust cycles that typify a state whose economic ups and downs have been as steep as its mountains and as deep as its canyons.

SILVER CITIES REBORN

A century later a few of the silver cities have resurrected themselves by mining a new resource—white gold (snow) and tourists. Aspen and Telluride have become world-class alpine resort destinations, offering not only winter sports, but also year-round festivals celebrating everything from food and wine to jazz and films. Towns like Leadville, Ouray and Silverton, while remaining small and relatively poor, attract tourists enthralled by little-altered antique mining towns.

The Denver and Rio Grande's narrow gauge steam engine still hauls some 200,000 tourists a year from Durango to Silverton along the spectacular Animas River Gorge on one of America's most popular rail excursions. The Colorado Historical Society restored another silver-era treat for rail buffs in Clear Creek County. The Georgetown Loop railroad climbs four and one-half miles of track through awesome mountain scenery seen from rustic trestles and numerous looping curves. Passengers can stop to tour an 1870s silver mine and thrill to the Devil's Gate High Bridge, ninety-five feet above Clear Creek.

The Georgetown Loop Railroad negotiates steep Clear Creek Canyon with its high bridge, allowing the train to loop back over its own tracks to gain elevation on its way to Silver Plume. Photo by Tom Noel

This Colorado Historical Society summer tourist
train, the Georgetown Loop Railroad, delights
youngsters, such as this tyke playing on one of the
line's narrow gauge steam locomotives. Photo by
Tom Noel

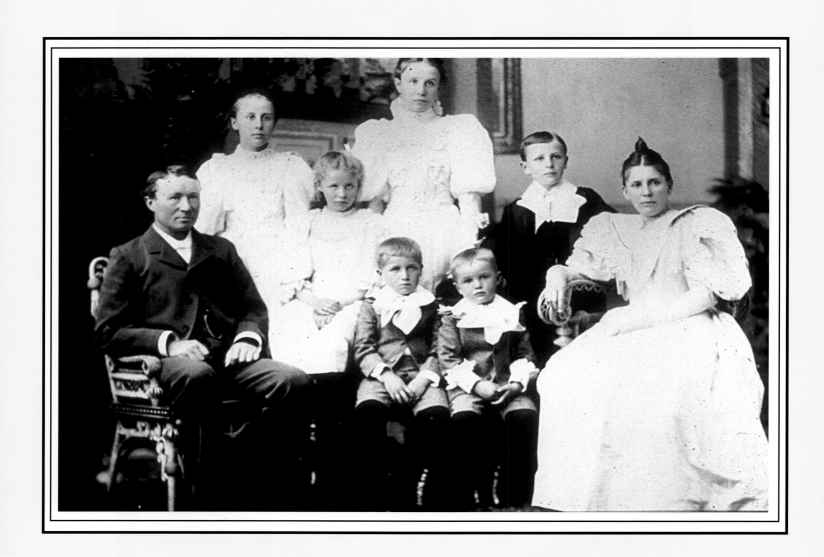

11

IMMIGRANTS

Successful immigrants often employed their countrymen, whom they trusted and understood. Adolph Coors, shown here with his wife and six children, employed primarily Germans. Courtesy, Tom Noel Collection.

On his 1880s visit to Colorado, Oscar Wilde characterized it as one of the few places in the world where practically none of the adult residents were native born. From the beginning, Colorado has been a state of newcomers.

While Native and Hispanic Americans had lived here for centuries, palefaces arriving after the 1858–1859 gold rush soon became the overwhelming majority of Coloradans. More people have become residents by choice than by birth. Many Colorado pioneers came from New York, Ohio, Illinois and Missouri. Among the early-day foreign- born, the Germans, Irish, English and Italians were most numerous, while Mexicans have become the largest group of foreign-born newcomers during the past century. Recently, the largest numbers of U.S.- born newcomers have come from California and Texas.

GERMAN COLORADANS

In 1868 a twenty-four-year old German stowaway landed in Denver, where he came to appreciate the frontier practice of not questioning a man's past. Orphaned at age fifteen, this youngster was running away from personal tragedies and long, compulsory—and often fatal—military service in the Prussian army. Like some 50,000 other foreign-born immigrants reaching Colorado before the 1920s, Adolph Kuhrs wanted a chance to start anew in a new world.

Kuhrs changed the spelling of his name to Coors and established what would become the world's largest single brewery. He arrived in 1868 along with some 55,000 Germans coming to the U.S. Germans were the most numerous of many immigrants coming to Colorado between the 1860s and the 1920s, when the U.S. began officially restricting immigration and the Colorado Ku Klux Klan began making foreigners feel unwelcome.

Of Colorado's immigrants, Germans were the most prominent and prosperous. In 1870 according to the census calculations of historian Stephen J. Leonard, Germans in Denver were richer than the English, Irish, Swedes and Scots combined. Typically, Germans arrived with more money, and earned and saved more after arriving.

Boulder's German House was typical of the Teutonic saloons to be found in many Colorado communities. As the state's largest foreign-born group from 1860 to 1910, Germans established many taverns where the food, drink, language, song and culture of the old country warmed homesick immigrants. Courtesy, Colorado Historical Society

Another German immigrant, Charles Boettcher, developed the mightiest and most successfully diversified financial empire in the Rockies. Rather than sink his money into one industry, such as mining, Boettcher concentrated initially on hardware and mining supplies. Moving into agriculture even before mining began to decline, Boettcher fathered the Great Western Sugar Company. To construct his sugar beet factories, he organized the Ideal Cement Company. Boettcher ventured into practically every Colorado enterprise, from ranching to utilities, from banking to meat packing, from insurance to the Denver Tramway Company.

Boettcher and other German-born immigrants were joined by Germans from Russia. The Volga-Deutsch, as they were sometimes called, had been enlisted by Tsarina Catherine the Great to settle in Russia's Volga Valley. Catherine, who was born in Germany, brought her countrymen, who were expert farmers, to turn the Volga River Valley into Russia's breadbasket. After she died, however, other Russian rulers were less kind to these Teutons, forcing them to join the Russian military and to otherwise become more Russian. Subsequently, thousands fled Russia. Many settled on

Colorado's Ku Klux Klan briefly controlled the Highest State during the 1920s, when Kluxers served as governor, U.S. Senator and mayor of Denver. The Klan, shown here burning a cross in Boulder, attacked Colorado's foreign born immigrants as "un-American." Courtesy, Denver Public Library

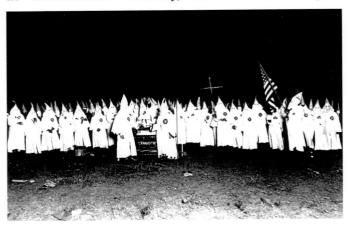

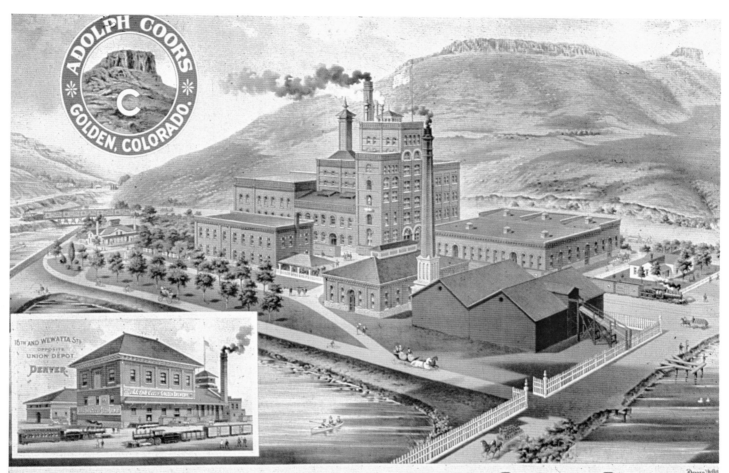

ADOLPH COORS GOLDEN BREWERY, GOLDEN, COLO.

the Great Plains of North America, including eastern Colorado's South Platte Valley. Christian Anschutz, one of these Germans from Russia, was the grandfather of Philip Anschutz who would become the wealthiest tycoon in 21st century Colorado.

Germans took a keen interest in public education, persuading the Colorado legislature to pass a law in 1877 requiring the teaching of German and of gymnastics in the public schools. The active German element led Colorado to print its laws in German, as well as in English and Spanish. Of several German newspapers published in Denver, the longest lived was the *Colorado Herald*, which championed German causes until it became a casualty of World War II.

German-born people owned roughly a third of Colorado's saloons before statewide prohibition closed their doors in 1916. Inside, customers spoke and sang in German, read German newspapers and

Adolph Coors, employed primarily Germans, who helped make his Golden, Colorado Brewery the premier suds-maker in the Rocky Mountain West by the 1940s. Courtesy, Tom Noel Collection.

magazines, consumed sauerkraut and strudel, and quaffed beer. Every city and many smaller towns contained establishments such as the Bavarian House, Deutsches House, the Edelweiss, German House, Germania Hall, Heidelberg Cafe, Mozart Hall, Saxonia Hall and Valhalla Hall. They offered not only "Dutch [*Deutsche* or German] lunches," but also the customs and culture of the old country.

Coloradans benefited from the Teutonic interest in music and culture. In 1873 the Kaltenbach family ordered a thousand-dollar orchestrion from Germany. When the elaborate instrument arrived a year later, the Kaltenbachs renamed their Denver

Germans gave much to Colorado's cultural life. This wagonload of Teutons is ballyhooing a performance at the Denver Auditorium by the German Singing Societies, along with a gymnastic exhibition from the German Turnvereins. Courtesy, Colorado Historical Society

tavern Orchestrion Hall. It took a week to assemble and tune the eleven-foot high machine and attach the reeds, horns, drums and xylophone. To celebrate the instrument's debut, hundreds crowded into the hall. "No one," an observer recalled, "had ever supposed there were so many Germans in the region and [all] were amazed that the beer held out through the long night." As Germans drank and sang along, the largest musical apparatus in the Rocky Mountain West ground out "Die Wacht am Rhein," George Schweitzer's "Yodel Hi Lee Hi Loo" and Ludwig von Beethoven's "Moonlight Sonata."

Although Germans had a more comfortable life in nineteenth-century Denver than most ethnic groups, the twentieth century changed that. The swelling prohibition movement tended to blame all evil on drink. Breweries and saloons, according to nativists, were un-American bastions where people spoke German, plotted against the established order and drank to dangerous excess.

Xenophobes hoping to crack down on foreigners and their "un-American" activities joined prohibitionists to vote for a statewide ban on alcohol. The dry spell began for Coloradans on New Year's

Day, 1916 and many Germans lost their jobs in the liquor business.

An even heavier blow came to the Teutonic community with U.S. entry into World War I. Germans became the target of a widespread hate campaign. Regardless of their professed and proven patriotism, Germans lost their jobs and were abused. Colorado school districts outlawed German language classes. Restaurants renamed sauerkraut "liberty cabbage" and hamburgers became "liberty steaks." After the double-barreled blast of Prohibition and World War I, this group that had contributed so much to Colorado's cultural, educational and social life never fully reemerged as a distinctive ethnic community.

IRISH-COLORADANS

Many poor Irish immigrants struck it rich in Colorado. But none became as wealthy or as philanthropic as John Kernan Mullen. When he was nine, Mullen's family fled famine-stricken Ireland for New York. After quitting school early to learn flour milling in New York, young Mullen moved to Colorado in 1867. He approached Charles R. Davis, proprietor of the West Denver Mill, one Saturday night when many of his countrymen were out carousing and asked for a job. When Davis said he had nothing available, young Mullen offered to work for nothing.

John Kernan Mullen (right), an Irish immigrant, made millions in flour milling and became a legendary philanthropist. "Myself and my wife," he explained, "came here when there were no old people. We were all young and because of this we consider ourselves pioneers . . . we wanted, before we passed away, to leave something." Mullen contributed all or most of the funding for many Denver landmarks, including the Broncho Buster statue (bottom right) in Civic Center and Immaculate Conception Cathedral (below). Photos by Tom Noel

"Well, if you want work that bad, you may begin tomorrow morning. If we get along all right, I will pay your room and board." Mullen made himself indispensable by doing the hardest work at the mill—breaking up ice in the mill ditch. On cold winter nights, ice often blocked the flow from the South Platte through the mill ditch. At the flour mill, Mullen always seemed to see the problem and know how to fix it. By 1875 Mullen was the head miller for Davis and also began leasing or buying other flour mills.

Thus began Colorado's greatest Irish immigrant success story, and one of the great fortunes of the Rockies. Mullen hoped to make Denver the Minneapolis of the west by dominating the flour business. Mullen erected the first grain elevator in Colorado and came to control grain storage and markets. In 1885 he consolidated his operations as the Colorado Milling and Elevator Company, which came to dominate wheat growing, harvesting, storage and processing in the Rocky Mountains and the High

The small two-mile-high City of Leadville commemorates St. Patrick with a march down Harrison Avenue. Because Leadville is snowy and cold in March, the city celebrates "St. Patrick's Practice Day" on the Saturday closest to September 17, when Leadville is warm and its aspen trees golden. Photos by Tom Noel

Plains. The acquisitive Irishman came to control more than 100 mills and grain elevators in an empire stretching from Oregon to Texas, from Missouri to California. His heirs sold out for another fortune in the 1950s to Omaha-based Consolidated Agriculture Co. (ConAgra), the nation's largest grain dealer.

Perseverance sometimes rewarded foreigners. Irishman Thomas Walsh prospected for years before discovering Ouray's Camp Bird Mine which made him millions. The Irish-born Gallagher brothers struck it rich in a Leadville silver mine, while Pat Casey found his fortune in a Central City gold mine. In the Cripple Creek mining district, Irishmen James Burns and James Doyle became millionaires, thanks to their Portland Mine.

The Irish proved to be one of the most prolific immigrant groups. Unlike Scandinavians, Italians, Greeks, Chinese and most other groups, both sexes of Irish came. Irish girls were in great demand as domestics and factory workers. Starving times in Ireland due to the potato famine led many families, however reluctantly, to send daughters as well as sons to America—their only hope for a decent life. With as many Irish women as men in the new country, the Irish tended to marry each other and raise large families. Many other immigrants came to make their fortunes and then return to their homelands and their sweethearts.

Most Irish came to Colorado as miners or as railroad construction workers. Colorado's Irish organized local chapters of the Ancient Order of Hibernians, the Daughters of Erin, the Irish Progressive Society, the Land League, a Ladies Land League, the St. Patrick's Mutual Benevolent Association and the Shamrock Athletic Club. Robert Morris, Denver's first Irish mayor, rewarded his constituency by sanctioning the city's first St. Patrick's Day parade in 1883.

Mayor Robert W. Speer made the parade an official city function in 1906, a practice continued until World War I. Anti-Catholic, anti-immigrant and anti-liquor interests suppressed St. Patrick's Day parades until the 1960s when the parade was revived. Since then, Denver's Irish parade has become one of America's largest, partly by welcoming any and all celebrants.

ANGLO-COLORADANS

Although the English were Colorado's third largest foreign-born group, they were not as visible as the Germans and the Irish, blending into the dominant Anglo society. Behind the scenes, the British reinforced an Anglophilic culture, underwritten by an estimated 50 million pounds, which Britons invested in Colorado before World War I.

Unlike non-English-speaking peoples, English-born Coloradans saw less need to organize ethnically. They, like U.S.-born Anglo-Americans, generally assumed they were the prevalent culture. Not only the language, but English capital prevailed, bankrolling Colorado mining, railroads and ranching. By 1890 twenty-five British mining firms were digging for Colorado pay dirt. Brits also bankrolled more than a hundred Colorado cattle companies. Ranching appealed to the English, who had no trouble appreciating the rewards of roast beef, butter and fresh cream.

Railroads, which were first developed in England, began criss-crossing Colorado with considerable financial support from the British Isles. The Denver & Rio Grande Railroad, for instance, was a favorite of British investors. Dr. William A. Bell, a London society doctor, became interested in the D&RG and promoted it among his patients. His son, Dr. William A. Bell, Jr., became so intrigued with this narrow gauge "toy" railroad that he came to America, where he wound up as the road's vice-president. Young Bell wrote a book, *New Tracks in North America* (London: 1870) explaining and promoting Colorado railroads to English readers and capitalists.

So many English people moved to Colorado Springs that the town unofficially became know as Little London. Brits did much to transform Colorado Springs from a raw western crossroads into a handsome and prosperous metropolis with solid Victorian office buildings, hotels, clubs, mansions and churches. Vacationers stayed at hotels such as Colorado Springs' Antlers or Broadmoor, and Denver's Brown Palace, Oxford and Windsor. Admiring handsome Episcopal churches and touring elegant Queen Anne and English Revival style

St. John's in the Wilderness, Denver's English Gothic Cathedral, attracts Anglophiles with its English clergy and traditional services. Exquisite stained glass and Gothic wood and stone detailing distinguish this Episcopal edifice. A particularly seductive "Eve in the Garden of Eden" window (left) distracted worshippers, necessitating the addition of a rose bush for modesty's sake. Photos by Tom Noel

mansion districts, visitors might well conclude that the English set the state's standards.

ITALIAN-COLORADANS

Immigrant communities often clustered around their churches. In Pueblo, for instance, the Italian community grew up around St. Ignatius Loyola Church. Father Charles M. Pinto S.J. founded the parish in 1872 to serve much of southeastern Colorado. Father Pinto lived in one corner of the church, screened by a curtain. This Italian-born Jesuit priest, who had studied philosophy in Spain and theology in France, invited the Sisters of Loretto to open a parish school in 1884. Fire destroyed the first church, but within a year the fast growing Italian congregation rebuilt a new church with a residence for the priest.

Italians emerged as Pueblo's largest immigrant group, working the smelters, farms and railroads, as well as the giant steel plant that made Pueblo "the Pittsburgh of the West." One Pueblo Italian

In Pueblo, Italian immigrant Augusto "Gus" Masciotra turned his house into a saloon that set the record, according to Ripley's Believe it or Not, for beer sales per square foot. His grandchildren still operate this famous blue collar bar which flies the Italian colors in its awning. Photo by Tom Noel

noted that "Americans went to the store for everything" while his people "had a bread man, a coal and ice man, a fruit and vegetable man, a watermelon man, and a fish man; we even had a man who sharpened our knives and scissors who came right to our home. Many peddlers plied the Italian neighborhood."

Eight Italian newspapers and seven Italian societies promoted solidarity among Pueblo's Italians. They also joined with their Denver countrymen to make Colorado the first state to declare an Italian-oriented holiday, the October 12 celebration of Christopher Columbus Day.

Italians who came to Colorado tended to be poor and were disliked for their dark complexions, Catholicism, foreign language, different food and homemade wine. Coloradans derided them as "macaroni eaters." Many lived in tents, shacks and shanties in river bottoms and worked hard, poor-paying jobs—building railroads, digging coal, tending truck farms and toiling in smelters.

Mother Frances Xavier Cabrini, the Italian nun who became the first U.S. citizen to be canonized a saint, visited Colorado in 1902 and reported:

Siro Mangini, on the left (above), a pioneer Italian entrepreneur, opened Christopher Columbus Hall (below) in 1872 to welcome his countrymen to Denver. Courtesy, Tom Noel Collection

CHRISTOPHER COLUMBUS HALL,

A CHOICE LINE OF

Wines, Liquors and Cigars,

ALSO DEALER IN

Imported Maccaroni, Cheese and Olive Oils.

2219 Larimer Street,

DENVER, - - COLORADO.

I drink at Christopher Columbus Hall.   **SIRO MANGINI, Prop.**   I don't, but will.

Here the hardest work is reserved for the Italian worker . . . they merely look upon him as an ingenious machine for work. I saw these dear fellows of ours engaged on construction of railways in the most intricate mountain gorges . . . Poor miners work year in and year out, until old age and incapacity creep over them, or at least until some day a landslide or explosion or an accident of some kind ends the life of the poor worker, who does not even need a grave, being buried in the one in which he has lived all his life.

To give Italian immigrants "the holy joys which in our own country the poor peasant has on Sundays at least," Mother Cabrini helped erect Our Lady of Mount Carmel Church in Denver's "Little Italy." This dignified Romanesque church, with its ornately painted and statue-filled interior, still stands at West 36th Avenue and Navajo Street in North Denver. One of the twin copper-capped towers houses the 1,000 pound bell known as "Maria del Carmelina" or "the heartbeat of Little Italy."

With the help of Mother Cabrini's church, as well as a school and orphanage, Colorado's Italians ultimately prospered. Hard-working immigrants sacrificed themselves to feed, clothe and educate their children, who often became professional white-collar workers. Italians slowly earned respect—and even admiration—for their hard work, ethnic pride and strong family ties.

OTHER IMMIGRANT GROUPS

Many other peoples make up today's Colorado. Among the most numerous immigrants have been Mexicans, Russians, Canadians, Swedes, French, Welsh, Scots, Swiss, Danes, Norwegians, Greeks, Yugoslavs, Poles, Czechs, Greeks, Japanese, Chinese, Africans and Vietnamese. Each group brought new skills, new customs, new food and a new culture to the Highest State.

Of the many immigrant groups, Japanese suffered perhaps the greatest persecution. During World War II they were locked up in relocation camps, including Amache in southeastern Colorado. Even American citizens, ninety-year-old grandmothers and babies, were removed from their homes, held behind barb wire and guarded by machine guns.

Louis DuPuy's Hotel de Paris in the mountain mining town of Georgetown brought the food, wine, language and culture of France to the new world, warming the hearts of Franco-Coloradans. Many non-French visitors were delighted by the accommodations as well, which included a fine library and wine cellar in what is now a National Register Landmark and museum. Courtesy, Tom Noel Collection

Colorado's small but relatively prosperous African American community enjoyed some leisure time. These couples are exploring Denver's South Platte River bicycle path on a 1908 excursion. Photo by Charles Lillybridge, Colorado Historical Society.

PRESERVATION

Every group, understandably, has wanted to preserve its heritage in Colorado, beginning with the Native Americans who constructed cliff palaces in what is now Mesa Verde National Park. Hispanic settlers, the largest single ethnic group, have contributed much to the state, including its name and oldest continuously occupied settlements.

To celebrate its historic ethnic treasures, Colorado has identified local, state and national register landmarks. The Colorado Historical Society, founded in 1879, has also established museums statewide that focus on ethnic history, including the Ute Indian Museum in Montrose, the Baca House Museum in Trinidad and El Pueblo in Pueblo. Even the smallest towns treasure their cultural landmarks. For instance, the tiny community of La Garita in the San Luis Valley boasts the Capilla San Juan Bautista and the Carnero Creek Indian Pictographs.

Preservation has been greatly enhanced by the Colorado Historical Society's State Historical Fund (SHF), which restores landmark structures statewide.

More than 2,000 national, state and local designated landmarks commemorate the achievements of the peoples of Colorado, be it a Swedish Evangelical Lutheran Church in Ryssby or the Trujillo Homestead of pioneer Hispanic sheep ranchers near Hooper, Georgetown's Hotel de Paris or the Egyptian Theater in Delta. In Denver, ethnic landmarks range from St. John's in the Wilderness Episcopal Cathedral to the Teutonic Denver Turnverein, from the Mosque of the El Jebel Shrine Temple to the Russian Orthodox Transfiguration of Christ Cathedral, and to all three synagogues of fast growing Temple Emanuel. Designated ethnic historic places include Lake City's Little Rome Italian mining camp, Lakewood's Jewish Consumptive Relief Society Historic District, the Sand Creek Massacre site, the Duck Creek Ute Wickiup Village, St. Patrick's Catholic Church in La Junta, the Amache Japanese Concentration Camp and Pueblo's Colored Orphanage and Old Folks Home. All the people of Colorado have made it a stronger, better and more colorful state.

For Purple Mountain Majesties   Above The Fruited Plain

America   America   God Shed His Grace on Thee

For Amber Waves of Grain

For Spacious Skies

Oh Beautiful

1876-2076

Women's Gold

THEATER

Their Heritage Gives Colorado Women Faith in the Future

12

REFORMERS

The Woman's Gold tapestry displayed in the state capitol features sixteen celebrated Colorado women whose faith in the future and love of beauty did much to mold the character of Colorado. Courtesy, Debra Faulkner Collection

The November 15, 1893 issue of the suffrage newspaper *The Queen Bee* proclaimed, "Western Women Wild with Joy over the Victory of Suffrage in Colorado." It had been a long fight. Female journalists such as *Bee* editor Caroline Churchill deserved much credit when the suffrage referendum passed in the November 7 election. Enfranchised in 1893, twenty-seven years before their sisters in most states were granted the vote by the 19th Amendment to the U.S. Constitution, the women of Colorado became full citizens. They wielded an unprecedented influence in politics and society that opened the way for social and political reform. Now, the real work began.

WOMEN'S CLUBS AND CIVIC HOUSEKEEPING

As newly invented household appliances liberated women from constant domestic drudgery in the late nineteenth century, they had time and energy to look outside the home for the first time. They sought the companionship of other women, and the women's club movement was born. Initially, these organizations concerned themselves with self-improvement, but then embarked on a larger mission of improving society.

Colorado embraced the women's club movement with gusto. At the second annual statewide meeting in 1896, delegates from fifty-eight organizations represented more than 2,000 ladies. By 1898 there were ninety Colorado clubs—twenty-four of them in Denver alone.

With the rise of women's clubs in the late 1800s came a new and wider recognition of women's roles. Middle- as well as upper-class ladies began to recognize that whatever touched their families in the outside world also touched their home. The meat or milk contaminated in unsanitary processing plants could make their families sick. The school building without fire exits endangered their children. Pool halls and gambling dens might lure their sons into vice. Saloons where men fraternized could send a husband home in a drunken stupor, or worse, a drunken rage. As women responsible for their families' well-being became aware of these outside threats, they joined women's clubs that ventured into civic affairs.

Reformers, including many women, crusaded to give females the franchise so they could clean up politically corrupt Colorado. Denver feminist Caroline Churchill, editor of the Queen Bee, proclaimed the Colorado legislature to be a "kindergarten" where men often "make an ass of themselves [while] a good sensible woman would have settled the question in about two minutes and a half and gone on with her knitting." However, Caroline added, "If this body of shaking mountain quaking aspen can be induced to give the suffrage to women, all is forgiven." Courtesy, Tom Noel Collection

DON'T FORGET THE WOMEN WHEN YOU VOTE ON TUESDAY.

Equal Rights! Equal Responsibilities! Equal Suffrage!

Although Wyoming's constitution was the first to give women the vote, Colorado in 1893 became the first state where men, encouraged by cartoons such as this, elected to enfranchise women, making the Highest State a model for the nation. Courtesy, Colorado Historical Society.

Women's clubs, such as this stylish group from Trinidad, Colorado, pushed women's suffrage and other reforms. Courtesy, Colorado Historical Society

The rhetoric of "civic housekeeping" implied that women were simply performing their traditional function outside the home. Before most men had fully grasped what was happening, entire communities had come under the purview of well-intentioned and determined housekeepers. They concerned themselves with public health and public schools, fire and food safety, inhumane conditions in hospitals and in prisons, even labor and union issues. They campaigned for public kindergartens and public libraries, and against alcohol and tobacco.

In Denver, municipal legislation outlawing prostitution and gambling had been circumvented for years by a police force as corrupt as many of the city's elected and appointed officials. But the municipal housekeepers were not to be deterred in their campaign to clean up both local politics and vice. As a direct result of their unrelenting and well-publicized efforts, the city's gaming and bawdy

Colorado College cadets marched with brooms, a symbol of women reformer's "housekeeping." They hoped to clean up public schools, housing conditions, public health issues, as well as unfair and unsafe labor conditions. It took a woman to clean house, they contended, and the vote would provide the metaphoric broom they needed to sweep away the dirty politics befouling the state. Courtesy, Colorado College Library, Special Collections

houses were officially shut down at last in 1913.

The gentler sex also maintained that poverty in their communities could no longer be ignored. Social workers and charitable organizations were mobilized. Denver's "Community Chest," the brainchild of Frances Wisebart Jacobs, was the progenitor of the nation's United Way network.

PROHIBITION

Denver's municipal housekeepers were able to successfully implement more reforms than their sisters in other regions of the nation, primarily because of their equal enfranchisement advantage. With citizenship and voting rights, Colorado females became more focused on Colorado's problems. One such evil, to the minds of many, was alcohol. Except for communities such as

Saloons were one of the major targets of reformers, who claimed alcohol was ruining men and causing them to neglect or abuse their families. The Pastime Saloon in Leadville, shown here, cleaned up for this 1900 photo, but regularly offered prostitutes and gambling, as well as liquor and cigars. Courtesy, Denver Public Library

Greeley, which were founded as temperance colonies, most Colorado towns had no shortage of saloons. As gathering places for fraternization, they served a social role. But all too often, alcoholic drinks came with corrupt chasers. Few could deny that violence, gambling, prostitution and crimes of every ilk blossomed at many of these watering holes.

Ellis Meredith, in a pamphlet published by the Women's Temperance Association in 1903, assured readers that women's entry into politics had de

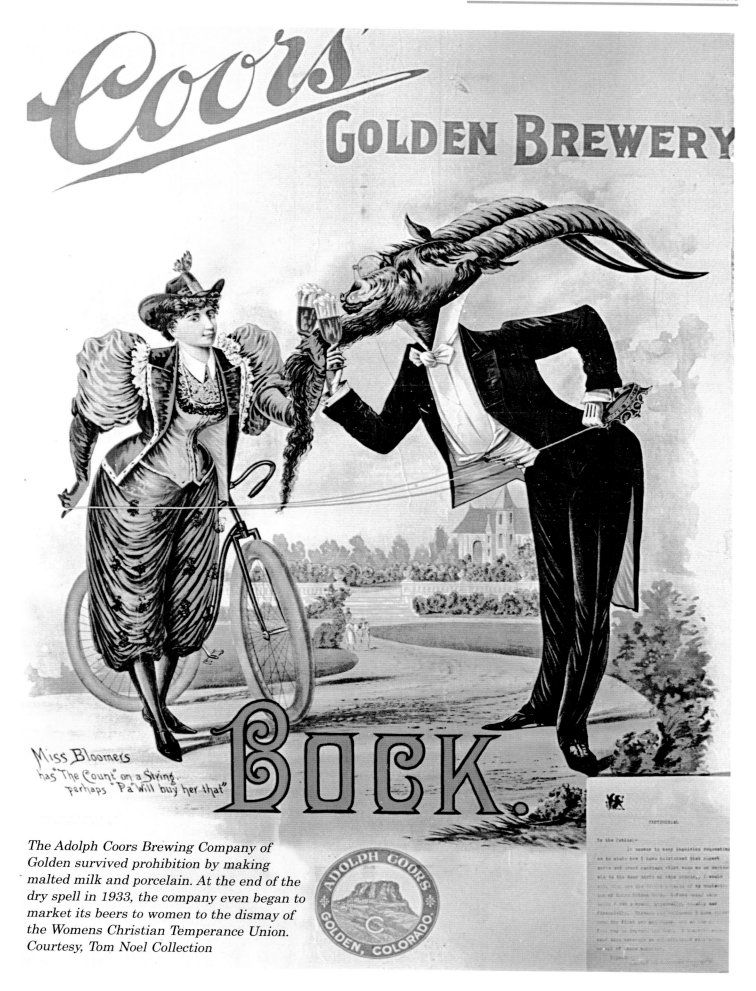

Miss Bloomers has "The Count" on a String, perhaps "Pa Will buy her that"

The Adolph Coors Brewing Company of Golden survived prohibition by making malted milk and porcelain. At the end of the dry spell in 1933, the company even began to market its beers to women to the dismay of the Womens Christian Temperance Union. Courtesy, Tom Noel Collection

creased crime by doing away with pool halls and saloons "in many small places." The more difficult challenge of doing the same in bigger Colorado cities remained. Meredith chastised churches with non-progressive pastors, whose "inaction for righteousness" compelled women "to do the work the churches ought to."

Some churches did ultimately join a coalition spearheaded by the Women's Christian Temperance Union that persuaded voters statewide to dry up Colorado. On New Year's Day 1916, Colorado undertook a statewide ban on the sale of alcohol, four years ahead of national prohibition.

In Denver alone, more than 400 saloons went out of business. Many became "soft drink" parlors or drugstores where bootleg booze could sometimes be purchased. Most of the state's once thriving breweries evaporated, leaving brewers, bottlers, delivery drivers and distributors out of work.

Rocky Mountain News reporter Ellis Meredith, who retained her maiden name through two marriages, used the power of the pen and the podium, becoming Colorado's preeminent woman booster in the process. As the "Susan B. Anthony of Colorado," she led the victorious 1893 campaign for women's suffrage. Courtesy, Colorado Historical Society

In Colorado mining, cattle and railroad towns, many saloons offered female companionship—for a price. These beer drinking "brides of the multitude" offered negotiable affections. Courtesy, Colorado Historical Society

Some sudsmakers, such as Denver's Tivoli-Union Brewing Company, survived by concocting and marketing non-alcoholic grain beverages. The Adolph Coors Brewery in Golden managed to stay in business by switching to malted milk and porcelain production.

Bootlegging flourished during Colorado's long dry spell. Rather than abolishing alcohol-related crime, as intended, prohibition merely obliged those who operated outside the law to adapt creatively and made criminals of the citizens who continued to imbibe. Prohibition proved to be a reform that failed. It was repealed nationally in 1933.

Emily Griffith, Denver's schoolmarm saint, realized that many parents of her pupils lacked the language and job skills to make them successful citizens. To offer them free public education, including night and weekend classes for working people, Emily opened Opportunity School in 1916. Courtesy, Tom Noel Collection

EDUCATION REFORMS

Among the fruits of women's enfranchisement was the election of clubwoman Mrs. Ione T. Hanna to the Denver Public School board. Mrs. Hanna wasted no time in fulfilling her campaign promise to incorporate kindergartens into the public school system. Other Colorado communities, large and small, likewise elected women to their school boards and extended education to pre-elementary children.

Mrs. Anna Louise Williams, center, founded one of Colorado's first kindergartens around 1900, the Stanley School. It still stands at 1300 Quebec Street in the East Denver neighborhood of Montclair. Courtesy, Tom Noel Collection

EMILY GRIFFITH

Not only kindergartners, but also people on the other end of the age spectrum had been neglected by the public school system. Adults who had missed out on an elementary education had no place to go to learn reading, writing and arithmetic. One visionary saw the need for adult education and did something about it. Emily Griffith, who began her teaching career in her teens as a prairie schoolmarm, recognized that many of the parents of her young students needed instruction in the "3 Rs" as much as their children. The purpose of public education, Griffith believed, was to "fit folks to life,"

to prepare them for a purposeful and satisfying role in society.

Gradually, persistently, Griffith persuaded influential people of the merits of her dream to open an "Opportunity School." Detractors predicted that a school with no age limits, no admission or attendance requirements, and no grades would lower the standards of public education. But supporters saw it as a way out of poverty and despair for those who wished to learn and make something better of their lives.

Pressured by public opinion, the Denver School Board approved Miss Griffith's "experiment" and made minor repairs to a condemned downtown Denver school for her use. Opened in September 1916, Opportunity School was one of the first in the nation to offer free public education in basic academics, English as a second language and vocational training to adults of all ages and backgrounds. In its first week alone, more than 1,400 people enrolled. Opportunity School was an idea whose time had come. To this day, it remains vital, offering a second chance to underserved populations in the community. To date, more than a million and a half people have passed through its doors.

LEGAL REFORMS

The fate of youngsters accused of crimes became another concern of the Progressive Era. Young criminals were locked up with seasoned felons. Helpless boys became prisoners in a veritable "school for crime." But Denver adolescents who ran afoul of the law were luckier than most. In 1902 Judge Benjamin Barr Lindsey succeeded in establishing one of the first juvenile courts in the land.

In his 1910 book, *The Beast*, Lindsey shocked the country with his revelation of "the abominable pollutions that had been committed upon the little bodies" of imprisoned children. At his suggestion,

Judge Ben Lindsey, left, was no bigger than many of the juveniles with whom he worked. Courtesy, Colorado Historical Society

the governor and numerous influential Colorado citizens listened to the testimony of boys who had been incarcerated. Their harrowing stories brought grown men to tears and inspired sweeping reform to the juvenile justice system.

The "kid's judge" fought relentlessly to create a more compassionate and effective way of dealing with under-age offenders. Lindsey's "contributory juvenile delinquency" laws opened the way for the prosecution of parents who neglected or abused their children, as well as liquor dealers and gamblers targeting the young. Judge Lindsey was also instrumental in improving child labor laws and their enforcement.

Under Lindsey's juvenile court system, young lawbreakers were sent to a detention school rather than jail, or were released on probation to responsible adults. "Our work, we find," said Lindsey, "is to aid the civilizing forces—the home, the school, and the church—and to protect society by making the children good members of society instead of punishing them for being irresponsible ones."

The judge once came across a policeman trying to arrest a couple of boys for stealing bicycles. The incident epitomized for Lindsey the difference between the criminal approach and the methods of his juvenile court. "Officer," he said to the policeman, "You are trying to save bicycles. I am trying to save boys."

JOSEPHINE ROCHE & LABOR REFORM

Labor conditions in the early 1900s cried out for reform. Miners worked ten to twelve hours a day for less than three dollars a day in dangerous places where injuries and deaths were common. Even if miners survived years of labor underground, they often suffered from lung problems due to breathing mine dust, not to mention other ailments due to cold, wet, exhausting underground labor.

Miners and other workers began striking for a minimum wage of three dollars a day, a maximum work day of eight hours, and safer working conditions. Most of these strikes failed until a remarkable woman decided to work with—instead of against—union employees in her family's coal mining company.

Union miners, such as these United Mine Workers of America in Louisville, finally found an ally in management when Josephine Roche took charge of the Rocky Mountain Fuel Company. After two decades of bitter labor wars between 1894 and 1914, Roche worked with—instead of against—organized labor. Courtesy, Colorado Historical Society

At the age of twelve, Josephine Roche had asked her father—the biggest stockholder of the Rocky Mountain Fuel Company—if he would show her one of his coal mines.

"It would be too dangerous," he told her.

"Then how is it safe for the miners?" the little girl asked. Her father did not have an answer.

When Josephine's father died in 1927, she inherited his Rocky Mountain Fuel Company stock. At that point, she tackled an issue that had troubled her for years. Josephine began touring coal mines. She found out just how unsafe they were and took steps to improve them. In 1928 she raised the base wage to seven dollars a day, the highest salary paid in the Colorado mining industry. Other mine owners criticized her and predicted that the Rocky Mountain Fuel Company would lose money and soon fail.

When the Depression of 1929 brought hard times, Josephine donated her salary as vice president to help keep the Rocky Mountain Fuel Company open. The United Mine Workers union also loaned money to the company so it could stay in business while many others were closing. Because Josephine had worked with the union instead of against it, the miners also volunteered to accept wage cuts and work fewer days so that no one would have to be laid off.

In 1934 Josephine Roche added another first to her long list. She became the first woman to run for governor of Colorado, narrowly losing the Democratic Party nomination to Edwin C. Johnson, a popular professional politician.

Roche's pro-labor solutions to Great Depression problems attracted the interest of President Franklin D. Roosevelt and his wife, Eleanor. They asked Josephine to come to Washington and become assistant secretary of the treasury. She accepted and became the second most prominent woman in the federal government (the first was Frances Perkins, the secretary of labor, who had been Josephine's classmate at Columbia University). Josephine later served as director of the National Youth Administration and the Public Health Service. In 1947 she became assistant to John L. Lewis, president of the United Mine Workers. A tireless booster of the poor and working class, Roche, like Emily Griffith, became a nationally known female reformer.

Mrs. Verner Z. (Mary Dean) Reed was one of many female philanthropists working to improve life in Colorado. She gave away millions, which her husband earned in gold and oil, to fund institutions such as a library at the University of Denver and a day care center in Denver's Five Points neighborhood. Courtesy, Pikes Peak Library District

Women's Clubs founded libraries in many communities, among them the Sarah Platte Decker Branch Library, named for one of Colorado's most active club women. This romantic, cottage-style landmark in South Denver features a cozy fireplace. Courtesy, Denver Public Library

POLITICAL REFORM

Women engaged in political as well as social and economic reforms. In 1894 the first three women in U.S. history to serve in a state legislature were elected in Colorado. Soon after taking their seats in the House chambers, the trio insisted on new rules banning cigars and foul language. By 1901 a total of ten women had served as state representatives. Helen Ring Robinson became the first female to serve in a State Senate in 1913. Robinson championed early legislation addressing food safety, minimum wage, and child protection.

Sarah Platt Decker of the Colorado Federation of Women's Clubs led the "ladies lobby" in reviews of pending legislation at the Capitol. Women legislators worked tirelessly to enact legislation to

Davis H. Waite of Aspen, the only radical reformer to govern Colorado, oversaw giving women the vote and supported working people in their crusade for a minimum wage of three dollars for an eight-hour workday. Courtesy, Tom Noel Collection

improve the welfare of women and children. Sometimes reform took decades. Not until 1944 did legislation introduced by Colorado State Senator Eudochia Bell Smith finally give women the right to serve on juries. Men had argued that women should not be subjected to the lurid details of criminal behavior often brought out in jury trials.

The Silver Crash of 1893 and growing social and economic unrest led in the 1890s to the creation of a third political party. The Populist Party captured the imagination and the allegiance of a growing number of voters in Colorado, as well as elsewhere in the country. The Populists championed the underdog and looked out for the interests of the common man . . . and woman. Nationally, most of their support came from farmers. In Colorado, the Populists appealed also to miners by advocating federal subsidies for the depressed silver mining industry, including government purchase of all available silver to make U.S. coins. The Populists also endorsed such reforms as a graduated income tax, government ownership and operation of railroads and utilities, as well as an eight-hour workday. The Populists argued further that both Republicans and Democrats had become tools of big business and had turned their backs on ordinary men, women and children.

GOV. DAVIS H. WAITE

Davis H. Waite, the Populist candidate for governor in 1892, was a former state legislator in both Kansas and Wisconsin. He had moved to Aspen in 1879 to work initially as an attorney and a Justice of the Peace, and later as the first Pitkin County superintendent of schools. Once a secretary for the Knights of Labor, Waite's sympathies lay with the working man. He found a public forum for his populist views in the *Aspen Union Era*, a radical weekly newspaper he acquired in 1891.

Iowan James B. Weaver was the Populists' candidate for President in 1892. Coloradans handed him a popular majority and all of their electoral votes in the national election. Populist candidates also swept the state races, winning not only the governorship, but also a one-seat majority in the state legislature and both of the state's new U.S. Congressional seats.

The victorious Colorado Populists enacted numerous changes in Colorado politics. U.S. Senators, who had always been appointed by the state legislature, would be popularly elected henceforth. The Populists also enacted voter referendums which allowed direct legislation by voters using petitions and initiatives to put reforms on the ballot when government would not do so. Populists passed laws addressing mine safety and inspections and requiring that workers be paid in cash instead of company scrip.

Governor Davis Waite inherited significant long-standing problems. When he tried to remove two gubernatorial appointees—who did nothing to suppress gambling, dance halls, brothels and opium dens—they refused to step down from the Denver Fire and Police Board. Instead, these crooked officials barricaded themselves in Denver's City Hall, where they were guarded by corrupt police and hastily deputized sheriff's officers. Tensions escalated when Waite called in the state militia. Four hundred troops surrounded the building with Gatling guns and cannons. With guns bristling on both sides, thousands watched as the "City Hall War" of March 15, 1894 developed into a volatile standoff. Finally, wishing to avoid bloodshed, Waite ordered the troops withdrawn and agreed to have the matter mediated by the State Supreme Court.

THREE GOVERNORS IN ONE DAY

Leading Colorado businessmen deplored Governor Waite's sensational efforts to clean up political corruption and helped defeat him in the 1894 election. Eleven years later the spectacle of three governors in one day further demonstrated the corrupt

Denver's City Hall War erupted in 1894 after Governor Waite called out the state militia to help oust corrupt city officials from the old City Hall at 14th and Larimer. Courtesy, Denver Public Library

and chaotic nature of Colorado politics. Alva Adams won the 1904 governor's race, but Republican supporters of James A. Peabody cried foul, alleging Democratic voter fraud. They were probably justified. The state's Democrats in those days employed "repeaters"—gamblers, prostitutes, derelicts and ex-cons who voted over and over again in different precincts under different names.

The Republicans were no better. Democrats accused mine and corporation owners of coercing their employees to vote for Peabody, a governor who had crushed striking mine workers and labor unions. Neither side had the corner on corruption.

With thousands of questionable Democratic votes thrown out by the Republican-controlled State Supreme Court, Peabody was declared the legitimate winner. But the whole debacle had turned many of his own party against him. Eventually, a deal was struck whereby Adams would be ousted and Peabody would take the governor's chair—but only if he agreed to resign within twenty-four hours and turn over the office to his Lieutenant Governor, Jesse McDonald. Adams sat as governor until 5:00 p.m. on March 16, when the legislature declared Peabody duly elected to that position. True to his word, at 4:45 p.m. the next day, Peabody stepped down and McDonald was sworn in five minutes later as Colorado's third governor in twenty-four hours.

HONEST JOHN SHAFROTH

Reformers, including many newly enfranchised women, did much to address the corruption that shamed Colorado. In a shady political era, one reformer stood out—a Coloradan who had actually resigned from the House of Representatives after serving three terms there because he felt his 1902 election was tainted. That man was "Honest John" Shafroth. Colorado voters, remembering his extraordinary honesty, elected him governor of Colorado, 1908–1912, and U.S. Senator, 1912–1918. The voters' faith was not misplaced. Shafroth did more than anyone else in Colorado history to lift politics out of the mire.

As a congressman, Shafroth introduced the Women's Suffrage Amendment, championed creation of Mesa Verde and Rocky Mountain National

John Franklin Shafroth, perhaps the most effective Colorado reformer, pushed passage of numerous state and national reforms, including controls on big business and limits to corporate control of politicians, that shape Colorado to this day. Credit: Colorado Historical Society

Parks and supported the Newlands Act, setting up the U.S. Bureau of Reclamation to benefit the arid West. As governor of Colorado, Shafroth signed the initiative and referendum law, pushed direct election of U.S. Senators by popular vote instead of by the legislature, and crusaded for the direct primary so voters had a choice in selecting their party's candidates. Governor Shafroth also persuaded the legislature to enact a Child Labor Act and an eight-hour day for miners and women.

Shafroth and other reformers had many agendas and varied motivations. Some were moralizers, some visionaries and some simply disgruntled citizens. The need for change was the only thing they all agreed upon. Yet their efforts to lessen political corruption and big business abuses, enhance the quality of life, improve the treatment of women and promote education, health and safety still benefit Coloradans today.

Among many progressive era reforms championed by Colorado's U.S. Congressman and Governor John F. Shafroth was the creation of Rocky Mountain National Park in 1916. This snowcapped playground straddles the Continental Divide, treating visitors to wonders such as Milner Pass, featured in this 1920 postcard. Courtesy, Tom Noel Collection

13

TRAVELERS AND TOURISM

Estes Park, a mountain-rimmed valley named for pioneer settlers Joel and Patsy Estes, offers breathtaking sunsets. Courtesy, Tom Noel Collection

Colorado's mountains held value beyond the minerals they yielded. Sightseers marveled at the grandeur of the two-mile high, snow capped Rockies. Among early visitors to the highest state were renowned world travel writers such as Isabella Bird, who rhapsodized in purple prose about Colorado's glorious mountains. Though unimpressed by Denver—"the great braggart city"—and the squalor of mining towns, this Englishwoman was enraptured by the wild beauty of Estes Park. "Guarded by sentinel mountains of fantastic shape and monstrous size, with Long's Peak rising above them all in unapproachable grandeur, while the Snowy Range, with its outlaying spurs heavily timbered, come down upon the park, slashed by stupendous canyons lying deep in purple gloom," she wrote in her classic book, *A Lady's Life in the Rocky Mountains*. "The rushing river was blood red, Long's Peak was aflame, the glory of the glowing heaven was given back from the earth."

The first tourists, like the first settlers, came by horseback or by wagon train. The establishment of stage lines, while expensive and often dangerous, made the trip faster and slightly more comfortable. The oldest building in Denver, Four-Mile House, welcomed greenhorns following the Cherokee Trail into 1860s Colorado. Here, the road-weary passengers could find refreshment and wash up before heading into Denver City. Now restored as Four Mile House Historic Park, this relic of the pioneer era welcomes visitors to a rural retreat surrounded by latter-day developments.

RAILROAD TOURISM

Beginning in the 1870s railroads made it much easier to sample the extraordinary sights of Colorado. The Denver and Rio Grande, in particular, aimed its advertising at excursionists considering a tour into the rugged Rockies. Spectacular photographs taken by William Henry Jackson for the D&RG graced brochures, posters, and postcards. Images of Pikes Peak, the Mount of the Holy Cross, Garden of the Gods, Mesa Verde's cliff dwellings, Glenwood Canyon, the Royal Gorge and other spectacles attracted rubberneckers to the western wilderness.

Postcard spectacles—like the Colorado Midland Railway's line through Hell Gate, between Leadville and Aspen, with a 1,000-foot granite cliff on one side and a steep, rocky mountainside on the other— thrilled tourists. Courtesy, Tom Noel Collection

Above and opposite page
The Royal Gorge suspension bridge spans the Arkansas River 1,053 feet below. The Denver & Rio Grande battled the Santa Fe to win access to this canyon leading from Cañon City up to the silver city of Leadville. The old D&RG mainline with its view of the bridge from below has been revived as the Royal Gorge Route with lunch and dinner rail excursions. Courtesy, Photos by Tom Noel

Opposite page
For decades, tourists posed with a photograher's sombreros and burros beneath Balanced Rock in Colorado Springs' Garden of the Gods. Courtesy, Tom Noel Collection

WILDLIFE: SHOOT AND STUFF

Colorado's distinctive flora and fauna attracted both naturalists and sportsmen. William F. "Buffalo Bill" Cody led prestigious parties of gentlemen on bison hunts as early as 1872, when he escorted Russia's Grand Duke Alexis on a High Plains safari. Participants shot an average of thirty-seven shaggy beasts each, and celebrated every kill with a bottle of champagne. Subsequent expeditions for the less wealthy gave amateur marksmen the chance to target buffalo from the comfort of their passenger train as it traversed Colorado's eastern prairie.

Field naturalist Martha Dartt Maxwell, an accomplished huntress in her own right, shot Colorado birds and mammals not for sport but for science. A skilled taxidermist, Maxwell's mounted specimen of Western wildlife—including antelope, beaver, bighorn sheep, elk, mule deer and prairie dogs—drew thousands to her exhibit representing Colorado at the 1876 American Centennial Exhibition in Philadelphia. When criticized for killing the animals to display, Maxwell emphasized that she was a vegetarian and took their lives only for educational purposes. "I leave it to you," she challenged her critics. "Which is more cruel? To kill to eat or kill to immortalize?"

THE CENTENNIAL STATE

When the territory of Colorado officially joined the nation as the thirty-eighth state on August 1, 1876, it added "The Centennial State"—denoting the one-hundred-year anniversary of the creation of the nation—to its list of nicknames. From then on, it became less of a frontier and more of a mainstream destination for visitors from across the country, as well as abroad.

Denver, the commercial hub located near the center of the state where the mountains met the plains, seemed a natural choice for the new capital city. But it was not the sole contender. The territorial legislature had used Colorado City (now part of Colorado Springs), Cañon City and Golden as meeting places. Tiny Capitol City and booming Pueblo also sought the honor. Ultimately, it may have been women who tipped the balance in Denver's favor. There were more of them in the "Mile High City" than in any of the other potential capitals to provide hotel and boardinghouse accommodations, meal and laundry services, and other amenities valued by the visiting legislators.

When Denver became the capital, consolation prizes were awarded to Boulder, which received the state university, and Golden, which became home to the Colorado School of Mines. Pueblo was given the state mental hospital, and Cañon City got the state penitentiary.

Henry C. Brown donated ten acres of prime property on Brown's Bluff as the site for the capitol building, assuming that it would boost the value of his surrounding real estate. Elijah E. Myers, architect of the Michigan, Texas, Idaho and Utah state capitol buildings, designed a traditional neoclassical edifice with a Greek cross design. Ground was broken in 1886, but not until 1908

Martha Dartt Maxwell of Boulder captured and taxidermied Colorado wildlife, which she exhibited in her Rocky Mountain Museum. Her fine specimens were also prized by the Denver Natural History Museum. Courtesy, Colorado Historical Society

Opposite page
The State Capitol can be seen from Civic Center's Voorhies Memorial Gateway, with buffalo murals in its blind arches. Courtesy, Denver Public Library and Roger Whitacre

Above
One of the largest of the sanitariums for tuberculosis victims was the Jewish Consumptive Relief Society in Lakewood. That campus remains largely intact, although it is now surrounded by the JCRS Shopping Center and the fast growing Denver suburb of Lakewood—Colorado's fourth largest city. Courtesy, Tom Noel Collection

Opposite page
The State Capitol's gold dome has been re-gilded to give a warm, golden glow atop the stately neoclassical structure. Courtesy, Denver Public Library and Roger Whitacre

was the impressive statehouse officially completed, with the gilding of the dome using 200 ounces of twenty-four-karat gold leaf—a $14,680 tribute to the precious metal that had first lured settlers to the state.

The capitol is a must-see for visitors, who pose for photos on the mile-high steps at the west en-

trance. For years, the high point—both literally and figuratively—of a capitol tour has been the dome, the gallery and observation deck around the outside of the rotunda. More than 200,000 people visit the capitol each year, Coloradans and tourists in roughly equal numbers.

INTO THIN AIR

Though many early vacationers came to Colorado for the breathtaking scenery, visitors with chronic respiratory problems discovered another reason to make the pilgrimage. In the thin, dry, high-altitude air, they literally breathed easier. The state became a mecca for consumptives, as tuberculosis victims were called, as well as for asthmatics and those with other bronchial afflictions. Special sanitariums and health resorts that catered to these "lungers" sprang up around the region, offering large, screened fresh air porches or tents and touting the benefits of the sunshine that Colorado enjoyed more than 300 days a year. The clear, crisp, champagne air would do wonders for the respiratory system. Boosters called it "air that only the angels had breathed before."

HOT SPRINGS HYDROTHERAPY

Hot mineral springs, too, appealed to health-conscious travelers, and the Rocky Mountain region capitalized on a plethora of these hydrotherapeutic natural wonders. Idaho Springs, Hot Sulphur Springs, Manitou Springs and Pagosa Springs built resorts where warm waters bubbled up from the earth with allegedly curative powers for everything from skin diseases to lost manhood. White entrepreneurs usurped the Utes' sacred Yampah (meaning "Big Medicine") hot springs and diverted the course of the Colorado River to create the renowned Glenwood Springs resort on the Western Slope in 1886. Glenwood's Vapor Caves, dripping with mineral-rich condensation to create a natural geothermal steam bath, are associated with a popular spa today. The historic Hotel Colorado, Hot Springs Lodge and the world's largest outdoor hot springs pool attract thousands of visitors year-round.

By 1910 more people came to Colorado seeking

Even in winter, the Glenwood Hot Springs pool, shown here with the Hotel Colorado in the background, is a place to soak aches, pains and troubles away. Photo by Tom Noel

its health benefits than its mineral wealth. Some found their maladies much improved by the salubrious climate, but many others did not. For them, hospitals were established to provide care beyond simple fresh air and sunshine. Frances Wisehart Jacobs, known as Colorado's "Mother of Charities," was particularly moved by the plight of the many Eastern European Jewish immigrants who contracted tuberculosis back East and made their way to Colorado in hopes of a miracle. For these often indigent and desperate newcomers, the Frances Jacobs Hospital opened in 1892. The ground-breaking speaker observed, "As pain knows no creed, so is this building the prototype of the grand idea of Judaism, which casts aside no stranger, no matter what race or blood. We consecrate this structure to humanity [and] our suffering fellow man." The

first invalid admitted was a non-Jewish tubercular young woman from Minneapolis

In the late 1800s and early 1900s tuberculosis (TB) was one of the leading causes of death in the U.S. Many children were orphaned by consumptive parents who came to Colorado, "the world's sanitarium," but never got better. A group of women philanthropists established the Sheltering Home for Children (eventually the National Home for Jewish Children) in 1907 to rescue these children from lives of poverty, ill health and neglect.

Denver's National Jewish Medical and Research Center, as the Francis Jacobs Hospital is now known, remains one of the world's leading facilities dedicated exclusively to respiratory, immune and allergic disorders. Ranked the nation's number one respiratory hospital, it continues to attract medical specialists, researchers and patients from around the nation and the globe.

Tuberculosis, the nation's deadliest disease, killed many parents, orphaning their children. The National Home for Jewish Children, at 3447 W. 19th Ave. in Denver, took in such youngsters from across the nation. Courtesy, Beck Archives, University of Denver

DENVER: THE CITY BEAUTIFUL

Big Thompson River looking east. Big Thompson River, east of the Estes Park Visitors Center, winds through the Estes Park Executive 9-Hole Golf Course before joining and emptying into Lake Estes. Courtesy, Estes Park Convention & Visitors Bureau

Robert W. "Boss" Speer, Denver's mayor from 1904–1912 and 1914–1918, was inspired by the 1893 Chicago World Exposition and his visits to Europe to transform a dusty, drab, unplanned town into "Paris on the Platte." His "City Beautiful" scheme included giving away 110,000 trees to any Denverite promising to plant and care for them, as well as doubling the city's parks space. To the new parks, the mayor added fountains, gardens, statuary and playgrounds, as well as a zoo and natural history museum in City Park. Working with the Carnegie Foundation, the Speer administration helped establish not only a central library but also branch libraries. Speer pushed construction of public bathhouses and swimming pools, as well as the Denver Municipal Auditorium. He cleared the trashy heart of the city to create Civic Center Park which included an outdoor Greek Theatre, despite local complaints that, "Denver ain't got that many Greeks. Why the heck do we need a Greek Theater?"

DENVER MOUNTAIN PARKS

Speer's ambitious vision also looked beyond the city limits to the majestic mountains in the west. In 1909 he suggested to the Chamber of Commerce that a road be built into the hills so that motorists could drink in inspiration from the Rockies. Promoter John Brisbane Walker helped form a coalition of the Chamber, the Colorado Mountain Club and the Denver Real Estate Board to urge a popular vote allowing Denver to purchase mountain park land outside the city limits. Ultimately Denver Mountain Parks came to include more than 20,000 acres and such tourist meccas as Buffalo Bill's Grave and Museum on Lookout Mountain and the Winter Park Ski Area.

MOTOR GYPSIES

The creation of Denver's Mountain Parks coincided with the rise of the automobile as the preeminent mode of transportation in Colorado and throughout the nation. Henry Ford's innovative mass production techniques combined with long-term financing made it possible by the 1920s for many upper and middle-class families to own cars. The freedom of individual transportation inspired "motor gypsies" to set out across the country. Tourists who previously might not have been able to afford a Colorado train trip could pack up a tent and a cookstove, load up the wife and kids in the Model T or farm truck, and head for the hills.

Businessmen in places like Denver and Estes Park quickly recognized the lucrative income potential of catering to these new adventurers and provided "motor camps" for them. Denver's City Park welcomed auto travelers beginning in 1915, and the local chamber of commerce distributed free maps and trip logs to campers en route to mountain splendors. By 1918 the swelling ranks of auto travelers prompted the city to add a second camp, Rocky Mountain Lake Park in northwest Denver, and by 1920, the enterprise was moved to Overland Park. The 800-space facility provided the road-weary with restrooms, showers, laundries and a clubhouse with a grocery store, barbershop, restaurant, billiard hall and even a state-of-the-art suspended dance floor. After the wayside stop attracted more than

59,000 campers in 1923, the city instituted a charge of fifty cents per night. That same year, an estimated 600,000 tourists stopped at 250 Colorado campsites.

During the Great Depression of the 1930s, the general character of auto nomads subtly shifted from middle-class motor gypsies to the less affluent "motor hobos" on cross-country quests for work. Unwilling to accommodate this indigent riff-raff, Denver authorities closed Overland Park. Never again would such a camp be operated within the city limits. During that decade, the Denver Mountain Parks system was completed with the help of New Deal agencies, particularly the Civilian Conservation Corps (CCC) and the Works Progress Administration (WPA).

One of the CCC's most impressive mountain parks projects was the creation of Red Rocks, near Morrison. Denver had acquired the property in 1928. George Cranmer, Manager of Parks and Recreation under Mayor Ben Stapleton, envisioned greater things for the site in 1935. Cranmer recognized that the unique arrangement of sandstone monoliths provided amazing natural acoustics on the mountainside overlooking distant Denver. The efforts of the CCC and the design by architect Burnham Hoyt combined to create a world-class outdoor amphitheatre that has hosted everything from opera to the Beatles, from classical dance to hip hop.

Auto tourism rescued many a fading mining town in the early twentieth-century. Hotels and "cottage camps" prospered in mountain resorts around the state. One of the most successful tourist destinations was Estes Park. First developed as a private hunting retreat by Englishman Windham Thomas Wyndham-Quin, the fourth Earl of Dunraven, in the 1870s, it annually attracted hundreds of adventurous visitors. In 1910 a new road up the Big Thompson Canyon led motorists from Loveland to the Park and its newest, finest hotel, the Stanley, built by the inventor of the popular Stanley Steamer motor vehicles. These visitors were as charmed by the area's breathtaking setting as Isabella Bird had been forty years earlier. The campaign to create a national park in the vicinity gained support from businessmen, the Colorado Chamber of Commerce, the Colorado Mountain

Club, the *Denver Post* and finally the entire state legislature.

The establishment of a national mountain park and game preserve above Estes Park was originally proposed and championed by local guide, nature writer and innkeeper Enos Mills. For more than two years, Mills sought support for his idea through speaking engagements, articles in national publications and a dozen books, such as *The Spell of the Rockies*. Yet Mills' refusal to negotiate with the mining, logging and grazing interests that opposed his plan nearly doomed the campaign. Denver lawyer and first president of the Colorado Mountain Club, James Grafton Rogers, however, drafted a bill acceptable to all parties and used his skill for diplomacy and political influence to gather support. The bill, designating 358-square-miles straddling the Continental Divide in Boulder, Larimer and Grand counties as the nation's tenth national park, passed in January 1915. When Rocky Mountain National Park was dedicated the following September, more than 2,000 people from all over the state made their way to Horseshoe Park in carriages, wagons and automobiles for the ceremony.

The park attracted tourists from around the nation. In 1920, when Fall River Road opened to the top of the Continental Divide, the park welcomed more than 116,000 visitors—28,000 from out of state. The Never Summer Range was added to the park in 1929. Construction of Trail Ridge Road, which traverses the entire park, began in 1929, but took twenty years to finish because crews could only work in the icy, snowy alpine ice zone about four months out of the year. Road builders used great care and expense to minimize landscape scars, preserve the delicate permafrost tundra and select local rock for road guards. Today, Rocky Mountain National Park stands as a monument to those with the foresight to see beyond its harvestable resources to its greater ecological, recreational and spiritual value. The park has grown to more than 415 square miles and annually attracts more than 3 million visitors.

Above and opposite page
Red Rocks outdoor amphitheatre, built between two natural megaliths in the foothills west of Morrison, is an architectural wonder that attracts the masses. Concerts begin as the sun sets and may feature a view of the moon rising over Denver on the plains fifteen miles to the east. Courtesy, Denver Metro Convention & Visitor Bureau.

Naturalist Enos Mills, the father of Rocky Mountain National Park, urged Americans to commune with nature. Mills, who definitely practiced what he preached, not only hugged trees but also climbed them because, he claimed, "a tree's greatest joys are the dances it takes with the wind." Courtesy, Denver Public Library

THE LURE OF THE MYTHIC WEST

Artists like Albert Bierstadt, Thomas Moran and Frederic Remington romanticized the Western landscape and lifestyle in their paintings and sculpture. But no one did more to mythologize the Wild West, especially cowboys and Indians, than William F. "Buffalo Bill" Cody. Elevated to celebrity status and coaxed into show business, Cody epitomized the Western hero. From 1883 to 1917, Buffalo Bill thrilled audiences that packed arenas across the nation and throughout Europe to witness his hugely successful "Wild West Show." The spectacular production captured the imaginations of both commoners and crowned heads of state such as Queen Victoria.

With his flowing hair and beard, extravagant costumes and thigh-high boots, Cody cut a striking figure astride his white horse. Ever the consummate showman, he presented buffalo hunts, Indian chiefs and lady sharpshooters, and reenacted everything from stagecoach ambushes to Custer's Last Stand, all to the rousing accompaniment of the Cowboy Band. For years, the show's grand finale recreated the final engagement of the so-called "Indian Wars" in Colorado, the 1869 Battle of Summit Springs, in which the dashing Cody helped rescue a captured white woman and killed the Cheyenne chief, Tall Bull.

The "Wild West Show" imprinted on the public psyche a portrayal of the vanishing West that persists to this day. Even in death, Cody was a tourist magnet. Recognizing his post-mortem potential, Harry Tammen of *The Denver Post* made Cody's widow, Louisa, an offer she couldn't refuse. Tammen paid for Buffalo Bill to be buried atop Lookout Mountain outside Denver, rather than on a bluff overlooking Cody, Wyoming, as Cody had wished. Together with the adjacent Buffalo Bill Museum, his gravesite continues to attract tens of thousands of fans each year.

Cody's mythic West lives on in films and television shows. People who sought their own Western experience spawned the "dude ranch" industry, popular in Colorado since the 1920s. Tourists snap countless photos of the bison herd at Genesee Park and flock to towns that offer a taste of the Old West. Savvy communities capitalize on their Western appeal: an arch spanning Golden's main street greets visitors with "Howdy, Folks! Welcome to Golden, Where the West Lives!"

Colorado owes much of its popularity as a tourist destination to this lure of the imagined West. Many cowboy wanna-bes come to visit and decide to relocate to the Highest State. Wealthier newcomers often corral a horse or two on "Mac-Ranches," which have cropped up in formerly rural areas all over the state. Rockmont Ranch Wear, longtime makers and retailers of Western snap-front shirts, still thrives in Denver's Lower Downtown Historic District, outfitting real-life wranglers as well as visiting "dudes" from around the globe in fringed, embroidered, colorful shirts and other western wear. Not only cowboy clothes, but trail rides, chuckwagon dinners, country music and rodeos perpetuate the Western experience, and Colorado reaps the financial rewards of feeding tourist fantasies.

Buckskin Joe is a movie set town near the Royal Gorge Suspension Bridge west of Cañon City, where tourists can see Wild West shootouts on Main Street, followed by a lynching. Photos by Tom Noel

14

COLORADO'S BOOM AND BUSTS

This abandoned gold and silver mill in the ghost town of Animas Forks reflects Colorado's boom and bust cycle. Courtesy Tom Noel Collection

Ever since its birth in a gold rush, Colorado has experienced a roller coaster history of economic ups and downs. The state's dependence on the riches of the earth—gold and silver, coal and molybdenum, oil and water—has subjected it to persistent boom and bust cycles. What goes up, comes down. The initial 1858–1859 gold rush led to economic stagnation during the 1860s; the 1970s oil boom ended with the 1980s oil bust when Colorado once again lost population and the economy faltered. Even more significant economic disasters rocked Colorado after the 1893 silver bust and the 1929 stock market disaster.

THE 1890s DEPRESSION

The Silver Crash of 1893 saw the price of that metal drop from about one dollar an ounce to half that. Silver mining, then the state's leading industry, collapsed. Many banks closed and a fourth of the population was thrown out of work.

As times grew tougher, management and increasingly unionized workers quarreled over who should receive dwindling profits. Workers insisted that companies pay a minimum wage of three dollars a day for a maximum work day of eight hours. Mine and smelter owners, like most other employers, rejected the very idea of a minimum wage and maximum work day. As both sides dug in their heels, strikes broke out around the state. Smelter workers in Colorado City and Denver and miners in Cripple Creek, Idaho Springs, Leadville and Telluride went out on strikes that turned violent in 1903 and 1904. In Idaho Springs, a dynamite blast at the Sun and Moon Mine on July 28, 1903 provided the excuse for the owners and businessmen of the Citizens' Protective League to run twenty-two union leaders out of town and crush the strike.

Union workers pointed out that in 1899 the Colorado General Assembly had passed an eight-hour workday law for mine, mill and smelter workers. That law however was undermined by the Colorado Supreme Court, which declared that it violated workers' rights to sell their labor as they saw fit. Three years later Coloradans countered the court's objections by voting—72,980 to 26,266—for a constitutional amendment permitting adoption of an eight-hour workday law. Under heavy

Above
To house an army of unemployed men thrown out of work by the 1893 silver crash, Denver constructed this relief camp along the South Platte River. *Courtesy, Denver Public Library*

Below
Mining towns, such as those in the Cripple Creek District, shown here on September 9, 1903, became campgrounds for the Colorado National Guard during the labor wars. The National Guard crushed the Western Federation of Miners union by arresting and deporting labor leaders. *Courtesy, Tom Noel Collection*

This Western Federation of Miners union hall and library in Victor, Colorado was attacked by the Colorado National Guard during the 1903–1904 strike. Bullet holes still scar the façade today as a reminder of the bitter, bloody struggle to unionize. Courtesy, Denver Public Library

pressure from corporate lobbyists, however, the General Assembly in its 1903 session adjourned without taking the action clearly mandated by the electorate.

Colorado Governor James Peabody sided with mine owners and sent in the state militia to protect scab labor and to arrest or deport union organizers. By the end of 1904 the Western Federation of Miners union was crushed. Coal miners in the northern fields, however, conducted a successful strike for an eight-hour workday.

LUDLOW MASSACRE

In the southern Colorado coalfields, miners faced not only the failure of the eight-hour movement but also payment of wages in company scrip rather than in U.S. currency. Coal miners encountered danger every day from collapsing shafts, explosions and poison gas. Colorado's foothills and mountains regularly rumbled with underground explosions, which added to the toll from accidents with mining machinery. Averaging more than 100 deaths a year, Colorado coal mines killed employees at twice the national rate.

In the fall of 1913 at least 8,000 members of the United Mine Workers walked off their jobs in southern Colorado's Huerfano and Las Animas counties. They struggled through driving snow and sleet to move their families and belongings from company housing in the foothill canyons to tent colonies on the open plains.

The course of the 1913 strike paralleled that of earlier strikes in which the state interfered on behalf of management. Governor Elias M. Ammons dispatched the National Guard in response to skirmishes between mine guards and armed strikers. The six-month standoff in the coalfields exploded on April 20, 1914, when a detachment of the National Guard opened fire on the tent colony at Ludlow. The battle on April 20 lasted the entire day before National Guardsmen, with two machine guns, routed the defenders from protected positions behind the camp. Five strikers and one militiaman fell in the fighting, one boy died from a stray bullet, and two women and eleven children choked to death on thick smoke in the cellar underneath one of the tents set afire by the National Guard.

The result was ten days of civil war. More than 1,000 armed miners swarmed over the hills to fight pitched battles with company guards and state troops. Over a twenty-mile stretch between Trinidad and Walsenburg, striking miners burned mine property and laid siege to mines. Not until President Woodrow Wilson assigned 1,600 federal troops to southern Colorado with orders to disarm everyone in the strike zone—militia, company guards and miners—did the warfare cease.

SMELTER GIANTS

While mining faltered, farming and ranching emerged as major industries. Other enterprises also helped the state bounce back. The American Smelting and Refining Company (ASARCO), formed in 1899 and capitalized at $65 million, absorbed Colorado's Omaha and Grant, United, Globe, Pueblo Smelting and several other firms. ASARCO controlled two-thirds of the U.S. smelting and refining capacity, with six plants in Colorado and nearly a dozen in other states. More consolidation came in 1901, when the Guggen-

Mother Jones led this 1913 demonstration in Trinidad in support of strikers protesting the Colorado Fuel & Iron Company's exploitive operations in southern Colorado. Courtesy, Colorado Historical Society

heims, whose industrial empire began with a Leadville smelter, joined the ASARCO team.

COLORADO FUEL & IRON

Coal mining was big business because of the huge fuel needs of western steam railroads and the growing demand for it as heating fuel and in power plants. The largest of the coal companies, Pueblo's huge Colorado Fuel and Iron Company (CF&I), produced coal, iron and steel. CF&I also became the leading western producer of railroad track, spikes, barbed wire fencing and pipe.

William J. Palmer was followed as CF&I's chief by John C. Osgood. CF&I owned 69,000 acres of coal lands, two iron mines, four coking plants and the largest steel plant in the west. With operations in over 100 Colorado communities and more than 15,000 workers, CF&I became the state's major employer by 1900.

The company also built better company housing in its twentieth-century towns than it had in the 1880s and 1890s. At the CF&I's showcase town of Redstone along the Crystal River in western Colorado, Osgood built an elegant Tudor-style boardinghouse for bachelors and fashionable cottages for family housing. These cottages featured electric lights, indoor toilets, running water and generous yards.

Soon after Osgood created that idyllic town, he lost control of it. To fund the modernization of CF&I, he borrowed from John D. Rockefeller, Jr., the richest man in the United States. By 1903 Rockefeller gained control of CF&I and annexed Colorado's biggest business to the nation's largest business empire.

THE MOFFAT TUNNEL

The Moffat Tunnel, a long dreamed of all-weather route beneath the Continental Divide, helped stimulate commerce. Entrepreneur David Moffat went broke in 1911 trying to build a railroad into northwestern Colorado and on to Salt Lake. Winter snow often blocked trains on 11,671-foot high Rollins Pass. Moffat's road needed a long tunnel under James Peak, but he could not afford to bore through more than six miles of mountain. After Moffat's death, his railroad hoped to build the tunnel at taxpayers' expense.

State legislators from Pueblo, whose Arkansas River rail route through the Rockies had been the main line, saw no reason to help rival Denver improve its rail connections until disaster struck in early June of 1921. The rain-gorged Arkansas River swept through central Pueblo burying parts of the city under twelve feet of water. Striking suddenly with scant warning, the torrent tore people from their homes. Property damage ran to $30 million, and at least a hundred people died. For years afterward, skeletons turned up downstream along the Arkansas River.

Pueblo asked the state legislature to approve a taxation district to raise money for flood repair and control. That gave Denver legislators the opportunity to pressure Pueblo into backing Denver's Moffat Tunnel taxation district. Votes were traded, and the assembly approved both taxation districts.

Pueblo's giant Colorado Fuel and Iron steel works were the largest in the American West. Courtesy, Tom Noel Collection

During the 1921 Pueblo Flood, the swollen Arkansas River destroyed much of the city, killed over 100 people and, as seen here, devastated the Union Avenue district near Union Station. Courtesy, Tom Noel Collection

Pueblo tamed the Arkansas, and Denver got a railroad tunnel under James Peak. This allowed the Denver and Rio Grande, which took over Moffat's old Denver and Salt Lake Railroad, to run trains on a direct, year-round route from Denver to Salt Lake.

THE GREAT DEPRESSION

Colorado had finally recovered from the 1890s crash and started growing again during the 1920s. Then came the Stock Market Crash of 1929. During the 1930s, Colorado, like the rest of the country, sank into the Great Depression. Trying to lift the country out of economic disaster, President Franklin D. Roosevelt established federal programs to create jobs that improved communities and public lands. One of Roosevelt's pet projects, the Civilian

Conservation Corps (CCC) hired young men to build trails, campgrounds and other amenities in public parks and recreational lands. Among the CCC's outstanding contributions were Red Rocks

Lowry Air Force Base in east Denver and Aurora became a huge training center during and after World War II. Closed as a military base in 1994, it has been successfully redeveloped as a residential, retail and office neighborhood. The hangar on the right has been recycled as the Wings over the Rockies Museum and many of the other structures seen here have been converted to commercial or residential space. Courtesy, Tom Noel Collection

outdoor amphitheatre in Morrison, Flagstaff amphitheatre in Boulder, and hundreds of other projects around the state, varying from building public bathrooms to fighting forest fires.

Another New Deal agency, the Works Progress Administration (WPA), put Colorado's unemployed to work repairing schools, building roads, planting trees and filling chuckholes. Larger WPA projects included installation of storm sewers and reinforcing the banks of flood-prone rivers and streams. The WPA hired unemployed women to make clothing, prepare school lunches and run nurseries. It supported weavers who repaired old Indian and Hispanic textiles at the Denver Art Museum. At the Colorado Historical Society, researchers gathered historical data and compiled an excellent book, *Colorado: A Guide to the Highest State*. Many hungry Colorado artists ate because of WPA's art program, which paid them thirty-five dollars a week to decorate schools, post offices and other government buildings. Among the WPA's most enduring and endearing legacies are the dioramas at the Colorado Historical Society in Denver depicting Indians, cowboys, mining, railroads and the two-year-old town of Denver.

The WPA spent more than $42 million in Colorado—$5 million more than the state produced in gold during the same period. By 1937 WPA workers were remodeling the Agnes Phipps Tuberculosis Sanitarium in east Denver as an Army Air Corps Technical School that evolved into Lowry Air Force Base.

When the WPA ceased operating in 1943, Denver's unemployed no longer worried about jobs. They knew the United States military wanted them. America was at war. Wartime industry and military installations transformed Aurora, Colorado Springs and Denver, generating thousands of new jobs.

SKI COUNTRY USA

Federal support for a Denver Mountain Park at Winter Park and for a World War II military base near Leadville jump started Colorado's ski industry.

Camp Hale, an army base near Leadville, trained the U.S. Tenth Mountain Division ski troops for World War II. After the war, some of these veterans returned to develop Colorado ski areas. Courtesy, Tom Noel Collection

The city of Denver opened Winter Park as a ski area in 1940. Accessible by train via the Moffat Tunnel, the popular Denver Mountain Park became one of the state's first winter resorts. But thrusting the ski industry into the forefront of Colorado tourist attractions took nothing short of military intervention.

To train soldiers for mountain and winter combat in Europe during World War II, the U.S. Army established Camp Hale near Leadville. Its ski facility covered 240 acres with ten downhill runs accessed by four rope tows. The camp housed 14,000 members of the Tenth Mountain Division, comprised of some of the most accomplished skiers in the nation. After fighting with distinction in Northern Italy's Appennine Mountains, many Tenth Mountain Division veterans decided to make Colorado their home.

Entrepreneurial Tenth Mountain alumni, including Larry Jump, Friedl Pfeffer and Peter Seibert, developed downhill playgrounds at Aspen, Arapaho and Loveland Basins and Vail, transforming Colorado into a world-class ski destination by the 1970s. Winter sports were boosted considerably by the 1973 completion of the Eisenhower-Johnson Tunnel and I-70, making it easier for ski enthusiasts to drive from the populous Front Range to the many Western Slope resorts without navigating treacherous passes over the Continental Divide in winter conditions. Today, Colorado's twenty-nine winter resorts continue to attract more skiers and snowboarders than any other state in the nation. With 60 percent of their business coming from out-of-state visitors, the industry generates more than $2.5 billion annually.

THE FEDERAL IMPACT

The World War II ordnance plant on West Sixth Avenue, between Lakewood and Golden, epitomized Colorado's post-war boom. After the war, it became a huge Federal Center for numerous agencies and thousands of employees. It also became the largest federal office center outside of Washington, D.C. Steady, high-paying federal jobs with good benefits brought many newcomers to the Denver area, both during and after the war.

After World War II military spending lifted Colorado out of depression and created many jobs, including civilian ones. Coloradans also strove to capture military institutions and contracts during the Cold War that continued for four decades after 1945. Pointing out that the east and west coasts were far more vulnerable to enemy bombs and missiles, Coloradans promoted the Rocky Mountain West as an unassailable bastion for military installations.

The Pentagon concurred. The Air Force Academy opened in 1958 followed by the North American Air Defense Command, both in Colorado Springs. That city became a hub of military installations, including what is still a very large army base—Fort Carson.

Coloradans lobbied effectively for two other major military installations: the Rocky Mountain Arsenal and Rocky Flats Nuclear Weapons Plant. At Rocky Flats in Jefferson County, plutonium triggers were manufactured and maintained for nuclear bombs. The Arsenal in Adams County made toxic weapons for chemical warfare. Both sites were regarded as heaven-sent boosts for the local economy. But with the end of the Cold War in the 1980s, Coloradans began the long, costly cleanup of contamination at Rocky Flats and the Rocky Mountain Arsenal to convert both to open space and wildlife refuges.

Oil booms and busts now rock Colorado's economy as gold and silver fluctuations once did. These Conoco refinery towers adorn the skyline of Commerce City in Adams County. Photo by Michael Gamer

OILY TIMES

Colorado's oil and natural gas fields fueled another boom from the 1950s to the mid 1980s. Colorado's resources and favorable tax laws for extracting companies attracted major oil companies, as well as wildcatters.

Colorado crude oil production soared from 5 million barrels in 1945 to 47 million by 1970. During the 1970s oil and energy companies bankrolled a gusher of downtown Denver high rises, including the forty-four-story Anaconda Tower and its swanky top floor Petroleum Club. Philip Anschutz and other Colorado energy kings erected the fifty-six-story Republic Plaza in 1984, which boasted almost as much prime office space as did all of downtown in 1950. Republic Plaza topped the fifty-four-story City Center Tower in 1983, as did fifty-two-story United (now Wells Fargo) Bank Tower in 1984.

The crash came in the mid 1980s as the price of oil slid from $34 a barrel to $9 a barrel. Unemployment and office vacancy rates soared. Some 13,000 Denver oil industry workers lost their jobs. By 1985 a downtown Denver, overbuilt during the energy boom, had the highest office vacancy rate in the nation—30 percent.

RECOVERY

If booms portend a bust, a bust also portends a boom. By the mid-1990s Colorado had recovered from the oil bust. The population and economy began soaring to new heights. Federal jobs and the rising tourism industry proved to be relatively depression proof. Until the federal government stops growing and Colorado's mountains no longer lure tourists, the state can bank on these old faithfuls.

Colorado's booms can be measured in downtown Denver high rises. During the 1970s downtown became the nesting place of the high rise construction crane. The fifty-six-story Republic Plaza is the tallest of the Mile High City's skyscrapers. Photo by Roger Whitacre (above). Photo by Glenn Cuereden (below).

MARY CHASE'S HUMOR BUOYED COLORDANS THROUGH THE HARD TIMES

Colorado's boom and bust cycle has inspired many attempts to cheer folks up during difficult days. One woman—who learned to write plays with the help of the New Deal's Depression-era Federal Theatre program—cheered up the entire country during World War II.

Mary McDonough Coyle Chase, a Denver native, won the 1945 Pulitzer Prize for her play *Harvey*. One of Broadway's most popular and longest running hits, it also became a blockbuster movie starring Jimmy Stewart. Chase learned storytelling from her Irish-born mother, father and uncles, whose fairy tale banshees, leprechauns and pookas would later reappear in her stories and plays.

The youngest of four children, Mary grew up in a modest one-story cottage at 532 W. 4th Avenue in a working class neighborhood. At age sixteen, Chase applied for a summer job at the *Rocky Mountain News*.

A confident young woman, Mary had deep brown hair, pearl white skin and large blue eyes. "She combined an exquisite profile with very nice legs," recalled longtime *News* columnist Lee Casey, "but that comely body housed a most unusual mind." Although initially confined to the feminine role of a society reporter, she later asserted herself as an investigative reporter.

Even after marrying *Rocky Mountain News* city editor Robert Chase and raising three children, Mary wrote plays in her spare time. The Federal Theater Project in Denver staged her first play, *Me Third*, in 1936. New York producer Brock Pemberton purchased the play, which was rewritten and renamed *Now You've Done It*. It opened on Broadway in 1937, directed by another Denver native, Antoinette Perry. It flopped, folding after seven weeks.

Hoping to bring laughter to wartime America, Chase wrote a comedy about a six-foot, one and

Denverite Mary Coyle Chase, shown here with her favorite character, captured the 1946 Pulitzer Prize for her play Harvey, *a smash hit Broadway comedy that cheered up Americans during World War II. Courtesy,* Rocky Mountain News

one-half inch tall imaginary white rabbit. She originally called her play "The Pooka," for the creature of Irish folklore. The play opened in Denver as *The White Rabbit*. The title was changed to *Harvey* for its November 1, 1944 opening at the 48th Street Theater in New York City. Rave reviews greeted this drama revolving around Elwood P. Dowd, an amiable alcoholic who found a drinking companion in Harvey. Dowd and his imaginary bunny buddy try to cheer up a war-torn, sad, lonely world. As Dowd puts it:

> Harvey and I sit in the bars and we have a drink or two and play the jukebox. Soon the faces of the other people turn toward mine and smile. They are saying: "We don't' know your name, mister, but you're a lovely fellow." Harvey and I warm ourselves in all these golden moments. We have entered as strangers—soon we have friends. They come over. They sit with us.

Dowd is a hopelessly cheerful fellow, never turning mean despite life's cruel tricks. His character is epitomized by his opening line in the play. "Hello," he says into a telephone, "You have the wrong number, but how are you anyway?"

Harvey enriched the Chases. They moved into a mansion at 505 Circle Drive in Denver's posh Country Club district. Mary called this Tudor castle "the house that Harvey built." In that castle, Mary died of a heart attack on October 20, 1981 at age seventy-five. Taking her sense of humor to the grave, she had picked a plot for herself in Crown Hill Cemetery next to a tombstone inscribed "Harvey." Mary Coyle Chase, who always believed that laughter heals, wanted the last laugh.

15

TRANSPORTATION

Denver's Union Station, the state's first great transit center, is being restored as a hub for not only rail, but light rail lines as well. As a multimodal transportation hub, it is also being expanded to accommodate motor vehicles buses, bicycles and pedestrians. Photo by Tom Noel

Situated far from any coast and near no navigable river, Colorado has long been concerned with transportation. Every town feared that if it did not attract a stagecoach and then a railroad, it would become a ghost. Since 1900 communities have fought for modern, paved roads. In recent decades Coloradans have focused on building a maze of freeways, an extensive light rail system and one of the world's largest state-of-the-art airports. From the beginning, expediting travel has been the key to development in a large and isolated state of long distances and mountainous obstacles.

Colorado's worst transportation nightmare came in the mid-1860s when the Union Pacific Railroad constructed its transcontinental line through Wyoming to avoid Colorado's mountain barrier. At that point Colorado's pioneer boosters staged a campaign that would be repeated in the automobile and air ages. Newspaper editors, the governor, town mayors and a chorus of boosters declared that Denverites must work together to build a railroad. Otherwise, Denver would become just another ghost town.

Coloradans celebrated the arrival of the Denver Pacific on June 24, 1870. This steel lifeline kept the town from becoming just another of the many ghost towns that haunt the Great American Desert.

Once the Denver Pacific arrived, other railroads also built to Denver. The city's population soared. By 1890 Denver's population of 106,713 was second in the West only to San Francisco, ahead of Los Angeles, Seattle, Phoenix or any town in Texas. Denver built a spider web of steel to become the regional metropolis of a vast Rocky Mountain and high plains hinterland.

FROM RAILROADS TO STREET RAILWAYS

Railroads thrived in Colorado, inspiring cities to build horse railways, as the first horse-drawn streetcars were called. Between 1871 and the 1940s, an extensive streetcar system was built in Denver. All classes of people rode the streetcar at all times of day, using them to get to work, school, shopping, recreation and back home again. Couples rented a Denver Tramway Company charter car for weddings and honeymoons. Many Coloradans took their

The California Zephyr *(opposite page top and below), the most fabled of a hundred different Colorado rail lines, offered the first vista dome windows (opposite page bottom) on its sleek stainless steel passenger coaches. Amtrak (right) has revived the legendary train as its* San Francisco Zephyr *which breezes through Colorado canyons and offers vista dome views of the Rocky Mountains as well as on-board meals (above). Photos by Tom Noel*

Horse-drawn streetcars, like this one, enabled city dwellers to move out to streetcar suburbs, setting a pattern for sprawling growth accelerated by automobile suburbs. Courtesy, Denver Public Library

final ride in Funeral Car A, which served Fairmount and Mount Olivet cemeteries. While the guest of honor and family rode in Car A with its solemn black paint and gold trim, mourners and the band rode in Funeral Car B.

Streetcars, not automobiles, first allowed people to move out of the core city into Denver's spacious suburban neighborhoods of single-family, detached housing. Not only the close-in ring of streetcar suburbs—Curtis Park, Highlands, Barnum, South Denver, Montclair, Swansea and Globeville—but also an outer ring of country towns—including Aurora, Arvada, Boulder, Englewood, Golden, Lafayette, Lakewood, Littleton, Louisville, Westminster and Wheat Ridge—were all served by streetcar and rail commuter lines.

At first horses pulled the streetcars, but the epizootic plague of the 1880s and the sturdier nature of mules led to their introduction. By the late 1880s most horses and mules were replaced by electric trolleys or trolley systems. Smaller, one-horse lines were ultimately absorbed by the Denver Tramway Company, which did not abandon its bright yellow electric trolleys until 1950.

STREETCARS STATEWIDE

Many other towns in Colorado also had streetcar lines, including Aspen, Boulder, Colorado Springs, Cripple Creek, Durango, Fort Collins, Grand Junction, Greeley, Leadville, Littleton, Manitou Springs, Pueblo and Victor. Aspen built a short-lived horse car line, the Aspen City Railway in 1889, but abandoned it after the silver crash of 1893. After an early horsecar failed and was converted to a lunch wagon, Boulder Railway operated a trolley (overhead electric power) system from 1899 to 1931.

The forty-one-mile system of the Colorado Springs and Interurban Railway also served Colorado City, the Broadmoor Hotel and Manitou Springs. Cripple Creek gold millionaire Winfield Scott Stratton financed this system, which operated from 1887 to 1932, when it was replaced by rubber-tired buses.

Cripple Creek, the last and greatest of all gold mining bonanzas, created an urban area of 55,000 people by 1900. To serve the Cripple Creek District and carry many miners to work, the Colorado Springs & Cripple Creek District Railway operated a line from 1898 until 1919. This CS&CCDR line served Cripple Creek, Victor and the smaller towns of Goldfield, Independence, Midway, Anaconda and Elkton.

While Durango had a single main street line, Fort Collins, Greeley, Pueblo and Trinidad had extensive streetcar networks connecting the business district with residential neighborhoods. All of these systems succumbed during the 1900s to the automobile.

Fort Collins, the last city in Colorado to operate a streetcar system, did not abandon its Municipal Railway system until 1951. In 1985 the city revived a mile and a half of the former Mountain Avenue line, running from City Park to the Old Town Historic District. Photo by Tom Noel

COLORADO'S LOVE AFFAIR WITH THE AUTOMOBILE

Streetcar ridership declined as more and more Coloradans purchased automobiles. Along with Californians, Coloradans have one of the highest motor vehicle ownership rates in the world, with almost one registered motor vehicle for every adult resident. Many families have sport utility vehicles as well as town cars, if not snowmobiles, motorcycles, motor boats or motorized all-terrain vehicles.

Cars have become the ultimate toy of teenagers and their favorite sixteenth birthday request. Middle-agers show they have made it by buying a new model every year or so. Older folks, likewise, cherish their automobiles, clinging to their cars and drivers licenses as long as possible. Some Coloradans have been conceived in motor vehicles, some born there and many will die in them.

Motor vehicles have reshaped Colorado, where cities are mostly paved over for driving and for parking. The skies are tainted with automobile exhaust and even the most remote rural areas are branded with tire tracks, if not roads.

The state of Colorado welcomed automobiles from their arrival in 1900. Today, road building remains one of the major concerns of state government. As early as the 1860s, private entrepreneurs started constructing toll roads. The dirt road networks continued to grow until the 1900s, when automobilists began insisting on paved roads. At first many felt that wealthy automobile owners should build their own roads, as millionaire Spencer Penrose did. Penrose, who bought a new luxury car each year, often complete with a chauffeur-mechanic, constructed a highway to the top of Pikes Peak as the ultimate challenge for motor cars. Still in use today, that road has hosted Colorado's most famous automobile race, the Pikes Peak Hill Climb, since 1916.

The Colorado Highway Commission, established in 1909, expanded after the Federal Highway Act of 1916 provided a 50/50 match for "primary roads." These state and federal matching funds were used

Poor road conditions and lack of services forced some pioneer motorists to get out and push and pull.
Courtesy, Colorado Historical Society

to construct the first paved road in 1918, a $73,939 concrete thoroughfare between Denver and Littleton.

Colorado highway construction accelerated with the use of convict labor beginning in 1905. Lime, gravel and stone for road building could be obtained from the quarry conveniently located behind the state penitentiary at Cañon City. Convicts built many of the first paved roads, including scenic highways in Big Thompson, Boulder, Colorado River and St. Vrain canyons. Prisoners also built the 1911 highway from Cañon City to the Royal Gorge Suspension Bridge and Cañon City's 1905 Skyline Drive. Colorado led the country in the use of convicts to build roads until the practice was abandoned in 1926 because of complaints from private contractors who wanted the work. Prisoners then began making Colorado's license plates, as they still do.

In 1919 Colorado became one of the first four states to tax gasoline to help finance road construction. The penny-per-gallon tax was doubled in 1923 and then raised to three cents in 1927, four cents in 1929 and twenty cents a gallon by the 1990s. Federal highways were the first paved, border-to-border Colorado thoroughfares. Thanks largely to federal funding and labor from New Deal programs during the 1930s, Colorado's paved roads increased from 500 miles in 1930 to 4,000 miles in 1940. The state bought the Berthoud Pass toll road in 1931 and made U.S. 40 the first paved crossing of the Continental Divide. This was followed by the paving of U.S. 50 over Monarch Pass. Denver, which began paving city streets before 1900, undertook an ambitious program to construct mountain roads, including the country's highest auto road to the summit of Mount Evans.

Colorado's first auto freeway was West Sixth Avenue, built during World War II from downtown Denver to the federal war production plant near Golden. A second expressway, the Boulder Turnpike (1952), proved so popular that tolls were removed in 1967 after the turnpike paid for itself.

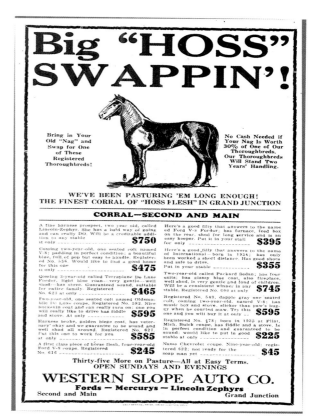

Coloradans were persuaded to buy "horseless carriages" by ads like this one in Grand Junction. Courtesy, Library of Congress

The automobile came to dominate twentieth century Colorado, from canyon bottoms to mountain tops. In 1913, this contraption even made it up to the shelter house atop Pikes Peak. Courtesy, Tom Noel Collection

Skyline Drive on the ridge west of Cañon City remains a spine-chilling example of the first automobile roads. They followed—rather than cut through—Colorado's precipitous, tough terrain. Photo by Glenn Cuerden

Colorado's north-south interstate highway, I-25 was completed in 1967; I-70 took much longer. Colorado's portion of this east-west freeway was delayed for five years (1968–1973) during blasting and burrowing under the Continental Divide for the Eisenhower-Johnson Tunnel. It took another twenty years to complete I-70 through the Glenwood Canyon of the Colorado River. Not only the deep, narrow canyon, but also protests from environmentalists delayed the Glenwood Canyon project, inspiring engineers to design I-70 as an eye-pleasing complement to the landscape.

RAIL TRANSIT RETURNS

As automobile congestion, pollution and other troubles mounted, some began to realize that rail transit had merit. Denver's privately owned Denver Tramway Company evolved during the 1970s into the Regional Transportation District (RTD), which served surrounding suburban counties as well as the core city. RTD initially confined itself to rubber-tired motor buses. However, as ridership and the density of the Metro Area increased, RTD inaugurated a light rail system reminiscent of the long-gone streetcars. Electric-powered light rail could carry more people faster and more efficiently, alleviating some of the traffic jams that made highway traffic slow and dangerous, especially at rush hour.

As this view of Denver's Colorado Boulevard suggests, growing motor vehicle congestion snarled traffic in the 1970s. Some began to look for alternative transportation. Photo by Glenn Cuerden

RTD opened the first stretch of its rail mass transit in 1994. That pioneer line roughly followed the town's first street railway system started in 1871 with a horse-drawn rail coach. RTD's electric light rail line now also runs from near the Platte River to Auraria and Five Points. A line opened in 2000 serves Englewood and Littleton in the metro southwest corridor as well as Denver's Union Station.

Streetcar systems of the late 1800s were reincarnated in 1994, when metro Denver introduced a light trail system, seen here at the Auraria stop in central Denver. Photo by Tom Noel

The Front Range RTD's reinvention of light rail service provides Coloradans both a ride back in time and into the future aboard sleek, fast coaches with picture-window views. Quiet, pollution-free, electric locomotives have replaced the horses and mules that pulled Colorado's first light rail coaches. RTD's reintroduction of the rail age even includes a recycling of historic rail stations in Boulder, Denver, Littleton and elsewhere as twenty-first century passenger depots. Once again, Coloradans are riding the rails just like their predecessors who originally settled along the tracks of railroad towns or in streetcar suburbs during the 1870–1893 boom.

RTD, which is financed by a 1 percent sales tax, won approval from voters in 2005 to build a metro-wide light rail and commuter rail system. By 2020 this network will whiz passengers to Boulder, Denver International Airport, Golden, Lakewood, Longmont and all quadrants of the metropolis. A line opening along the I-25 corridor in 2006 will serve the southeast corridor, including Douglas County.

COLORADO AVIATION

Airplanes, like autos, intrigued Coloradans. They welcomed aviation as a fast, direct way to fly over the many geographical obstacles in the Highest State. Initially, Colorado hosted "Birdmen" who experimented with balloon ascensions. In 1894 the Army Signal Corps built a balloon station at Fort Logan in southwest Denver, which housed the nation's entire "air force"—a single tethered hydrogen-filled balloon. Denver's Overland Park hosted the first flight in a "heavier-than-air machine" in 1910 when French aviator Louis Paulhan made six short flights to the cheers of thousands of spectators.

Flying fever led many towns and individuals to rig up primitive airfields. Communities endeavored to construct airports just as they had once built depots to capture railroad service. Denver's first "aerodrome" opened in 1910 in the Park Hill neighborhood, where various other short-lived private airports were also established. In 1921 Colorado's first commercial passenger service connected Denver with Estes Park, Colorado Springs and Cheyenne, Wyoming. Denver had at least nine different private airports before Denver Municipal Airport opened in 1929 and consolidated most air activity.

Post office airmail contracts first made flying profitable and led to the establishment in 1926 of Colorado's first postal route from Denver to Pueblo's Heinshon Field. In 1927 Colorado Springs welcomed the first airmail service to Nichols Field. The Springs also boasted a second airport, that of the local Alexander Aircraft Company, maker of the Eaglerock, a popular early airplane. Aviators in Pueblo launched an annual air show in the 1940s and opened the Pueblo Historical Aircraft Society Museum in 1978.

By 1930 Colorado had twenty-seven airfields and landing strips, ranging from the American Legion field in Akron to the original Lowry Army Air Corps Field in Park Hill. Eleven were municipally owned, while six were private. By 1940 the number of airplanes in Colorado had grown from 91 to 143, and 4 more airports had opened. Following World War II, Colorado Springs, Pueblo and La Junta bought local army air bases, which they converted to municipal airports. By 1960 Colorado boasted more air service to small communities than any other state; twelve cities offered regularly scheduled public flights, and thirty-two others provided private aviation.

The air age aspirations of small towns were shot down in the 1980s when the Federal Aviation Administration deregulated airlines, allowing carriers to abandon less profitable rural routes. Although smaller commuter airlines picked up some of the towns, regularly scheduled passenger service was abandoned to Cañon City, Craig, Delta, Glenwood Springs, Grand Lake, Greeley, Fort Collins, La Junta, Leadville, Salida and Trinidad. Many small airports deteriorated and some closed, while bigger cities such as Denver, Durango and Grand Junction improved or built new facilities. Airports in Aspen, Centennial, Cortez, Eagle-Vail, Telluride and Steamboat Springs have all been built since 1940.

STAPLETON AIRPORT

In 1929 Denver flew into the air age with the construction of Denver Municipal Airport. Mayor Benjamin Franklin Stapleton encountered shrill opposition led by *The Denver Post*, which ridiculed "Stapleton's Folly" and dubbed the proposed Sand Creek site in northeast Denver "Simpleton's Sand Dunes." Why build an airport so far away from downtown when there were better, closer sites? This boondoggle, fumed the *Post*, had been conceived to allow the mayor to squander municipal money buying out landowners—most notably the mayor's crony, H. Brown Canon of Windsor Farm Dairy—at inflated prices.

"Rattlesnake Hollow," as other cynics called the site at East 32nd Avenue and Quebec Street, was blasted as a taxpayer subsidy for a few rich kids who liked to play with airplanes. Sure enough, the power elite, whose offspring flocked to the new sport of aviation, endorsed the plan. Denver's first families

Aviation began with small, single-engine, open cockpit machines, like this Varney Air biplane. Although initially concerned primarily with delivering air mail, some pilots sold spare seats to passengers. As more people grew interested in air travel, Varney evolved into United Airlines and introduced ever larger aircraft such as the four-engine CDC-8 jet in the background. Courtesy, Tom Noel Collection

swamped the grand opening celebration, October 17–20, 1929—one week before the stock market crash. The city paid $143,013 for the 640-acre site and another $287,000 to build the airport with four gravel runways, one hangar, a tiny terminal and a wind sock.

Three days of dedication festivities drew crowds estimated at 15,000 to 20,000. Rubberneckers watched the climbs and dives, the loops and rolls of airplanes overhead. Sightseers thronged around Boeing's "Leviathan of the Air," a fourteen-passenger bi-plane equipped with Pullman sleepers, a kitchen and a dining room. Coloradans celebrated "The West's best airport . . . a model for further airport development . . . a great center on America's aerial map . . . large enough and level enough to meet all future needs of long distance passenger flying."

To feed the flyers, "Mom" Williams opened her Skyline Buffet next door to the terminal. Mom, the original airport concessionaire, was replaced in the 1960s by Sky Chef, which opened one of Denver's fanciest restaurants. Shrimp boat dinners and ice cream sundaes made Sky Chef famous, as did its orchestra and after-dinner dancing. Denverites held their children's birthday parties at the airport, toasting the air age future. To honor the mayor, who had braved considerable opposition to build

it, Denver Municipal was renamed Stapleton Airport on August 25, 1944.

By the mid-1980s, Stapleton International Airport, as it was renamed after flights were added to Mexico and Canada, had become the seventh largest airport in the world. It was the fourth busiest in the nation, after Chicago, Atlanta and Dallas-Fort Worth; Coloradans decided it was time to build a new airport. One reason was to keep up with rival states such as Utah, where Salt Lake City had improved its airport to attract skiers and other tourists.

SKI COLORADO

Air age activity was the key to many of Colorado's dreams of prosperity and national prominence. Ski resorts, for instance, relied on airborne customers

The Skyline Café and Mom's Diner, the original 1930 concession at Denver Municipal Airport, has evolved into more than 100 different shops in Denver International Airport. Photo by Ralph Morgan, courtesy, Tom Noel Collection

to become one of Colorado's largest and steadiest growth industries. Unlike gold and silver, coal and oil, and other non-renewable riches of the earth, snow reappears annually. It also can be artificially increased by cloud seeding and snow-making machinery. By the 1990s Colorado attracted some 10 million skiers a year to the state's twenty-nine ski areas. Thanks to the ski boom, Colorado's tourist industry became a year-round bonanza.

Utah boosters of the Beehive State stung Coloradans in 1987 by creating a new Utah license plate. Instead of the old beehive drawing and "Beehive State" license representing Mormon industry, the new plate was snow white and featured a skier and the slogan "Utah! Greatest Snow on Earth."

Salt was rubbed deeper into Colorado's thin skin when Salt Lake City captured the 2002 International Winter Olympic Games. Ironically, Coloradans had voted against funding the 1976 games, thus ending the state's efforts to attract the winter Olympics. Many Coloradans began to regret the environmentally minded vote against the Olympics as they saw jobs, visitors and the world flock to Utah in 2002.

To humble Salt Lake, Las Vegas, Phoenix and other rivals, Denver opened in 1994 what boosters claimed was "the World's Largest State-of-the-Art Airport." With fifty-five square miles, DIA was one of the world's largest airport sites, but in buildings and passengers it was still behind Chicago, Atlanta and Dallas-Fort Worth. The terminal's billowing white tent-like roof is constructed of translucent, Teflon-coated fiberglass. Sunlight streams into the airport by day, and by night, DIA is visible from a hundred miles away. Its snowy white peaks echo the white-capped Rockies and commemorate the Arapaho, Cheyenne and Ute *tipis* pitched here long ago.

Skiing, snowboarding and other winter sports have replaced mining as the economic mainstay of Colorado's high country. Ski areas open in November and, when blessed with abundant spring snowfall, stay open into May. Courtesy, Winter Park Resort

16

AIMING HIGHER

The old Mile High Stadium still stood next to the new stadium during the fall 2001 season. The sky often turned Bronco blue and orange during the twilight games of Colorado's most popular big league team. Courtesy, Tom Noel Collection

Longtime Denver Broncos fans approached the team's Super Bowl XXXII appearance in January 1998 with mixed feelings. Although cheering its AFC championship, they cringed at the memories of four previous Super Bowl defeats—all humiliating blowouts. Still, diehard devotees kept the faith and proudly donned the blue and orange as they crowded not only the stadium in San Diego, but also sports bars and living room parties. Denver fans fancied quarterback John Elway's explosive flashes of athletic brilliance and nerve-wracking ad-lib style of play. His last-minute game winning heroics were legendary.

The NFC champion Green Bay Packers put up a valiant fight, but the Broncos prevailed in a 31-24 nail-biter. Their SuperBowl XXXII victory was all the sweeter for the hard knocks they had taken previously. At the post-game ceremony, team owner Pat Bowlen hoisted the Lombardi trophy and triumphantly proclaimed, "This one's for John!"

The Broncos' defeat of the Atlanta Falcons 34-19 in SuperBowl XXXIII was icing on the cake. At 36, Elway was the oldest player ever named Super Bowl Most Valuable Player. He retired at the top of his game, having given avid Colorado football fans one heck of a ride during his Bronco career.

ECONOMIC ROLLER COASTER

The football team's fate resonated with Coloradans who had long weathered economic ups and downs. The 1970s had been flush times, as the Arab oil embargo set the stage for Colorado's emergence as an oil and energy giant. The fiscal optimism of that decade, however, led to disaster when oil prices plummeted in the 1980s. Over-extension in the good times led to massive foreclosures and savings and loan collapses when the bottom fell out. Oil shale operations in Parachute on the Western Slope, a billion-dollar operation in the previous decade, abruptly shut down in May 1982. The three largest airlines operating in the state—Frontier, Continental, and United—all filed for Chapter 11 in the wake of deregulation.

The decline of the sugar beet and cattle industries made things worse. The 1979–1980 strike at the odiferous but prosperous Monfort feedlot crippled Greeley. The Gates Rubber Company's decision to cease its manufacturing operations in the state let the air out of Denver's tires. In Pueblo, both the State Hospital and U.S. Ordnance Depot announced major layoffs. But the demise of Colorado Fuel & Iron hit the "Pittsburgh of the West" hardest of all. CF&I shut down in 1984, throwing thousands of Puebloans out of work. Partial reopening of the plant, for decades Colorado's largest employer, brought back only a tiny portion of the workforce in the early 2000s.

Buyouts, mergers, and bankruptcies changed the face of business in Colorado in recent decades and led to the state's gradual economic recovery. Public projects like Denver International Airport created employment for many. The demand for new prisons in addition to the State Penitentiary in Cañon City gave at least twenty struggling Colorado communities a much needed economic shot in the arm.

The state's natural and economic climates both appealed to the emerging cable communications and high tech industries. Bill Daniels, John Malone

Above
Colorado's oil boom of the late 1970s and early 1880s fueled construction of new Denver high rises. The Amoco Building, shown here at 17th and Broadway, is a glistening stainless steel, thirty-seven story tower featuring six sides, which provided more corner offices for executives. Photo by Jim Havey

Left
Oil booms in the 1970s and 2000s kept Colorado's Commerce City oil refineries humming night and day, seven days a week. Photo by Tom Noel

and other cable television moguls made Colorado a global leader in twenty-first century telecommunications. In 1960 Hewlett-Packard had built a manufacturing facility in Loveland, the first outside of Palo Alto, California. Information technology pioneer, International Business Machines's (IBM) Boulder facility dated back to 1965. These companies paved the way for subsequent high tech giants who built Colorado campuses in the 1990s—Storage Tech, Compaq, EchoStar, Level 3 and Sun Microsystems among them.

Aerospace companies, including Lockheed Martin and Ball Aerospace, launched major operations in the state and helped to fuel the 1990s rebound. In 1999 Space Imaging in Thornton, a booming Denver suburb, became the first private company in the nation to market pictures from space captured by its own satellite. Federal defense department contracts fattened many Colorado wallets, especially in Colorado Springs. That city, the second largest in the state, is home to the army's Fort Carson, the United States Air Force Academy, the North American Air Defense Command and many military contractors.

CULTURE COMES TO COWTOWNS

Colorado's recent cultural renaissance stemmed from a unique sales tax that has become a model for others struggling to sustain their cultural assets. The Scientific & Cultural Facilities Tax, approved in 1988 by voters in Adams, Arapahoe, Broomfield, Boulder, Denver, Douglas and Jefferson counties, is a 0.1 percent (one penny of every $10) sales tax which distributed over $38 million in 2005 for various facilities. It provides for the enlightenment and entertainment of the public through the production, presentation, exhibition, advancement or preservation of art, music, theater, dance, zoology, botany, natural history or cultural history.

Sixty percent of the SCFD funding goes to the metro area's five major institutions: the Denver Art Museum, the Denver Botanic Gardens, the Denver Center for the Performing Arts, the Denver Museum of Nature and Science, and the Denver Zoological Gardens. The SCFD tax, voter renewed for another decade in 1994 and 2004, also generates

Despite ups and downs in the ranching business, the National Western Stock Show celebrated its centennial in 2006 and drew an all-time record crowd of 650,000. As part of the centennial celebration, sheep were driven down Denver's 17th Street in the annual Stock Show Parade. Courtesy, Tom Noel Collection

The Colorado Historical Society Museum in Denver displays some of the Wetherill Family's Mesa Verde collection, as well as dioramas depicting life at Mesa Verde. Baby Doe Tabor, the museum's cover girl (pictured far left) had her wedding gown showcased inside. Photo by Tom Noel

increasing monies for some 300 other organizations, such as small theaters, orchestras, art centers and natural history, cultural history and community groups. These range from the Littleton Historical Museum, the only Colorado museum to earn a partnership with the Smithsonian Institution, to the Central City Opera House Association, and from the Colorado Railroad Museum in Golden to the Hiwan Homestead Museum in Evergreen. Hunger Artists are fed funding and so is Dinosaur Ridge, with its awesome hogback trails following the footprints of the giant lizards that once roamed a swampy Colorado.

A 2004 study by Deloitte & Touche found that the cultural facilities outdrew the Denver Broncos, Denver Nuggets, Colorado Avalanche and Colorado Rockies combined. Groups funded by the Denver metro area's SCFD attracted more than 11 million visitors in 2005. The following are among the most popular destinations.

DENVER ART MUSEUM

In 1971 the Denver Art Museum (DAM) found a permanent home within its Civic Center castle, a dramatic design by Gio Ponti of Milan and James Sudler of Denver. The DAM had earlier struggled to find gallery space in nooks and crannies of the City and County Building. Besides European, American, Asian, Latin American and African collections, the museum has one of the world's finest collections of Native American pieces. The DAM claims to be the first museum in America to have established a separate Native American collection.

The DAM garnered international attention with the 2006 opening of a dramatic addition designed by world famous architect Daniel Libeskind.

DENVER BOTANIC GARDENS

The Gardens sprouted in the 1940s, thanks to a coalition of socialites and plant lovers who first tended gardens in City Park. In the 1950s the city had acquired the Catholic portion of the old City Cemetery on the east edge of Cheesman Park for $80,000. As part of the deal, the city agreed to remove the remaining 6,000 corpses to Mount Olivet Cemetery. Crews worked rapidly at night to transplant most of the remains, yet expansion of the Botanic Gardens unearths a corpse every now and then. The well-fertilized gardens have expanded in recent decades to cover more of the former boneyard with alpine, cutting, herb, high plains, Japanese, vegetable and water gardens. DBG's large domed Boettcher Conservatory shelters an extensive garden of tropical plants.

THE DENVER MUSEUM OF NATURE AND SCIENCE

Founded in 1900 on a hill at the east end of City Park, the Denver Museum of Nature and Science (as the Museum of Natural History was renamed), is Colorado's largest and most popular museum. This museum has more than doubled its space in recent decades, adding the Gates Planetarium and the IMAX Theater. The Museum's famed life-sized dioramas and dinosaur exhibits are among a hundred exhibits ranging from Colorado building stones to butterflies, from a lifesize diorama of a Cheyenne camp to the cavernous Coors Mineral Hall with its replicas of treasure-filled mines and caverns. Some 2 million visitors a year make this America's fifth-largest natural history venue.

DENVER PERFORMING ARTS COMPLEX

Soaring glass canopies shelter the theatres of the Denver Performing Arts Complex (DPAC) at 14th and Curtis streets. Once known as Denver's "Great White Way," Curtis Street lost all of its old theatres, including the fabulous Tabor Grand Opera House, to urban renewal.

The DPAC complex boasts four theaters, a television studio, and even voice research laboratories. This four-block complex and park is the second

The glass-topped Boettcher Conservatory of the Denver Botanic Gardens offer a year-round tropical haven for Coloradans—and their teddy bears. Courtesy, Tom Noel Collection

largest performing arts complex in the country, after Lincoln Center in New York City. The DCPA's cornerstone is Mayor Speer's 1908 Denver Municipal Auditorium, now renamed the Mayor Quigg Newton Memorial Auditorium. The auditorium received a major facelift between 1995 and 2005 when the $100 million Ellie Calkins Opera House and the Temple Hoyne Buell Theater were built into it. The Buell, named for the Denver architect and developer whose fortune posthumously helped fund it, is a state-of-the-art roadhouse for Broadway touring presentations.

Boettcher Concert Hall hosts the Colorado Symphony Orchestra. In this $13 million hall, the 2,600 seats are arranged in asymmetrical banks in a 360-degree surround, so that 80 percent of the audience sits within 65 feet of the 2,400-square-foot stage. The DCPA's Helen Bonfils Theater Complex contains four theaters with production space and rehearsal rooms. The resident Denver Center Theater Company is the largest professional resident ensemble between Chicago and the West Coast.

OTHER MAJOR MUSEUMS

The Colorado History Museum in Denver has eleven branch museums scattered around the state, including reconstructions of Fort Vasquez and Fort Garland. Colorado Springs boasts a super Fine Arts Museum, the American Numismatic Museum, the Cheyenne Mountain Zoo, the Van Briggle Pottery Museum and the Carriage Museum at the Broadmoor Hotel, among many other fascinating sites. The Colorado Railroad Museum in Golden, the Butterfly Pavillion and Insect Center in Westminster, the Sangre de Cristo Museum in Pueblo, and the Museum of Western Colorado in Grand Junction are also among the top tourist stops.

WATERWAYS REBORN

Coloradans traditionally dammed, ditched, diverted and trashed their waterways. After the 1859 Colorado gold rush, clear streams became muddied with mining and human waste. Since the 1970s, however, many Colorado communities have been cleaning up their waterways as scenic, recreational and alternative transportation routes. Denver mayors Bill McNichols, Federico Peña and Wellington Webb, all worked to clean up the South Platte and Cherry Creek and gave Denver the state's first river and creek greenway trail system. Confluence Park, at the junction of the two waterways, opened July 4, 1976 as the centerpiece of a greenway system that has inspired many other waterway parks and trails.

Littleton launched its Arapahoe Greenway following the river from Denver to Hudson Gardens, which showcases spectacular plantings along a former riverbed. The Arapahoe Greenway leads up to Waterton Canyon where the Platte bursts from the mountains. There, hikers and bicyclists follow

The Colorado Historical Society's statewide sites include the restored Healy House and Dexter Cabin in the two-mile-high silver city of Leadville. Courtesy, Tom Noel Collection

the old grade of the Denver, South Park & Pacific Railroad as it snaked its way into the high country. This is also the start of the Colorado Trail, which wanders all the way to Durango. Waterton Canyon feeds the Highline Canal, whose cottonwooded banks shade a seventy-one-mile-long pedestrian and bicycle trail that meanders through Denver and its suburbs to Denver International Airport. On one of the South Platte's major tributaries, Golden has transformed once unclear Clear Creek into history and water parks where you can pan for gold, tour a log village, or ride the white water.

The state's most ambitious project is the historic Arkansas Riverwalk of Pueblo, a twenty-six-acre urban park in the heart of the old, rusting steel city. The $26.6 million ongoing project has transformed the Arkansas as it flows through town. After the 1921 Pueblo flood killed more than a hundred people and destroyed much of the urban core, the Arkansas was diverted through a monstrous concrete canal. Water from that canal is now diverted back to its original streambed. There rivergoers can now stroll or take a boat ride to the public plazas, the Sangre de Cristo Art & Conference Center and the Union Avenue Historic District. From the

Pueblo's Historic Arkansas River Project, which returned the river to its old bed, abandoned after the 1921 flood, is the most elaborate of many waterway revivals rejuvenating Colorado cities. Visitors now boat through what was once a flooded wasteland. Courtesy, Photo by Tom Noel

Riverwalk, the Arkansas River Trail leads west to City Park, the Pueblo Zoo and Pueblo Reservoir with its water sports and fishing.

Since Colorado's river renaissance began, it has flowered to embrace more than a hundred trails along irrigation ditches, gulches, creeks, rivers and lakes. Aspen, Boulder, Breckenridge, Steamboat Springs and Telluride have some of the best-developed waterway trails, lined by gardens, libraries, music tents, outdoor cafes, parks and greenway links to other major attractions.

Smaller, poorer, less glamorous towns are also cleaning up their waterways. Tiny Minturn, a blue collar town of miners and more recently of service workers for nearby ski resorts, celebrated its turnaround in the summer of 2005. "Mines had really killed the river," admitted former Mayor Earle Bidez. "The joke was that you could catch more fish with a magnet than a fishing pole." With mitigation funds from the Eagle Mine which had polluted the river, the Eagle River has undergone a $70 million cleanup. Now the brown trout and the fishermen have returned to the river as it flows

through town. Like many other communities, Minturn is coaxing motorists from crowded, polluted, hostile highways to try walking, running, bicycling or boating Colorado's reborn waterways.

Breckenridge's Blue River Walk brings thousands of visitors and locals to its historic downtown, which includes a summer music tent. Photo by Tom Noel

MALLS MOVE IN

Elegant department stores lined the downtown streets of big cities, and locally owned, family-run businesses crowded Main Street in countless smaller Colorado towns as the twentieth century dawned. Shoppers patronized these local commercial districts until the 1950s, when Denver architect Temple Buell decided to follow Kansas City's lead and developed the state's first shopping mall. His Cherry Creek Shopping Center was a marketplace of a different color. Stores clustered around a central space were surrounded by ample parking. Major retailers moved their operations from downtown or established branch stores to the new, upscale location. Shopping would never be the same. Today a seemingly unending procession of shopping

malls open up in fast growing suburbs, only to face competition from big box chains, such as "Mall-warts," as Colorado critics dubbed the retail giant. Downtown shopping districts shriveled and died as everyone flocked to the newest mall.

MAIN STREET PEDESTRIAN MALLS

Things began to turn around when communities undertook concerted efforts to revitalize their former economic hearts. Grand Junction opened Colorado's first Main Street Mall in 1962, followed by Aspen, Boulder and other towns. In Denver, 16th Street, formerly home to the most fashionable department stores, closed off twelve blocks to

Architect Temple Hoyne Buell (above left) built Colorado's first shopping center in Denver's fashionable Cherry Creek neighborhood in 1954. Buell, one of Colorado's longest lived and most flamboyant architects, is also remembered for the extravagant mausoleum he designed for himself at Denver's Fairmount Cemetery (lower left). Buell posthumously funded the state's fanciest theatre, the Temple Hoyne Buell in the Denver Performing Arts Center (above).

motorists in 1982 and transformed the thoroughfare into a pedestrian shopping mall. Free electric shuttle buses, like the old streetcars, transport foot-weary shoppers up and down its entire length. Nearby, the 1400 block of Larimer Street, home of Denver's first two city halls and other historic buildings, was saved from the wrecking ball, refurbished and marketed to upscale retailers and restaurants. Dubbed Larimer Square, it has become not just a place to window shop, but a genuine destination. Annual special events include Oktoberfest and La Piazza 'dell Arte, a unique summer exhibition of chalk art on the street's pavement.

Smaller towns, too, have worked to reclaim and revitalize their Main Streets. Fort Collins' downtown renaissance began in the 1980s with brew pubs and micro-breweries that brought people back to the heart of the community. Today its Old Town bustles with galleries, jewelers, boutique retailers, antique shops and outdoor concerts and festivals. Many other Colorado towns have leveraged Colorado Historical Society preservation grant funds to restore old storefronts and rehabilitate their historic retail districts.

Today, most of Colorado's venerable old department stores—The May Company, Daniels & Fisher, The Denver Dry, Neustetters, and Joslins—have disappeared, swallowed up by national mergers and acquisitions. Major outlet centers draw bargain hunters from miles away. New shopping complexes built to serve expanding urban areas no longer funnel customers into central interior corridors and food courts. These "lifestyle centers" are

Grand Junction, the largest city on Colorado's western slope lies at the junction of the Colorado and Gunnison Rivers. Grand Junction in 1962 became the first Colorado Community to convert its main street to a pedestrian-friendly mall. Since then the mall has become a major sculpture garden with beautiful and humorous people- pleasers, such as this scrappy locomotive. Photos by Tom Noel

designed instead with adjacent stores and eateries connected by outdoor landscaped sidewalks with park benches, ironically reminiscent of yesterday's Main Streets.

COLORADO IN THE NEWS

In recent decades, a few unfortunate tragedies have thrust Colorado into the national spotlight. On July 31, 1976—the eve of the state's 100th birthday—a freak deluge dumped an unprecedented amount of rain on Estes Park in three-and-a-half hours. As the water rushed downstream toward Loveland, steep and narrow Big Thompson Canyon became a giant funnel, concentrating and accelerating the flow. The flash flood came on so fast

Like many Colorado communities returning to their urban cores, Fort Collins has restored its original Old Town as a pedestrian-friendly historic district and retail area. The old Angell's Deli is now Coppersmith's Brewpub, one of the most popular of some 100 brewpubs to have sprouted up in Colorado since 1990. Photos by Tom Noel

that there was little time for warnings, and those that were issued were largely ignored. The "Big Thompson" is a relatively small, shallow river. How bad could it be?

As the rising waters encountered obstacles such as bridges, it backed up before surging onwards. The wall of water grew, battering cabins and roadbeds with accumulated debris as it grew in strength. By the time the flood surge reached the mouth of the canyon, it was sixty feet high.

Dark clouds hung ominously over the canyon for days afterwards. The Big Thompson Flood of 1976 left 144 residents and visitors dead. Seven refrigerated semi-trailers behind the Loveland Hospital held bodies and body parts awaiting identification. Hundreds of people lost their homes, and the roadbed of Highway 34 up the canyon was washed out along several stretches by the worst natural disaster in Colorado history.

The shocking murder of little JonBenet Ramsey on Christmas night 1996 brought unwanted attention to Boulder, Colorado. The six-year old blonde was a veteran of child beauty pageants. Her parents found a ransom note in the kitchen early that morning and called local police. Later that afternoon, JonBenet's father and a friend found her body in the basement of their home. Boulder police and a large proportion of the world's media believed that

her wealthy and successful parents, John and Patsy Ramsey, were responsible for her brutal death. The Ramseys vehemently denied any guilt and launched a major PR campaign in their own defense. The case became a national obsession, but critical mistakes by investigators muddied matters severely. Upon Patsy Ramsey's death in 2006 the case remains unresolved.

The Columbine High School massacre on April 20, 1999, in Littleton, stunned the nation. Two teenage students, Eric Harris and Dylan Klebold, carried out a shooting rampage, killing twelve fellow students and a teacher and wounding twenty-four others, before committing suicide. The deadliest school shooting in U.S. history provoked much debate over gun control laws, high school cliques and bullying, and the effects of heavy metal music and violent movies and video games on young people. Two-thousand people gathered seven years later to honor the thirteen victims at a ground-breaking for the Columbine Massacre Memorial. Thunder crashed and light hail punctuated the steady rainfall as keynote speaker Bill Clinton recalled, "one of the darkest days Hillary and I had in the White House." The memorial, on a hilltop overlooking the high school, will consist of an outer wall known as the Ring of Healing and an inner circle known as the Ring of Remembrance.

GOVERNING THE HIGHEST STATE

Colorado's governors in the last half of the twentieth century made important contributions to the state's progress and improvement. Dan Thornton, a champion Hereford breeder elected in 1950, was a close personal friend of Dwight D. Eisenhower. Thornton's influence with the president helped to win the Air Force Academy and other federal agencies for Colorado. His administration focused on tourism promotion and infrastructure development, particularly long-range highway plans. Thornton's successor, Stephen McNichols, one of the most active governors, greatly improved education at all levels and health care, especially for the mentally ill.

John A. Love, the first Colorado governor elected to three terms, served from 1963–1973. The challenges for his administration included resolving contentious water rights issues that divided the

Governor Dan Thornton, a champion Hereford breeder elected in 1950, poses with his prize winning $50,000 bull in Denver's Brown Palace Hotel in 1945. Courtesy, Tom Noel Collection

eastern and western slopes of the state. His "Sell Colorado" campaign brought new businesses and national attention to the state. But Love's proposal to bring the 1976 Winter Olympics to Colorado was thwarted by residents concerned about the effect such a huge event would have on the mountain landscape and quality of life. In 1972 voters passed an initiative forbidding any state funding for the games. Known for his moderation and conciliatory skills, Love resigned the governorship in 1973 to become the nation's first "energy czar" for president Richard M. Nixon.

As a member of the Colorado legislature, Richard D. Lamm first gained statewide attention leading the successful campaign against the 1976 Olympic games. Governor from 1975–1987, Lamm served longer than any other Colorado chief executive. The outspoken young Democrat was always controversial, notably in his support of physician-assisted suicide. While governor, he supported no-fault insurance, decriminalization of certain abortions, zero population growth, and environmental protections.

Roy Romer became governor after serving as a Colorado legislator and as state treasurer. Romer

This break dance competition in the Denver Center for the Performing Arts drew an animated throng in 1984. Photo by Tom Noel

became the last Colorado governor elected to three terms, as the result of voter-adopted term limits Serving from 1987–1999, Romer's administration focused on reforming and improving both K-12 and higher education in the state. While working to maintain a healthy economy, he also coordinated with local governments to plan for and direct Colorado's rapid growth and to protect its beauty and environment. After years as a national leader in education policy, Romer accepted the position of superintendent for Los Angeles public schools.

Colorado's fortieth governor, William F. "Bill" Owens, was elected in 1998. The conservative Republican's initiatives have addressed tax relief for Coloradans, transportation and health care issues, technology and the economy, wildfires and drought. Perhaps the most pleasant of his gubernatorial duties was overseeing the launch of the Colorado quarter in 2006. First lady Frances Owens chaired the advisory commission that selected the "Colorful Colorado" design, featuring a view of Longs Peak and a stand of evergreens.

Colorado began the twenty-first century booming. As in the gold rush days, immigrants were arriving from all over the nation and the world. The state's population, which officially reached 4.3 million 2000, looks like it will climb to over 5 million by 2010. True to their optimistic character, through good and bad times, Coloradans are still aiming higher.

Denver International Airport's terminal peaks are made of teflon-coated fiberglass which admits light and solar radiation and which sun-bleaches whiter with age. Courtesy, Tom Noel Collection

Civic Center Park, created by Mayor Robert W. Speer a century ago, remains a clean, green hub for downtown Denver's civic buildings, including the Colorado History Museum, Denver Public Library and Denver Art Museum. Courtesy, Denver Metro Convention & Visitors Bureau

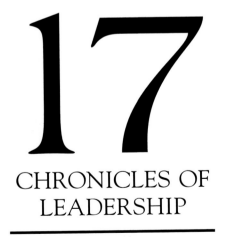

17

CHRONICLES OF LEADERSHIP

Colorado, the highest state, was named by the Spanish for its reddish soil and stone. They navigated its colorful major river centuries ago to find fantastic cliff cities—the state's first great communities.

Native Americans occupied Colorado for at least 3,200 years before the discovery of gold in 1858–1859. That strike launched one of the the great mass migrations in U.S. history. Some 100,000 rushed into Colorado and a third of them stayed to create a new state.

Two Spanish missionaries led the first party to explore, map, and report on Colorado in 1776. French trappers and traders explored the Platte and Cache La Poudre Rivers and they claimed these tributaries of the Mississippi River were part of French Louisiana. After President Thomas Jefferson bought most of eastern Colorado as part of the Louisiana Purchase in 1803, Zebulon M. Pike was sent to explore the new purchase. Both Pike and Major Stephen H. Long, who explored the South Platte Valley of northeastern Colorado in 1820, found a dry, rugged land that Long labeled on his map as the "Great American Desert." After the Mexican War ended in 1848, Mexico sold the United States the rest of what is now Colorado.

Americans avoided the "Great American Desert" and the rugged, remote Rockies until gold was found near the present site of Denver in 1858. Thousands of gold seekers settled in Denver and in the smaller towns. To feed the miners, some began ranching and farming. Others developed large scale ore mining and milling operations. In 1861 Congress created Colorado Territory and the railroads came in the 1870s, providing safer, faster, cheaper travel. Railroads also made mining more efficient and profitable. They brought in heavy mining machinery and took gold and silver ores to huge smelters. Due to railroads and new gold and silver strikes, Colorado's population jumped from 39,864 in 1870 to 194,327 in 1890.

A booming population made statehood possible in 1876. The bonanza years lasted until the 1893 silver crash. Gold mining remained important until the early 1900s. Mining declined partly because areas were mined out and partly because of labor conflicts that arose when miners refused to work ten or twelve hours a day underground or in equally dangerous smelters for less than three dollars a day.

While mining sank, farming and ranching thrived. Farmers learned to grow wheat, sugar beets, and other crops on Colorado's dry, high plains with the help of water ditches and dry-land farming skills. The agricultural boom busted during the 1930s. The Great Depression dried up markets for farm crops and ranch livestock. Dust storms and grasshopper plagues added to the problems that have left the eastern plains of Colorado littered with abandoned farms, ranches and ghost towns.

The New Deal and World War II transformed Colorado by giving many people federal jobs. Moreover, the federal government built or helped to build dams and parks, military bases and government buildings, roads and airports. These improvements helped attract a million newcomers to the state between the 1950s and the 1990s and another million during the 1990s alone.

The mining bonanza boom has been repeated in recent decades as Colorado became one of the nation's fastest growing states. Tourism, notably skiing, snow boarding and white water rafting, and booming coal, oil and natural gas production, as well as hot electronic, computer and cable television markets have propelled growth. Between 1990 and 2000 the population mushroomed from 3,294,473 to 4,301,261.

In a state of deserts and high mountains, of long distances and unpredictable weather, people have met unusual challenges. They persisted, however, and made Colorado one of the most prosperous and fast growing states. Among the key players are the organizations whose stories are detailed in the following pages. These firms and the people behind them have chosen to support this project, by contributing their own unique stories, preserving them for future Coloradans. They illustrate how individuals and their enterprises have shaped Colorado. These businesses, educational institutions, and government agencies take pride in their own histories and in making Colorado a better place to work, go to school, play and live.

PIONEERS

In addition to the businesses, organizations and institutions that have a distinguished presence in Colorado communities, this chapter also introduces some of the pioneer families that have shaped the state from its earliest days. A pioneer is not only one of the first settlers in a new region, but also one of the first to search out new types of enterprise and development.

The Bonfils, Evans-Cheesmans, Fulenwiders and Van Gilders have embodied the pioneer spirit. Each family translated their loyalty to Colorado by becoming instrumental in transforming barren plains and Rocky Mountains into welcoming cities and towns. To this day, these families demonstrate their responsibility to the community through philanthropy, community service and sustaining their businesses that serve vital functions in the state.

The stories of these families attest to the notion that history is shaped by individuals with vision and will and that communities are simply families and individuals living together and working towards a greater good. With an understanding of their role in history, these pioneer families continue to serve Colorado while remembering that every great accomplishment is grown from the desire to plant roots.

To convey trains under the Continental Divide, the Moffat Tunnel opened in 1928. Many coal and passenger trains, as well as Amtrak's Denver-Salt Lake-Oakland line, still use this route through the Rockies. Photo by Tom Noel

BONFILS BLOOD CENTER

For many people across Colorado who give blood or have received blood transfusions, the Bonfils family name has become synonymous with life itself through their nonprofit organization Bonfils Blood Center. With one in ten people entering a hospital requiring blood, the 225,000 units of blood Bonfils collects per annum are of great importance to the health of the community and beyond. Blood, a vital fluid, fights infections, helps heal wounds, carries oxygen and nutrients through the body and brings the body's waste products to the lungs, kidneys and liver for disposal. Before establishing Bonfils Blood Center, the Bonfils family was known for providing another key service to the community. They pioneered the *Denver Post*, which became not only a central news source for Denver but in turn helped the blood center become what it is today.

In 1892 Frederick Bonfils and Harry Tammen founded the *Denver Post*, a daily newspaper for the second largest city in the west. It was a time when gamblers, western bartenders and lottery sharpies were running wild in the Mississippi Valley. Bonfils and Tammen made a name for the paper—and for themselves —even in the face of strong competi-

Belle Bonfils Memorial Blood Bank opens February 28, 1943.

tion from the *Denver Rocky Mountain News*.

On New Year's Day 1928, Bonfils, co-publisher and editor of the *Denver Post*, used the paper as a platform to announce the establishment of the Frederick G. Bonfils Foundation for the "Betterment of Mankind." The decision earned him the January 9, 1928 cover of *Time* magazine. Bonfils said, "I want the Foundation to be so administered that it will result in better homes, better schools and more intelligent people, healthier and happier conditions of

life, greater morality and more widespread regard for the love of God and the Gospel of Christ."

Bonfils and the *Denver Post* survived the Great Depression, but Bonfils did not survive a severe ear infection. In 1933 the *Denver Post* trumpeted the biggest news story in its history. Three big, black front page banner lines thundered, "Frederick G. Bonfils, Editor and Publisher of the *Post* Dies at Home Early Thursday." President Herbert Hoover publicly mourned the passing of Bonfils who he felt contributed greatly to Denver.

Bonfils daughter Helen continued the family's rich legacy in the Mile High City. Helen was true to her father's wishes and took over the newspaper he labored to build, but she also focused heavily on philanthropy. She donated generously to countless causes, including the Central City Opera, University of Denver, Denver Zoo, Denver (now Colorado) Symphony Orchestra, the Dumb Friends League, and, of course, Belle Bonfils Memorial Blood Bank.

Plans for the blood bank were started when American troops battling in World War II increased the awareness for the need of and demand for blood plasma worldwide. When the war moved to the

In Bonfils' early days the collected blood was stored in glass jars.

home front with the bombing of Pearl Harbor in December 1941, the need for a blood bank became more pressing than ever. During World War II many communities felt a social responsibility towards ensuring a safe and adequate blood supply for anyone who needed it.

Although the Denver community embraced the concept of a homegrown blood bank, there was an outstanding obstacle between the vision and its reality: funding to get the project underway. Carrying on her father's philanthropic tradition, Helen donated $10,000 on behalf of the Frederick G. Bonfils Foundation and in honor of her mother Belle, who had passed away in 1934. The contribution funded the creation of Belle Bonfils Memorial Blood Bank on February 27, 1943. The funds allowed Colorado doctors William Rettberg and E.R. Murgage, along with Osgoode S. Philpott to establish what today is known as Bonfils Blood Center.

Belle Bonfils Memorial Blood Bank was originally located at Colorado Gen-

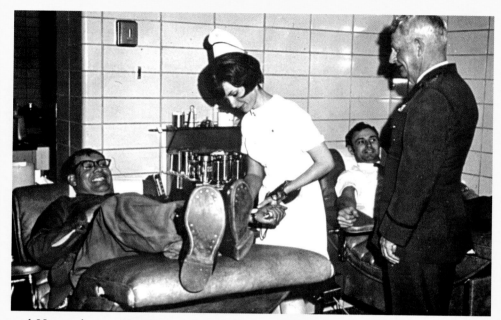

eral Hospital, now University Hospital. At the time offering only whole blood and blood plasma, Bonfils hoped to meet the blood needs of the local community and the military forces fighting overseas. In its first year of operation, Bonfils collected 1,645 units of blood.

Bonfils Memorial Blood Bank's early challenge was educating the public about the need and ease of donating blood. Drawing from its financial backer's experience with the media, Bonfils tapped into the publishing platform to spread the word. Bonfils was one of the first community blood centers to use paid advertising to recruit donors, relying heavily on radio to educate and advertise. They continue to foster strong media relations. Coupled with stories written in local newspapers and other community outreach efforts, this strategy to involve the community has helped the center to expand its current active donor base to nearly 112,000 volunteer blood donors.

The initial growth plan also called for targeting groups of people to support blood donation rather than individuals. The Denver Teacher's Club, Denver Catholic Register, and the Denver Police Department were some of the first groups to participate. The plan worked so well that Bonfils quickly outgrew its space because of the high demand for its

A lab technician hard at work in Bonfils' founding years.

A blood donor during Bonfils' initial years of operation.

services and its expanding research department. In 1954 the organization moved to new facilities where it could nurture its expanding role in the community. Soon after, the name changed to Belle Bonfils Memorial Blood Center to better reflect its services, especially in the area of transfusion medicine.

In the 1980s the AIDS crisis hit the world, creating an urgent need to ensure the safety of the blood supply. In response, Bonfils initially adopted appropriate screening methods and in 1985 began testing for the virus. Along with the Food and Drug Administration (FDA) and the Red Cross, Bonfils was at the forefront of organizations protecting the blood supply through infectious disease testing. Testing today includes monitoring for new threats, such as the West Nile virus and conducting twelve FDA mandated tests on each unit of donated blood. There is a tremendous cost associated with continually guarding the blood supply against new strains of diseases and new outbreaks. The challenge is balancing science, medicine and economics. To best play its vital role, Bonfils is committed to investing in technological testing models that keep the blood supply safe.

Before 1980 Bonfils routinely imported blood products as they could not meet the demand with their own supply. Dr. William Dickey, the CEO and medical director at the time, made a concerted effort to recruit donors and hire staff to ensure that none of Bonfils' Colorado healthcare partners would experience a blood shortage. The plan was so effective that now Bonfils supports other parts of the country and is even called upon to supply the military. After the September 11th terrorist attacks, Bonfils was the first blood center to send blood to New York. The center also sent more than 750 units to the hurricane-battered Gulf Coast Region in 2005.

In the mid 1990s a process was initiated to redevelop the former Lowry Air Force Base in a mixed-use fashion—to include both business and residential development. In 1995 Bonfils was the first business to bring its operations to the former base when the blood center moved its headquarters to a 150,000 square-foot facility into what was once the commissary.

Bonfils Blood Center's vision is to advance healthcare to a higher level of excellence. Bonfils is carrying out that

Bonfils' modern day blood storage facility.

vision with: the addition of a donor testing laboratory where specialized tests for blood donors are performed; the Colorado Marrow Donor Program, which participates in bone marrow and umbilical cord transplants and where the Colorado registry of 65,000 bone marrow donors is maintained; Laboratories at Bonfils, which offers organ and tissue testing for transplantation; and Hemo-Net, which provides technical computer experience with an emphasis on blood donor management and transfusion medicine software applications.

Although many changes have occurred throughout the years, Bonfils Blood Center still maintains the same vision: to advance healthcare to a higher level of excellence. With only 4 percent of Coloradoans donating blood, Bonfils currently provides more than 80 percent of Colorado's blood supply. Additionally, Bonfils supplies blood and blood products to more than 200 hospitals nationwide. Because it provides the invaluable service of helping to save lives and its loyal donor base, Bonfils has thrived. "Blood is not a commodity but a community resource," Thomas C. Puckett, CEO, said.

Following Dickey's retirement in March 2006, Thomas C. Puckett, retired colonel in the Medical Service Corps, Bonfils' former chief operating officer and a board member of the National Blood Foundation, assumed the CEO position. With thirty years in hospital and healthcare management, Puckett has strong associations within the blood banking industry. The blood center's board of trustees also felt community-minded Puckett would compliment Bonfils' goal of improving donor loyalty.

The center made a concerted effort to not use a "critical appeal" as a way to

Bonfils Blood Center's headquarter facility was once the commissary of the former Lowry Air Force Base.

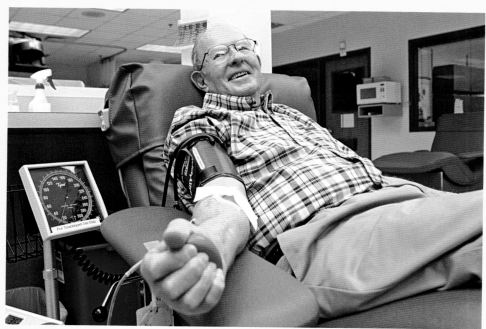

Donation technology has come a long way since Bonfils began in 1943. Today, donors can comfortably view movies as they donate.

generate blood donations. Instead they create campaigns and promotions throughout the year to bring in new donors and increase repeat donations by showing the ease and expedience with which almost anyone can donate blood. With someone in the U.S. needing a blood transfusion every two seconds, such campaigns are imperative to replenishing the blood supply and preparing for unexpected events. Ideally, the center could collect 4,350 donations per week.

Puckett wants Bonfils to be the most phenomenal steward of the blood supply for the community. He aims to ensure that blood is safe, adequate and affordable. To achieve this, the blood center will continue to work with the community, hospital partners and the media. By bringing the community together and helping people understand their vital role in saving lives, the functioning of the blood supply chain could become seamless—blood products will be available to those patients who need it on demand.

Because blood donations tend to decline up to 20 percent in the summer months due to increased activity and travel, Bonfils created an annual unique event that both educates and inspires the public. Held in May, before the summer blood drive, Community Lifelines introduces a local blood recipient to his or her life-saving blood donors. In 2006 Bonfils introduced a local man who suffered a near-fatal ski accident in February 2003 to nearly 40 of the 130 blood donors who helped save his life. Three years after his accident, Denver Haslam personally thanked each of these donors for their selfless life-saving act.

October 2006 will mark the ninth installment of Drive for Life, a blood drive in partnership with the Denver Broncos Football Club. It is the state's largest single-day blood drive. While he was chief operating office, Puckett helped an employee who now works for the Broncos, Cindy Galloway, implement her idea about creating a blood drive event with the team. The annual event brings the football team, their cheerleaders and Denver together for a fun day that also serves the community. Over the last eight years, Bonfils has collected more than 14,000 blood donations to support the community during the event. Denver Broncos Wide Receiver Rod Smith, whose daughter suffers from sickle-cell anemia, has served as spokesperson for the event since its inception.

Throughout Colorado, Bonfils Blood Center has become an important part of the healthcare system. It now operates 9 community donor centers, serves more than 200 healthcare facilities, and offers a variety of services to better meet the needs of the community. Bonfils Blood Center expects to continue growing with and adapting to the changing needs of the Colorado community.

Platelets are collected and stored in bags and must be in constant motion prior to transfusion.

THE EVANS-CHEESMAN FAMILY

"Develop the country!"
— *Governor John Evans*

Evans, Cheesman, Elbert, Davis, Hayden, Sanger, Freyer, Moore—it is impossible to read Colorado history and not see the names of these related families who gave generously of their time and money to put down roots, bring institutions and services to the foot of the Rockies and build a community.

The Evans-Cheesman family has a diverse and distinguished heritage that played a distinctive role in the development of Colorado. Beginning, on the Evans side—with Governor John Evans, born 1814, who was the second territorial governor of Colorado; through to his son William Gray Evans, successful entrepreneur; to William's son John Evans II, First National Bank and International Trust Company president; to John Evans, Jr. (III), of Evans Investment Company and director on numerous civic boards—it is easy to see the tradition of civic involvement carried on by the current generation of Freyers and Moores.

Like John Evans, Walter S. Cheesman, arrived in Colorado when it was still a territory. Both he and Evans were

Walter S. Cheesman.

Governor John Evans.

the sixth generation of their families in this country. An astute business mind, Walter contributed greatly to the development of the future state. His daughter, Gladys Cheesman, became the wife of John Evans II in 1908, joining two families with imagination, education and shared commitment to building a thriving community in the Rockies.

In the mid-1800s John Evans, living in Chicago, had become a noted physician who won national recognition for pioneering the humane treatment of the insane and identifying cholera as a contagious disease, helping to combat the epidemic that swept the Midwest in 1848. In the 1840s Dr. Evans was active in inducing the State of Indiana to construct its first home and school for deaf mutes, and later the Indiana Lunatic Asylum. He pioneered the medical education of African Americans and women of all backgrounds. And he invented several surgical instruments still used in their original designs—the best known, the obstetrical extractor. As one Evans descendant says, "Today we see him as an outstanding pioneer, but everything he did then was out of a sense of necessity."

Evans campaigned for Abraham Lincoln and became a delegate to the Republican convention in 1860. In 1865

he was elected by the Legislature to the U.S. Senate and spent two winters in Washington, D.C. before he was appointed Governor of the Colorado Territory. By 1867 the gold rush that had sparked life in Denver was over. Denver was referred to as "too dead to bury." Evans could have returned to an established, high-standing life as a medical pioneer in Chicago, but he was enchanted by the Rocky Mountains.

Evans faced many political problems in his new governorship. Chief among these was keeping the new community safe from Indian raids on ranches and settlements. During a trip to Washington to promote Colorado statehood, hundreds of innocent encamped Cheyennes were killed by militia he had ordered to protect the community. This cost him his governorship and political aspirations. Still, he stayed.

He devoted his energies to the growth of Denver and the state. In 1864 he founded a second Methodist university, the Colorado Seminary, for which he donated four lots on Arapahoe and 14th Street. In November 1864 some fifty students commenced their studies. Regrettably bankrupt, the seminary was closed in 1867 but reopened in 1880 as the University of Denver after the *Rocky Mountain News* scoffed at Coloradans for sending their children east for higher education. The university moved to its current location in 1890. Founding and opening a university was nothing new for Evans, who had established and developed Northwestern University in Evanston, Illinois, which opened in 1855 with ten students. Between 1870, when the first railroads arrived, and 1890, Denver's population exploded from 4,759 to 106,713. In one generation, it became the most populous city in the West second only to San Francisco.

In 1853, at age thirty-nine, Evans married Margaret Gray, his second wife and with whom he parented William, Evan Elbert, Anne and Margaret. Both Margaret Gray Evans and her friend Elizabeth Byers—wife of William Byers who established the *Rocky Mountain News*—had unshakable faith in the fledgling community of Denver. In addition to their traditional duties at home, these civic-minded women saw the need for education and community services. Together they fostered schools, taught church classes, sponsored charities, and directed funding drives. Evans men and women were building Denver together.

Perhaps John Evan's greatest contribution to Colorado was developing the mile-high town as a railroad center. He helped build four lines. The first, joining the Transcontinental Railroad at Cheyenne, prevented Denver from fading into oblivion. The second and third made it an outlet for rich mining lodes in the Rockies. The fourth created a north-south line that tied the city to the trading wealth of the Gulf Coast ports. With associates, he founded the Denver, South Park and Pacific Railroad (DSP&P) in 1872. The DSP&P was organized and financed by Evans together with a Who's Who of Denver capitalists that included financier Walter Scott Cheesman, banker Joseph E. Bates, and U.S. Senator Jerome Chaffee.

Denver Union Water Company. From the left: Mr. Moffat, Mr. Robinson, Mr. Cheesman and Mr. Miller.

Anne Evans.

The steam-powered, narrow-gauge line never reached its goal—the Pacific Coast—but it served Denver well, bringing in South Platte River Canyon lumber, Morrison sandstone, South Park hay and cattle, and Gunnison granite, coal and gold.

Having taken a leading role in building the railroad that connected Denver with the Union Pacific's transcontinental line, Evans attempted to capture the rail freight markets of the Front Range's biggest ore producers. With the best route to the nearest mining district tied up by competition, Evans decided to build a new line to the next closest mining center, which was near Fairplay on the western fringe of South Park. With David Moffat and Walter Cheesman, the three became known as the Iron Trail Trio.

From the money he made in railroads and

real estate, Evans invested in other industries necessary for development. He built and endowed churches and other civic institutions, foremost among them his seminary. Evans' wife Margaret was a patron of the arts and she, too, became one of the seminary's most ardent supporters.

After the 1893 depression, heavy investments in the Denver and New Orleans Railroad wiped out much of Evans' once substantial fortune. The responsibility for pulling the family and company back together went to the governor's son, William Gray "Napoleon Bill" Evans, who resuscitated the governor's crumbling empire, became a millionaire in his own right, then lost his fortune in an effort to tunnel through the Continental Divide. Despite these setbacks, the pioneering tradition of the Evans family never faltered.

Growing Denver gained much from the Governor and Margaret's grown children. Josephine, his daughter from his first marriage, married Samuel Elbert, who served as territorial governor from 1873 to 1874. Then, the governor's son, William G., who at first had no intention of becoming involved in his father's hectic business world, returned to Denver and followed in his father's footsteps. After graduating from Northwestern in 1877, he worked as a bookkeeper for the Denver and New Orleans railroad, then as a stockbroker and secretary of the Denver Tramway Company, later building it into a multi-million dollar transportation monopoly. He married Cornelia Lunt Gray in 1883 and became the father of John II, Josephine, Margaret and Katherine.

Tramway earnings fell drastically with the introduction of the automobile, making the value of Will's tramway shares, once marketable for more than a million dollars, decrease to a value below Evans' indebtedness. After suffering a nervous breakdown and resigning from the tramway and railroad companies, Will Evans returned, more determined than ever, to complete the Moffat tunnel—a direct east-west rail line through the Continental Divide, which Denver badly needed. He died financially exhausted but with great faith that his dreams would become a reality. "They were dreamers and believers in the future," said William's son, John II. "How much finer to leave that kind of heritage than to bequeath a great fortune." As a present-day descendant said, "Someone had to do this work. You need utilities, transportation and culture or people won't stay. We take these things for granted today."

Anne Evans had a great passion for arts and culture and devoted her energies to ensuring that the people of Denver would have access to these treasures. To this end, she worked to bring the Denver Art Museum into existence, and to make certain that arts were taught at the university. Traveling through the Southwest, she saw the beauty and value of Native American culture as expressed in the handwork they created and collected these works, which have since been donated to the Denver Art Museum. She also helped establish the Denver Public Library. Never marrying,

John Evans II, banker.

Captain John Evans II and Family, 1918

she spent her life promoting the cause of the arts and artists in Colorado and the greater Southwest and also worked to improve Denver's parks. Always involved in a cultural project, in 1931 Anne conceived of an annual summer Central City Opera House festival to revitalize the old mining camp and restore its historic, crumbling opera house. In 1932 actress Lillian Gish starred in a production of *Camille* at the opera house.

Anne later served on the Women's Council of Defense, a group of stalwart women who supported U.S. troops during World War II.

Anne's nephew, John Evans II, born to William G. and Cornelia in 1884, became a pillar of the Denver banking industry. He attended the University of Denver, then graduated from the Massachusetts Institute of Technology in 1907 with a degree in electrical engineering. He returned to Denver and became chief engineer and general manager of the Tramway Company. John helped build the First National Bank of Denver. In 1903 he formed the Evans Investment Co. to manage and conserve the remainder of his father's estate. By buying and selling property, stocks and bonds, John regained what his father had lost.

In 1908 John Evans II married Gladys Cheesman, daughter of Denver business leader Walter S. Cheesman, who came to Denver in 1860 as a pharmacist. He retired in 1874 from the drugstore business to participate in building the Denver & Pacific Railway project. He, Governor Evans, General Carr and D. H. Moffat together urged the Union Pacific directors to complete the Denver Pacific. They sold its bonds and purchased iron for the rails. In 1869 track-laying began from Cheyenne southward. Cheesman also began purchasing lakes and building reservoirs. The Cheesman Dam is an extraordinary engineering achievement that today continues to supply pure water to Denver. In the pioneering spirit of the times, Cheesman, like Evans, risked everything he owned on Denver's future—and won.

John and Gladys Cheesman became the patriarchs of the current Evans-Cheesman family, which living descendants perceive as the beginning of their chapter.

In 1917 the Selective Draft Act was passed by Congress and became law. John Evans II was appointed Provost Marshal of the state to handle all matters pertaining to drafting the army. Evans did well and was then put in charge of the Liberty Loan Drive, a war savings drive that encouraged the citizenry to invest in war bonds.

With the city torn apart by World War I, Denver sought to put itself back together in the early 1920s. Evans II aided in Red Cross work at the time and was instrumental in bringing Fitzsimmons Hospital to Aurora and establishing the flying field near Clayton College. In 1919 Evans II became chairman of the State Railroad Commission. In 1927 he finally saw completion of the Moffat Tunnel that his father and D.H. Moffat had struggled to achieve.

Gladys Cheesman, a knowledgeable and devoted arborist, believed that the city should be endowed with as many gardens as possible. Among her many civic-minded achievements, she and fellow garden club members brought the Denver Botanic Gardens into being, an important gift of beauty and botanical education to the community. Gladys and her mother, Alice Foster Cheesman, finished the design and also built the beautifully architected Cheesman residence on 8th and Logan that is now the Governor's Mansion, housing Colorado's current governor.

In 1928 John Evans II joined the First National Bank of Denver and, at age thirty-two, became its fifth president. He is remembered for astute financial leadership, responsible for the bank's survival of the 1930s Great Depression, and later merging it with Denver's International Trust Company. Carrying on the tradition of civic involvement, John II was a trustee of the Denver Museum of National History, a director and longtime president of Colorado History Society, and a director of many more organizations. Named by *Fortune* magazine in 1966 as one of

The Cheesman Dam.

Engine Room of the Denver Tramway Central Power Plant.

nineteen of America's "grand old men of business," Evans held many board positions in industry. *Fortune* wrote, "He ran the bank with a conservative hand, although he also showed imaginative willingness to accept good risk." First National Bank was the first bank in the region to risk a loan to an airline. John Evans II built no tunnels through the Continental Divide, nor a railroad from

Denver to the Gulf of Mexico, but when he died in 1978 at the age of ninety-three, the family's financial affairs were in order.

John and Gladys had three children; a son, John Evans Jr., and two daughters, Alice Evans Moore and Anne Evans Freyer. Alice and Anne remembered how their father had implanted the "Evans obligation" into his children's lives as well as the family history. "It was all around us. President Lincoln's framed appointment of Governor Evans was in the library, right over the telephone," said Anne. "We spent our summers on the ranch looking at Mount Evans. We grew up knowing what was expected of us, that we should live in Denver and work for the community."

John Evans Jr. remembers being between six and seven when his parents started training him in the geology and botany of Colorado. "Of course, I learned about Governor Evans' career, and that Mother had the Cheesman Memorial built in honor of her father." John went to Princeton University to broaden his horizons, but at the end of his junior year, he returned to Denver. He went to work for his father in the Cheesman

Mount Evans. Photo by Steven Blecher.

Realty Co. office as a $60-per-month bookkeeper. He didn't know much about property management when he started, but thirty-two years later, he was considered a real estate management expert working sometimes fourteen hours a day. He was also director of the Rio Grande Railroad, president of the board of trustees of the Uni-versity of Denver, a director of the Denver Public Library, member of the managing board of St. Luke's Hospital, on the board of the Mountain States Employers Council and the board of the Colorado Outdoor Development Association.

The Evans name is everywhere in Denver: Mount Evans, the most impressive peak of the Front Range west of the city; Evans Avenue, a major east-west thoroughfare; the Evans Chapel on the campus of the University of Denver, a treasured landmark and preferred wedding chapel; and the Byers-Evans mansion, a Victorian home on the northeast corner of 13th Avenue and Bannock Street. And there are many institutions that do not bear the Evans name but stand today because of the family's involvement and efforts. John Evans II headed the Trust for the Denver Public Library Western History Department. Thanks to the donation of the Byers-Evans house by the Evans family to the Colorado Historical Society, the historic residence has been converted into an educational venue and museum of Colorado history. Evans Ranch in Clear Creek County was Colorado Open Lands' first conservation project to preserve and enhance the wildlife habitat and historic significance of the property.

Current family members agree that what the members of their family do today is maintain the institutions that were built by their predecessors—such as Denver University, Denver Public Library and the Museum of Natural History. "Through happenstance or out of necessity, the family has done a lot for the society in which they've lived," says one descendant. "If there's a legacy, it has to do with someone setting their roots somewhere and making a place for their family to be. If you move city to city, you don't have the opportunity to do that. You can help future generations feel like they're a part of something if you set your roots into one location. The more attractive the location, the easier it is to set those roots."

The current generation continues to be actively involved in the well-being of Denver, maintaining the institutions that will determine the success and appeal of Colorado. A quote from John Evans II speaks to the natural wonder of Denver that inspires the family's ongoing devotion: "One thing remains unchanged—the mighty rampart of the Rockies, appearing to us exactly as they appeared 100 years ago to the Pikes Peak gold-seekers, as it appeared thousands of years ago to prehistoric man, as it will appear a thousand years hence."

*Pikes Peak, America's most famous mountain,
was painted by George Caleb Bingham. Rising in
solitary splendor, the 14,110-foot-high wonder is
generally the first Alpine sentinel seen by travelers
as far as 150 miles away on the eastern plains.
Courtesy, Tom Noel Collection*

THE FULENWIDER FAMILY

"I take the legacy that has been passed down to me very seriously. The values of my father and grandfather continue to be the foundation of our approach today. We take a long-term view, and we treat people with respect."
—*Cal Fulenwider*

The first industrial park in Denver, the first condominiums of any kind—including the first high-rise condos in Colorado—from business parks and residential communities to ski resorts, the Fulenwider family, on its own and with partners, has had a series of firsts that helped shape the Colorado real estate industry. Over 100 years, the Fulenwider name has remained synonymous with innovative business practices.

L.C. Fulenwider Sr. came to Denver in 1903 and began to practice his irrigation engineering skills and techniques on Colorado farm and ranch development with increasing success. A year later he and his brother D.P. Fulenwider rode on bicycles to visit their first clients, later in a horse-drawn buggy; and in 1907, they invested in an automobile. In 1930 the company became L.C. Fulenwider, Inc. and became the landmark developer of Box Elder Farms, which sixty-five years later would become the location for Denver International Airport.

In 1939 L.C. Fulenwider Sr. was elected president of the Colorado Asso-

The barren plains of Colorado.

ciation of Real Estate Boards, and served on the Board of Directors of the National Association of Real Estate Boards from 1939 to 1940. His son, L.C. Fulenwider Jr., also served on the Colorado Real Estate commission for eighteen years, nine as chairman. He too cared deeply about ethical real estate standards and provided leadership for industry organizations including the Denver Board of Realtors, the Colorado Association of Real Estate Boards and the International Real Estate Federation.

L.C. Fulenwider Sr. died in 1949, and his son, L.C. Fulenwider Jr. took over.

He led the company in the development of Greenwood Acres, today known as Greenwood Village.

In 1959 Denver's first industrial park, the 200-acre Mile High Industrial Center, was another first for Fulenwider. That same year, the company opened Park Villa Homes, Colorado's first residential condominiums. In 1962 Fulenwider opened Cherry Knolls, in partnership with Writer Homes, and in 1963, the first high-rise condo in Denver, La Fontana Apartment Homes, was completed. Fulenwider is also responsible for introducing Colorado to the first recreational/resort condos and was involved in more condo development in Aspen, Vail and Breckenridge.

As if this whirlwind of activity were not enough, under L.C. Fulenwider Jr., the company branched out and offered residential and commercial brokerage services, office leasing, shopping center development and management, insurance and securities. Its holdings continued to grow and included a major share of Copper Mountain ski resort. The 1970s provided more success with the Cherry Hills North residential development.

L.C. "Cal" Fulenwider III, who runs the company today, said, "I started as an intern during my college years doing market research for a guy who worked for my dad. Post-Army and college, I got into the family business in the early 1970s. We were involved in brokerage and property management, which was my father's specialty. Although my father had been involved in a number of development projects, it was never in a hands-on way. When I moved out of downtown to work with the company on the development of Polo Club North in the late 1970s, Fulenwider became a development organization. While development was not what we had done full-time in the past, it's now all we do. The reason is that I enjoy this work and one day asked myself, 'Why am I doing this other stuff?'"

Under Cal's leadership during the 1980s and 1990s, the company changed the silhouette of the downtown Denver skyline with the development of two buildings: The Bank One Building, a

Harvest in Colorado, 1920.

twenty-five story, 500,000 square-foot office building, and the thirty story luxury condo project, Larimer Place Condominiums.

During the mid- to late-1980s, Fulenwider redeveloped the Security Life Building. The company then returned to its core of experience with the new Denver International Airport location, about 40 percent of which was purchased from Box Elder Farms. In the 1990s Fulenwider developed Polo Field West, seventeen high-end homes in Cherry Creek and The Heights, a 220-unit luxury apartment complex.

Impressive as its business outlook and achievements have been, the Fulenwider family has also always had a broad perspective on how to benefit Colorado. Since Fulenwider Sr., the family has placed great importance on contributing to the ethical standards and practices in the real estate industry. In 1925 L.C. Fulenwider Sr. had been named president of the Denver Real Estate Exchange, which eventually became the Denver Board of Realtors. He participated in the enactment of Colorado's real estate license law and was appointed by the governor as one of the first commissioners of the Colorado Real Estate Commission, created to administer the new licensing law.

In 2002 more than airplanes were taking off at the airport. So was the Denver International Business Center. Several years after the opening of the airport, restaurants, hotels and corpo-

Globe Investment Co.,1904; L.C. Fulenwider, Sr. and Associates.

rate offices now stand where winter wheat fields once grew. This is the outcome of the work of three generations. He said lightly, "We are developing the family farm," but still finds the land remarkable. "When you've got that much ground, you take it with a huge sense of responsibility."

Reunion is a 3,000-acre plot of land near Denver International Airport, and its history began twenty years ago. The Urban Land Institute set the stage for current airport activities and set parameters for the airport itself. In the mid-1980s Cal was building a condo at Polo Club North for Rob O'Donnell, one of the original founders of the Urban Land Institute. Box Elder Farms consisted of 30,000 acres at that time. There were six different sites being evaluated

for the airport. Fulenwider owned pieces of five of them. "I sat down with Rob O'Donnell," said Cal. "Who said he would assemble a Who's Who of airport development if I could bring in political players as co-sponsors. We brought in presidents from master-plan airport and beltway development communities from all over the country who had come to critique our plan. No one believed we would build our airport or beltway E-470."

One of the lessons they learned from the outstanding panel is that to attract Class A companies, one needs a state-of-the-art master plan community. "I made a commitment to Commerce

Annual outing of the Denver Real Estate Exchange, Indian Hills, Colorado. September 15, 1923.

City," said Cal, "that we would keep our property intact, in one piece, so the site would be large enough to build Reunion. It took two years just to develop a master plan, and the City was involved in the entire process. We could have sold those acres five times over and earned a great deal of money," said Cal, "but we would have messed up the area. That would have been the true definition of sprawl." What kept him on track? "When you've been around that along," he said, "it's your responsibility to go the extra ninety yards."

Learning from sessions with the Urban Land Institute, Cal Fulenwider III refined his plans for Denver International Business Center (DIBC), a 450-acre master-planned business park right at the airport. A founding member of the CU Real Estate Council, Cal realized that early planning for DIBC created a unique educational opportunity. In 1992 he approached Professor John Prosser, former dean of the University of Colorado Graduate School of Urban Design, and suggested allowing graduate students in the design program to use DIBC as a case study for urban planning. They convinced the city to give students a

L.C. Fulenwider Sr. and his brother D.P. Fulenwider in one of Denver's first automobiles, 1907.

full semester to work on this piece—and insisted that officials would not be influenced simply because the students had been asked to do this. According to Cal, "We said, 'You do everything. We'll give you facts you need. But you tell us what you think works and what doesn't, and why.'" The students and the city brought in commercial, restaurant and office people to consult with

them. "And the outcome," said Cal, "verified and reinforced our original thinking."

DIBC is currently home to Frontier Airlines' corporate headquarters, an eight-story Marriott Courtyard, a Marriott Fairfield Inn, a La Quinta Inn, in addition to the Bennigan's restaurant. A 174-room Embassy Suites is now open as well as a Village Inn restaurant, restaurant Ruby Tuesday, two new hotels and an office building. "Also, the Denver voters passed probably the largest mass transit project in the country—maybe the world," said Cal. It's a $4 to $5 billion project that will cover the entire city. One of its main lines will go to the airport and hook up with Union Station. There will be a stop at DIBC coming from the airport. "This forces us to rethink our master plan for DIBC, but that's not a problem for us," Cal said. "You have to roll with the punches."

Despite a downturn in the national economy in 2002, Cal Fulenwider predicted that the pieces were in place for the northeast metro area to grow. His belief was based on Colorado's highly skilled and educated workforce, the explosion of residential development in

L.C. Fulenwider Sr. and sales associate in 1904 on a farming tour by horse and buggy.

the northeast area, and the final leg of highway E-470 linking the area's newest beltway with Interstate 25.

A few years ago the Reunion location was nothing but prairie and a few farms. Now there is a golf course and several hundred homes. The airport corridor is alive and well today because of the L.C. Fulenwider family. The new Denver business community is emerging due in large part to the land holdings of this family. On November 1, 2004, the City Council of Denver passed Resolution 82, honoring the 100th anniversary of L.C. Fulenwider, Inc., founded in 1904 as Globe Investment Company, a full-service real estate firm specializing in farm and ranch transactions.

Many of Cal's employees have been with him for forty years; his senior executives, at least fifteen years each. "We've worked on this together," he says. "You all pitch in together and create solutions to problems and negotiate your way out of trouble. It has all been a company-wide effort. If I'm hit by a

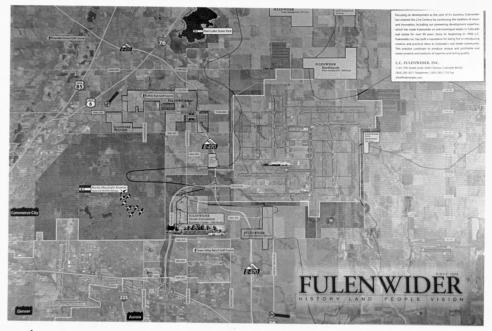

Aerial photo of Fulenwider land developments.

truck tomorrow, we won't skip a beat. They are all technically great at what they do." As for the company profile, he says, "We're pretty low-key—on purpose. We will sometimes take a high-profile position when we need to. We're there with the business leaders working on things as a team. We're good at what we do, intimately involved in the work of Colorado, and responsible."

Fulenwider boasts a staff of broad experience, and the company is geared toward helping clients and partners get the most out of their real estate experience. An ambience of team spirit pervades all the work, and the modest size of L.C. Fulenwider Inc. ensures that clients and partners work with decision-makers throughout the entire process.

The company's reputation for a pioneering spirit and commitment to high standards continues today. Still notching company guns with a series of firsts, the company is leading the development of new territory around Denver International Airport and, after more than 100 years in business, Fulenwider Inc. retains its sense of tradition.

John Freyer, another notable Denver family, says, "The Fulenwider company has always tried to do what is in the best interest of the city and the state. Real estate helps develop a city into what it becomes, and so the people who are developing that are going to have a large impact." With holdings of more than 7,500 acres surrounding the airport, L.C. Fulenwider, Inc. is likely to make an impact on the city's real estate for a long time to come.

Denver International Airport at night.

THE VAN GILDER FAMILY

"Take care of the customer, and the customer will take care of you."
—*Hal D. Van Gilder, 1905*

John W. Van Gilder, the son of Isaac and Elizabeth Van Gilder was born in Island Creek Township in Jefferson County, Ohio (present day Akron, Ohio), in the year 1851. In 1874, the year that Alexander Graham Bell invented the telephone, John and his farming family moved to Melrose, Iowa. John met and married Isadore Stuart in Melrose that same year. Together they had three children, Hal (1876), Dell (1878) and Isadore (1882). By 1880 the Van Gilder family had moved to Albia, a city of dirt streets but also electric lights, telephones and sidewalks made of wood. Isadore, a trained pianist, wrote music at a time when parlor music was popular. In fact, between 1870 and 1885 more than 47,000 pieces of sheet music were registered in the United States.

Hal (left) and Dell W. Van Gilder strike this elegant pose in 1893 while living in Chicago. Hal had taken a position with the Chicago Record, and Dell was attending Rush Medical College. Both brothers sport derbies and gloves, the rage of men's fashion during the 1890s. Courtesy, the Van Gilder Collection.

Dell Williamson Van Gilder (left) and Hal Van Gilder on the right pose for this photo taken in Iowa around 1878. The original image appeared on a tin. Courtesy, the Van Gilder Collection.

Despite the onslaught of the depression in 1893, the Van Gilder family, believing strongly in the importance of a good education and sent their son Hal to Chicago. A city of more than 1 million people, Chicago was a center of economic and social power. Hal took a position with the *Chicago Tribune*, a prominent newspaper, running errands for the education department. In 1895 he took courses at Morgan Park Academy, then at Bryant and Stratton Business College. Later, Hal attended the University of Chicago.

By this time the entire Van Gilder family had moved to Chicago. Dell W. Van Gilder studied medicine at Rush Medical College and graduated as a doctor in 1899. After enduring brutal Chicago weather extremes and competition for jobs in the growing city, the family seized an opportunity to start fresh in a young city. In the spring of 1900, John and Isadore faced hard times. Isadore left John, boarded a train to Denver with their children, Hal and young Isadore, to start a new life at the foot of the Rocky Mountains.

In 1880 Isadore's brother Thomas Benton Stuart had moved to Denver to practice law. By 1900 he had become a highly recognized judge. Upon the arrival of Isadore, Hal and young Isadore, Thomas Stuart welcomed his sister and her children with open arms and encouraged them to stay with him at his new residence at 3659 Marion Street, a home that still stands. Isadore, Hal and young Isadore lived with Judge Stuart through the summer and fall of 1900. At the end of that year, Dell W. Van Gilder arrived in Denver and set up a medical practice.

At age twenty-four, Hal Van Gilder started his first job at the People's Bank Building in Denver working in the office of his uncle, Judge Thomas Benton Stuart, who would later become speaker of the Colorado House of Representatives. Hal left the bank but continued to work for his uncle at the Rockland Hotel in Palmer Lake, Colorado.

In 1901, when Judge Stuart earned the title to the Rockland Hotel—a sixty room, three-story building—Hal Van Gilder seized the opportunity to manage this large organization and meet a variety of people. The elegant hotel was the first of its kind in Colorado and had such modern conveniences as telephones, steam heat, baths and a unique acetylene lighting system.

In the early 1900s there was a Rocky Mountain Chautauqua in progress that drew hundreds of people and business opportunities to the area. Chautauquas, which flourished at the time, were gatherings that provided popular education combined with entertainment in the form of lectures, concerts and plays, often presented outdoors or in a tent. Their scope and diversity reflected and influenced American culture.

Hal's understanding of the Chautauqua movement was strong since he had studied its moral and ethical principles at the University of Chicago and appreciated the movement's demonstration of the effective power that large organizations can have when they mobilize to influence public policy and social mores.

The youngest American president ever elected, Theodore Roosevelt, created new vitality in 1901. There was ongoing urban growth, and a new reform movement that encouraged social justice and order during this period of rapid industrialization.

Hal closed the Rockland for the winter and returned to Denver. The following year he was introduced to Judge Frank Johnson who hired him to be his clerk and assistant. Hal observed existing norms of municipal corruption from the echelon of Mayor Speer down. He also became acquainted with fiduciary and other surety bonds that had to be posted.

Much of Hal's responsibility as district court clerk required attention to certain legal instruments called surety bonds, more specifically fiduciary and litigation bonds. Sureties are financial guarantees that protect the consumer against loss in case the terms of a contract are not filled. Hal Van Gilder was fascinated

Captured by an unknown photographer, Isadore Stuart Van Gilder holds her grandson, Dell George Van Gilder. This photo taken in 1905 is one of very few photos of the courageous family matriarch. Courtesy, the Van Gilder Collection.

by them. In the course of his employment with Judge Johnson, he learned the detailed mechanics of sureties and the reputation of the companies and agents who utilized them.

In 1905 Hal started a surety general agency, the Van Gilder Agency, which represented United Surety Company of Baltimore. Local agents and lawyers went to him for various surety bonds and he split the commission with them. Because the income potential was small, Hal learned the property and casualty business from Charles Cobb, a founding father of insurance in Colorado. While learning the business he became involved with George Pullman Sanger, and Hal and George formed a partnership called the Sanger-Van Gilder Insurance Agency, from 1911 to 1914. When the partnership failed, Hal renamed his company the Van Gilder Agency.

To counter the pressures of clerical tasks and learning the inner workings of both civil and criminal proceedings, in 1902 the social-minded Hal Van Gilder founded the Arapahoe County Courthouse Social Club. Having inherited his father's charm, he got along well with everyone—from executives to office clerks. He organized formal galas and became the most popular bachelor in town. In 1902 Hal met and married Mildred Slack, a student at Denver's Manual Training School, who shared musical interests with Hal's mother. Hal's $125 per month salary made for a modest living.

They had two children, Dell Sr., named after Hal's' brother, and Beatrice. They lived in north Denver until 1915 when they moved to 5th and Race in east Denver. Young Dell went to East High School and then to Colorado University. He excelled in all scholastics, but his true love was baseball. He lettered four years at Colorado University and tried semi-pro ball but was injured and had to quit the game. After he graduated as a business major from CU, he went to work for his father at Van Gilder Agency. He discovered early on that the company was near bankruptcy. He immediately eliminated all brokerage with other agents and started selling insurance to new automobile owners and cold-called people he read about in the newspapers.

At the same time, Dell picked up a new passion: golf. Every weekend he played seventy-two holes and within a short time became a scratch player. Later on, during the Depression, he relied on his golf skills to supplement his income. More importantly however, he found out how to use golf as a means to develop relationships.

The Denver area population had now doubled. While the electric tram moved most people to and from work, shops, theaters and amusement parks, automobiles were becoming popular. The mile-high city was fast becoming a large, growing metropolis.

With a call by President Wilson to support allied powers in 1917, Dr. Dell W. Van Gilder administered to the wounded and sick of the 40th Division.

Dell George Van Gilder, East Side High School graduation picture, 1922. Courtesy, the Van Gilder Collection.

He wrote his brother Hal in November 1918 of the "sensation" of "being under fire." When the Great War ended, Dr. Dell W. Van Gilder returned home in 1920 and lived with Hal, Mildred, Dell G. and Beatrice for a short while. Then, he moved back to Ohio.

In 1930 Dell met and married Lucia Lee Spencer. They had four children, Dottie Lee (1932), Margot (1934), Dell Jr. (1940) and Lucia (1941). All four children went to college and afterwards married. The three girls moved out of state.

During the 1920s, 1930s and 1940s the Van Gilder Agency grew slowly but steadily. In the 1940s Hal helped found the Independent Insurance Agents of Colorado. Its primary principle was to maintain ethical standards within the industry, a reputation it has maintained. Today, the association is best known for education facilities and legislative activities. Dell became president in 1945.

Hal Van Gilder stands with his secretarial staff outside the new building on 18th Avenue in Denver around 1950. Hall was seventy-five years old at the time. Courtesy, the Van Gilder Collection.

Hal D. Van Gilder (left) and Dell G. Van Gilder stand in front of their new office building on 18th Avenue in Denver. This photo was taken around 1955. Courtesy, the Van Gilder Collection.

The Van Gilder Insurance Agency survived the Depression years and adjusted to the economic shift. In 1950, after leasing space for many decades, Hal and Dell moved into their own building located at 825 E. 18th Avenue. Attention to serving clients distinguished their agency from other brokers. Their dedication and integrity brought them client loyalty and new customers.

In 1963 Dell Van Gilder Jr. joined his father and grandfather in the agency after graduating from the University of Colorado. The agency had five employees, $500,000 in annual sales and $120,000 annual income. They were well respected by clients as well as the insurance companies it represented. Dell Jr. developed his insurance product knowledge and started building the business.

In 1969 Hal Van Gilder passed away. The partnership was dissolved and Van Gilder Agency incorporated. Van Gilder hit Dell Sr's. production goal of $1 million in annual sales and received its first offer to sell the company to Frank B. Hall.

By the mid 1970s the company either had to grow or sell. National Insurance Agencies were buying up all the good local agencies and offering services and prices that Van Gilder found to be stiff competition. Van Gilder Insurance Corporation, as it was now known, had sales of $3.5 million, revenue of $600,000 and seventeen employees. They decided to dramatically expand the company, and made Dell Jr. the new CEO.

Over the next decades, Van Gilder grew through acquisitions of other insurance agencies and opening new offices. On January 1, 1978 the company moved to 700 Broadway. That year Van Gilder Insurance Corporation purchased Steel, Jacobs and Gardner Insurance Agency folowed by Fulenwider Insurance Agency. In 1982 Schoelzel Insurance Agency was acquired. Van Gilder purchased the Dowis Agency of Sterling, Colorado in 1988, their first acquisition located outside Denver. Van Gilder Insurance Company started an office from scratch in Kansas City in 1989 and two years later purchased Day, Webb and Taylor followed by Tri City Insurance in 1998 and CBS in Colorado Springs. Three

Dell Van Gilder Jr. joined his father and grandfather in the business in 1963. He represented the third generation of the family for over three decades, most of which he served as the chairman & CEO.

long ago that you can handle only so much business. I differentiated by turning over my accounts to other people we hired. This has allowed us to bring in new people and grow our business at the same time. When the company started, we had 5 employees. Today we have more than 270."

Integrity is the key word at Van Gilder. "That's all we have as human beings," says Dell, "is the integrity of doing what's right for our fellow man and ourselves. The Golden Rule applies in business as well as in individual life."

Michael Van Gilder took the helm of the Van Gilder Insurance Corporation as had the three generations before him.

years before his death, Dell Van Gilder Sr. saw Van Gilder Insurance Corporation achieve Dell Jr's annual goal of $100 million in sales in 1993. In 2000 Van Gilder Insurance Corporation purchased Aero Insurance, an aviation-only agency, and in 2005 added to the aviation division by purchasing AirSure Limited. These acquisitions, plus aggressive organic growth have increased the corporation to annual sales of $450 million, with annual revenue of $43 million and more than 270 employees in seven different offices as of 2005.

After forty-three years of leading the company, Dell Jr. stepped aside to allow a younger Van Gilder to lead the organization. Dell's son Michael Van Gilder assumed the duties of CEO in 2006. The advice that Dell Jr. gave to Michael was to retain 10 percent of revenue every year, to learn to delegate and then step aside. Dell says, "Probably the most important thing I did was delegate responsibility. I learned

ACCENT WINDOWS

With a bustling manufacturing plant and headquarters on Denver's Pecos Street, another in St. Louis and a franchise network comprised of seven locations in nearly as many states, it would be easy to think of Accent Windows as just another corporate entity. However, Accent Windows actually began humbly, with one man's desire for professional growth and excellence. Those traditions are continued to this day at the now-booming family business. The company has always had a staunch commitment to providing the highest level of customer service through its quality products and conscientious workmanship. By maintaining the personalized service characteristic of the small business it evolved from, Accent has earned its customers' respect and business, while giving back to the Adams County community it calls home.

In 1982 Tim Marcovich had reached the apex of professional growth at the Colorado Springs glass business where he was employed. With a desire to expand his own horizons, he relocated to Denver where he and his wife, Sherry, created Accent Windows. After locating an ideal manufacturing space, which would house the business for more than twenty years, Tim Marcovich set to work building quality products with an initial staff of only four employees. His son, Terry Marcovich, joined him as a

Co-presidents Richard Roeding and Terry Marcovich.

minority partner in 1983, and the family business was well on its way.

Accent Windows' original product offerings were limited to interior vinyl storm windows. Interested in expanding, Accent Windows bought a storm window line in 1984 from a supplier who was closing that particular division. Along with the new product line came another asset: Richard Roeding, who would become an instrumental part of the Accent Windows family. Richard helped diversify Accent's product line even further. It soon included products ranging from insulated custom windows and glass to storefronts and screens.

By the late 1980s Accent Windows returned to its roots, selling off most of its individual product lines to focus on

replacement windows. From its inception through the early 1990s, Accent worked as a wholesale supplier, providing its products primarily to contractors and distributors. At the time, selling directly to the public was not considered an option, as it would have put Accent in direct competition with its own clients.

Over time, however, several frustrating business patterns arose that inspired drastic change. Of great concern was the loss of quality control inherent in the wholesale stream of commerce. Providing their distinct products to a myriad of contractors and distributors, who worked directly with the final consumers, made ensuring the highest level of customer satisfaction nearly impossible. Another factor was the constraint on growth. Many contractors ran small operations, but the demand for relatively small numbers of custom products was costly. With so many middlemen involved, the numbers weren't adding up.

The management team at Accent Windows was increasingly frustrated with the limits on the business—and an overall feeling of the work devolving into a daily grind. One staff member succinctly summed up the sentiment in an internal communication by flipping the letters in "fun" to reflect how he was starting to feel about work: 'N-uf. After a few years of careful consideration,

Accent Windows' corporate headquarters on 12300 Pecos Street in Westminister.

and even, at times, high anxiety, management decided to make a complete change. Though it was a risk—and an expensive one at that—everyone at Accent was in agreement: they wanted to feel good about the products and services they were providing to the public, and the old model of delivery just wasn't going to cut it any more. Accent Windows gave its wholesale customers six months notice that their $12 million a year wholesale operation was being scrapped, and that they would now be providing their custom products directly to the public. "We went from hero to zero, so to speak," said Richard Roeding, who was a top executive at Accent by this time.

The management felt that, in a way, it was a logical step: Accent already custom-made windows that were sold through contractors, who would then turn the installation back over to Accent. All the company lacked was a sales and marketing staff. By cutting out the middlemen contractors and distributors, Accent would be able to oversee every aspect of the presentation and upkeep of their product, making sure customers had the best experience, from sales through the life of their windows.

On January 1, 1995 Accent Windows shifted its entire business model. The

Accent's Signature Series windows, installed in a Denver downtown high rise.

company began aggressively selling and marketing to the public with the tagline: "Built. Installed. Guaranteed." Since Accent became responsible for the entire job, the company felt comfortable guaranteeing satisfaction and the highest quality—for the life of their products. Richard Roeding summed it up, telling customers: "Congratulations, your window problems are over for life."

At that point, Accent Windows was operating true to its triangular logo. The first edge of the triangle represented

Accent's clients and a commitment to delivering the service that each particular client desired. The second side of the triangle represented Accent's employees—at that time, 125 strong at the original manufacturing plant and company headquarters. As the expansion demonstrated, the company wished to foster an environment of professional growth, not just for the bottom line of the business, but for the people who worked there. They strove to ensure that no one would be stymied in their professional ambitions—as Tim Marcovich had been, prior to starting Accent Windows. The final side of Accent's triangle represented a committment to sustain the business itself. It vowed not only to keep providing quality and value to its customers, but also to make sure that since it guaranteed its products for life, it would still exist to make good on its promise. In a volatile industry rife with shifting and short-lived businesses, Accent felt a strong responsibility to remain a lasting presence.

One way of ensuring this longevity was to continue to develop and offer the finest quality products. Accent Windows produces the number one rated window for thermal performance in North America, as assessed by the National Fenestration Rating Council (NFRC), a nonprofit organization committed to providing "fair, accurate and reliable energy performance ratings." This designation was earned after comprehensive testing of approximately 67,000 window units submitted from across the United States, making the distinction all the more impressive. Accent's award-winning window is made with a special glazing system that gives it unique reflective properties, keeping homes cooler in the summer heat and warmer in the winter. It was this component that *Popular Science* magazine deemed one of the twentieth century's "Most Useful Inventions."

Accent 's Legacy Series windows grace the front of a suburban Denver home.

In addition to becoming a bit of a maverick in Denver's business community, Accent Windows has also made its presence known in the Adams County civic community. Accent Windows is actively involved with numerous philanthropic groups. They have worked with Rebuilding Together, an organization that provides and installs windows to low income, elderly or handicapped individuals who are in need of assistance in maintaining their homes—all free of charge—creating warmer, safer and dryer places for these people to live. In addition, Accent Windows supports the efforts of employee—and former Bronco Ring of Famer—Karl Macklenburg in his work with the REACH (Rewarding Experiences for All Children) program, which strives to provide Denver-area youth with the educational opportunities and resources needed to excel in both the classroom and in life.

Accent Windows is particularly proud of its involvement with the nonprofit Colorado Energy Sciences Center (CESC), which, in conjunction with the National Renewable Energy Laboratory (NREL), runs the K12 Program. The innovative program utilizes home energy use as a springboard for teaching students about math and science. Accent Windows participates

A four-point robotic welder operates at Accent Windows' new production facility.

in CESC's Home Energy Investigation Contest, challenging small teams of students to complete home energy audits. The winning team gets, among other prizes, the windows replaced in the home they audited, courtesy of Accent Windows.

More than ten years after the momentous 1995 switch, much has changed for Accent Windows. Its founder, Tim Marcovich, retired in 1998, leaving active minority partners Terry Marcovich and Richard Roeding to carry on as co-presidents. Tim's daughter, Tracy (Marcovich) Klein, joined as a partner in the mid-1990s as well.

When asked if any younger family members might be interested in continuing in the family business, Richard Roeding laughs, "Well, my son's only two and a half!" Terry's two children, both in their teens, are still discovering their own paths, which may or may not lead back to Accent. However, Roeding notes that the Marcovich family is now entwined with his own through the business. Richard's wife Jodie is active in the business and several other close relatives, spanning two generations, are also a part of the Accent family.

While Tim Marcovich continues to advise the younger generation, Terry Marcovich and Richard Roeding are firmly in command of their posts, having both grown up in the glass and window industry and worked their way up from the mailroom, as the saying goes. The two work synergistically and interchangeably in every aspect of Accent. Under their guidance, Accent Windows now sells more products directly to the public than it ever did in its wholesale incarnation. Yet their greatest success lies in taking Accent Windows from a small family business to a national brand without compromising its small-business integrity, an accomplishment that is a well-earned source of pride.

The company's former factory in Denver served as its production floor for over twenty years.

ADAMS STATE COLLEGE

For more than eighty years, Adams State College has provided exceptional education to students in the remote, rural San Luis Valley of Colorado. Until its founding in 1921 as the Adams State Normal School, there were few local options for attending college. The lack of educational opportunities was acutely evident to Billy Adams, a Colorado legislator who would later become governor.

Adams moved to Alamosa in 1879 at the age of seventeen and became a rancher. Although Adams had no more than a grade school education, he was determined to become a learned man. He read constantly in his spare time, particularly history, economics, law and government.

His interest in government led to a career in politics. Elected mayor of Alamosa at age twenty, Adams was later elected to the state legislature and then to the state senate before being elected governor in 1926. From the time he was elected mayor of Alamosa, Adams was determined to use his political power to increase educational opportunities in the area. It took more than three decades for his vision to come to light.

In all the time he served in the legislature and senate, Adams introduced only a single bill. That bill eventually authorized the creation of the Adams State Normal School, dedicated to educating teachers. Once the bill passed, the real work began—building the campus,

Adams State was named for its founder, former Colorado Governor Billy Adams, a rancher who never completed high school.

The original building on Adams State's campus was built on the edge of Alamosa in 1923. In the early days, rows of Russian olive trees were planted to keep out herds of horses.

hiring instructors, developing the curriculum and more.

In 1921 the cornerstone was laid on what would become Richardson Hall, named after the college's first president, Dr. Ira Richardson. Now the college's administration building, the structure originally housed the administration, faculty, classrooms, library and dormitories. When state funding to get the college off the ground was withheld due to some political maneuvering, local families and businesses stepped in to contribute. The local community pledged $27,000 to help bring the college to life and donated more than 1,000 volumes for the school's library.

Adams State Normal School opened its doors in June 1925 for its first summer session. Helen Eagle of Monte Vista was the first of 119 eager students to register. That fall, another forty-two students enrolled at the teaching college, which had only three instructors at the time. The campus began to take on a truly collegiate atmosphere with the creation of student clubs

and athletic teams as well as the selection of school colors: green for evergreens and white for snow.

In 1926 Adams State held its first commencement ceremony, awarding the first degree to Harriet Dalzell Hester. Nobody could have been more proud than Billy Adams. His dream of providing education to students in the remote San Luis Valley had become a reality.

Since then, thousands of area students have graduated with a solid education. Among them were the five children of Dr. Luther Bean, one of the college's first instructors. One of them, Glen Bean, who graduated in 1936, still recalls the close-knit feeling at the small college where instructors knew the names of every student and personalized their instruction.

This has remained a hallmark of education at Adams State, which boasts one instructor for every eighteen students. Even as the college has grown from a few hundred students to more than 2,500, Adams State has retained that small-college atmosphere. The intimate feeling persists although the campus has

expanded from a single building to more than thirty, including residence halls, a performing arts center, a visual arts building, and advanced science and computer laboratories. Traces of Adams State's original Spanish-style architecture remain in the historic president's residence. It was recently dubbed "Marvel House" in honor of the service of former president Dr. John Marvel and his wife, Frances.

A host of individuals who shared Adams' dedication and perseverance in bringing the college to life have helped fuel the college's expansion. A number of past presidents persevered through turbulent times that threatened the college's very existence. For instance, in

Over the last six decades, Adams State has built two new science buildings to keep pace with technology.

Named for its first president, Dr. Ira Richardson, Richardson Hall was the college's only building when classes began in 1925. Today, it houses administrative offices on a ninety-acre campus with more than thirty buildings.

the 1940s enrollment dropped dramatically due to World War II and only four degrees were granted in 1944. In the tumultuous 1960s student unrest peaked with a bomb explosion in Richardson Hall. Strong leadership helped the college survive these challenges.

The college's leaders have often taken unique approaches to problem solving. For instance, when a new library was built in 1973, the college was faced with an obstacle: how to transfer 140,000 library volumes to the new structure. The school's president joined students and faculty members to form a human chain in a "bucket brigade" to move the

volumes over half a mile to their new home.

More recent challenges have included remodeling and replacing some of the original buildings and updating technology campus-wide. Adams State has invested millions of dollars to build a new backbone for technology. Now, every building, including residence halls, is wired for high-speed Internet access. Students can also take advantage of "smart classrooms," where instructors teach via the Internet or share lecture material through Web sites.

As Adams State evolved from a little teaching school into a thriving liberal arts college, it never veered from its commitment to providing educational

Adams State science students enjoy very high rates of acceptance into pre-med programs, owing to modern labs and dedicated faculty members.

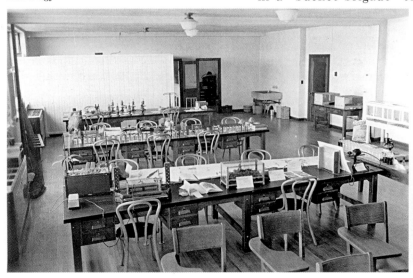

opportunities to the San Luis Valley. In particular, the college has preserved its tradition of working with underserved populations, including underrepresented minorities, first-generation college-goers and low-income students. In keeping with this mission, it has one of the state's lowest tuition rate among four-year institutions. About one-third of undergraduates come from neighboring San Luis Valley high schools and 37 percent of the student body is from minority groups.

With a large percentage of Hispanics in the San Luis Valley, Adams State has always reached out to this population. The U.S. Department of Education recognizes Adams State as a Hispanic Serving Institution. In 2000 it awarded the college a $1.85 million Title V grant. Through this grant, Adams State created the Center for Excellence in Learning and Teaching (CELT), designed to help professors create more learner-centered classrooms. The 2000 grant helped pave the way for a second Title V grant in 2005 totaling $3.4 million, earmarked for a cooperative project with two junior colleges and intended to increase Hispanic participation in higher education.

Adams State's long-standing mission to serve the area was reinforced by receiving Regional Education Provider status in 2003. This designation emphasizes strengthening educational opportunity, economic development and cultural enrichment across southern Colorado. Adams State has more than lived up to the region's academic needs.

Its success as an educational provider is undeniable and has also had a tremendous economic impact on the area. With 325 on-campus employees, the college ranks as the San Luis Valley's largest employer. In addition, the spending power of the college, its students and employees adds up to more than $70 million in the region—equal to almost 20 percent of all the personal income in Alamosa County.

While Adams State has achieved success with its educational mission, it has also found victory on the field. The NCAA Division II "Grizzlies" support fourteen intercollegiate sports, including the top-notch men's and women's cross

country teams. Coached by Dr. Joe I. Vigil, an Adam's State emeritus professor and graduate of the class of 1959, the men's team won the 1992 national championship in its first year of NCAA Division II competition with an unprecedented and unduplicated perfect score. The Vigil tradition of turning average runners into national champions continues to this day with head coach Damon Martin, nineteen-time NCAA Division II National Coach of the Year. The men's team has won a record-breaking seventeen national championships, and the women's, fourteen. Adams State's women's cross country team was recognized as the best NCAA Division II team in the past twenty-five years.

Adams State's quality academics are complemented by a dynamic campus with many avenues for student involvement. Thanks to Adams State's unique location in North America's largest alpine valley and its Adventure Program, students can participate in dozens of recreational activities, including backpacking, snowboarding, skiing, kayaking and river rafting. They can also round out their education through numerous clubs and activities.

Equally dedicated to its off-campus learners, Adams State has been offering courses to students throughout Colorado, the United States and beyond since the mid-1960s. Today, more than 12,500 students across the globe participate in the Extended Studies program's undergradu-

Key to Adams State's mission is promotion of the San Luis Valley's unique history and culture. Now in its thirty-fifth year at Adams State, Semillas de la Tierra keeps the folk dance traditions of Mexico alive. The college also sponsors Corazon del Valle, a student Mariachi group, and works to stimulate local arts through its Office of Community Partnerships.

ate and graduate degree programs, professional development courses, and non-credit courses. Developed in cooperation with regional community colleges, Adams State's Rural Education Access Program allows place-bound students with associate's degrees to complete an Adam's State bachelor's degree in their communities as well.

It's evident that Adams State has come a long way from its beginnings as a small-town teachers' college. Although it continues to award more degrees in education than any other major, its School of Business is quickly narrowing the gap. The real proof that Adams State is achieving its mission lies in its graduates. The college has produced such notable alumni as William Porter, the founder of E*TRADE; John Salazer, congressman; William Moyers, renowned cowboy artist; and Judge Carlos Lucero, the first Hispanic appointed to the U.S. Court of Appeals for the Tenth Circuit in Denver. It's clear that Adams State College has not only met but far surpassed the vision of its founder, Billy Adams.

AET ENVIRONMENTAL, INC.

AET Environmental, Inc. (AET) has a short but rich history in providing solutions for the cost-effective and responsible handling of hazardous materials in Colorado. Headquartered in Denver, adjacent to the historic Lakeside Amusement Park, the firm is the largest independently-owned and operated environmental services and waste management specialist in the Rocky Mountain region.

Each of the principals of AET—Lori DeVito, president; her husband, Arthur Clark, technical director; and Frank Virginia, their vice president—came from different fields. Lori DeVito had taught at the Berkeley College in Manhattan for twelve years and, prior to that, was a radio station disc jockey. Art Clark, a native of Golden, Colorado, and a graduate of the Colorado School of Mines, was an engineer with a doctorate in biochemistry, who had conducted research on new drugs and worked as a senior project manager for a geotechnical engineering firm. Frank Virginia was an engineer with an MBA and ten years of experience working for nationally known environmental service and waste disposal companies.

Two of AET's principals—Frank Virginia, vice president, and Art Clark, technical director.

Lori DeVito (right) is presented with a WBE award by Channel 4 news anchor Kathy Walsh.

How did AET become the largest independent environmental service firm in the region? Initially, a Denver-based chemical distributor offered Clark, who had been looking for a new challenge, a management position. The seventy-year-old firm was having financial difficulties, and the owners believed that new management would help turn the situation around through fresh ideas and innovative technologies. Clark accepted the challenge; however, the distributor's financial struggles continued.

Seeing the challenge as an opportunity, the husband and wife team established AET Environmental in 1993, using $20,000 of DeVito's savings. "The distribution company [that Clark was working for] sold chemicals to a large group of customers. We knew these companies had to contract with someone to dispose of their chemical waste and to deal with environmental compliance issues," says DeVito. "We contacted these companies and asked them how they managed their hazardous waste and if they'd be willing to give us the opportunity to handle their requirements."

Convincing the defunct chemical company's clients to try AET's services was not as difficult as the couple thought it would be. "It was a time when small companies could not get service from the large national hazardous waste firms, who wanted to deal with big businesses like themselves. They simply were not interested in servicing small clients," explains DeVito. AET won new clients over by describing their "small but competent team of professionals who would give them the individual care, attention, and help they needed to carry out their environmental responsibilities."

For the first few years, the company worked with a factorer, who each Friday would give them 80 percent of the face value of their invoices for the week. With the high interest rates, DeVito was motivated to wean the company off borrowed money. She targeted small-scale manufacturing and industrial operations, such as local print shops and auto repair businesses. "We got started by providing individual assistance to firms who could not get a return call from the large companies doing what we do," continues DeVito. In this way, AET developed a reputation as a place where small industries could go for answers.

Frank Virginia joined the firm in 1996, bringing his knowledge of the industry to further enhance AET's offering to its clients. When the large environmental companies consolidated in the 1990s, AET survived. In fact, some of their small competitors ended up giving AET their customer lists because they wanted their customers to be in good hands.

Today AET has a customer base of more than 2,000 companies, comprising both large and small clients. The company works with government agencies at the federal, state and local levels. Included among its federal clients are the Environmental Protection Agency, the United States Geological Survey and the Drug Enforcement Agency. In the commercial sector, AET still works with print shops and auto body repair shops, but now counts metal finishing, printed circuit board manufacturers, pharmaceutical companies, research laboratories, hospitals, universities and utility companies among its extensive client list. In addition to transporting chemical waste to treatment facilities, AET performs environmental compliance audits; facilitates decontamination and remediation of sites; provides lab packing, industrial cleaning and sanitary surveys; and operates water treatment facilities.

Company officials are particularly proud of AET's rapid response to waste removal emergencies. Their teams of chemists and compliance specialists remove hazardous materials from the environment and help clients deal with regulatory agencies. They also collect confirmation samples at sites to determine if further decontamination or remediation is needed. "There aren't a lot of firms who offer all the services

An AET employee handles materials in the lab.

Staff members from AET's Denver office pose in front of historic Lakeside Amusement Park.

that we do," says Frank Virginia, vice president of AET. "Our clients can feel confident when their company receives a compliance inspection. We want them to have good environmental compliance because their success is a reflection on our business and our environmental stewardship."

AET has worked on numerous projects in Colorado including storm water treatment and the removal of hazardous materials from buildings slated for demolition for the Interstate-25 road-widening project (TREX). A team of senior field chemists was also sent to New Orleans to lab pack chemicals at Tulane University in the aftermath of Hurricane Katrina. At times the company has been involved in unique projects, such as the tracking of bird species for the U.S. Bird Aircraft Strike

Hazard (BASH) team. AET also operates the Avian Hazard Advisory System (AHAS) to reduce and eliminate the incidents of bird collisions with aircraft.

As a way of giving back to the business community, DeVito speaks to other women entrepreneurs and mentors those interested in starting their own companies. She encourages small business owners not to be afraid of hard work, long hours, and Saturdays spent balancing the books. "If you have a great business idea and you've looked at the cons as well as the pros, move on it," she advises. "When your days consist of getting the children off to school, going to work, picking up the children after school, making dinner, and then returning to graduate school at night, expect it and embrace it! Believe in your purpose, because your success will be immensely satisfying, not only to you, but also to your family."

Along with the Denver corporate office, AET has regional offices in Salt Lake City, Utah; Las Vegas, Nevada; Albany, Georgia; and Panama City, Florida. The guiding principal of AET's foundation is that every single customer deserves individual care and attention. With a history of researching new—as well as time-honored—approaches to environmental stewardship, AET Environmental plans to move forward by providing superior leadership in environmental services and hazardous waste management.

AIMS COMMUNITY COLLEGE

Aims Community College has evolved into one of the most comprehensive two-year colleges in Colorado. In the past forty years, its professional and caring faculty and staff have provided a variety of educational programs and services for more than 300,000 students. Since opening its first building in Greeley in 1967, Aims has added eighteen buildings and established additional campuses in Fort Lupton and Loveland.

Over the years, the public, post-secondary institution has responded to local, regional and even global educational needs. The college offers 2,000 day, evening and weekend courses to an average of 14,000 credit and non-credit students each year. Different programs provide students the opportunity to earn Associate's degrees in Applied Science, the Arts, Science, or General Studies, or work toward career or technical education certificates. Aims Community College confers more than 1,000 degrees and certificates annually.

Although some of Aims' students spend only nine to eighteen months at

The Sunrise Building, shown here in 1967, was the first building to house Aims Community College.

the college, mastering relevant work skills that will allow them to enter the job market, about half the student body attends the college for two years before transferring to a four-year program elsewhere. Not only are core curriculum units guaranteed to transfer in state, students appreciate the fact that they can save up to 50 percent on tuition by starting at a community college. For many, Aims offers a second—and sometimes third—chance to those students who, for financial or academic reasons, haven't been able to easily transition to a four-year institution. Recent documentation from a study done at the University of Colorado showed that community college students who transferred in ended up with a GPA equal to or higher than those who started there as freshman.

However, not all of Aims' students pursue degree or certificate programs. Unique in its student body, the average Aims student is thirty-three years old. Celebrating diversity in society, the college makes educational opportunity accessible to anyone who may benefit from its programs and courses. A leading source for career education and workforce development, Aims enables its students to improve their abilities for career advancement. Still, thousands

Students at Aims 2006 graduation.

of working professionals seek out courses to enhance their performance and efficiency on the job, while others enroll in courses they simply find interesting, pursuing a lifelong love of learning.

It's hard to believe that only forty years ago, northern Colorado didn't have a two-year college. It wasn't until the summer of 1966 that a citizen's committee representing school districts in Weld County recommended the formation of a junior college district. Both district voters and the Colorado State Board of Education approved of the idea. The committee, wishing to name the college something that represented its "high and worthy goals," settled on "Aims." In March, 1967 a governing board was elected, which selected Dr. Ed Beaty as the college's first president. The first building erected on the Greeley Campus was eventually named in his honor.

Aims held its first day of classes in a makeshift building on September 27, 1967, boasting an enrollment of 949 students—and fifteen full-time staff

An aerial view of the Aims Community College Greeley Campus.

Students in microbiology lab.

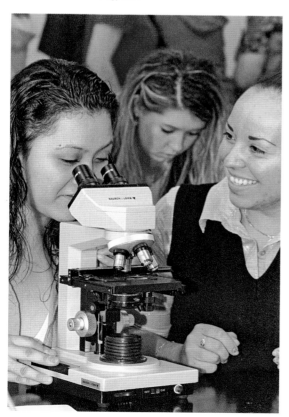

members. Aims found a permanent home in 1971, after purchasing a 175-acre site on the western edge of Greeley. In July 1981 the Aims Southern District Office was opened in Fort Lupton, and three years later—after completing a $1.9 million, 27,000-square-foot complex—the sixty-acre South Campus opened there. Still expanding in 1990, Aims added a West Campus in Loveland, offering classes in the remodeled 14,400-square-foot White Building.

As with its physical growth in order to serve the community, Aims has had a fundamental drive to change in order meet the needs of its students. In the early years programs like pottery and music were a large draw. While those programs continue today at Aims, the college has expanded into high-tech areas like Graphic Technology, 3-D Computer Aided Drafting, Cyber Protection, Computer Information Systems, Web Design and more. Microsoft founder Bill Gates was impressed enough with the college's technology to remark, "Schools like

Aims Community College are real leaders." In addition, Aims is the only community college in the country with a full-motion flight simulator. The college teaches both students and airline pilots, providing the training necessary for FAA certification.

Recently, when the local healthcare industry reported drastic shortages of well-trained medical personnel, Aims responded by rapidly developing at least five new programs and certificates to meet the needs of the medical community. In no time, most of those programs were filled to capacity, with waiting lists of four to five years. Under the leadership of current president Dr. Marilynn Liddell, Aims is using capital reserves and certificates of participation to erect the college's first new building since 1993. The $20 million center for Allied Health programs will be located northeast of the College Center. Dr. Liddell's hope is that "in five years, when bioscience emerges as one of the fastest growing fields, we will have the flexibility to be on the cutting edge."

Through continuous program review, Aims ensures that it is offering the programs students want and that the business community needs. In fact, the college's accreditation is based on the Academic Quality Improvement Program, as instituted by the Commission on Institutions of Higher Education. Instead of waiting every ten years to do a report, Aims submits annual reports and systems portfolios in order to demonstrate their progress toward continuous improvement goals.

The school's adaptability would not be possible without its team of talented and dedicated faculty, staff and administrators. Unlike some large universities, Aims faculty prides itself on providing a personalized experience, with fewer than thirty-five students per class. Among students, the college's instructors are consistently rated as Aim's best feature. Their ability to explain subject material in a simple but thorough manner allows students to increase their comprehension levels, resulting in higher grades.

Aims' students and staff are also extremely loyal to the school. An example of this loyalty is Art Terrazas, who was the second student to register for classes in the fall of 1967. After completing an Associate of Arts degree at Aims, Terrazas went on to complete both undergraduate and graduate level study, finally returning to Aims to serve students as a faculty member. He remained at Aims for his entire career, recently retiring after thirty-three years in the classroom.

Likewise, all of Aims' employees are

Students in microbiology lab.

College Center building on the Aims' Greeley Campus.

willing to do what ever it takes to serve Weld County. As a local, tax-district-supported college, Aims has very strong ties to its immediate area and belongs to most of the community's civic and business organizations. Aims also participates in or hosts a variety of public events, such as the Weld County Relay For Life, the annual Water Festival, the Healing Field, the Greeley Independence Stampede, the High Plains Chautauqua and many others activities.

In one of its more unusual public "initiatives," Aims' former Public Information Director, Mark Olson, took to the steps of the Denver Capitol on April 2—since April 1 had already been booked—and made an impassioned plea to have Aims' mascot, the aardvark, named Colorado's official state animal. With tongue firmly in cheek, Olson addressed a crowd of radio, television and newspaper reporters. In the end, the state Legislature decided not to take the title away from the Big Horn Sheep. Still, Aims Community College was recognized nationally in the media.

Aims is thankful for its community, whose citizens have eagerly and generously supported the college. The benefit of continuous financial support from local taxpayers has been especially appreciated in the past three years, during which 25 to 40 percent of the college's funding allocation has been cut from the state budget. "Those changes impact learning processes and the ability of colleges to provide quality and quantity of experiences," Dr. Liddell notes. "Within the next five years there will need to be a major reconsideration of how we fund the business we're in."

The year 2007 will mark Aims Community College's fortieth anniversary. However, more changes and innovations are just around the corner. As Aims serves the needs of emergent industries and their future employees, the school will continue to develop new programs and refresh the programs currently offered. As the saying goes, the only thing that is a constant at Aims is change. One thing is certain, though: Aims Community College will remain a dynamic and innovative organization, ready to serve its students and the community.

COLLINS CASHWAY LUMBER

Before Home Depot was known from coast to coast, Collins Cashway Lumber was a household name in Fort Collins. The full line lumber and hardware store has been catering to general contractors and do-it-yourselfers alike since 1972. That's when its founders, Floyd Wernimont, Eldon Garrett and Elmer Jannsen opened the first Collins Cashway Lumber in Fort Collins. The trio literally built the business from the ground up with hard work, good old fashioned business sense and flexibility to change with the times.

Wernimont was no stranger to the timber business when he launched Collins Cashway Lumber. The young entrepreneur learned the ins and outs of the industry while managing a lumberyard called Johnson Cashway in Lincoln, Nebraska. During that time, he discovered the impact of supply and demand and proved his ability to keep a business in the black. Also, he learned what customers want from a local lumber supplier.

Emboldened with experience, Wernimont found two business partners and launched his own lumber empire. The trio opened for business with about $50,000 in cash and a dream to become a leading force in the independent lumber industry. Wernimont also leveraged

Left to right: Floyd Wernimont, Jerry Haller, Doug Frost and Kevin Pazdernik.

relationships with young up and comers who could help the trio transform the business from a dream into reality. In 1976 a second store in Loveland was formed. Doug Frost, secretary and treasurer of the Loveland-based lumber retailer, was one of the company's five founding employees.

Frost and Wernimont weren't strangers, either. Doug learned the lumberyard ropes as Floyd's employee at Johnson Cashway. He and nearly a dozen of his fraternity brothers worked part-time at Johnson Cashway to help pay their way through school. Having made a good impression on his lumberyard boss, af-

ter Frost graduated college Wernimont hired him as a salesman at Collins Cashway Lumber. Frost still remembers painting the Fort Collins building for the grand opening. At twenty-three, he was ready to tackle the business world.

In line with its name, Collins Cashway Lumber emphasized the cash aspect of the business in the early years. No other lumber wholesaler or retailer in the area employed this tactic, which became the company's key competitive differentiator. While there were strong competitors in the general contractor side of the lumber business, no other Fort Collins company catered to the do-it-yourself market. Instead, local handymen were forced to take the forty-five-mile drive to Denver to buy the materials they needed for home repair or construction projects. One might say that Collins Cashway Lumber was the Home Depot of its day. The company's two-pronged marketing strategy also grabbed a small share of contractor business from local competitors.

Collins Cashway Lumber rose to success quickly. Frost still remembers Collins Cashway Lumber's first significant milestone: winning contracts with two large, local builders in 1974. By 1975 the company was a large player in Fort Collins. The store was doubling and tripling annual volumes. Cashway

Inside a Collins Cashway Lumber store.

The company then purchased land and opened its second store in Loveland in 1976 with five partners. At 20,000 square feet, it was three times the size of its original store.

Frost moved from Fort Collins to Loveland to manage the new store and admits to feeling challenged by the high goals the owners set. Though he describes his youth as one of the biggest obstacles in the business, Wernimont's wisdom balances the scales. Everyone told them the business wouldn't make any money in its first three years, but the Loveland store was profitable the first year it opened and it was onward and upward from there. As the decade came to a close, business was booming, the economy was strong and the future looked bright. Success was an attitude at Collins Cashway Lumber, even in the face of personnel issues, financial issues and economic issues.

Collins Cashway Lumber was recognized for its attitude of excellence. *Home Center* magazine presented the company with two of its nineteen annual international awards in 1979 for its Loveland store. One was an Award of Honor for the overall exterior of the building, which is constructed from the wood it sells. Collins Cashway Lumber also received an Award for Merit in the Total

Collins Cashman Lumber store in June 2001.

Home Center category. Both awards sit on Frost's desk today as a reminder that all things are possible.

Within just a few years, Collins Cashway Lumber had carved out a niche in the local lumber industry with the do-it-yourself market. Despite its growing success with that model, not a single competitor copied the strategy and Collins Cashway Lumber dominated in that market sector. Collins Cashway Lumber also took a different approach to selling to contractors. The sales team did everything they could to get their foot in the door, even if it meant splitting up large lumber packages and selling individual pieces. That strategy went against the grain of most lumberyard business philosophies of the day. It has since become a well accepted practice in megastores like Home Depot and Lowe's that put service first.

Not only business strategies, but also hard work helped Collins Cashway succeed. Frost describes it as a blue collar mindset that wasn't afraid of long day of rigorous labor. That mindset would come in handy in the 1980s when recession was the word of the day. Interest rates ran up to 18 percent. Borrowing capital became more difficult, causing construction lending to decrease. Only 111 permits were issued in Loveland in 1980. With five lumberyards competing for the business, the outcome was devastating for the local industry.

The hard times caused other serious changes. Collins Cashway Lumber closed the Fort Collins store in late 1990 after the prolonged economic downturn. For those companies that remained in the lumber industry, it was a time of rebuilding. Even large competitors with dozens of stores fell prey to the economic pressures of the times. But Collins Cashway Lumber was left standing with loyal customers, many of whom were independent builders rather than monolithic contractors. The change in business scope was a smart move, especially with the construction of the Denver International Airport (DIA).

Wernimont and Frost credit Denver Mayor Federico Peña with helping turn around the region's construction industry. Under Peña's leadership, federal officials authorized the outlay of the first $60 billion to construct DIA in 1989. In 1990 the construction industry saw another breakthrough when voters

Inside the Collins Cashman Lumber store in June 2001.

from the six-county Denver area approved a 0.1 percent sales tax to fund Coors Field, a baseball-only stadium that is home to the Colorado Rockies which cost $215 million to construct. The Denver Broncos' $364 million INVESCO Field at Mile High, widely known as Mile High Stadium, was also constructed during that period. The Colorado economy was officially bustling again and Collins Cashway benefited from the turnaround.

But more problems for the local industry would emerge when a millwright strike and political issues of cutting timber in the early 1990s. Environmental groups launched a series of lawsuits alleging that federal timber sales in the Northwest violated the Endangered Species Act by harming the northern spotted owl. Judge William Dwyer placed an injunction on federal timber sales and restricted logging on most national forests and some private timberlands in the Northwest. The injunction was lifted in 1994.

About that same time, the company started aggressively giving back to its community through donations to charities and religious outreaches, including various chapters of Campus Crusade for

Doug Frost on roof of Collins Cashway for a balloon rally in 1980.

Christ and Wing Shadow, an organization that helps wayward kids. Currently, Collins Cashway Lumber donates to about thirty local charities. Wernimont and Frost are also active in industry associations like the Home Builders Association, National Federal of Independent Businessmen and the Chamber of Commerce.

The company's independent status has allowed it to move quickly with new trends in the marketplace. One new strategy has seen the company launch into service provision. Collins Cashway Lumber started installing insulation for contractors in 1999, and it began a kitchen cabinet installation department in 2002. Next, the company opened a hardware store, called Drake

Hardware, in Fort Collins in 2004 followed by a truss shop, called Building Components, in the Platteville area in 2005. Collins Cashway Lumber has slowly come to meet more and more of its contractor customer needs.

The management of Collins Cashway Lumber looks much different today. One of the original partners passed away and the other two partners were bought out. Frost bought minority interest in the business he helped launch. Wernimont, the last original living partner, still owns majority interest. Frost, runs day-to-day sales operations while Wernimont focuses his experience on broader business operations.

Although much has changed in the past thirty years, Wernimont's and Frost's goal remains the same: to serve its niche in the marketplace, with hard work, fair prices and quality service. The owners are constantly exploring new opportunities to serve its builder customers better. The motto now is "Slow and steady growth." Through the ups and downs, Collins Cashway Lumber's owners have learned to give back to the community with humility. The owners and employees are on a mission to continue learning about the industry they serve so that they can better serve it for another thirty years and beyond.

Professional football player Sammy Winder helping with a group of children in 1992.

ALBERTA DEVELOPMENT PARTNERS

Alberta Development Partners, LLC, located in Greenwood Village, is a land development firm which acquires, develops and invests in retail and residential real estate throughout the Front Range. The relatively young company has completed an impressive 220 projects with a combined value of more than $1.5 billion. In its fourteen years of operation, the firm has grown from developing smaller projects—acquiring modest amounts of land for retail shop space—to purchasing opportunistically located land parcels and creating "mixed-use lifestyle villages." The one man who has experienced this remarkable growth first-hand is founder and principal, Donald G. Provost.

Provost has always been connected to the Denver area. He attended grade school and high school there, and then continued his education at the University of Denver. His college studies focused on finance, not on land development. However, shortly after receiving his bachelor's degree, Provost embarked upon a thriving career in real estate acquisition and land development. His strong ties in the Denver community were paramount to his success.

In 1992, two years out of college, Provost was working for his father who owned an established heavy construction firm in the Denver area. Even

Donald G. Provost, founding principal, Alberta Development Partners.

Grand amenities including outdoor sculptures, signature clock tower, interactive pop-jet fountain all make Southlands a great place to gather.

though he was gaining experience and using his skills organizing his father's real estate endeavors, Provost knew he eventually would seek an occupational path of his own. About this time, an old high school friend presented Provost with an opportunity that would not only challenge him, but would become his life's vocation. It was a chance to purchase a fourteen-acre parcel of land located to the west side of the city of Denver. The idea was to purchase the property for retail shops anchored by a major grocery store and then sell the developed property for a profit. His finance skills quickly came into play as Provost created a budget for the project, calculated investment dollars necessary and determined the breakdown costs to complete the venture. After

deciding the risk was worth it, Provost formed his company and began looking for investors.

Twelve investors, each committing a unit of $50,000, was the goal. Provost's likeability quotient and his personal commitment to the Denver community are what secured the dollars necessary. "These were men who knew me, trusted me," stated Provost, "At that point in the game, you're investing in character." He approached established businessmen who believed in the project, but who also trusted Provost to keep his promise of a return on their investments. By 1993 investment money was in hand and the project was under way.

Because this was a new endeavor, Provost had to develop pertinent skills to drive the project from beginning to end. At that time, the business had only one employee: Provost, himself. As sole owner and operator of the company, he had to acquire the various skills necessary and wear all the hats. "I had to put the land under contract, design it, entitle it, lease it and then sell it." Provost gives credit to those earlier experiences for his company's achievements. He added, "Gaining experience in all the facets of the land development business is the number one reason for my success to date."

That first project set precedence and was the beginning of many land development projects to come. He made a profit, returned money to his investors and built equity to repeat the pattern again and again. In 1995 Provost took on a partner, Peter Cudlip, who had fifteen years experience in the Denver real estate development community. The partnership's projects continued to grow in size and scope.

Now the company has twenty-seven employees, including five principles with varied expertise. David J. Goldberg is focused on entitlements, public finance, leasing and project management; Bryan C. McFarland is in charge of development; Jerry B. Richmond III is primarily responsible for residential properties; Joseph M. Bellio is responsible for all operations and property management; Provost remains focused on retail, mixed-use land development

and master planning communities. In addition to the company's staff, Alberta Development Partners employs several consultants and contributors on a project by project basis.

Alberta Development Partners' commitment to Denver's greater sense of community is evident in the design of their projects. Take the Southlands project, for example. Southeast Aurora is the fastest growing region of metro Denver. It is a sprawling expanse of subdivisions with beautifully planned, high-income homes, but has no real destination of a hometown center for the families who live there. Southlands is designed to fill that void. "You've got all these great master-planned communities, and in and of themselves they're great places to live. But they don't provide an overall town center," stated Provost.

Southlands' unique plan will give these communities a sense of place. With great amenities including gardens, mature trees, outdoor sculptures, a clock tower and large plaza, the seventy-five store, four-block Main Street is created for the whole family to enjoy. Quality retailers, restaurants, a cinema and a twice-weekly Farmer's Market will line the main promenade. While meeting

The Streets at Southglenn, a $360 million mixed-use development and retail destination, will be as varied and vital as the city and as convenient and comfortable as the suburbs with cutting-edge residential condominiums, parks and promenades.

shopping needs for the growing area communities, Southlands will also be a destination for special events, strolling or watching children play in the Plaza's interactive pop-jet fountain. Once completed, the $350 million Southlands project will be Colorado's largest completely outdoor town center destination which provides shopping in a uniquely nostalgic, main street atmosphere.

Another project that addresses the needs of its surrounding communities is The Streets at Southglenn. The long-time landmark of Southglenn Mall will soon be renovated into a "casually eclectic" outdoor center featuring bistros and sidewalk cafés, specialty shops,

The Streets at Southglenn features a gourmet grocery store, a bookstore, a movie theater, a library, bistros, fast-casual restaurant favorites and unique apparel boutiques.

movie theaters, bookstores and a gourmet food market. Like Southlands, it will be a destination spot for special occasions, festivals, concerts and other community events. Provost commented, "Our main goal is maintaining a sense of community while providing a new, improved and diverse shopping experience for area residents."

In recent years, Alberta Development Partners has completed the development of Jefferson Village, Highlands Ranch Village Center and Saddle Rock Marketplace, among others. Presently, Alberta is developing three large-scale projects, all of which are in line with the company's track record of impressive design and attention to community enhancement. These are Northlands, Cornerstar and Wheatlands. As the projects continue to grow in scope and scale, so does the desire to accommodate the growing needs of Denver's greater community. "We have the one-time opportunity to make a difference in the communities that are home to our projects," passionately stated Provost, "If we have successful tenants, happy residents and the places are enjoyed for generations, we've done that."

ALVARADO CONSTRUCTION, INC.

The only daughter in the Martínez family, Linda Alvarado was raised with five brothers by parents who had high expectations for their children. Valuing education and leadership, Linda's parents instilled in their children a love for learning, as well as a competitive spirit. Perhaps that explains why, for more than twenty-five years, this Hispanic entrepreneur has been president and CEO of Alvarado Construction, a Denver-based commercial general contractor and development firm. The road that led her there was anything but ordinary, and the direction she has taken has been very much her own. In her non-traditional career path, there were few role models to be found.

In the late 1500s Linda's maternal family settled in the geographic area that is now southern Colorado and northern New Mexico. Her grandfather, Benedícto Sandoval, was a Presbyterian minister who traveled on horseback as a

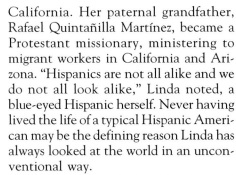

Linda Alvarado, president and CEO of Alvarado Construction.

circuit rider to small Hispanic religious gatherings in rural areas of the New Mexico Territory. Descended from a mixed heritage—that includes Spaniards, Sephardic Jews and later Native Americans in the New World—the family was one of many who were forced to leave Spain during the Inquisition. Linda's father's family received a small Spanish land grant to settle in Baja

California. Her paternal grandfather, Rafael Quintañilla Martínez, became a Protestant missionary, ministering to migrant workers in California and Arizona. "Hispanics are not all alike and we do not all look alike," Linda noted, a blue-eyed Hispanic herself. Never having lived the life of a typical Hispanic American may be the defining reason Linda has always looked at the world in an unconventional way.

Linda's parents, Luther Martínez and Lily Sandoval, were resourceful people with limited material possessions but were "rich in values." Her upbringing was focused on church, school and athletics. At age ten Linda started a small yardwork business with her brother, trimming bushes and raking leaves. "My brother and I picked tons of weeds. This childhood experience was not about an investment in a bank account," she said, "but rather an investment in our character. Even at a young age, my parents taught us that we have an obligation to actively help others. They insisted we do things to demonstrate that commitment. The money we earned was given to other needy children, not us. . . . Now, in my business, I recognize that it is not just about Alvarado Construction or me; it is also about what we do in the communities where we conduct business."

Linda became a sports enthusiast early on. "When you live with five brothers, you don't have tea parties; you build forts, wrestle, play baseball, joke, and learn to roll with the punches." Rather than feeling like a victim, Linda's life with her brothers taught her how to be a team player. "Boys typically learn early about teamwork and strategies for winning in sports and I was included in this experience." Linda also learned that she didn't have to easily give up. "There would be another game, another season, and another opportunity to pursue down the road."

"My parents possessed a strong sense of ethics and values. They helped their children see the best in themselves and in others." While Linda is bilingual, there is no trace of her heritage when she speaks. During her New Mexico education, children were not allowed to

The Denver West Side Courthouse located at Speer and Colfax. This structure was built in 1921 with several courtrooms, the office of the Denver District Attorney and the Sheriff's headquarters. After historic restoration the building was designated as a national landmark. It was rededicated in 2001 as the Bernard A. Valdez Hispanic Heritage Center.

The Colorado Convention Center spans nine city blocks, 2.2 million square feet of space and a roof that encompasses 13.7 acres. The 5,000 seat auditorium features luxurious seating and a grand stage that resembles the famous Colorado Red Rocks Amphitheater. The ballroom is designed with no columns inside the entire 584,000 square-foot space.

speak Spanish in school. "Our goal was to speak English without an accent—to become part of the mainstream." Still, she and her brothers learned Spanish "Dichos" (wise sayings) from their parents that filled them with a sense of pride in their family and Hispanic heritage. "¡Empieza pequeño, pero piensa grande!" her parents would say, "Start small, but think big!"

To earn money while attending college, Linda took a job with a landscape contractor because she enjoyed working outdoors. "When I first started working in the construction field," she recalled, "it certainly was not a career that women considered." Linda later worked for a development company and construction management firm. Although she did not have an engineering or architectural background, she worked with a project engineer as a contract administrator, keeping track of submittals, requests for design and construction information and tracking subcontractor and supplier applications for payment. Defying convention, Linda began to dream

about pursuing a career in this non-traditional field.

While Linda knew she could not yet construct buildings, she was captivated by the process of how a conceptual

Denver Botanic Garden Boettcher Memorial Conservatory. Originally built in 1966, the structure was demolished on the interior and rebuilt with extensive restoration of the large atrium frame and glass. This conservatory is one of only a handful of displays in the United States to re-create the ambiance of a tropical forest.

project becomes a detailed design which in turn becomes a permanent structure. "I was enamored with the creative elements that go into the design of a building and the construction management components from ground-breaking to the excitement of the ribbon-cutting," she said. She took classes in estimating, surveying and, most importantly, computerized scheduling—at a time when few had the skills to use the new technology she was learning. Starting small, but thinking big, she began as a small concrete subcontractor and eventually grew her firm to a multi-million dollar commercial general contractor and development company.

In 1975 Linda moved from California to Denver with her husband Robert, who had an opportunity in Colorado to pursue his dream of owning a restaurant business. Construction cranes were on almost every downtown block of Denver. The economy was booming. "Colorado was growing rapidly. This enabled the company to make inroads into the expanding construction market during this period of high demand." Alvarado Construction's first Colorado commercial project was as a concrete subcontractor, placing all the horizontal concrete for the building and site work of the Colorado Judicial Heritage Center, headquarters of the Colorado Historical Society located on 12th and Broadway. Next came an opportunity at the new downtown bus terminal located at 16th and Champa. The company placed all the new terminal's concrete flatwork including the parking structure, bus ramps, curbs, entrances and walkways.

Linda refocused the company's growth strategy from a subcontractor to becoming a commercial general contractor. The first structures Alvarado Construction built were eighty bus passenger shelters for the Denver Regional Transportation District. The company constructed only twenty at a time—the number the firm could afford to finance. "Even though these were small twelve-feet by six-feet structures, it gave me an adrenaline rush," Linda exclaimed. At the same time, she knew she needed cash in order to grow the business, develop a stronger track record and demonstrate the ability to work on larger projects. After being rejected by several banks, her parents mortgaged their small

Invesco Field at Mile High.

The Burnsley All Suite Hotel.

home and loaned her $2,500 that opened the door to expand the firm.

Alvarado Construction took on larger commercial construction contracts and development of office and retail projects. Linda found new ways to market the firm's capabilities, while continuing to fight myths and stereotypes about the ability of women to succeed in the construction field. Having encountered many challenges over the years on a construction site, she recalls, "It is not easy for anyone to be the 'first' or 'only.' You can resent this or you can find ways to stay focused on changing that mindset and achieving your personal and professional goals." Aside from being a busy commercial general contractor, Linda has been opening doors for other women in business and defying myths about what women are capable of achieving.

Today Alvarado Construction is a multi-state commercial general contractor, providing construction management, program management development and design/build services. With offices in Colorado, California, Arizona and New Mexico, the firm's track record includes numerous multi-million dollar commercial, transportation, manufacturing, communications, retail and technology projects. Alvarado has constructed convention centers, high-rise office buildings, airports, research laboratories, multi-family

residential housing, schools, hotels, restaurants, aquariums and correctional facilities.

Alvarado Construction is focused on delivering the highest quality construction services on schedule and within budget. The company believes a team approach is critical to the successful completion of all projects. Construction requires the development of positive working partnerships. Alvarado's first commitment is to the owner, but there is also a need to form positive partnerships among the architects, engineers, subcontractors, suppliers, government agencies and many other interfaces. Alvarado Construction frequently assumes a primary role in the planning process by identifying potential design, construction or budgetary issues at the earliest possible stage, providing alternative solutions and being instrumental in the efficient implementation of those solutions. "This input in the planning and decision-making phase can have greater impact on achieving the desired schedule and project cost savings than any management activity initiated at a later date in the project," said Linda.

Over the span of twenty-five years some of the firm's Colorado projects include the 1988 Phase I of the Colorado Convention Center and the 2004 Phase II Colorado Convention Center Expansion that together comprises 2.2 million square feet of space; INVESCO Field at Mile High; Colorado's Ocean Journey Aquarium; the 37-story, 1,100 room Convention Center Hyatt Regency;

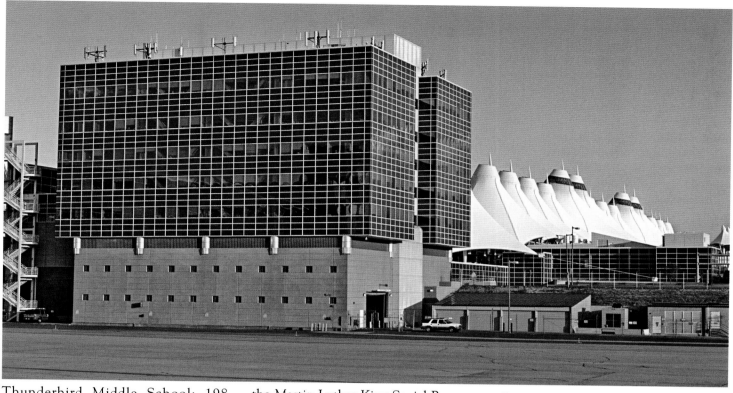

Denver International Airport office building.

Thunderbird Middle School; 198 Inverness Drive office high rise; the $25 million commissary at Buckley Air National Guard Base in Aurora; the Denver International Airport office building; Peterson Field Wing Command Headquarters; the Trinidad Correctional Facility; and the historic restoration of the 1921 landmark Denver West Side Courthouse on Speer Boulevard and Colfax Avenue, re-dedicated in 2001 as the Bernard Valdez Hispanic Heritage Center.

Alvarado Construction has been recognized with many industry accolades including the Gold Hard Hat Award, Awards for Excellence by the Concrete Institute of America, the Downtown Denver Partnership Award of Honor for construction of the Colorado Convention Center and several awards from the Army Corps of Engineers for safe work practices. Civic and community involvement has also been a hallmark of Alvarado Construction and its C.E.O. The company has received several honors including the Denver Opportunity Head Start Leadership Award, The Denver American Jewish Committee Humanitarian Award and the Martin Luther King Social Responsibility Award.

Just as she would not have predicted owning a construction company, Linda states, "I never imagined I would have the opportunity to be an owner of a major league sports team!" In 1991 she became a member of the ownership group vying to win a new National League Baseball franchise. In June 1993 the new franchise was awarded to launch the Colorado Rockies Baseball Club. Alvarado became the first Hispanic—male or female—owner of a professional sports team and the first female to achieve ownership as an entrepreneur, rather than inheritance.

With the growth of Alvarado Construction, a host of other opportunities have come Linda's way. She serves as a member of the board of directors of Qwest Communications, 3M, Pepsi Bottling Group, Lennox International and Pitney Bowes.

Linda has also been pivotal in the growth of Colorado. She was founding trustee of the Rose Community Foundation, and has participated in many civic and community boards including Mile High United Way, Boy Scouts of America Denver Council, The Children's Museum and The Denver Partnership. Linda is a founding member of the Denver Hispanic Chamber of Commerce and first female chair of its board. Recognized by *Colorado Biz Magazine* as one of Colorado's twenty-five most powerful people, she is an inductee in both the Colorado Woman's Hall of Fame and National Women's Hall of Fame, Honorary Dean of the Real Estate and Construction Management school at the Burns School of the University of Denver and recipient of the Horatio Alger Award.

Alvarado Construction has grown not just in revenues, but has also expanded the type of large projects undertaken across the U.S. and Latin America. "Colorado has afforded me the opportunity to travel a road not typically taken by women in pursuit of the American dream," Linda Alvarado points out, "It is important to me as the principal of Alvarado Construction that I not just break through a number of barriers for the company, but also open doors for others to achieve their dreams."

267

ASPHALT PAVING CO.

Asphalt Paving Co. serves the Denver metropolitan area, the entire state of Colorado and adjacent states. The company has contributed to the creation of local highways, area subdivisions, the roads and runways at Denver International Airport and even the top of Vail Pass. They not only perform aggregate mining and processing, but also act as a full-service construction company and materials supplier, with three asphalt plants to their name. By using new equipment with cutting-edge technology, Asphalt Paving Co. is able to do everything from site preparation and laying asphalt to recycling. In addition, their full mining and crushing operation allows them to make any size rock—chips to boulders—and to meet any gradation or specification that a job may require by screening and combining aggregates.

Asphalt Paving Co. is dedicated to maintaining the highest standard of quality workmanship in the industry. According to their mission, they strive to "successfully serve the complete needs of all of our customers by providing excellence in service satisfaction, construction and superior aggregate resources." The vision to "provide excellence" is as strong as it was over

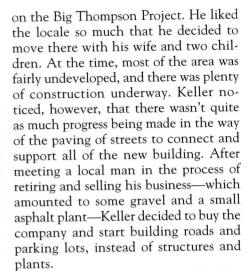

John H. Keller, founder of Ashpalt Paving Co.

fifty years ago, thanks in no small part to the fact that Asphalt Paving Co. has remained a family-owned business for three generations.

In the late 1940s John H. Keller, a light industrial builder, came to Colorado in order to work as a subcontractor for the U.S. Army Corps of Engineers

on the Big Thompson Project. He liked the locale so much that he decided to move there with his wife and two children. At the time, most of the area was fairly undeveloped, and there was plenty of construction underway. Keller noticed, however, that there wasn't quite as much progress being made in the way of the paving of streets to connect and support all of the new building. After meeting a local man in the process of retiring and selling his business—which amounted to some gravel and a small asphalt plant—Keller decided to buy the company and start building roads and parking lots, instead of structures and plants.

John H. Keller wanted to build a company that could provide jobs and contribute positively to the community and so, in 1955, he started Asphalt Paving Co. Initially, the company consisted of about fifteen employees and took on small, local paving jobs. John's son, Bill, was involved in the business from 1958 on. In 1968, though, Bill struck out on his own, creating Keller Construction Co., which focused on structures, curbs, gutters and sidewalks. Bill's new company operated independently of Asphalt Paving Co., but often subcontracted to his father's company, as needed.

John H. Keller retired in 1970, at which point Bill purchased some of the company's assets as well as the company name, taking the helm of the new Asphalt Paving Co. Bill quickly found that working with the company's original equipment, Asphalt simply couldn't keep up with the demand that its good reputation had created. By 1974 Bill had invested heavily in the business, buying a larger asphalt plant, upgrading the company's existing equipment and rebuilding their fleet of trucks. Throughout the next three decades, the company flourished under Bill's vision and strong leadership.

As the area developed and the times changed, the design requirements of roads and parking lots became much more detailed and technically-advanced. Bill responded by upgrading the company's technology in order to stay one step ahead of increasingly stringent standards of quality. He realized, how-

Entrance to Ashpalt Paving Co.'s Ralston Quarry.

ever, that technology was only one piece of the puzzle. The business depended on its resources. Thus, after a hard work putting together leases, getting permits and obtaining local and state government approval, in 1975 Bill successfully started a new aggregate quarry located just north of Golden, on Highway 93. The site was rich in high quality aggregate deposit and had great reserves.

The addition of the quarry truly put Asphalt Paving Co. on the map. The company quickly became known for producing the best aggregate in the area, mining a wide variety of high-quality aggregates for both aesthetic and functional uses—from roadways to parking lots to fireplace linings. Unparalleled in durability and strength, their materials enhanced concrete and extend the wear of surfaces and seal coats. With the boost in business that their new quarry provided, in 1979 the company added its first portable asphalt plant.

It was not long before Asphalt Paving began to be awarded difficult jobs that, in turn, ranked it at the top of its industry. In 1984 Asphalt Paving Co. performed the first night-specified

A portable asphalt plant, set up and working, at Denver International Airport in 2002.

Left to right: Jeff Keller, John M. Keller and Bill Keller in 1986.

paving job in the Denver area and subsequently received widespread recognition for its quality workmanship. The company's high level of attention to quality lead to additional projects and, in 1987 Aspahlt Paving Co. traded in its stationary plant for a larger, higher production facility.

Bill Keller's vision and perpetual investment in the company allowed Asphalt Paving Co. to grow and remain competitive. He continued to change

with the times, adding equipment that had the capability to do specific blends of aggregate, converting the plants to a computer-controlled system and even installing computerized mechanisms in the lay-down equipment. That technology was a critical part of the company's active role in several major projects during the construction of Denver International Airport between 1991 and 1994. After the completion of the airport, Asphalt Paving Co. worked on an impressive thirty-two-mile stretch of the E-470 Tollway between 1996 and 1998. It was no small feat: to this day, it is the largest asphalt paving job to be performed under a single contract in the state of Colorado.

At that point, Bill decided to hand over the reins to his oldest son Jeff, who had started with the company in high school, sweeping floors in the shop. Jeff had worked for Asphalt Paving Co. every summer through high school and college, becoming full-time in 1982, when he graduated from Colorado State University with a degree in Construction Management. Although Bill stayed on with the company until 2004, Jeff became president in 1998. (Bill's second son, John, was also a president— at Alpine Rock Co., an affiliate of Asphalt Paving Co.)

As a relatively small, three-generation business, the company has always thought of its staff as family, too. Depending on its workload and seasonal demands, Asphalt Paving Co. employs nearly 250 people—some of whom go back with the company as far as 1969. "One of the keys to our success is our people, who are very loyal to us," says Jeff Keller, remembering a controller who started with Jeff's grandfather in 1965 and retired in 2005. "They're the ones who make it happen, year after year after year." One of the company's current paver operators started working for them at the age of seventeen—and is now fifty-three. There are numerous other truck drivers, equipment operators and maintenance workers who have track records that are just as impressive. Keller notes, "We have a bunch of great people who have worked—and continue to work—with the company. That's what makes it great."

Asphalt Paving Co. feels the same way about its community as well—a long-time sponsor of local youth athletic leagues and a supporter of the National

The paving operation of E-470 in 1998.

Western Stock Show and Junior Livestock Auction. In addition, Asphalt actively participates in annual fundraisers and provides various financial and labor donations to the community. In fact, all of the company's employees feel strongly about giving rather than receiving. In December of 2005 the staff decided to donate the amount of money normally spent on employee and customer gifts to a church in New Orleans that had been devastated by Hurricane Katrina.

A large part of contributing positively to the community is Asphalt Paving Co.'s concern for the environment. In order to protect the area's ecosystem, portable asphalt plants are used for on-site processing whenever possible. Proud of being part of the solution toward cleaner air, production facilities utilize state-of-the-art pollution control equipment. Asphalt conserves natural resources by reclaiming aggregate mining areas and recycling existing pavements into new work.

By using the best materials and maintaining the highest standards of workmanship, the company has become a nationally recognized quality award winner. Compared to its competitors,

Asphalt Paving Co. is considered a relatively small company. Even so, it has an impressive reputation and has garnered widespread recognition. Asphalt Paving Co. has received numerous local and national awards for its dedication to quality work, workforce development, compliance to stringent safety standards, integrity and innovation. It has also been recognized for its commitment to assisting in the achievements of other subcontractors to complete joint projects with the "Excellence in Partnering Award."

In 2003 the company was awarded the Colorado Asphalt Pavement Association's (CAPA) prestigious, annual, statewide Quality Award for the overall smoothness of its I-70 Chief Hosa to Floyd Hill overlay project—a job that also won the "Best in Colorado Stone Mastic Asphalt (SMA) Surfacing Award." CAPA also recognized Asphalt Paving Co.'s work along Highway 58, which held up for an impressive twenty-three years without needing repair.

Asphalt Paving Co. also won the National Asphalt Paving Association's (NAPA) "Quality in Construction Awards" in 2004 for its Hot Mix As-

Part of Asphalt Paving Co.'s fleet getting ready to deliver materials from the Ralston Quarry.

phalt (SMA) overlay of Highway 74. The project was a pilot of the Colorado Department of Transportation (DOT), designed to test the effectiveness of a surfacing material in prolonging road life. DOT found that HMA was a durable and cost-effective alternative to mill and fill projects.

In fact, Asphalt Paving Co.'s ability to supply superior materials has been one of the keys to their growth. First and foremost, the company's private quarry provides a superior level of aggregate. In addition, over the years, they have developed the necessary experience to work with experimental materials, handle innovative jobs and take on projects that have stringent specifications. In recent years the company has served as the paving contractor for the new international runway at Denver International Airport as well as for almost eight and a half miles of paving on Central City Parkway, which connects I-70's Hidden Valley Interchange (Exit 243) directly to Central City. But, as

Jeff Keller points out, materials aren't the only thing that matters. "We've got our people and the materials. We willingly give our customers the level of service that they deserve, and they appreciate us for it. We get a lot of return business because of it."

Part of that commitment is Asphalt Paving Co.'s dedication to completing projects on time. The company is stringent about its construction management. By finishing early, clients save on construction costs, and are often able to open sooner, potentially increasing their revenues. Jeff Keller states the company is often able to stay ahead of the curve because they are "a smaller, locally owned company, with fewer people and less overhead, which gives us an advantage over a lot of our competition."

Even so, these days, there is a lot more competition than there used to be. Although the company's clients are comprised of a blend of public and private business owners, nearly all of the jobs involve a bidding process. The amount of available work has been a driving force, and has made the importance of safety paramount. Meeting an

increasing number of regulatory requirements adds another challenge. "You have to change the culture of the people who work for you and understand the expectations of your customers." Jeff Keller notes. "We can't just make little rocks out of big rocks anymore. We have to meet and exceed our customers' expectations, so that when we have the opportunity to serve them in the future, they're glad we're their paving contractor or material supplier."

Still, Jeff Keller considers the company lucky. "We've been very fortunate that we have the people, the resources and the equipment to compete on small jobs as well as extremely large ones." That kind of diversity keeps the company thriving year after year. What he is truly thankful for, though, is the determination and dedication of his father, Bill, without whom, Asphalt Paving Co. would not be what it is today. Though the technologies and specifications may change, Jeff Keller sees Asphalt Paving Co. continuing on in the future much the same way it was shaped by his father: with an ongoing dedication to quality, safety and productivity.

AURARIA HIGHER EDUCATION CENTER

Located in downtown Denver, the Auraria Higher Education Center (AHEC) has proven to be an innovative and successful model for urban-centered higher education everywhere. AHEC consists of three educational institutions—including the Community College of Denver (CCD); Metropolitan State College of Denver (MSCD); and the University of Colorado at Denver and Health Science Center Downtown Denver Campus (UCDHSC) —each with a distinctly separate set of goals.

The birth of AHEC began in 1968, when the Colorado Commission for Higher Education first explored the idea of merging together the physical campuses of the three state educational institutions. In 1969 voters approved a $6 million bond issue for the construction of the campus. When the AHEC board and the three institutions reached agreement on nonacademic programs being administered centrally, ground was officially broken on October 4, 1973.

The title given to the new campus, "Auraria," actually dates back to the name of an old town on which the campus resides. Derived from the Latin word for "gold," the town of Auraria was

Three institutions of higher learning share the largest campus in Colorado.

established back in 1858, when gold was first discovered along the banks of Cherry Creek. The discovery was made by miner William Greene Russell and his brothers, who panned out seven ounces of gold. News of the discovery traveled far and wide and soon a town of 35,000 fortune seekers was formed. The Russell brothers named the town after their

hometown in Georgia. As the years went on, Auraria faded into the shadow of a much bigger hamlet rising just across the creek—the burgeoning city of Denver.

According to the Auraria campus Web site, "the Mission of the Auraria Higher Education Center is to support the Community College of Denver, Metropolitan State College of Denver and the University of Colorado at Denver and Health Sciences Center Downtown Denver Campus and to facilitate the achievement of their goals and objectives." The Auraria Higher Education Center is governed by an eleven-member board of directors. Nine directors are voting members and two are non-voting members. The voting members are (1) the chancellor of the University of Colorado at Denver and Health Sciences Center Downtown Denver Campus, (2) the president of Metropolitan State College of Denver, (3) the president of the Community College of Denver, (4) an appointee from the State Board for Community Colleges and Occupational Education, (5) an appointee from the Metropolitan State College Board of Trustees, (6) an appointee from the

Auraria, hosting 38,000 students, lies just across Cherry Creek from downtown Denver.

Regents of the University of Colorado, and (7-9) three lay members, appointed by the governor, who are residents of the Denver metropolitan area. The two non-voting members are a student representative and a faculty member, who are elected by their respective organizations.

More than 38,000 students attend the Auraria campus (the largest campus in the state) with 95 percent of the students coming from the seven-county metropolitan Denver area. About one in every five of the college students in Colorado take courses on the Auraria campus. Students range in age from sixteen to eighty years old, with the average age being twenty-eight. Eighty percent of all students attending Auraria hold either a full-time or part-time job. Approximately 8,800 (27 percent) of the students attending classes on the campus are ethnic minorities, including students of Hispanic, African American and Asian origin. These students represent 22 percent of the ethnic minority students attending college in Colorado.

The Community College of Denver, a two-year school, offers associate's

Dean Wolf, executive vice president for Administration.

degrees and certification programs, general and remedial education and GED preparation courses. CCD also provides career training in computer science, paralegal studies, nursing and graphic arts. The college also guarantees job competency to employers and assures the automatic transfer of core classes to all four-year Colorado educational institutions. Nearly half of all students graduating from CCD go on to obtain their bachelor's degree, with many continuing their studies at one of the other two institutions on the Auraria campus.

Metropolitan State College of Denver is a comprehensive institution offering baccalaureate degrees in arts and sciences and business, as well as a myriad of other

professional courses and programs. MSCD's mission is to provide high quality education, which prepares students for successful careers, postgraduate education and lifelong learning. Courses and programs include accounting, teacher certification, nursing, entrepreneurship and professional pilot training.

The University of Colorado at Denver and Health Science Center downtown Denver campus is one of four campuses in the CU system. UCDHSC offers both undergraduate and graduate programs, with an emphasis on doctoral studies at the Auraria campus. Many of these programs are nationally accredited and world-renowned. UCDHSC in particular serves the business, cultural, government and industrial fields through a variety of partnerships involving both students and faculty. UCDHSC is also the home of the only graduate-level programs offered in architecture and planning and public affairs in the state of Colorado. It is also known for its MBA program.

Some of the courses that are offered to students from all three institutions include: physics, meteorology, education, journalism, Chicano studies, African American studies, women's studies, arts management, pre-medical, criminal justice, business and nursing.

Not surprisingly, one of Auraria's greatness achievements is its success in effectively utilizing the space available on the campus. Approximately 21 percent of the 7,0000 combined courses taught on the campus are open to students from all three institutions. Many of the programs and services available on campus are also shared between the three schools including: campus recreation; assessment and testing; gay, lesbian and transsexual services; grants in technology and faculty training; an art studio, a photo lab, a sculpture lab; and a computer access center. In addition, to meet the growing educational demand in the seven-county area, Auraria is putting together a feasibility study to assess how and where they might build more physical classroom space.

"Right now we are sitting here with a shortage of an estimated 600,000 square feet of instructional space," states Dean Wolf, executive vice president for

Rocky Mountain background.

Administration of AHEC, who was appointed to his position in May 1996. "We're looking at how we might leverage assets on the campus, and are working toward new joint partnerships and the possibility of creating some public-private ventures for some of the space on the campus. We are bringing a team onboard to look at that and come up with some creative ideas and approaches. We are trying to find a way to minimize or not pass those costs on to the students."

Currently classrooms are operating at just over 92 percent capacity. Classes begin at 7:00 in the morning and run until 10:30 at night, totaling ten class periods in a day. The result is that, during certain hours of the day, there are no vacant classrooms to be found anywhere on the campus. A typical class size today is forty to forty-five students. Wolf estimates that Auraria could easily spend $200 million on additional facilities to meet the growing educational demand.

As Auraria has grown in both physical and student size, its reputation as a model for urban education has also stretched beyond the Rocky Mountain region. Currently the city of Buffalo, New York is working actively to create a similar concept together that might include Erie Community College, the State University of New York at Buffalo and Buffalo State College.

"We are visited probably three to four times a year by groups from other areas of the U.S. and as well as from around the world to see how this system works,"

Auraria early learning center.

states Wolf. "Their biggest question is, 'How do we put this together?' The most significant statement I can make is that the Auraria concept is really no different than any other organization complex—it will succeed if those people who are in leadership positions of the various elements want it to succeed. They will make it work."

Wolf meets every two weeks with the three institutional college presidents to discuss, among other things, operational issues and challenges. Wolf and the three college leaders enjoy a very good working relationship. "If one of the institutions wants to offer some new and unique course work, we discuss how this will impact the sister institutions and how will it impact space, which is my concern," explains Wolf. "A lot of these requirements are the responsibility of campus operations."

The current campus, which was formally dedicated on January 21, 1976, was constructed from a master plan. Many of Auraria's buildings have won architectural or design awards. Amid the newer buildings on the 126-acre campus is the Ninth Street Historic Park, a group of century-old restored residences, with some structures dating back to 1872. The fourteen

buildings, used today as administrative offices for the campus, represent one of the most complete views into what a nineteenth century neighborhood looked like in middle-class America. Six of the structures were built before 1876, the year in which Colorado gained statehood. One building represents the commerce of the time, the old Groussman Store, the area's local grocer.

Listed on the National Register of Historic Places, the 1976 restoration of the historic area was led by Historic Denver, Inc., a private, nonprofit corporation. A total of $750,000 was spent on the exterior restoration and interior refurbishment of the Victorian structures, with landscaping along a "village green" design costing an additional $200,000.

The park also includes a number of historic places of worship. The 1879 construction of St. Elizabeth's, the area's first Catholic Church, was built in response to the growing population of German immigrants. St. Elizabeth's is the only structure on campus that is not owned by AHEC. As Irish immigrants began to arrive in Denver, a new Catholic Church, St. Leo's, was established in 1890. A third church in the area, St. Cajetan's, began saying mass in 1926 to

Ninth Street historic park.

accommodate the growing Spanish-speaking population. St. Cajetan's was one of the first churches in America to offer services in Spanish. The Emmanuel Chapel, the oldest standing church structure in Denver built in 1876, has gone through many phases. Originally an Episcopal church, the property was sold in 1903 to a group of Jewish immigrants, who formed the Shearith Israel Congregation or Remnant of Israel. In 1973 the building became the Emmanuel Gallery, which today offers exhibits by Auraria students as well as traveling exhibitions.

Another structure of note is the former residence of the late Israeli Prime Minister, Golda Meir, which was moved onto the campus in 1986 from a nearby neighborhood. The Golda Meir Museum House is the only known U.S. residence of the leader and is a tribute to her undying commitment to peace, freedom and truth. Golda was the daughter of Russian Jewish immigrants who settled in Milwaukee to escape religious persecution. She eventually spent a year in Denver, living with her sister, Shayna and brother-in-law, Sam Korngold. "It is believed that it was during her time in Denver that Golda Meir formed her philosophical base that carried her

through the rest of her life," Wolf adds. The structure now houses the Golda Meir Center for Political Leadership program operated by MSCD's Department of Political Science.

Dean Wolf administers the Auraria campus with a $44 million dollar budget. In addition to the 38,000 students attending class each day and evening, there are approximately 4,000 full and part-time faculty, classified and professional staff. In addition, the campus employs some 350 students during the year in all departments of campus operations,

Fitness class.

including accounting, facilities management, facilities master planning, media center, telecommunications, early learning center, bookstore, mail and delivery services, campus police and parking. Each day the campus provides parking for some 12,000 educational commuters.

"The Auraria campus is a real asset in downtown Denver," states Dean Wolf. "The 38,000 students and 4,000 plus faculty and staff are a significant economic generator to downtown Denver. The campus provides many employment and educational opportunities for the members of the Denver area workforce. The labor pool that is generated from this campus has proved to be quite a boon to the Denver business community." Wolf also stresses that Auraria's value to the well being, enrichment and prosperity of the community is immeasurable. "The Auraria campus serves many students who are first generation graduates. It is a place of opportunity where many can achieve their educational goals and improve their lives. This, in turn, creates a stronger workforce and enriches the community for everyone."

You can learn more about Auraria Higher Education Center by visiting their Web site at http://www.ahec.edu.

Ninth Street Fair.

AURORA MENTAL HEALTH CENTER

Since 1975 the Aurora Mental Health Center has been providing quality, affordable mental health services to the citizens of Aurora. With an emphasis on programs geared to children and families, the center is committed to improving the mental health and overall well-being of people from all walks of life and of all ages. After more than thirty years of service, the center has enhanced the lives of thousands of Aurora residents.

Prior to 1975 it wasn't as easy for the citizens of Aurora to find mental health care as there weren't any facilities in or near the city. Residents seeking care were forced to travel several hours by car and all day by bus to reach the nearest center. Because of this inconvenience, many people who could have benefited from mental health services chose not to seek them.

This problem did not go unnoticed by Ellin Mrachek, an active citizen who served on the Aurora school board. One day, in the late 1960s, Mrachek saw a young girl playing on the street on a school day. Concerned, Mrachek asked the girl why she wasn't in school. The child explained that her mother couldn't take her to school be-

Ellin Mrachek, founder of Aurora Mental Health Center.

cause she was traveling to the mental health center.

The chance encounter resonated with Mrachek, who wanted to help Aurora residents in need of mental health services. The community activist quickly went into action. Initially, Mrachek's volunteer efforts included driving patients to and from clinics outside of Aurora. But soon she realized that the city needed its own clinic and was determined to make that dream a reality. She began phoning other community activists she knew from church and from

school to organize a committee to try to create a mental health clinic in Aurora. Approximately thirty people showed up at her first meeting.

In 1968 Mrachek and these other concerned citizens presented a proposal which was rejected. The setback didn't discourage Mrachek, who continued fighting for the cause. By the mid-1970s the community activist finally earned the support necessary to establish a mental health care facility.

With $35,000 from the Aurora City Council and additional funding from county, state and federal grants, the Aurora Mental Health Center was established on July 1, 1975. With just eight staff members, the center offered three services—outpatient, emergency and consultation—and helped 175 patients that year. In 1976 the center received a federal grant, which allowed it to expand to twelve services, including emergency response, assessment, outpatient, consultation, education, geriatrics, children services, partial care, hospitalization, after-care and alcohol and drug programs.

Once the center had gotten under way, Mrachek took on more of an advisory role, allowing their executive director and board of directors to take the lead. However, she stepped into a more active role once again in 1978 following the untimely death of the first executive director and also lead the search for a successor.

Normally, searches for executive directors at nonprofit organizations can take several months, even years. But Mrachek was a decisive woman and set a time limit of twelve weeks for her search. Living up to her word, she found a new executive director within the designated time frame. The man she selected, Randy Stith, Ph.D., remains executive director of the center to this day.

When Stith first joined the center, the staff numbered about forty-five and the annual budget was slightly less than $2 million. At the time, the center had only three locations: a clinic housed in a school building, another clinic located in a law office building, and one 10,000-square-foot building of its own.

Bemis Hall, Dayton Street and East 16th Avenue, in North Aurora, was the site of many early meetings of a citizens committee to establish a mental health center in Aurora.

Under Stith's leadership, the center has flourished with expanded facilities and additional staff members, including highly trained psychiatrists, psychologists, nurses, social workers and master's-level counselors. Stith has also overseen the creation of numerous award-winning programs that focus on children and families.

In 1980 the center opened the Adolescent Day Resource Center, a pilot project and the first of its kind in the state of Colorado. The project met with success and has since been renamed Hampden Academy. Today, Hampden Academy is a therapeutic school offering a structured educational and therapeutic program for teens. In addition, it provides intensive outpatient services to teens and caregivers.

The 1980s saw additional expansion of the centers programs and services geared to children and teens. In 1986 the Child Day Treatment Program was launched and was eventually renamed Metro Children's Center. The Therapeutic Preschool, now called the Early Childhood and Family Center, debuted in 1989.

Randy Stith, Ph.D., executive director, Aurora Mental Health Center.

A meeting of the 1983 executive committee of the board of directors. Left to right: John Fluke, Kate Tauer, Larry Davila, Pat Weddig, Bill Davis and Anne Robinson.

As the center expanded, it began receiving recognition for its unique and innovative programs and services. In 1982 the center's Older Adults Program earned Program of the Year accolades from the Colorado Mental Health Association. A few years later in 1985 the Community Living Program, a service for persons with chronic mental illness, was named Program of the Year in the United States by the National Council of Community Health Centers.

The 1990s was a decade of tremendous growth for the center, including the addition of a number of residential facilities. In keeping with its commitment to children and families, the center created a groundbreaking program designed specifically for adolescents with dual disabilities. Perhaps the biggest reason behind the center's rapid growth in the 1990s is the fact that it won the state contract to provide mental health services to Medicaid-eligible clients. This alone nearly doubled the size and scope of the center. The decade culminated with the center being named the top community mental health center in Colorado.

For its twenty-fifth anniversary in 2000, the center hosted a large celebration with the community. And it had much to celebrate. The center, which helped 175 clients in its first year of service, was now serving 5,600 clients with its growing range of programs and services.

The growth hasn't stopped and now, after more than thirty years of service to the Aurora community, the Aurora Mental Health Center is reaching more than 7,200 clients. In addition, the center boasts 300 staff members, twelve facilities within Aurora, and a $19 million annual budget. The center is currently the only mental health center in all of Colorado to have an elementary school, a high school, a dual disability program and an early childhood program.

Throughout the years, the center's programs have continued to expand in order to provide the best and most up-to-date care possible. For Stith and the rest of the staff, it is important to reach people in need of help as early as possible and to include a person's family or support system in the treatment. The center's leaders believe that positive relationships and strong family bonds are important in achieving and maintaining good mental health. For these reasons, programs focusing on children and their families have remained at the core of the center's services.

The Early Childhood and Family Center addresses emotional and behavioral difficulties at the earliest age. This program offers a comprehensive range of services for children under the age of six. Therapists involved in this program have special training and education, qualifying them to work with infants, toddlers and preschoolers.

Among other programs for children and their families is the Childhood Trauma Treatment, designed to address the needs of children suffering from traumatic stress disorders. The Metro Children's Center is a day treatment program where children from first to eighth grade receive individual, group and family therapy. In addition, these children attend school in a special education setting with very small classes. The center also provides therapy at many of Aurora's public schools as part of the Child & Family Outpatient Services.

For adolescents, there is Hampden Academy, a high school that provides therapy within a structured educational environment. Teens and their

Randy Stith and Bill Davis break ground for the Southeast Counseling Center.

Randy Stith, right, accepts a federal grant for the Colorado Adolescent Research Study from Congressman Dan Schaefer and State Representative Peggy Kerns.

families, along with foster families, can also receive intensive therapy services through Adolescent Intensive Services.

One of the most unique programs geared to children and adolescents at the center is the Intercept Center. This center, which opened in 1996, provides services to young people with dual disabilities, including a developmental disability and a mental illness. Often unable to attend public schools because of their behavior, these children are welcome to attend the day treatment program at the Intercept Center.

In addition to its emphasis on children and families, the Aurora Mental Health Center provides programs for adults as well as the community at large. A Community Wellness Program offers ongoing wellness groups and classes to any members of the community hoping to improve their relationships and well-being. For adults, the center provides a comprehensive range of services, including counseling, education and outreach services. A Dual Disability Program for adults, similar to the one for children and teens, offers treatment for those with a developmental disability and a mental illness.

The center also currently boasts seven residential facilities for adults. These home-like settings are designed for adults who are homeless, undergoing an emotional crisis or a major life transition, or suffering from chronic mental illness. The goal of the residential facilities is to encourage independent living for these adults.

In an effort to provide the most comprehensive services to serve the community of Aurora, the center teams up with other mental health centers throughout the metropolitan Denver area. If a person's needs fall outside the scope of the center's programs and services, a referral can be made to a neighboring center. With this cooperative arrangement, the center is able to meet the varied mental health needs of the residents of Aurora.

As the Aurora Mental Health Center has expanded and evolved in its efforts to meet the needs of the community, its overall mission has remained unchanged. While most mental health centers focus on adults, the Aurora Mental Health Center keeps its focus squarely on children and families. What has evolved throughout the decades is the definition of "family." Traditionally, the notion of family centers on parents and their children. But in today's fast-paced, fast-changing world, that definition encompasses the relationships in a person's support group.

Because of its focus on families, the center also makes a tremendous effort to keep families together as they work through trying times and emotional difficulties. The center's therapists focus on ways to support a family through a crisis or ongoing

The Center's Viewpoint Plaza Counseling Center on East Bethany Drive.

Aurora Mental Health Center has supported and been involved in the Aurora community for decades.

challenge so the family can remain intact.

This focus on family and children can be traced back to Mrachek, whose initial concern for a little girl out of school was the impetus to establish the center. Her interest in helping young people has been carried on by Stith, who was originally trained as a child and family psychologist. From the time he took over as executive director back in 1978, he has encouraged treatment geared to children and families. His contributions to the center's growth and impact on the community of Aurora haven't gone unnoticed. In 2003 Stith was awarded the Lifetime Achievement Award for Excellence from the National Council of Behavioral Healthcare.

His efforts, and those of everyone involved with the Aurora Mental Health Center, have resulted in a tremendous community resource for the people of Aurora. Since its debut more than thirty years ago, the center has helped thousands of Aurora residents with its wide array of treatment programs. And in keeping with Mrachek's initial vision for the center, it will continue to provide access to affordable, convenient and effective care for decades to come.

BEST CARE, INC. HEALTHCARE AT HOME

When Anna Zarlengo, founder and president of Best Care Inc., opened the doors to her in-home health provider company in Englewood, the second-generation Coloradoan may have been on the forefront of a broad healthcare trend, but she had a focused mission.

Bringing medical services into the home had become a burgeoning industry in the early 1990s. But Zarlengo, who had worked for other private home-health companies, wanted to do things a little differently. She understood the commitment it would take to operate a profitable business; however, as a registered nurse for thirty-five years, Zarlengo knew that her success would lie in bringing dignity, compassion and quality to her clients, on an individual basis. "I had been working in homecare for several years and I felt like, with my clinical experience, I could do it better. I believed in homecare—the necessity and the goodness of healthcare going into the home from the wealthy to the indigent," said Zarlengo.

The enterprising RN teamed up with a business partner and formed Best Care, Inc. in October 1995 in a small office located on South Downing Street. What Zarlengo and her co-owner lacked in capital, they made up for in ambition. Although they started out with just $30,000, they had an abundance of

In 2001 Best Care moved into a new 6,800-square-foot facility.

Best Care adopts two families every Christmas, providing food, clothing, toys and gifts.

desire. "Our mission was true and our desire for quality was pure. I never had the slightest idea in my head that it wouldn't work. And once you get that ball rolling, you can't stop it."

In the beginning, Best Care had eight people in the field, including Zarlengo, and two administrative employees. The founding staff members functioned as a team to make the company a success, and Zarlengo felt the importance of being a responsible leader. She decided that the culture of Best Care would include caring for her team members as people, not just employees. "I needed to be the boss that I always wanted to have. When you hire people, you need to take care of them to the best of your ability." Like any successful company president, Zarlengo also knew that contented staff members meant satisfied customers. Even beyond a focus on the bottom line, Zarlengo's dedication to her team helped keep the mission of Best Care on track through some tough times.

Best Care's first year of operation was difficult, due in no small part to a bureaucratic delay. The agency was assured it would have its Medicare certification by December 1995, but before that much-needed paperwork could be processed, the federal government went on furlough. Because of the hold up, Best

Care's employees worked for several months without pay. Understandably, some were forced to find employment elsewhere—including Zarlengo's business partner, who left the company after a year and a half. "It was six months by the time we got our certification. We started getting paid by Medicare by the end of June 1996. As we started to make money, I was able to pay everybody back for what they did for me, even if they were no longer an employee."

The business found its footing and began a steady but controlled growth. Best Care purposefully kept its patient count low, to ensure the goal of quality service was maintained. Since Zarlengo had never owned her own business before, she focused on learning operations, in preparation for continued growth. Still, even three years after opening, Best Care found itself in an extremely competitive climate. "We were sitting on pins and needles, not really sure we were going to make it," Zarlengo said.

Best Care reacted quickly, hiring the agency's third marketing professional. With increased outreach to consumers and second-party referral sources—such as physicians and hospital discharge planners—Best Care saw a rapid turnaround as a result of its strategic moves. Since finding a good balance of sales

Best Care has an open house in their new offices.

Anna Zarlengo, R.N. is the president and CEO of Best Care, Inc.

drive and personality in the marketing communications department, Best Care has experienced a growth trend of 25 to 30 percent annually, while continuing to deliver superior quality.

The Best Care, Inc. of today is a company that has evolved as an industry leader—despite some serious challenges, and because of a deliberate approach to growth. With more than 120 employees, the firm is now based out of its own 8,200-square-foot office building on Englewood's Ithaca Avenue. Admissions exceed 1,800 per year, and Best Care's healthcare employees provide up to 30,000 visits to patients each year.

People are living longer and, due to insurance issues, hospital stays are becoming increasingly shorter. To bridge that gap, Best Care's carefully selected staff specializes in geriatrics, wound-care management, telemonitoring, disease management for diabetes, CVA, joint replacement, pulmonary disease, anodyne therapy and PT/INR.

From elderly and terminally ill patients to those recovering from surgery or an injury, Best Care's Health Care at Home allows for medical healing and also offers the emotional benefits of dignity and independence. After an on-site evaluation, a client's specific needs are met with a wide array of services that range from complicated nurse management to medication assistance, exercise therapy to photo light therapy, and from cardiac telemonitoring to light housekeeping and meal preparation. Clients are able to avoid hospitalization and, instead, be treated in the comfort of a familiar environment—their own home.

Keeping close tabs on the industry, and what affects it, has been paramount to the company's success. "You have to be on top of what's happening and what's new," Zarlengo noted. "[The business of healthcare] is an ever-changing product, delivered to society based on the continual changes in insurance coverage and governmental process." Still, it is Best Care's focus on its clients' needs that has really been the key to its growth. The company has a heart and soul based in exceptional service.

There is little doubt that the company's growth will continue as Best Care stays focused on looking forward. But, when Anna Zarlengo stops to look back, she knows her journey is a big part of her success. "I think I was always pointed in the right direction. I believed in something better, in quality care. Today Best Care, Inc. has a solid reputation in the community that what we do is appropriate and our care is truly the best."

CANINO'S SAUSAGE COMPANY

As the nineteenth century was coming to a close, Italian immigrants began settling in Denver, Colorado. Lena Pagliano was one of those immigrants. A nine-month-old Pagliano came to America with her family in 1897. She grew up in a quarter of downtown Denver known as Little Italy and married her sweetheart, Joseph J. Canino, in 1917. Little did they know they would soon launch a sausage empire that would outlive them both.

It all began when Joseph's mother, Assunta, gave the young couple the treasured old-world sausage recipe that she brought to America from Calabria, Italy. Pagliano perfected the sausage for her husband and children. Eight years later, in 1925, Joseph and Lena launched Navajo Meat Market on the corner of 34th and Navajo, as they pursued the American dream. The site is now a Denver landmark.

The Navajo Meat Market was truly a 50-50 partnership between husband and wife. While Joseph cut the pork, Lena measured, mixed, kneaded and stuffed 500 pounds of meat every day. Lena added the aromatic spices that transformed the salty pork into succulent sausage. Passersby could often hear Lena singing her favorite Italian ballads as she prepared the hand-made sausage while her five children watched and learned.

Lena's strong voice would come in handy as she set out to peddle her edible product on the streets of Denver's Little Italy. With sausages wrapped around her arms and neck, Lena called out to the community that her delectable sausages were officially for sale. They didn't last long. Navajo Meat Market's sausages quickly became a staple of the neighborhood diet and would soon garner attention from spicy meat lovers in other cities.

Lena became just as famous as the sausages she shaped and sold. Even during the most difficult economic times, she refused to let people go hungry. Lena is legendary in Little Italy for

Lena Canino inside the Navajo Meat market at 3514 Navajo Street.

helping families survive the depression and for feeding homeless beggars and rail transients during World War II. Lena's strong relationships with meat suppliers ensured Navajo Meat Market a steady supply of pork despite stringent government restrictions.

Joseph and Lena built the successful family business under the Navajo Meat Market name for thirty years. In 1957 the couple changed the name of its local sausage-making kingdom to honor the Canino heritage. The new name was Canino's Italian Sausage Company. About that time, the food service firm began to expand its line of sausages to include new flavors.

After a full life, Joseph passed away in 1969. Lena sold the business to her grandson, Joe Tarantino, a year later. Joe and his dear friend Mike Payne set out to take Canino's to the next level. Though not a member of the Canino family line, Payne had an undeniable passion for the sausage business, along with a vision for what the Canino's Sausage Company could be. The duo developed new sausage recipes over a period of eighteen years as they strove to make Canino's a household name from coast to coast.

Payne began investing in the business bit by bit. Joe finally sold him the re-

Charlie Casey, plant manager, and other employees traying breakfast sausages.

maining shares of the company in 1988. Payne immediately changed the name to Canino's Sausage Company, Inc. to embrace the company's many successful non-Italian sausage varieties. The future looked bright for Canino's under Payne's watch. Tragically, however, he died just a year after buying the company. Payne left full interest in Canino's Sausage Company to his widow, Diana.

Diana knew very little about running a business—especially a sausage business. As a longtime homemaker, Diana knew she needed to take on the challenge to provide for her family and preserve the vision of her husband. She went to work right after her husband's funeral and hasn't looked back since. She admits she was scared, but says she found a new purpose and quickly became a sausage company operational pro. Indeed, Diana dedicated herself to learning everything there is to know about management, meat prices and marketing. Today, she remains president of the company.

While Canino's is certainly operating in a new era—and in a different building one mile north of the original location—Diana is loyal to the Canino family. She still maintains the corporate name and uses the same recipe carried from the toe of Italy's boot by its founders' family. You can still smell

Canino's emplyees in front of the company's building.

fennel, paprika, chili carribe and garlic escaping from the spice room just like in Lena's days.

While Italian sausage remains the hallmark of Canino's Sausage Company, it also offers Bratwurst, Polish, German, Chorizo and other custom blend varieties of sausage. That's not the only change that came under Diana's watch. She also switched to leaner meats to reduce the fat content, lowered the salt content and refuses to use preservatives or artificial colors. The company continues to formulate new recipes.

Of course, Diana does not measure, mix, knead, stuff and sell the sausage the

way Lena did. Instead, she has seventeen employees that help make 8,500 pounds of sausage daily at Canino's Denver plant. The employees don't stuff the sausage by hand, either. Canino's now depends on state-of-the-art, stainless steel, Vemag stuffers. The production process now involves ice, which improves shelf life and enhances color, texture and flavor.

Canino's sausage is no longer sold exclusively on street corners, but in grocery stores across the country. In fact, Canino's Sausage can be found at Sam's Club, Costco, Safeway, Albertson's and King Soopers. Local restaurants, cart vendors and caterers throughout Colorado also serve Canino's sausages.

Colorado Biz Magazine ranked Canino's Sausage Company forty-seventh on its list of top 100 women-owned Colorado Businesses. Diana is proud to be the owner of a company that has touched so many lives on its journey through Denver history. Canino's has emerged as a stable and trusted brand on grocers' shelves and family dinner tables.

The way Diana sees it, it's important to maintain the connection to the past traditions. She stays in touch with the Canino family members, who tell her that Joe and Lena would also be proud of what she has done with the eighty-year-old company.

A package of sausage being labeled.

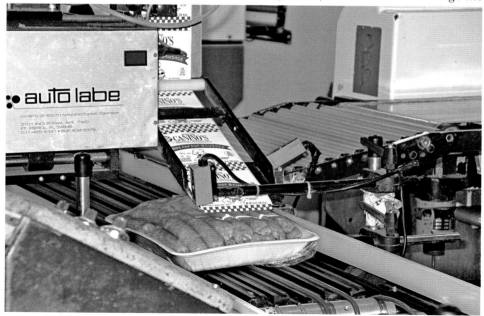

CATHOLIC CHARITIES AND COMMUNITY SERVICES

From the dark days of the Great Depression to the chaos of lives turned upside down in the aftermath of Hurricane Katrina, Catholic Charities and Community Services has been providing help and creating hope for those in need for nearly eighty years. Headquartered in Denver, the organization is now the largest nonprofit provider of social and human services in the Rocky Mountain region.

Catholic Charities offers nearly two dozen services that touch families and individuals in every stage and walk of life. The knowledgeable and compassionate staff served one-quarter of a million people in Denver and northern Colorado in 2005. They provide assistance by finding housing for the homeless, helping the poor, enriching the lives of seniors and youth, arranging child care, placing hurting children in the homes of loving foster and adoptive families, counseling the troubled, furnishing safe housing for seasonal and migrant workers and brightening the lives of the developmentally disabled.

"Our primary focus is to work with people so they can become self-sufficient," says Catholic Charities President and CEO James Mauck. "We have a history of great staff and great volunteers and a board that is willing to take reasonable risks in an effort to better serve people."

The organization was founded in 1927 by Bishop J. Henry Tihen, who saw the value in placing all the organized charitable activities in the diocese under one umbrella, to be called Catholic Charities.

The USO poses outside Catholic Charities' offices, during World War II.

The Mission in Fort Collins houses the homeless and northern offices.

He appointed Father John R. Mulroy to head the new organization, but only on a half-time basis. Mulroy spent the other half of his time serving as a pastor in two parishes. A two-room office was opened in downtown Denver.

In the early years, the shoestring operation concentrated on providing medical clinics, assistance centers, and resettlement houses for poor immigrant families. Turning to child welfare, Catholic Charities opened an adoption agency, operated a summer camp for underprivileged children and oversaw Denver's several Catholic orphanages.

In 1934 Catholic Charities moved into a larger home, the George C. Schleier mansion, which had been given to the diocese. It was good timing, as the Depression saw hundreds of unemployed persons and hungry families walk in the front door for food.

Following World War II, the organization began what would be a decades-long dedication to resettling refugees, becoming one of the top twenty largest refugee settlement agencies in the country. Beginning with Eastern European refugees and continuing with Hungarians, Cubans, and the Indo-Chinese, Catholic Charities participated in every refugee resettlement since World War II. Closely associated with the resettlement efforts was the opening of an immigration counseling program that certified immigrants for legal entry into the United States. It was the first immigrant counseling program connected to a social service agency in the country. Immigrants from over 100 nations have now come to Catholic Charities for help with immigration.

In the 1970s two studies—one local and one national—had a dramatic impact on Catholic Charities. The Whelen report called for a total reorganization of the agency to better meet the needs of people. The Cadre study urged Catholic Charities offices across the country to reexamine their mission, direction and services.

The result was a decentralization of services and a focus on involving

The historic Margery Reed Child Care Center is one of four such centers run by Catholic Charities.

parishioners in a network of advocates for the poor and marginalized. Satellite emergency assistance offices were opened in the city's low-income neighborhoods, and youth and senior centers were established. Professional counseling service offices were moved to parishes.

Under Catholic Charities' leadership, core groups of parishioners rallied to shape public policy and to change laws that made it difficult for the poor to better their lives. At the same time, the agency organized families on public assistance to work together to change the regulatory and governmental barriers that hindered them from leaving welfare. Partnerships were formed with institutions and agencies in the community to jointly address significant social justice issues.

Workers package food in the SHARE Colorado warehouse.

Another reorganization occurred when Colorado Springs became a diocese, eliminating the need for the Denver agency to provide services in the area. Catholic Community Services Northern in Weld and Larimer counties, which operated two homeless shelters, emergency assistance and an outreach to migrant workers, then became part of the Denver organization. Samaritan House, a downtown shelter built by the Archdiocese of Denver, also came under the auspices of Catholic Charities and Community Services, Inc.

Acutely attuned to the needs of the community, the newly expanded organization began a period of overall program growth. It opened a center for the developmentally disabled; created Hospice of Peace; formed the Farm Labor Housing Corporation; established transitional housing for homeless individuals and families ready to leave the shelters; initiated SHARE Colorado, a food and community service program; and opened four child care centers and five Head Start centers.

Today, the organization continues to provide a broad spectrum of services throughout northern Colorado. Since 2000 the agency has built two migrant and seasonal housing complexes, opened a shelter for single mothers and children, purchased a Western Slope office, and expanded social ser-

vices into 1,100 housing units for low-income families as well as the elderly and disabled.

In June 2005 the seventy-unit Mount Loretto Family Housing complex and community center opened. Renovations are currently underway to convert a thirty-four-unit complex into a facility that will house primarily military veterans. Land has also been purchased in the Greeley area for a new Guadalupe Shelter and for the development of forty residential units that will provide independent living opportunities for formerly homeless and disabled adults.

The growing need for affordable housing became even more critical in the fall of 2005, when Hurricane Katrina and Rita evacuees from Louisiana sought to

A family appreciates Samaritan House, a shelter for the homeless.

rebuild their lives in Colorado. Catholic Charities, in cooperation with state and federal government agencies, located and leased temporary housing for more than 1,000 displaced families. They also worked with other church ministries to provide outreach and follow-up services to every Hurricanes Katrina family in Colorado.

With an annual operating budget of approximately $25 million, Catholic Charities uses only 8.7 percent of the budget for administration and delivery of services and 3.7 percent for fundraising. In 2002 *Worth Magazine* ranked Catholic Charities as one of the top nonprofit organizations in the U.S. to make the biggest impact with their donations.

CREDO PETROLEUM CORPORATION

James T. "Jim" Huffman, president and co-founder of CREDO Petroleum, says he was born to be in the oil business. The West Texas native grew up working in the oil fields around Odessa and Midland, Texas, including working in his family's oil field service business. In fact, as soon as he was old enough to hold a broom, Jim's father had him sweeping the floors of the family business. In the generation before his father, both his maternal and paternal grandfathers worked in the oil business. One worked in the West Texas oil camps for Phillips Petroleum and the other was an Oklahoma wildcatter responsible for a number of discoveries in and around Oklahoma City. Today, Jim's brother, Dan, runs the family oil field service business which is one of the leading manufacturers of special purpose heat exchangers for refineries; and Jim runs CREDO.

In addition to his entrepreneurial drive, Huffman wanted to find a place to call home and raise his family. Colorado with its majestic, mountainous terrain, good weather, and dynamic growth offered Huffman and his employees a healthy business environment as well as desirable quality of life.

In 1978 during the oil boom that occurred in the aftermath of the second Arab oil embargo, Jim Huffman, at age thirty, was ready to leave his job as an oil and gas industry specialist with Price

The company's patented Calliope Gas Recovery System brings new life to oil gas wells. The J. C. Carroll well had been dead for over six years when Calliope brought it back to life. The Carroll well has produced almost a billion cubic of gas using Calliope.

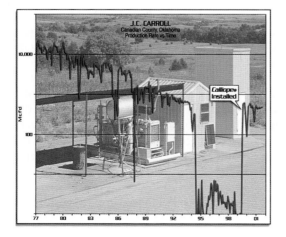

Ken DeFehr, engineering manager (top left), Jeff Carlson, operations manager (top right), Torie Vandeven, exploration manager (bottom left), Jim Huffman, president (bottom right).

Waterhouse and go out on his own. Jim put up his $20,000 savings. He then turned to private investors, mostly family and friends, to put up the rest of the capital, and with $200,000 in assets, CREDO began its existence as an oil and gas E&P company. Jim quickly decided to take advantage of the boom times to take CREDO public in 1979 on the NASDAQ for $1,500,000 at $0.10 per share. CREDO was one of the first of a large group of small companies that went public during those boom times.

Today CREDO Petroleum is a thriving independent oil and gas exploration and production company based in Denver, Colorado. By staying debt free and profitable, CREDO has flourished through the boom and bust cycles of the last twenty-five years when many other companies, large and small, went under.

Weathering the "boom and bust" cycles of the oil industry with style, Huffman and his staff have built a record of excellence acknowledged both inside and outside of the oil and gas industry and over a wide range of performance metrics. Under Huffman's leadership, CREDO has become what *Forbes* magazine calls one of the "200 Best Small

Companies" (2001 and 2004) and CREDO is the only oil and gas company to rank as one of *Fortune Small Business* magazine's 100 "Fastest Growing Small Companies" for each of the last four years. In addition to the distinctions from *Forbes* and *Fortune Small Business*, CREDO has consistently been ranked by John S. Herold as one of the top performers in the oil and gas industry based on its low finding costs and high profitability per unit of production.

CREDO's business focuses on two core projects: exploring for natural gas and application of its patented Calliope Gas Recovery System. CREDO's success comes from a rigorous application of science that is focused on creating value where none previously existed. Above all, that requires talented and innovative teams of professionals. "We have an extraordinary group of scientists and support staff working for CREDO," Huffman said.

For fourteen years, Ken DeFehr, engineering manager, has been responsible for leading CREDO's scientific team. In addition to his reservoir engineering duties, Ken is responsible for keeping a keen eye on the big picture and assuring that all relevant information has been properly considered before major commitments are made. "Metaphorically speaking, Ken drills our dry holes on paper," Huffman said. "That makes them a lot less expensive."

In the oil business, it is often said that 10 percent of the geologists find most of the oil. For eight years at CREDO, Torie Vandeven, exploration manager, has proven time and again to be one of those 10 percent. In northwest Oklahoma, she developed a new geologic concept which proved correct and has resulted in discovery of many billions of cubic feet of gas. She recently completed two of the best wells drilled in Harper County in recent years.

In the oil business they also say "no lease, no grease," meaning that if the landman doesn't get the leases, the best geology goes undrilled. That's where CREDO's land department has played a pivotal role by amassing over 60,000 gross acres in the Anadarko Basin. Jeff Carlson, operating manager, oversees drilling wells and the day-to-day field operations that occur in the aftermath. Working as a team in tandem with Jim's leadership, this core group of scientists is responsible for CREDO's success.

The company's patented Calliope Gas Recovery System is another example of creating value where none existed before. Named for the instrument it resembles, Calliope is a new generation of fluid lift technology designed for deep gas wells. Calliope brings many old wells back to productive life by pulling down reservoir pressure far below levels achievable with other fluid lift technologies. In fact, Calliope has recovered billions of cubic feet of stranded gas from wells that other companies believed were completely tapped-out. CREDO's operations manager at the time, Don Reitz, invented Calliope, and he continues to be a Calliope partner and to oversee many of the company's Calliope installations and field operations. "Calliope worked perfectly on the very first well and has never been in the red," Huffman said. "Don is a mechanical genius, and Calliope is an

Cheyenne Rig number fifteen drilling for CREDO in the Northern Anadarko Basin of Oklahoma, a core drilling area for the company.

amazing technology due to the elegance in its simplicity."

One of Huffman's proudest business accomplishments is that CREDO has been a steady and reliable work place for twenty-five years, with employees counting over twenty years with the company. Huffman says that, unlike most companies in the oil and gas industry, CREDO has never needed to reorganize or layoff employees. CREDO takes care of its employees by providing a good and reliable workplace. In return the employees have made CREDO one of the top performing companies in the oil and gas industry.

As individuals, this group of scientists with Huffman at the helm have achieved, but not sought, public recognition. "In the community, we are a low-profile, service oriented group of people," Huffman said. He is very proud of CREDO's commitment to corporate responsibility and that CREDO has given enormously to the community for over twenty-five years by being a growing, steady and reliable employer with a reputation for honesty and integrity in its business practices.

CREDO continues to perform with excellence year in and year out. Over the past five years, production has increased 25 percent annually, reserves have increased 17 percent annually, revenue has increased 46 percent annually, and net income has increased 58 percent annually. Perhaps the success of CREDO is attributed to innovative science and a focus on fundamentals. Perhaps it is because Jim has looked after the interests of his employees and shareholders like one would look after the needs of a family. Essentially, like Calliope, which creates new value where none previously existed, Huffman has brought a team of people together who, through their dedication and scientific innovation, have created a company with an extraordinary record of excellence.

The Calliope Gas Management Platform is connected between a standard oilfield compressor and the wellhead. The platform controls the direction and timing of gas flows between the compressor and the chambers in the wellbore.

DENVER ART MUSEUM

With an impressive collection of more than 60,000 works of art, the Denver Art Museum is regarded as one of the premier institutions of its kind in the western United States. From its Native American crafts to Asian and African artwork to modern sculpture, the museum houses a diverse range of masterpieces from around the world and offers engaging programs that appeal to both novices and art connoisseurs.

The museum's rich history dates back to 1893, when a group of Denver painters and sculptors established an arts association to exhibit the work of local artisans. The Artists' Club, which was renamed the Denver Art Museum thirty years later, received strong support from municipal and cultural leaders, and one year later, became the official art agency of the city.

In the early years, temporary exhibits and educational programs were the major focus of the organization as it struggled to settle into a permanent location. The museum's collections were moved around from the public library to the historic Chappell House, and later to the City and County Building. It was

"Ponti Finished"—Covered in more than 1 million gray glass tiles, the North Building anchors the southern end of Denver's Civic Center Park alongside the Denver Central Library. Photo courtesy of the Denver Art Museum.

The Denver Art Museum has one of the most comprehensive and important collections of American Indian art in the world and was the first museum to collect these objects for their artistic value. Dream Shields / No da khi/ho ma ni yoo, 2003, by Gordon Yellowman and William O'Connor. Photograph; 35-1/2 x 38-1/2 inches. Collection of the Denver Art Museum.

not until the 1940s that the museum was finally able to gather all of its collections under one roof at a site south of Civic Center Park. The Denver Art Museum moved into its current home on 14th Avenue Parkway in 1971.

The two-towered, seven-story building is a work of art in itself. Designed by Gio Ponti of Italy in cooperation with James Sudler Associates of Denver, this castle-like structure has twenty-six sides covered with more than one million shimmering gray tiles specially made by Dow Corning.

While the exterior of the museum evokes a sense of grandeur, the inside is warm and welcoming with a friendly staff and an eye-pleasing arrangement of collections. In fact, enhancing the art experience for its visitors is a primary objective of the museum's directors. Through tours, classes, and various interactive programs, people of all ages and backgrounds discover that a trip to the Denver Art Museum is both educational and fun.

The Denver Art Museum's display of Pre-Columbian artwork is termed a "study gallery" because most of the department's 7,000 objects are on view and available for study by researchers and scholars from around the world. Photo courtesy of the Denver Art Museum.

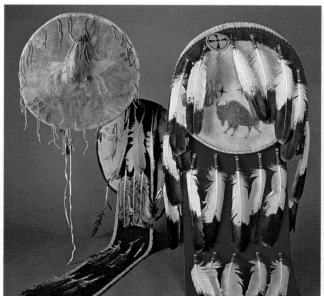

This rendering shows the completed Denver Art Museum complex, including the 146,000-square-foot expansion designed by Daniel Libeskind on the left, and the North Building completed in 1971. Image by Miller Hare.

"From young school children to senior adults, from first time visitors to art aficionados, we want to reach out to everyone in the community," said Andrea Fulton, Public Relations Director for the museum. "Some people feel they have to be educated about art before they can come to a museum. Our philosophy is the exact opposite. We say come even if you don't know a lot about art, and you will learn while you are here."

Eight curatorial departments make up the museum's permanent collection: Architecture, Design, and Graphics; Asian; Modern and Contemporary; Native Arts; Pre-Columbian and Spanish Colonial; American and European Painting and Sculpture; the Institute of Western American Art; and the Department of Textile Art.

The Native Arts department houses what is considered one of the largest and finest collections of North American Indian handicrafts in the world. The 19,000 objects make up the principal group of works in the museum, and represent all aspects of American Indian life and culture. From utilitarian objects to fine art, the ever-growing collection includes Navajo weavings, Pueblo pottery, Eskimo ivory carvings, Plains beadwork, contemporary art, and much more.

The Pre-Columbian and Spanish Colonial collection is also highly regarded and contains over 8,000 objects from the ancient cultures of Central, South, and Mesoamerica. Paintings, sculpture, furniture, and an exceptional collection of silver and decorative objects from the Spanish Colonial Period are all on view.

Inside the museum gift shop, a variety of art-related merchandise, books, and jewelry are available for purchase. A restaurant and a café are also located on the site.

With so much to see and do, a number of innovative programs can make a tour of the museum engaging for families and school groups. The "Just for Fun" Family Center offers hands-on fun at seven play stations, where children can learn about various world cultures through interactive games and activities. Especially popular with children are the "Eye Spy Games," in which kids of all ages can play detective, and the "Family Backpacks" program, which leads children on a voyage of discovery as they use the items in their backpack to learn about objects of art on display in the galleries. The backpacks are free and can be checked-out near the Kids Corner on the first floor.

Like other cultural institutions in Denver, the museum has reaped the benefits of being part of a community that places a high value on the arts. In 1988

Activities for children and families can be found throughout the Denver Art Museum, including the "Eye Spy" game seen here, which lets visitors search the galleries matching the clues on the games to paintings or objects in the museum.
Dream of Arcadia by Thomas Cole, collection of the Denver Art Museum.

the Scientific and Cultural Facilities District (SCFD) was created by voters in the seven-county metropolitan area to help support over 300 nonprofit organizations involved in the arts, sciences, and cultural activities. A penny sales tax on every $10 spent goes directly to the SCFD and is distributed to qualifying organizations in proportionate amounts. Funding for approximately one-third of the operating budget for the Denver Art Museum is derived from this program.

Exciting times are ahead as the museum undergoes a major expansion that will nearly double the size of the existing facility. The 146,000-square-foot Frederic C. Hamilton Building will span the length of a city block and is slated to open in the fall of 2006. It will be situated south of the North Building, with the two structures connected by a second-story bridge.

Clad in titanium with a series of angular forms likened to origami, the Hamilton Building's striking architecture will become a celebrated landmark on the Denver cityscape. It was designed by renowned architect Daniel Libeskind, designer of the Jewish Museum Berlin and other current projects in Canada, Germany and Japan. Once completed, the Hamilton Building will house three changing exhibition spaces, feature new galleries, and offer magnificent mountain vistas from its third floor sculpture garden.

The Denver Art Museum is an architectural gem in the heart of downtown Denver, offering two of the most unique structures in the state. With collections spanning the world and activities for all ages and levels of art experience, it is a worthwhile destination for all types of culture-seeking visitors.

THE DENVER BRONCOS

How do you measure the soul of a city? In Denver, for the better part of five decades, it's been by the Broncos. From the first nationally televised Monday night game in 1973, through postseason games that include back-to-back World Championships and four other Super Bowl appearances, the Broncos arguably have provided the Mile High City's primary identity on a national level.

Not only did the Broncos win consecutive Super Bowls in 1997 and 1998, but they established all-time pro football records for most wins in two seasons (thirty-three, now second to New England's thirty-four), most playoff wins in two seasons (seven), and most wins ever in three seasons (forty-six, from 1996–98), all records that will be very difficult to challenge.

The attachment of Denver's fans to their football team stands out as unusual even in a city that has as strong an affinity for all its teams as does Denver—whether judged by thirty-seven consecutive seasons of sellouts (with the last non-sellout being in 1969), by the highest local television ratings of any NFL city during that time frame, or just by the impact of Bronco wins and losses on Denver's collective Monday morning psyche. Denver's love affair for and support of the Broncos certainly helped

John Elway celebrating following his first Super Bowl win (XXXII).

spawn the eventual arrival and fan loyalty to the other professional teams here, but the term "Broncomania" was born out of necessity as a response to the genuine fanaticism surrounding pro football in the Mile High City.

The nation's first truly regional sports franchise, the Broncos were the first major league team to call Denver home,

beginning play as a charter member of the new American Football League, with its first season being 1960. The next year the team was sold to Rocky Mountain Empire Sports, a syndicate headed by Gerald and Allan Phipps. In 1965 the Phipps family became sole owner. Ownership of the Denver Broncos passed to others in 1981 and, three years later, to current owner Pat Bowlen.

Bowlen, a businessman with interests in oil, gas and real estate and an avid amateur athlete in his own right, is actively involved in the team's day-to-day operations as president and chief executive officer. Widely praised throughout the National Football League as a dynamic chief executive, during his ownership Bowlen has stamped the Broncos as a dominant team in the AFC West, posting more division titles (eight), conference Championship Game appearances (seven), and Super Bowl appearances (five) than any other division club from 1984–2005. The Broncos have posted the best home record in football from 1974 to the present, with 199 regular and postseason wins (and an overall winning percentage of .750), and that home win total represents the highest number posted by any team, in any thirty-one-year period of play, in professional or college football history.

Given the dynamics of modern stadium design and the financial imperatives of professional sports in the 1990s, the need for a new football venue was obvious, and the Broncos moved into their new stadium INVESCO Field at Mile High, for the 2001 season. The new stadium assures a prominent place for Denver as professional football moves into the twenty-first century.

The Denver Broncos played their first winning season in 1973, which was also the year of their first nationally televised game. Since then, the team has served as the lightning rod in helping to focus the attention of the nation and the world on Denver. In fact, when it snows in Denver during a televised game, calls making reservations at the state's ski resorts go up 50 percent. Televised Bronco games from Denver offer the

2005 Denver Broncos Walter Payton Man of the Year nominees.

A beautiful gameday at INVESCO Field at Mile High.

entire nation incredible vistas of the Rocky Mountains. An internationally popular team, the Denver Broncos have represented the NFL, the city and the region in seven American Bowl games since 1987—playing in London, Berlin, Barcelona, Mexico City, Sydney and twice in Tokyo.

In 1977, a defense composed of five Pro Bowl Players known collectively as the "Orange Crush" propelled the Denver Broncos to the team's first Super Bowl game, validating the faith of the team's loyal and long-suffering fans. In 1983 legendary quarterback John Elway joined the team, the first player taken in that year's NFL draft.

During the 1980s, the Denver Broncos became the only American Football Conference club to appear in three Super Bowls—1986, 1987 and 1989. In all, the Broncos have won ten AFC Western Division titles, made eight AFC Championship Game appearances, and played in Super Bowls XII, XXI,

XXII, XXXII and XXXIII. The team also earned wild-card playoff berths in 1979, 1983, 1993 and 1997.

The Denver Broncos organization operates from the Paul D. Bowlen Memorial Broncos Centre, located on 13.5 acres of land in the Dove Valley Business Park in southern Arapahoe County. This state-of-the-art office and training facility opened in 1990.

The organization employs several people full and part time, including stadium employees. The team is regularly listed as one of Denver's top 50 private companies.

Furthermore, Broncos' president Pat Bowlen has demonstrated an amazing

Safety John Lynch meets with Boys and Girls Club participants for a Lynch's Leaders meeting.

commitment to the Colorado community off the field over the years as well, serving as honorary chairman of the Colorado Special Olympics and leading efforts to benefit St. Joseph's Hospital and the Rose Medical Center. He is also president of the Denver Broncos Charities Board, which was established in 1993. His wife, Annabel, has been equally committed to serving the community and has been an integral part of the advancement of the Beacon Center, a residential treatment center for adolescent youth.

In 2001, the Denver Broncos Football Club, together with Broncos Charities, charted a new philanthropic course, honing in on a proactive and succinct mission: to improve the lives of Coloradans through youth, health and hunger relief initiatives. In keeping with this mission to support Colorado's youth, The Denver Broncos Boys and Girls Club was established in August of 2003 with a $1.2 million investment over a minimum of five years. Additionally, the Broncos have committed to integrating community programs and player visits into the Club's operations, truly building upon a legacy of investment that transcends mere monetary contribution. Currently, the Club's membership has

swelled to capacity with over 1,500 members and an average nightly attendance of over 200 children.

The Denver Broncos are also committed to promoting and supporting youth football throughout Colorado. In this spirit, the Broncos established a Youth Football Task Force in 2004, comprised of major youth leagues in the metro Denver area, to address common issues such as expansion, new programming and cross league play. NFL programs such as Junior Player Development and High School Player Development continue to

2005 Denver Broncos Holiday party benefiting the Denver Rescue mission.

grow as they have proven their effectiveness in successfully engaging youth players. In addition, the Denver Broncos host an annual Broncos Bowl—a preseason celebration of youth football held at INVESCO Field at Mile High that kicks off the youth seasons with an invitation to teams across the state to scrimmage one another in a Broncos game day atmosphere.

Kids Caravan, established in 2004, is a traveling "road show," bringing the excitement of the Denver Broncos to the young fan base in the Colorado community. Broncos players, cheerleaders, and miles are just a few of the perks of the Caravan. Gatorade Junior Training Camps along with organized activities and inflatables round-out an action-packed day for children ages six to twelve living in areas such as Pueblo, Colorado Springs, Fort Collins, Greeley and metro Denver. Participants are recruited from local Boys and Girls Clubs chapters and through marketing and sponsor giveaways.

The Broncos are also committed to literacy in supporting the youth portion of their mission. In so doing, Broncos Reading Corners were born as a program that provides a library reading corner with Broncos-colored kid-friendly

Youth preparing to participate in Broncos Bowl 2005 at INVESCO Field at Mile High.

furniture in elementary schools throughout the Denver Public Schools system with the future goal of reaching elementary schools across the state. The program hopes to establish five to seven reading corners every year.

In supporting the health portion of its mission, The Denver Broncos Community Blood Drive—Drive For Life—is the pinnacle program. Since 1998, Drive For Life has been held during the football season at INVESCO Field at Mile High. In partnership with Bonfils Blood Center, Drive For Life has grown into one of Denver's best Broncos traditions, with record numbers of donors helping to bolster Colorado's blood supply just in time for the difficult winter months. "Drive for Life" has become the largest single-day blood drive in the history of Colorado, and one of the largest in the nation.

Moreover, in support of Colorado's health, the Broncos have identified prostate and breast cancer awareness as major areas of focus. Working in collaboration with the Prostate Cancer Education Council, the Broncos promote prostate cancer screening and early detection throughout the month of September. October, in turn, traditionally features a pink hat awareness campaign for the Susan G. Komen Breast

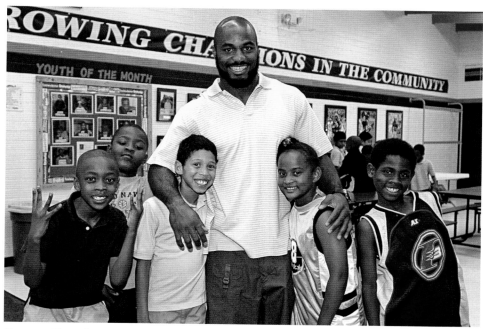

Cancer Foundation at Broncos home games.

For support of the Broncos' commitment to alleviating hunger, the annual Broncos Wives Food Drive is perhaps the best-known Denver Broncos Charities program. Since 1981, the wives of Broncos players, coaches and staff have collected cash donations and non-perishable food items at the stadium from generous Broncos fans before a designated home football game. Furthermore, since 2003, the Denver Broncos have invited families of the Denver Rescue Mission and other local hunger relief

Linebacker Ian Gold with members of the Denver Broncos branch of the Boys and Girls Club in Montbello.

agencies to enjoy a holiday meal alongside Broncos players and cheerleaders during the holiday season at INVESCO Field at Mile High. Families are selected based upon need and given a holiday gift bag with gift certificates and small gifts to enjoy.

Finally, Denver Broncos Charities, the 501c3 arm of the Denver Broncos, works in tandem with the Denver Broncos' community mission to assist citizens of Colorado through grants to designated programs in the areas of youth, health and hunger. In so doing, wonderful partnerships have been established as a long-lasting legacy of collaboration and investment in the community, directly benefiting elementary schools in Denver Public Schools and throughout the state in the future, Inner City Health, Denver Rescue Mission and the Colorado youth football community, to name a few. It is their hope to be "Champions in the Community" for many years to come.

Before the Nuggets, before the Rockies, before the Avalanche—the Denver Broncos Football Club was here, the primary force in defining Denver's transition from "cow town" to major metropolis.

Linda Lynch accepting a donation for the Denver Broncos Wives Food Drive.

DENVER HEALTH

From a modest log house in a fledgling settlement along Cherry Creek to becoming the principal safety net institution for Colorado, Denver Health has been committed to providing the highest quality healthcare to vulnerable populations for nearly 150 years. In June 1860 Dr. John Hamilton and Dr. O.B. Cass, two East Coast physicians, responded to a need for health care in the rough frontier town and opened the City Hospital at what is now Nineteenth and Larimer.

It is no surprise that one of the hospital's first patients was a dueling victim. F.W. Bliss, acting governor of Jefferson Territory, was shot by Dr. J.S. Stone, the judge of Central City's miner's court, when settling a disagreement at thirty paces with double-barreled shotguns. Bliss survived the initial wound, but died seven months later.

In 1863 fifteen percent of the $15,000 operating budget was spent on health care for smallpox victims and on care for the poor. To displace the burden of caring for "paupers" onto Arapahoe County, in which Denver was the principal city, the post of City Physician was abolished in 1864. However, by 1870 it was clear that an established health care institution was crucial to the health of Denver. County Physician Dr. John Elsner answered this call by securing $8000 from the county to purchase land, equipment and to build a new hospital. Since all goods were hauled by ox team and money

This two-horse ambulance delivering patients to the emergency tent circa 1890 was replaced in 1910 by the first automobile ambulance.

The old Denver General Hospital, constructed in 1898, had sixty beds and a steam plant for heating.

was scarce, Elsner's hospital was furnished with beds made from dry goods boxes, mattresses stuffed with dry grass from the banks of Cherry Creek, pillows made from the cheapest cotton batting and army blankets. In October 1873 Denver Health, then known as Arapahoe County Hospital, opened its doors on West Sixth Avenue and Cherokee Street, the same location it occupies today.

In 1887 Dr. McLauthlin and Chicago nurse Miss Hattie Shepard established the Colorado Training School for Nurses, the first of its kind west of the Mississippi. With the completion of the training school building in 1889, the crowded hospital's bed capacity increased from thirty-five to ninety-one. Two years later an average of 141 patients came through the hospital daily. The majority of patients were treated for pneumonia, typhoid fever and insanity.

Dr. W.H. McLauthlin, the City Health Commissioner, made the great contribution of improving the staffing patterns by inviting reputable physicians and specialists to treat specific cases in the hospital. In 1891 twenty-seven nurses, five of whom were male, a visiting staff of thirty physicians and a druggist assisted the two resident physicians. In 1892 a horse-drawn ambulance answered the call for emergency service and the Steele Hospital for contagious diseases was built.

Around this time, the Home Rule Amendment combined Denver as a city and county. Soon, the County Hospital and the City Health Department came under the same jurisdiction. The hospital's name was officially changed to Denver General Hospital (DGH). Construction continued to accommodate the public need. During the 1930s, a new five-suite operating pavilion, a teaching theater, a new service building and the Robert Speer Memorial Building for pediatrics were built. Still, overcrowding was a problem, as visits increased due to the Depression.

Being linked with the City Department of Health and Charity did not allow DGH the autonomy it needed to thrive. The expenditures of the City Department of Health, which included the public health department, Steele Hospital for contagious diseases, a tuberculosis hospital, a county farm, a detention home and DGH, had only increased $73,000 between 1929 and 1934. In 1947 Mayor Quigg Newton began a necessary reorganization of Denver's health system under the advisement of the U.S. Public Health Service.

Following Mayor Quigg in the post-war years, Dr. Florence Sabin, manager of Denver Health and Charity, made decisive changes that led DGH to the success that Denver Health knows today. First, the Department of Welfare was created so healthcare, solely, could be looked after by the Department of Health and Hospitals. City leaders helped Dr. Sabin implement a 911 emergency response service. Also, voters approved an independent policy-making Board of Health and Hospitals. In 1956 the Rocky Mountain Poison Center opened. Other changes included the remodeling of the tuberculosis building to house the public health administration offices, a reorganization of the health department, the creation of the Visiting Nurse Service and an agreement with the regents of the University of Colorado that DGH would be a teaching hospital. Denver Health is now recognized as one of the top fifteen teaching hospitals in the nation.

Dr. Sabin's mission to combine personal and public health was carried on by the hospital's current CEO and Medical Director Dr. Patricia Gabow, a graduate of Seton Hill College and the University of Pennsylvania School of Medicine. She joined the staff of Denver Health in 1973 as the Chief of the Renal Division and worked as a doctor and

The Denver Health Pavillion for Women and Children opened in 2006.

principal investigator of the National Institute of Health Program Project Grant in polycystic kidney disease. In 1992 she accepted the post of Denver Health's CEO. "Being a doctor is perfect training for being an administrator because you treat a problem just like you treat a patient," says Dr. Gabow, who also serves as medical director.

Dr. Gabow initiated the information technology system that allows Denver Health and its affiliated health centers to create an electronic medical record. Denver Health's integrated delivery system—including the Level I trauma center, nine community health centers, twelve school-based clinics, the 911 system, poison center, the public health

Open wards were typical of Denver General at the end of the nineteenth century.

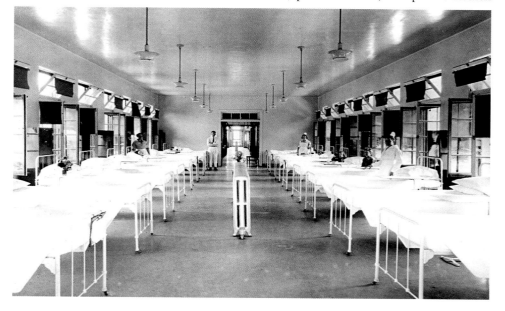

department and a center for disaster preparedness—is a national model for integration.

One of the most significant changes under Dr. Gabow's management was the 1997 action to finally make the DGH politically independent from the city, changing the name to Denver Health. At the hospital, they say they didn't divorce the city, they just needed to live in different houses, which assures Denver citizens of the health system's continued commitment to the community. Dr. Gabow believes that if this change had not occurred, Denver Health could not take the actions needed to survive in a competitive environment. Currently, Denver Health employs 4300 people and stays in the black with a $475 million annual operating budget.

History has proven that Denver Health has achieved success by keeping true to its high standards and commitment to the community. Echoing the spirit in which the first hospital was founded before Colorado was a state, a plaque in the hospital lobby reads, "Dedicated to the people of Denver, a Center for health care so that they may find ready help in time of need in an atmosphere of enlightenment and kindness...a place where...crisis is met and life is celebrated."

DENVER METRO CHAMBER OF COMMERCE

For nearly 140 years the Denver Metro Chamber of Commerce has provided business leadership for Denver and Colorado. Beginning in 1867, when members of the Denver Board of Trade raised $300,000 to construct a rail spur to Cheyenne, Wyoming to prevent the bypass of Denver by the Union Pacific Railroad as it moved west, the Chamber has taken the bold actions needed to secure Denver's future.

Denver Metro Chamber members saw, as far back as 1885, that they needed a library and opened their own doors to house the first one. In 1898 the Chamber persuaded the National Stock Growers Association Convention to meet in Denver, which eventually led to the creation of the National Western Stock Show. The Stock Show draws an international audience of more than 600,000 people and is now celebrating its 101st anniversary.

In 1908 the Chamber raised funds to prevent closure of the Denver Museum of Natural History and was one of the first homes for the collections of the Museum. The Denver Museum of Nature and Science, as it is known today, is one of a small percentage of museums nationwide honored with accreditation

In its early days, the Chamber was instrumental in ensuring the growth of Denver by helping to bring the rail lines through the city. Courtesy, Denver Public Library, Western History Collection, X-1887-1.

Today, the Chamber Building is at 1445 Market Street in Denver's LoDo neighborhood. Courtesy, Pro-Pix Photography.

by the American Association of Museums and houses more than a million objects in its 500,000-square-foot building. The museum opened its doors to more than a million visitors in 2005.

The depression of the late nineteenth century stirred corruption in the local police department, prompting the City Hall War, fought by Chamber of Commerce members who stepped in to negotiate a peaceful resolution. On the lookout for economic recovery after this rough time, the Chamber convinced the U.S. Department of the Treasury to relocate the U.S. Mint to Denver to be near the state's gold mines. The Denver Mint is one of six such facilities in the country and is one of two that produces all denominations of coins for general circulation.

Connecting the growing metro area dominated the Chamber's efforts between 1960 and 1980. In 1968 the Regional Transportation District (RTD) was created by the Chamber to provide transportation options throughout the region. In 1964 Denver's airport, Stapleton Field, was renamed Stapleton International Airport. By 1979 Stapleton was already too small and the Chamber's Airport Task Force recom-

mended that the city build a new airport much farther east. The Chamber led the charge and, in 1996, Denver International Airport (DIA) opened, now the sixth busiest airport in the country and eleventh busiest in the world. DIA also boasts a 16,000-foot runway—the longest in North America.

In 2004 the Chamber led the campaign to approve FasTracks, the largest simultaneous construction of a mass transit system in U.S. history. Scheduled for completion in 2016, FasTracks will build-out metro Denver's entire light rail system in twelve years, adding six new lines and extending routes to include 119 miles of new track. The plan also includes expanded bus service and construction of new parking at rail and bus stations.

Through the years, the Chamber has been the voice of the region's business community, representing major corporations and small entrepreneurial ventures in the seven-county metropolitan area.

On behalf of its member businesses, it advocates on issues critical to the economical vitality and quality of life within the region, including economic and workforce development, education, transportation, health care and small business services.

The organization's objectives are accomplished by the work of many dedicated volunteers and through the efforts of its affiliates: The Metro Denver Economic Development Corporation (Metro Denver EDC), which focuses on metro-area economic development activities; the Denver Metro Chamber Foundation (DMCF), whose mission is the development of leadership; the Colorado Competitive Council (C3), a statewide lobbying organization focused on growing core Colorado industries; and the Denver Metro Small Business Development Center (SBDC), which provides assistance and a variety of counseling services to small business and entrepreneurs.

In addition to its role as a community steward, the Chamber helps its 3,000 member businesses secure their future by providing them access, visibility and expertise. More than 200 Chamber programs and special events provide opportunity for member busi-

Denver's City Park offers beautiful views of both the Rocky Mountains and the Downtown Denver skyline. Courtesy, Pro-Pix Photography.

nesses of all sizes to grow and become more profitable. The Denver metro area has a booming small-business economy and a reputation for being entrepreneurial, thanks to the Chamber's efforts.

The Chamber has helped turn metropolitan Denver into one of the most vibrant places in the country to work, live and raise a family. Its mission is to collaborate and convene with other community organizations to achieve mutual goals, to represent members' interests in government and legislative issues, to enhance the region's global competi-

tiveness and to ensure the highest standards of business leadership.

Chamber President Joe Blake is proud of the organization's "legacy of leadership" but is more focused on the future.

"The Denver Metro Chamber of Commerce is a venerable institution and our litany of accomplishment is historic and remarkable," said Blake. "But what drives us is the future and the unique opportunity to align our hopes, aspirations and pride to create a better Colorado for business, our economy and our families."

As the City of Denver begins making plans to celebrate its 150th birthday in 2008, the Chamber is asking the question: "What is the next big idea that will move the metro area and Colorado forward in the future?" In June the Chamber published "Business for a Competitive Colorado" as the business agenda for the November 2006 election. The document clearly highlights the strengths and outlines the challenges ahead for the state. The Chamber's focus is on ensuring that everything possible is done to place Colorado in the best competitive position for today and tomorrow.

Denver International Airport (DIA) is currently the sixth busiest airport in the country with high traffic growth every year.

DENVER REGIONAL TRANSPORTATION DISTRICT

The Denver metropolitan area ranks among the nation's most desirable places to live, but the Mile High City is also the seventh most congested city in the country. In the next twenty years there will be nearly 1 million new residents in metro Denver, and the area's existing transportation system cannot handle the coming population boom. The Regional Transportation District (RTD) is coming to the rescue with a transit expansion strategy that facilitates smart growth, offers viable transportation options and helps the local economy thrive today and in the future.

In fact, RTD has been on a mission to meet its constituent's present and future public transport needs by offering safe, clean, reliable, courteous, accessible and cost-effective service throughout the district since 1969. That's when the forty-seventh session of the Colorado General Assembly created the regional authority to plan and build a public transportation system for the Denver metro area.

Nearly forty years after its inception, RTD develops, operates and maintains a mass transportation system for the

Denver Union Station in 1924 showing the newly added center section, which remains in full use today. The arch marked the entryway to the station on 17th Street and read "Welcome" on the opposite side to greet passengers as they left the station. "Mizpah" was placed on the side through which departing passengers would travel. It is a Hebrew salutation meaning "The Lord watch between me and thee, when we are absent from one another." Note the trolley car tracks in the foreground.

benefit of the metro area's 2.5 million residents. It has 2,500 employees, along with 1,400 private contract employees. To be sure, Denver's RTD has emerged as a model transportation authority.

To fully understand RTD's impact on its community, it is first necessary to look at the circumstances under which it was created. RTD was organized at a time when automobiles were overwhelming the transportation landscape. Private for-profit companies, which had long operated buses from coast to coast, were eliminating routes because riders were opting to drive their own vehicles. A long-term transportation crisis was in the making as public buses were threatened with extinction, just like public trolley lines before them.

Denver Union Station as seen today. In the future the station will be transformed into a mixed-use development which will be the hub of the RTD FasTracks rapid transit corridors serving bus, light rail, commuter rail and bus rapid transit (BRT).

Denver officials had witnessed this scenario before. Once a thriving passenger depot where hundreds of regional and cross-country trains passed through its hub each week, Denver Union Station traffic dwindled to one Amtrak stop daily after the automobile drew the public's adoration beginning in the 1950s. Influenced by RTD, breadth of public transportation has changed dramatically since that time. RTD's active bus fleet totals nearly 1,100; its total ridership averages almost 300,000 a day; and its annual operating budget is nearly $400 million. RTD's 2,327 square mile district includes all or parts of eight counties.

Indeed, RTD has played a vital role in its district's transportation needs from the beginning. In October 1970 RTD participated in a comprehensive transportation study for the Boulder Valley area. The District would need to establish its Northern Operations Group, which would include intercity, Boulder and Longmont service.

Even in 1971 the urban areas of the district clearly needed more than private cars and buses to meet growing transportation needs. RTD's Phase I report also recommended planning and development of a future fixed-guideway transit system, which would be supplemented by an efficient, dependable local bus system. By the end of 1972 the transportation plan was completed. This significant accomplishment complied with the RTD's 1969 legislative mandate to plan and build a public transportation system for the region.

RTD's plans were well-received by the community. In 1973 citizens voted for RTD's plan to finance the development of an integrated regional public transportation system through a dedicated sales tax. About that same time, public transportation industry consolidation got underway. The Denver Metro Transit system became part of RTD in July 1974. The District then consolidated its acquisitions to provide an interim system of routes, schedules and common fares. Consolidation paved the way for expansion as of 1975. The following year RTD focused on improving service frequency, taking over several routes

Artist's rendering of what the rear portion of Denver Union Station (DUS) could look like with the full FasTracks improvements in place. DUS will be the hub of nearly all of the rapid transit corridors from around the metro area, once again reclaiming its position as the crown jewel of public transportation for the metro region and beyond.

previously serviced by commercial carriers and trying new service techniques.

Continued growth, improved performance and innovation in transit service resulted in a new grid system of routes that went into effect in 1978. Increasing inflation during that period led RTD to develop and implement a new fare structure aimed at encouraging ridership while maintaining service levels. At the same time, the new grid system placed buses on arterials and important collector

Community leaders and RTD officials joined together on June 8, 2006 for the first official walk across the RTD's new US 36 and McCaslin pedestrian bridge connecting the two sides of the Park-n-Ride lots located in Louisville and Superior. From left, RTD Board member Lee Kemp, Louisville Mayor Chuck Sisk, RTD Board member Dick McLean, Superior Mayor Andrew Muckle (in tie), and RTD General Manager Cal Marsella (waving, in tie). The opening of the new bridge marked the first construction element of the $4.7 billion FasTrack's twelve-year major rapid transit expansion program approved by voters in November 2004.

streets where the routes could be better understood, the buses and transfer points more easily seen and where the buses could travel faster. RTD's innovation spoke to its dedication to serving the needs of the community.

In 1979 RTD developed detailed plans and applied for federal funding for the transitway/mall on the heavily congested 16th Street through downtown Denver. The 16th Street Mall project would allow regional and express bus productivity to double by directly connecting Civic Center and Market Street Stations with high frequency bus service and also serve as a distribution system for a future rail system, further demonstrating the District's long-term perspective. The 16th Street Mall would also serve as a key anchor for the economic health of Downtown Denver.

RTD had a breakthrough year in 1980. The agency received federal funding to begin 16th Street Mall construction, reached a record number of passengers per weekday, expanded the Park-n-Ride system, acquired 127 new transit buses and 89 articulated buses and made RTD's bus system, then known as "The Ride" more accessible to handicapped and elderly passengers. RTD became the first large transit agency in the country to order wheelchair lift-equipped intercity buses and was the first to have a fully lift-equipped bus fleet. The Americans with Disabilities Act of 1990 saw RTD enhance its services for disabled passengers with the new Access-a-Ride, a curb-to-curb transportation system with door-to-door assistance.

As the transportation needs of the Denver region have changed, so has RTD's vision. RTD has refined and improved its original vision for rapid transit development by conducting numerous studies that reflect the changes in the region's land use, population growth and employment center locations. Each study carefully examined the benefits associated with rapid transit, such as increased mobility, reduced air pollution, and less congestion. RTD's studies of rapid transit corridors, modes and financing options have resulted in significant progress in the region. By the

Northbound and southbound Central Corridor Light Rail trains pass the Colorado Convention Center in downtown Denver. RTD relocated the light rail station underneath the recently expanded Convention Center to provide even better access to Light Rail for conventions and for special events at the adjacent Denver Performing Arts Center.

1990s RTD was prepared to advance public transportation to a new level.

In 1994 the Downtown Express/High Occupancy Vehicle (HOV) lanes that RTD helped build were opened to buses, and, a year later, the HOV lanes opened to carpools. During the morning and afternoon rush hours, the $228 million Downtown Express lanes carry approximately 1,600 cars and buses in each direction.

The Denver metro area entered a new transportation age on October 7, 1994, when RTD opened the 5.3-mile $116.5 million Central Corridor Light Rail line on time and on budget, the region's first experience with light rail technology. This line allowed RTD to take more

than 200 bus trips each day off the congested Broadway-Lincoln corridor. The line easily exceeded rider projections, immediately reaching 17,000 daily passenger trips. Shortly after opening day the agency ordered six more light rail vehicles to alleviate the crush loads.

Despite the warm public welcome of the Central Corridor, fewer, but very vocal skeptics remained. Many were awaiting the first suburban line to judge the success of the new system. In September 1995 the fifteen-member RTD Board of Directors led by General Manager Cal Marsella, approved spending $4 million to complete the final design of the Southwest Corridor Light Rail Project. The new $177 million line opened to the public on July 14, 2000. Critics claimed light rail would soon be dead in the water, but the new line has been a tremendous success by any measure. Ridership exceeded original forecasts by nearly 70 percent and now averages 18,000 riders a day. To keep up with the demand, RTD purchased twelve

The new Elati Light Rail Operations Center was developed on the abandoned General Iron site in Englewood. The Elati facility helped revitalize the neighborhoods around the long-dormant, former military supply factory site.

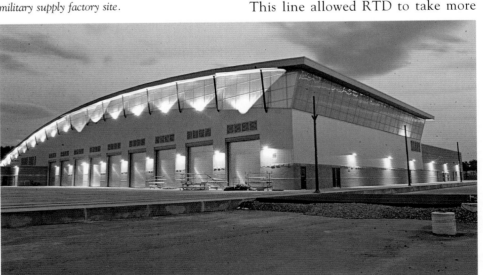

additional light rail vehicles for the 8.7-mile line.

Building on the overwhelming success of the Southwest line, the Southeast Corridor Light Rail Line will open to the public in November 2006. Dubbed the Transportation Expansion (T-REX) Project, the $1.67 billion highway expansion and light rail project includes the 19-mile light rail line, interstate widening, and the rebuilding of several bridges and interchanges. It will connect the two largest employment centers in the Denver region. RTD worked in cooperation with the Colorado Department of Transportation to complete the intermodal project. Average weekday ridership on the new light rail line is expected to total nearly 38,000 by 2020 and will serve as a model for the rest of the nation.

RTD faced additional criticism when it formed a public-private partnership to purchase Denver Union Station and nineteen acres of land around it in 2001. This futuristic move is making way for an intermodal hub for a new mass transit system: FasTracks. When RTD purchased the station, there was no support for a regional system and no indication that Denver would approve a regional mass transit system in the near-term. RTD's board took a risk and it paid off. It overwhelmingly won the election in November 2004 to build FasTracks.

Of all the projects RTD has embarked upon over the years, RTD's Board of Directors, chaired by Chris Martinez, is most proud of FasTracks, a twelve-year comprehensive plan overwhelmingly approved by voters in 2004 to build and operate additional passenger rail lines, expand and improve bus service and Park-n-Rides throughout the region. FasTracks includes 119 miles of new light rail and commuter rail, 18 miles of bus rapid transit service, 21,000 new parking spaces at rail and bus stations, and expanded bus service throughout the metro area. FasTracks will cost $4.7 billion to construct with the first line scheduled for completion in 2013 and the last line set to open in 2016.

RTD's board believes FasTracks is a major part of Denver's ability to thrive and compete in a global economy.

The Southeast Light Rail Line was constructed as part of the T-REX Project. Here, a Southeast Light Rail test train zips past Denver Tech Center buildings near Orchard Road.

FasTracks will allow riders to transfer from one line to the next, and with access to the expanded bus system, will provide the ability to travel almost anywhere in the metro area. It will feature a hub at Denver Union Station where local and Greyhound buses will co-locate with taxicabs. The hub will also offer a bike rental station, ski area buses, Amtrak and the Ski Train. It will even host pedicabs and horse drawn carriages. In short, one site will feature every mode of transportation available in the region.

RTD remains on the leading edge of the transit industry in its work with alternative fuels and pollution reducing technology. Starting more than fifteen years ago, RTD began to experiment with various alternative fuels, including methanol, propane and compressed natural gas (CNG), in the daily operation of its standard passenger buses and support vehicles. In 2000 RTD introduced a fleet of thirty-six new mall buses that operate on CNG in a hybrid-electric configuration, which now gives RTD one of the largest fleets of hybrid-electric buses in the entire nation. The agency

also introduced four new hybrid-electric buses into regular local bus service in 2006 to give an updated comparison of alternate fuels in daily operation.

Last year, RTD began experimenting with biodiesel in partnership with the National Renewable Energy Lab. RTD is preparing for "ultra-low sulfur diesel" fuel in compliance with advanced technology emissions reduction requirements, which will reduce 97 percent of its sulfur content in diesel fuel and result in diesel exhaust emissions reduction of 90 percent. RTD has taken delivery of 183 new low-floor transit buses that meet the most current Environmental Protection Agency stringent emissions regulations. In other efforts to minimize vehicle emissions, RTD continues to phase out the use of old, higher emission buses. Over the past five years, RTD has procured more than 759 new buses, mostly to replace the old buses.

RTD has a proven track record for on time, on budget projects that have proven mass transit critics wrong time and time again and continues to serve as a model for other public agencies across the nation. This record has directly led to RTD's ability to earn the trust and respect of the voting public. The transit agency has made innovative and visionary decisions that have benefited the community for nearly four decades. RTD has proven that if you build it—and build it according to the current and future needs of the community—they will come. RTD's strong relationships with area cities and counties, other agencies and the public help ensure a bright future for the entire region.

The next element in RTD's long-range transportation vision is NexTracks. The District has already trademarked the name, which describes the future planning phase for possible transit projects beyond FasTracks. Meeting the transportation needs of the growing metro area requires forward thinking and advance planning. As RTD has learned, it is never too early to prepare for tomorrow.

EMILY GRIFFITH OPPORTUNITY SCHOOL

Located in downtown Denver since 1916, Emily Griffith Opportunity School is a testament to the American Dream. Through two world wars, the industrial era, the Great Depression and into the 21st Century, Opportunity School has remained a fixture in the landscape of Denver, a place where dreams are nurtured and lives changed. Opportunity School represents the chance for a better life "for all who wish to learn" just as it did ninety years ago when legendary educator Emily Griffith opened the doors to the first-of-its-kind adult vocational school

Opportunity School too was born of a dream. A young woman who began teaching in a sod school house in Broken Bow, Nebraska came to Denver in 1895 and observed that the parents of the children she taught struggled with reading, basic math and English language proficiency.

Emily Griffith said she envisioned a school where, "The clock will be stopped from morning 'till midnight...I want the age limit for admission lifted and the classes so organized that a boy or girl working...may come to school, study what he or she wants to learn to make life more useful...I will be laughed at, but what of it? I already have a name for that school. It's Opportunity."

Emily Griffith, founder of Emily Griffith Opportunity School.

In the original Longfellow school building, Emily Griffith Opportunity School enrolled over 1,400 students on its first day of operation. Instruction in courses such as basic math, industrial millinery and telegraphing were offered.

It wasn't until 1916 that Emily's dream came to fruition. Griffith worked as a teacher in the Denver Public Schools for nine years and eventually was elected State Superintendent of Public Instruction for the state of Colorado in 1904. One Christmas, while serving free dinners to the poor, Griffith told journalist Francis Wayne of her lifetime ambition to create a school designed for adult learners.

Nine months after the journalist reported Emily's dream in the *Denver Post*, Opportunity School opened its doors. Expecting just 100 students, Emily was pleased to personally register over 1,400 students in courses such as addition and subtraction, industrial millinery and telegraphing. The school was open thirteen hours a day, five days a week. Unlike the pedagogical style of her contemporaries, Emily insisted that no one in the school should frown and that the staff should never accentuate a student's weakness, but rather emphasize his or her achievement.

Emily expressed genu-

ine care and empathy for the people who sought an education at Opportunity School. In the original Longfellow school building, donated by Denver Public Schools, Emily greeted students with messages written on the blackboard such as You Can Do It and Help One Another. She welcomed working adult students by writing, "Don't worry about attendance, come when you can. We know you are learning wherever you are, or you wouldn't be seeking our help." After observing a hungry young man faint in class, she and her sister Florence began cooking and serving free soup nightly.

Throughout her tenure, Griffith was committed to the ideal that education should be "for all who wish to learn," a motto that is still embodied by the school she founded. For ninety years, Opportunity School has served this purpose with the supportive spirit of Emily Griffith herself to become one of the oldest and largest adult vocational schools in the United States.

Emily Griffith Opportunity School has continued to respond to the demand for relevant education for the job market throughout the years. In the 1920s automotive and welding classes proliferated. During World War II programs such as machining and nursing were developed to support the war effort. In the 1950s plumbing, pipefitting, iron working and electrical apprenticeship programs were established.

Today, Opportunity School serves as Denver's technical college, providing career and technical training in over forty different areas including business, health sciences, aircraft maintenance, cosmetology, auto mechanics and welding. A nationally accredited technical college, Opportunity School offers transferable college credit with the most affordable tuition in the region. In addition, it boasts the largest English as a Second Language program in the state, serving over 2500 immigrant and refugee students annually. Opportunity School also offers adult basic education, corporate training and nearly twenty apprenticeships.

Since 1916 more than 1.5 million students have attended Opportunity

School—that's one of every three residents of Denver today. Approximately 11,000 students annually pass through the doors of Opportunity School and 69 percent of students who begin a program graduate. The success rate of students is astounding—89 percent obtain a job upon graduation. Through a dropout retrieval program, approximately 350 students graduate from high school each year. The numbers, like the name of the school, speak for themselves. As Emily Griffith intended, Opportunity School empowers students to actively shape their role in society.

Current Executive Director Les Lindauer is an example of what Emily Griffith envisioned when she opened her school. Lindauer attended Opportunity School and graduated from the ironworker's apprenticeship program in 1974. After a fifteen-year career in ironworking, he earned a teaching degree and then a master's degree before returning to Opportunity School to carry on the legacy of "linking learning and earning." Lindauer knows first hand the difference Opportunity School can make and is dedicated to the school's mission to provide a relevant education to

Still in its original location, Emily Griffith Opportunity School occupies an entire city block in the heart of downtown Denver.

students in a supportive environment while keeping tuition affordable.

Still in the original location, the school now spans an entire downtown block adjacent to the convention center. One of its greatest assets, its long-standing presence in the central downtown community, has also grown into one of its major challenges in the new century. "Our school has a rich history and an aging facility," explains Lindauer. To address this challenge, Lindauer and other school administrators are working with community and business leaders to develop a Master Plan for the rehabilitation of Opportunity School in its current historic location. The reconstructed facility will allow the school to expand and continue providing career and technical education in Denver.

Emily Griffith's dream, an American Dream, is realized on the block of 1250 Welton Street. Opportunity School has evolved from a drop-in learning site into an established technical college with national accreditation. With the same pride as Emily Griffith herself, who showcased the talent of student milliners by wearing their new creations, Emily Griffith Opportunity School continues to champion its students by working to meet educational demands and by providing students with a compassionate learning environment in an innovative setting. It is still a place where everybody is welcome and all who wish to learn can make a better life for themselves and their families. As its founder would have insisted, Opportunity School continues to serve the public purpose in Denver.

Opportunity School has continued to respond the demand for relevant education for the job market throughout the years.

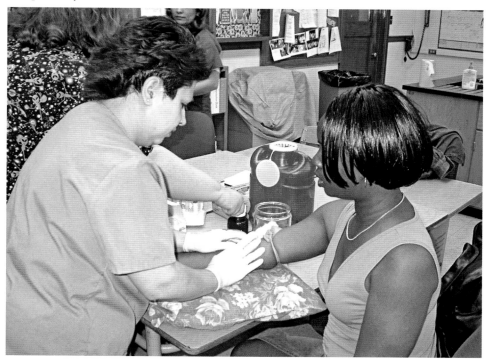

engineering-environmental Management, Inc. (e²M)

Very few companies are created with the goal of remaining small, but Dr. Jose Merino had exactly that in mind when he founded engineering-environmental Management, Inc. (e²M) in April 1989 in Lakewood, Colorado. Prior to starting his own company, Dr. Merino had worked for large companies as an ecologist researching the behavior of small mammals. He felt the businesses had become too big and unwieldy to provide excellent service. He felt they had lost the ability to be flexible and fully in control of their projects.

Dr. Merino planned to offer environmental consulting on a niche area of the National Environment Policy Act (NEPA) and only grow e²M to a fifteen person firm. Initially specializing in studies for natural resource management and threatened and endangered species, he teamed with other small companies as he received requests for services he could not provide. He realized the time was right to grow and began looking for partners who could provide expertise in related areas.

Michael Cassio and Neil Botts became co-owners of e²M in 1995. Mr. Cassio, a geologist, has a background in operations and regulatory compliance. Mr. Botts, also a geologist, brought experience in the investigative and restoration fields.

e²M senior vice president Brian Hoppy holding a falcon used as part of March Air Reserve Base's bird aircraft strike hazard reduction program in California.

"I make sure a project adheres to local, state and federal laws," says Cassio. "This division develops hazardous waste and spill management plans, creates bio-terrorism response plans and even provides training for our clients."

The restoration business area includes remediating mold, asbestos, lead-based paint abatement; and also conducting preliminary assessments, delineating and characterizing sites, remediating soil and groundwater, risk screening and other environmental engineering activities. Botts' and Cassio's compliance and restoration experience complemented Dr. Merino's environmental conservation and planning services and set e²M on a course of steep growth.

By 1997 Cassio had taken over as president, and the company began to seek out lucrative government contracts. e²M's customers include the Departments of Homeland Security, Interior, Defense and Commerce, as well as the U.S. Geological Survey and the Environmental Protection Agency.

Staying true to Dr. Merino's concept of retaining flexibility and control by staying small has allowed e²M to stay competitive. "The government classifies you as a small business as long as you have under 500 employees," Cassio explains. Once you go over that number, you could have 501 employees

e²M Archeologists on-site at Williams Fork Reservoir, Grand County, Colorado. This site was occupied at two different periods. First, around 8,000 years ago and, second, circa 1,000 years ago. Interesting finds include an 8,000- year-old bottle gourd.

e²M owner and president Michael Cassio and geologist Craig Vrabel studying plans to demolish an old World War II army hospital at Fort Carson Army Post south of Colorado Springs.

and be expected to compete with companies that have 18,000 employees."

The company, now headquartered in Englewood, Colorado, has grown from three to over 300 employees located in 22 states and the Territory of Guam. e²M regularly wins government contracts and provides defensible NEPA documentation and studies, beating out companies earning $5 billion in yearly revenue.

Cassio also credits their employees for the company's success. Management believes in selecting and hiring talented individuals with good technical and management skills to effectively interact and satisfy client needs. Employees must understand project budgets, produce quality products, meet contract deadlines, direct and mentor assigned technical staff. In addition, e²M has never lost a key employee to a direct competitor.

Another factor in e²M's success is simply that regardless of economic or political climate, the services they provide in the areas of regulatory compliance, conservation planning and restoration are in constant demand all over the world.

After Hurricane Katrina devastated the Gulf Coast in 2005, the Louisiana National Guard contracted e²M to cleanup the spilled chemicals, oils and fuels spread throughout Jackson Barracks in the lower Ninth Ward of New Orleans. Several homes had floated into the area before collapsing. In addition, parts of the Barracks had been covered in five to twenty feet of water. There had also been fuel leaks. e²M provided damage assessments and chemical cleanup and helped restore the barracks so that the reconstruction process could start.

On the finite amount of land that is Guam, excess garbage dumps and landfills are not an option. The island utlilized e²M's sutainability services and, along with the company's compliance division, provided training and education to help Guam combat the trash problem and protect land for future generations.

e²M is also proud of the environmental impact statements they

Ash pile sampling at Fort Riley, Kansas.

developed that assist large oil companies (Shell, Chevron-Texaco, Exxon) in moving liquid natural gas (LNG) ports and lines offshore into deep water. When the Coast Guard became part of the Department of Homeland Security, e²M conducted the environmental studies for the implementation of new security measures for ports, rivers, lakes and oceans. The four approved applications to date for LNG ports were documented and prepared by e²M.

Sticking with Dr. Merino's goals of being small and flexible has worked well for e²M. The company earned more than $30 million in revenue last year. In the past five years, they completed environmental protection projects in forty-eight states, three Territories (Guam, Puerto Rico, Virgin Islands) and the District of Columbia. e²M also completed environmental project work in Japan, Korea,

Preble's Meadow Jumping Mouse survey in Colorado.

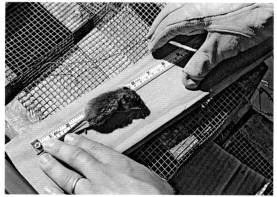

Mexico, Italy, Portugal and throughout the Federated States of Micronesia. Yet, there are challenges to be met.

A number of key clients allowed competitive bidding for contracts in the full and open arena rather then releasing the contracts as small business set-asides. e²M responded by building a competitive team and merging talents with those of multi-billion dollar environmental companies. However, they did win multi-million dollar full and open contracts for the Arkansas Army National Guard and for the Corps of Engineers in Fort Worth, Texas without adding a large company.

"Our goal is to grow at 10 percent per year. That should put us at 500 employees in 7 years. Then it comes down to getting into the acquisition mode to start buying smaller companies to get to a 3,000 person plus company to compete at the large company level," explains Cassio.

Because of a core belief in good service with flexibility, e²M continues to grow and thrive. By providing solutions to environmental problems, creating sustainable solutions to protect natural resources, designing innovative and common sense environmental management programs, the company is committed to only providing the best. e²M is on the leading edge of our future, making the world better for everyone.

EXEMPLA SAINT JOSEPH HOSPITAL

Founded in 1873, Exempla Saint Joseph Hospital was born of the vision of Bishop Machebeuf. In 1868 he approached Mother Xavier Ross of the Sisters of Charity of Leavenworth, Kansas about opening a hospital, but she did not have enough Sisters to commit at the time. Finally, in 1872 was she able to send four Sisters into the Wild West with the mission to serve the newly bustling region by establishing a school in Central City and a hospital in Denver. This pioneering spirit was the foundation upon which the first private teaching hospital in Denver would be built.

With just nine dollars in hand, the Sisters embraced the challenge. Upon arrival, the Sisters provided healthcare in a cottage at 14th and Arapahoe. They quickly expanded to a location on what would become Market Street. In 1876 they built a hospital at 18th Avenue and Humboldt Street, property the hospital still occupies.

The Sisters treated all members of their community with respect, extending care to families and workers as well as prostitutes and gamblers. They accepted all in need of care and ventured into the community to ensure medical care was available to all.

Soon, the hospital expanded by leaps and bounds. In 1899 the *Denver Times* noted that this growth could be attributed to the organization's non-sectarian

Located on the same site in downtown Denver for more than 130 years, Exempla Saint Joseph Hospital is committed to serving the Denver community with clinical excellence and preeminent patient care.

The original twin towers of Saint Joseph Hospital in 1904.

nature, the efficiency of the medical personnel and the dedication of the Sisters to accomplishing their mission. The hospital was also establishing itself as a leader in medical innovation. A brass sterilizing machine and state-of-the-art X-ray equipment were installed by 1899, just four years after the discovery of the X-ray procedure.

Saint Joseph Hospital remains on the cutting edge. Employing 2,400 people and with 1,268 staff physicians, the hospital's presence in every aspect of the Denver community is undeniable. The original goals of the Sisters of Charity of Leavenworth are in full force. Saint Joseph Hospital's mission is clear: "To foster healing and health for the people and communities we serve, particularly those medically underserved, through preeminent patient care and medical education."

Saint Joseph Hospital houses 565 licensed beds. The hospital also hosts over 50,000 emergency room visits and welcomes over 5,000 new babies annually, more than any other Colorado hospital. Awards for exceeding patient expectations within such a bustling facility are not only impressive, but a testament to Saint Joseph Hospital's excellence.

The hospital has developed numerous programs to bring its mission to life. It trains nearly 100 medical residents each year in its Graduate Medical Education Program. Saint Joseph Hospital also takes pride in fostering employee opportunities through its Workforce Development program. The Baby Bootique, an award-winning program that encourages proper prenatal care, and Boot Camp for New Dads, an intensive program for first-time fathers, promotes education in the challenging voyage into parenthood.

Saint Joseph Hospital is now a part of the Exempla Healthcare family, which includes Denver-area hospitals Exempla Lutheran Medical Center and Exempla Good Samaritan Medical Center. Saint Joseph Hospital endeavors to carry on the legacy of the Sisters of Charity of Leavenworth, Kansas by serving the needs of the metropolitan city it calls home with excellence in care and innovation.

EXEMPLA LUTHERAN MEDICAL CENTER

Exempla Lutheran Medical Center began in 1905 as an answer to a pressing health problem. Tuberculosis, known then as the white plague, was afflicting millions across the globe. People from around the country flocked to Denver's dry climate in search of relief.

Sanitariums that were committed to providing care for those afflicted with tuberculosis had been operating throughout the United States since the late 1880s. By the turn of the century Colorado had yet to open a single facility. In 1903 members of St. John's Lutheran Church began plans for the Evangelical Lutheran Sanitarium. The sanitarium opened two years later, built on a budget of $17,500, a significant investment at that time. The facility consisted of an open-air tent colony and was located in Wheat Ridge, just a few miles outside of Denver's city limits.

From its inception, the health facility was committed to serving a specific need within its community. When antibiotics were developed decades later for the treatment of tuberculosis, sanitariums quickly became obsolete. However, Jefferson County's burgeoning population had other health needs that had to be served. With no hospital of its own, the blooming county that linked the City of Denver to the Rocky Mountains still had plenty of use for the facility.

In 1961 the Evangelical Lutheran Sanitarium closed its doors. In 1962 a newly remodeled Lutheran Hospital and Medical Center opened as a 220-bed facility.

The "Tucker Tents" on the grounds of the Evangelical Lutheran Sanitarium were considered cutting edge treatment at the turn of the century.

The 1980s saw the addition of Colorado Lutheran Home, a long-term care and assisted living facility, as well as West Pines behavioral health center. Lutheran Medical Center has also stayed on the cutting edge of medical advancement, with state of the art cardiac care offered at The Heart Center, which opened in 2003. Lutheran's Diagnostic Imaging Center and Radiation Oncology Center are also recognized as elite facilities in Colorado.

Exempla Lutheran Medical Center is now owned and managed by Exempla Healthcare, a nonprofit organization that includes Exempla Saint Joseph Hospital, Exempla Good Samaritan Medical Center and Exempla Physician Network. With a mission "to foster healing and health for the people and communities we serve," each entity provides vital services for the Denver metro area.

Lutheran continues to expand its services even further. In 2006 Collier Hospice Center was opened at Lutheran

Today, Exempla Lutheran Medical Center advances the art of healing and the science of medicine by offering a comprehensive spectrum of personalized care.

Medical Center. This twenty-four-bed in-patient facility compassionately supports the end-of-life needs of terminally ill patients and provides southwest Denver/Jefferson County residents with the safest care, most advanced technology and best service right in their community.

Today, Lutheran has 2,500 employees, 800 physicians and 1,200 volunteers who provide service at its 400-bed facility. Lutheran is consistently recognized for patient care and excellence in service, having been selected seven times for the *100 Top Hospitals, Benchmarks for Success* by Solucient, which maintains the most comprehensive healthcare database in the world. Lutheran was even named "Favorite Hospital of Denver Metro" in a consumer poll.

By adapting to the needs of its patients, Lutheran has made itself indispensable. By putting patients first in every step of its evolution, Exempla Lutheran Medical Center provides Denver/Jefferson County residents with the safest care.

FAMOUS BONANZA CASINO

Casinos are not traditionally known as family establishments, but the Famous Bonanza Casino is a model family-owned and run business. The Famous Bonanza Casino was founded in 1992, after limited stakes gaming was legalized in Central City, but Ross and Nancy Grimes established the Famous Bonanza gift shop in the same location in 1959. The casino now has over 100 employees and is managed by their daughter Ann Dodson. In addition to Ann, during the fifteen years of its existence, their daughter Sue Hentschel, son Reed Grimes and their spouses Ed Dodson, Brad Hentschel and Kathy Grimes have been involved. Keeping the business close to the heart of family serves the Famous Bonanza well—they were recently voted as having the friendliest staff in Colorado.

The Famous Bonanza name comes from the mining era, when gold was plentiful in Central City and more than one bonanza became famous. The Famous Bonanza gift shop earned its own distinction as the result of a sculpture of a gold miner crafted by a local artist. He sat in the window prompting locals and tourists from around the world to take memorable photos with him. Today, many travelers return to visit

Ross and Nancy Grimes in their Victorian finest.

the Famous Bonanza specifically because they had photos taken as children with "Old Pete."

The Grimes family's success can be attributed to Ross and Nancy's decades of experience in business. In 1950 they purchased Evergreen Crafters from Nancy's parents, Willard and Mary Helen Crain. During their fifty-five years, they operated gift and clothing stores, a toy store and a hamburger stand where the kids worked as soon as they were old enough to hold a potato peeler. A pacesetter for commerce on Main Street in Evergreen, Ross was president of the Chamber of Commerce, took a leadership role in founding the volunteer fire department and was fire chief for many years. He also served as president of the water and sanitation districts for over thirty years. Ross, Nancy and her parents, created the local newspaper, the *Canyon Courier*, in the 1950s.

Central City was a mining community of considerable wealth and importance. After mining declined it became a tourist attraction, home of the Central City Opera and numerous businesses. Unfortuately, business was seasonal and therefore unprofitable. The town deteriorated over the years. The entire back of the Famous Bonanza gift shop building had fallen off; the

façade had pulled away from the front of the building; and the interior required modernization. Like many old prospector towns in Colorado, Central City had seen better days.

After owning and operating the Famous Bonanza gift shop in Central City for five decades, Ross and Nancy Grimes felt a duty to respond to the need for restoration of the charming Victorian town. The Grimes family and many others became involved in the effort to pass the Limited Gaming Act. Passed by popular vote in November 1990, this constitutional amendment legalized limited stakes gambling in Cripple Creek, Central City and Black Hawk. The intent behind the Act was to use the casino generated revenue to revitalize these towns, with particular emphasis on restoring their historical integrity. Initially, the Act created a boom. Over thirty casinos sprung up in Central City alone. However, by 2005, Central City had returned to a diversified economy of casinos, gift shops, restaurants and museums.

In 1991 the Famous Bonanza gift shop underwent a year of refurbishment and reconstruction. The renovations were completed with the history of the town in mind. The 1875 building had been a restaurant, a boarding house and almost certainly a house of ill repute. The façade was restored to its Victo-

In the 1870s this storefront was the home of Rachofsky's New York store and the eventual location of the Famous Bonanza Casino. It sold dry goods and clothing. In May 1874 the town was destroyed by the Great Fire.

rian glory, as was the interior. During the restoration, the Grimes family kept intact many of the original architectural details and fixtures. They added two elegant wooden bars, reminiscent of the Victorian era. The casino is decorated with Tiffany glass, bronze statues and antiques from the Colorado mansion of the famous "Unsinkable" Molly Brown. As a result of the town-wide refurbishment, people returned, not just to gamble in Central City, but to stroll down Main Street and absorb the history of the small town. Revenue from gambling has given new life to Central City. Along with important historic preservation efforts, many new jobs have been created and the visitor season is now year-round. Residents have shared in the benefits as well. The casinos pay very high local taxes which have allowed residential property taxes to become among the lowest in the country.

Grimes asserts that the intent of the act was not to create gambling towns for gambling's sake, but to restore and preserve the rich history of the region, as well as give back to the community. Unfortunately, the nearby town of Black Hawk interpreted the Act differently and allowed the establishment of Las Vegas-style casinos, creating

Employee Tracy Yanchunis and Pete the Miner share a moment inside the Famous Bonanza Casino.

new problems for Central City. As Black Hawk was a mile closer to Denver and unimpeded in its ability to provide large, traditional gambling facilities, the Famous Bonanza and other Central City casinos housed in historic buildings faced an unfair competitive disadvantage.

Ross Grimes was instrumental in responding to this need. As there was no direct road to Central City, much potential business was lost to Black Hawk due to its primary location. As the Chairman of the Business Im-

provement District, Ross guided the construction of a four-lane highway connecting Central City with Interstate 70. The Central City Parkway, which opened in November of 2004, gives travelers direct access to Central City and provides both towns with a desperately needed alternative route.

Throughout the years the Grimes family has been in business, they have succeeded and given back to the community. Ross attributes the resilience and success of his casinos to his experience as a businessman and to the help and dedication of his family and loyal employees. Working for a family-owned company has been a positive experience for many. The Famous Bonanza and Easy Street enjoy low turnover; many employees have been there since the beginning. The Grimes family mission has remained the same since opening: Give customers the best possible gaming and hospitality experience in Colorado, preserve the unique atmosphere of Central City and work together as a family to be successful. The Grimes family and the Famous Bonanza Casino are committed to caring for places and faces that they hold close to their hearts.

The Famous Bonanza Casino today.

FIRST UNITED BANK

First United Bank is a modern American success story fueled by pioneering spirit. Through commitment to its clients and good old-fashioned hard work, the bank is a shining example of a great Colorado business. First United Bank was founded by Chairman and CEO Stephen Baltz in 1983. When the bank opened, its first and only account belonged to Mr. Baltz. Today the bank hosts 18,000 accounts and holds $180 million in assets. More importantly, this family business is actively involved in the Colorado communities it calls home.

In the mid-1970s Aurora, Colorado was one of the fastest growing cities in the United States. Stephen and his wife, Marty, wanted to be a part of this vibrant, expanding city. Aurora seemed like an ideal location to start a new banking venture. Whether it was intuition, business acumen or a combination of the two, the Baltz's decision was right on the money, so to speak.

Mr. Baltz was already quite accomplished by the time he decided to open the bank. A native of Los Angeles, California, Mr. Baltz attended Valley College and was a student of The University of Southwestern Law School. Mr. Baltz had already been working in the banking field in California. At that time, he held the distinction of being the youngest bank branch manager in all of California. However, when a new job was offered, he and his college sweetheart, Marty, picked up and moved to Colorado in 1975. The banking job that brought the Baltzes to Denver paid less

This picture of the original lobby of the First National Bank of Denver (1908) was given to the builder and architect by Stephen Baltz to replicate the lobby that is used by First United Bank today.

than Mr. Baltz's managerial position in California. Yet there was definite promise in the cool, clean Colorado air.

By 1979 it seemed a natural step for Mr. Baltz to take his years of experience and talent to the next level. Mr. Baltz bought a failing bank and began his career as a turn-around specialist and banker extraordinaire. In 1983 he founded a new Aurora bank on the northwest corner of Mississippi and Chambers in the Aurora Plaza. This single site was rented. When the bank opened, it had only three employees and a legal lending limit of just $135,000.

These humble beginnings are remarkable compared to the bank's current statistics. It is now comprised of eleven full-service branch locations, the property for each office owned outright by the bank. First United Bank now employs approximately 125 people across the State of Colorado. And in twenty-three short years, the bank's lending limit now borders $3.5 million.

One of the offices in the downtown branch of First United Bank is an exact replica of the office that was once used by Thomas Keeley, assistant cashier of the First National Bank of Denver in 1908.

What factors contributed to the bank's standout success? Stephen Baltz doesn't think it was anything mysterious. Rather, success was a natural result of hard work, dedication and commitment. This focus was aimed at providing premier customer service and managing the bank prudently.

The bank became profitable within one year of opening due to Mr. Baltz's complete commitment. Mr. Baltz is well known for making things happen. He prides himself on still picking up the telephone and bringing in new business, and on being available to each and every current customer should they need his personal attention. This hands-on style

A close-up of decorative plaster in the downtown branch crafted by Nostalgic Stone, a local company.

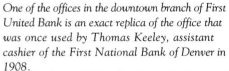

is evident in every aspect of the bank's management and growth.

First United Bank has also elevated the level of bank service available to its customers. From its inception the bank has prided itself on trying to find ways to make loans rather than turning people down. Over the years, the bank has helped hundreds of people buy homes and begin new businesses. Most banks are only willing to make loans with little risk. But First United Bank makes it a point to try to find a way to make every loan that is presented to it without risk to the bank's capital and that is not in violation of regulatory guidelines. Mr. Baltz has a special intuition about his customers. It allows him to get a sense of the person in front of him before looking at the financial bottom line.

In order to facilitate these loans, First United Bank's loan committee meets three times a week. The bank feels a weighty responsibility to serving its customers by giving them timely and fair consideration for their lending needs instead of the hassle of long wait times and red tape.

The thirty-seven ton round vault door, circa 1900, was taken from an old building in Chicago that was being razed. This door took twelve hours to install, five of which were spent balancing it so it could be opened manually every day. The door is functional and used to access the safe deposit box area

First United Bank has also kept an open lending mind when it came to construction loans. Many other banks were afraid to follow this course, but for First United Bank the risk has paid off. With the steady growth of population and economy in Colorado in the past twenty years, construction has proved to be a wise, and profitable investment. Using Return on Average Assets (ROA) as the primary indicator, First United Bank was the ninth highest earning bank in the United States between 1995 and 2000, an impressive distinction to say the least.

The management of the bank has

Stephen Baltz, founder, CEO and president, and his daughter Kimberly Baltz, future president.

been vital in ensuring not only its success, but its continued existence. Vigorous competition from other banks required First United Bank's management to aggressively monitor its own expenses and continually offer elite customer service. Between 1985 and 1990 the five banks in the immediate vicinity of the Aurora location failed. While one was recapitalized by its parent organization, the other four remained closed. Smart management and the best service in town further distinguished First United Bank from the crowd.

The 1980s brought other challenges to the First United Bank family. A national recession made the banking landscape bleak. But savvy management and smart purchases and sales of locations, made with chess-master vision, kept First United afloat. In 1992 when Colorado began to allow branch banking, the Baltzes were able to merge their individual locations into their current incarnation under the First United Bank moniker.

Stephen Baltz and First United Bank extended a wonderful benefit in appreciation of the excellent service rendered by its many employees. In 2000 United Banks of Colorado, First United Bank's holding company, purchased Kickapoo Lodge. The Grand Lake, Colorado, property had belonged to Dorothy "Nursie" Young. Ms. Young had been a celebrated nurse in the Army Nurse Corps during World War II before returning to Colorado and becoming the head school nurse for all of Grand County.

Kickapoo Lodge is now a corporate retreat for all First United Bank employees. The property includes lake access with boat docks, fully upgraded cabin lodging, and many other amenities and activities. Bank employees can enjoy Kickapoo Lodge with their families as a complimentary benefit for their loyal service. When the Lodge is not being used by bank employees, it is rented out. All proceeds from the Lodge are then donated to the Rocky Mountain Repertory Theatre.

The theater, which has been providing live entertainment since 1966, relies on patrons to maintain the high level of production quality it offers to its Grand Lake audiences. First United Bank has contributed over $80,000 in the past six years, helping the theater put on such productions as the classic *Singin' in the Rain*. Theater management has gratefully

The D&F Tower in downtown Denver, the restoration of which was financed by Stephen Baltz in the early 1980s.

acknowledged this contribution as playing a significant role in the theater's continuation.

Over the years, the bank has used its position to benefit the Colorado communities it calls home. The bank has

purchased five failing banks over the years and returned them each to profitability within twelve months' time. This has translated into rescuing personal banking services in diverse communities in order to maintain neighborhood banking options. This has been a particular boon considering that banks have become more impersonal and automated. The needs of the community have no place in such homogenized, arms-length transactions. First United Bank has continued to attempt to bridge this gap in service.

The bank has also actively contributed to the historic preservation of Colorado landmarks. One such example is the D&F Tower in Denver. Built in 1910, the D&F Tower was the tallest structure west of the Mississippi at that time. The primary building, home to the Daniels & Fisher department store, was demolished in 1980. Thanks largely to First United Bank, the clock tower was saved. Today it remains a beautiful part of Denver's downtown skyline.

Even more recently, in 2002, the bank has completed the painstaking and loving restoration of its branch in the historic Equitable Building, also in downtown Denver. Built in 1892, the Equitable Building was a hub for some of the most significant Denver businesses at the turn of the century. The restoration included an exact duplication of the floor plan of the building's original bank, which occupied the space from 1896 to 1911. This included barred tellers' cages and a thirty-seven-ton circular vault door, a replica of the bank of yore.

The cost of the property purchase and restoration was approximately twice the cost of the original building prices in 1892. This put the price tag on the new bank location at over $500 per square foot! However, the price was well worth the effort. The restoration was recognized as one of the best achievements in that field by Historic Denver, a citizen's organization dedicated to preserving Denver's history.

The Equitable Building Branch also attracts numerous visitors for tours. Many Chambers of Commerce from local communities bring in guests to the notable site. Tom Noel, considered Colorado's

The lobby of the downtown branch in the Equitable Building. Everything from the teller cages to the decorative plaster was restored.

The historic Equitable Building on the corner of 17th Street and Stout Street where the downtown branch is located.

State Historian and also known as "Dr. Colorado," has been so impressed with the preservation that he makes the bank a regular site of interest when taking visitors on tours of Denver. *Westward* newspaper named the Equitable branch the "Best Old-Style Banking Experience" in Colorado.

The bank, led by Mr. Baltz, has also made a concerted effort to clean up its surrounding communities. It has played an integral part in eliminating numerous establishments that contributed to the crime level on East Colfax. In appreciation of Mr. Baltz's efforts in this regard, he was named an Honorary Lieutenant of the Denver Police Department in 1980.

First United Bank has another notable community project currently underway. The bank has founded a nonprofit organization specifically to create a Christian youth camp. An initial contribution of $5 million will be followed with another donation of $8.5 million in order to give young people from throughout the Denver metro area the opportunity to enjoy the youth milestone of camping. Ideally, the camp will host 1,200 to 1,500 children when fully built.

The Baltz family believes in uphold-

ing the values the United States was founded on: ethics, honesty and morality. They have endeavored to follow these principals each and every day in their management of the bank. Coupled with love, care and concern for the state of Colorado, the Baltzes believe this human approach keeps the bank in tune with the customers it serves. As time has passed, more and more local banking institutions have been purchased and become assimilated into corporate banking institutions. This care and commitment to seeing customers as not only real people, but neighbors, has made First United Bank even more unique.

First United Bank has the distinction of being the nineteenth largest woman-owned corporation in Colorado, represented by Marty Baltz and the two Baltz daughters, Kimberly and Jennifer. Marty Baltz is active in the corporation,

managing the many properties and making sure they are maintained to the highest standards. The corporation is also the ninety-seventh largest privately owned corporation in the state. Among Mr. Baltz's greatest achievements is handing the reigns over to a second generation. Keeping the bank in the family assures that the years of hard work and level of dedication will be scrupulously maintained.

Kimberly Baltz has followed easily in her father's accomplished footsteps. She is a graduate of both the prestigious Wharton School of Business at the University of Pennsylvania, with an emphasis in accounting, and Colorado University Law School. With business smarts and legal expertise, Ms. Baltz is uniquely qualified to take over daily operations at the bank, a transition expected to occur in 2007. With the love of the bank and pride in the family-run business, the Baltz legacy seems assured.

The bank plans to add more branches in the near future. A new office is planned in Woodland Park and Mr. Baltz has a running list of about thirty other potential branch locations. The Baltzes have big plans for the future, but have no intention of forgetting what has buoyed First United Bank in the past. This means continuing to extend the best service possible and taking responsibility for their place in the greater Colorado business landscape.

The Denver Tech Center branch is the main branch. It is located at Belleview and Ulster in Englewood.

THE FORT

When patrons dine at The Fort, located in the Rocky Mountain foothills of Southwest Denver, they feast on robust delights from an era gone by while embarking upon a journey into living history. The structure is a replica of Bent's Fort, Colorado Territory's first fur trading post, built in 1834. Authentic and detailed in its design, The Fort pays homage to a trade and time past and cultivates an appetite for the cuisine of the old frontier.

The history of The Fort is as unique as its dining experience. It began when Sam and Betty Arnold, founders of The Fort, happened upon a line drawing of Bent's Fort while looking through historical photographs and documents at the Denver Public Library. "It looked just like an Adobe Castle," remembers Arnold. "I thought, wouldn't it be great to live in something like that?" So in 1961 Arnold bought a seven-acre stretch of land overlooking southwest Denver and began the daunting task of building the replica of the historical trading post that was to be the home for Arnold and his family. He hired a twenty-five-man crew from Taos to build the structure, using 80,000 forty-five-pound adobe bricks (each made on the site), supported by hand-hewn beams. He wanted every

Proprietors Samuel Arnold and Holly Arnold Kinney pose in front of The Fort.

feature to be as authentic as possible. Even the floors are the same color as the original "blood floors" of the period.

Unfortunately, funding ran out before his castle was complete. Refused by banks for a residential loan, Arnold reasoned that a business loan would insure him the remaining financing necessary to complete the job. The stipulation, of course, was starting a business. He obliged by opening a restaurant on the first floor, while he and his family inhabited the upper level of The Fort.

Arnold had a fascination with food and a passion for history. The Fort afforded him the opportunity to indulge both interests while creating a unique and profitable business. He became engrossed in the study of Bent's Fort and researched the diaries and journals of early nineteenth-century settlers, trappers and traders. His idea was not only to recreate the types of foods and recipes of the 1830s and 1840s, he wanted his customers to be immersed in the atmosphere—to step foot into another time and place.

Arnold's vision has become his patrons' reality. From the moment they enter the massive front gates of The Fort, history engulfs them. A fire glows in a rock pit in the center of the courtyard. An Indian tepee reminds visitors that Bent's Fort was once a real trading center licensed to trade with the many Indian tribes that inhabited southeastern Colorado as well as fur traders and pioneers moving west and south. On special occasions and most weekends, a

Blackfeet flutist plays original romantic songs throughout the dining rooms. Music of the Indian flute fills the courtyard and spills into separate dining areas where visitors enjoy expertly prepared "new foods of the Old West."

The menu itself is a lesson in frontier history and way of life in the early Colorado territory. Bent's Fort, in particular, was an oasis of civilization in the Western wilderness; fine wines and candlelit tables with elegant tablecloths became expected by its patrons. The same is true at The Fort more than a century later. Special dishes such as peanut butter and pickled jalapenos, Buffalo Bone Marrow (also known as Prairie Butter—the restaurant's award-winning guacamole) and Rocky Mountain Oysters are favorite appetizers. Old West Classics such as the Gonzales Steak stuffed with green chiles and the Game Plate featuring a sampling of elk, teriyaki quail, and tenderloin of buffalo are also served. The Fort's most famous dessert is the Negrita, a dark chocolate ganache with dark rum, served in a tulip cup. Patrons also enjoy the huckleberry crème brulee and chile chocolate cake. Traditional and sometimes long-forgotten ingredients such as: Anasazi beans, purple potatoes and a blend of chiles are served as delicious side dishes. Meals are prepared and presented with authenticity, yet also possess the style of modern-day, cutting-edge cuisine. More information about the menu can be found at The Fort's Web site, www.TheFort.com.

One food synonymous with The Fort is bison—American buffalo. Since 1963 over 1 million buffalo dinners have been served at the restaurant. That averages out to about 70,000 dinners per year. Amazingly, when Arnold first started serving bison, only about 30,000 of the animals were even in existence. The modern buffalo industry has grown right along with The Fort. Now, bison number over 250,000 head and there are bison ranches in all fifty states. The Fort

Diners enjoy a romantic dinner in the Tower Room.

has contributed much to the education about bison's healthful qualities as well as its fine taste. Today, The Fort even sells its famous buffalo steaks online at www.FortTradingCo.com.

Arnold's own culinary education is quite extensive. He studied cooking with James Beard and culinary skills at La Varenne Ecole de Cuisine in Paris. He also attended cooking classes in Sri Lanka, Thailand, and China. Arnold has spoken and cooked around the world, hosted radio and television shows, won countless awards, and has been featured in top culinary publications and national newspapers such as: *The New York Times*, *Americana*, *Newsday*, *People* and *Sunset*. He's made appearances on *The Today Show*, ABC and NBC News, CNN, TNN, *Discovery*, and *Live with Regis and Kathie Lee*.

Co-proprietor and daughter, Holly Arnold Kinney, had the distinct advantage of learning the family business from the time she was a child. She has held many positions at the restaurant, including busser and tortilla girl. She shares her father's interest in travel and often accompanied him to London, Vienna and Switzerland, which helped Kinney develop culinary knowledge at an early age.

The Fort is lit with Farolito lanterns.

As an adult, Kinney gained experience in public relations and the media. In 1981 she founded Arnold Media Services (AMS), a firm focused on specialty food products and the restaurant industry. AMS' accounts were national and international and, for more than twenty years, Kinney's company provided public relations, marketing, advertising and promotional services for clientele including: Nestle Specialty Foods Division, National Bison Association, Hatch Chile Company, Colavita and Monari Federzoni Balsamic Vinegar. In 2002 Arnold Media Services became the in-house public relations, advertising and graphic design agency for The Fort restaurant.

In 2001 Kinney became her father's business partner and 49 percent owner of The Fort restaurant. Active in the day-to-day operations of the restaurant, Kinney manages over ninety employees who she says are "very much like an extended family." Some of the employees have worked at the restaurant for more than fifteen years. One started as a busboy and now is in a top management position. "It's almost as if The Fort sort of chooses its caregivers," says Kinney. "There's just something about the rock, the building—the spirit of the place."

The rich history that intrigues both Kinney and her father inspired The Tesoro Foundation, a nonprofit organization committed to protecting and making available to the community the artistic treasures and history of the American past in the Southwest. Kinney has created a series of living history events including: the Indian Market and Powwow in mid-May; the Spanish Market and 1830s Rendezvous in late September; the Historic Dinner and Lecture Series, January through May; and The Christmas Eve Las Posadas reenactment. The Tesoro Foundation also has an educational outreach program through which historians lead K-12 school groups on tours and present a trunk show, demonstrating life as it was in the 1830s. These events bring to life the traditions that have shaped Colorado's history and the Southwest's heritage.

The Fort has hosted a summit dinner with eight leaders from the leading industrial nations of the world. It also has given tours to grade school children. Even though its visitors are diverse, the appeal of The Fort is universal. Its environment is welcoming and its culinary delights exceptional. It transports its patrons to another place and time, reminding them that even though more than a century has passed, the value of good food and good company has remained the same.

Onlookers observe the grand entry procession into the Indian Market and Powwow.

HOWELL CONSTRUCTION

When James R. Howell was in his teens, he began his career as a professional boxer. After many "rounds" of punches being thrown and being received, James decided to change his career path and enter into the construction industry where he found "victory."

In its seventieth year of business, Howell Construction, a Denver-based general contracting firm, continues to specialize in full-service construction, design-build, tenant finish, renovations, mechanical and electrical systems, as well as project management for new buildings. Its varied projects include commercial buildings, laboratories, medical facilities, industrial complexes and historical restorations along Colorado's Front Range, as well as parts of Wyoming.

The company's longevity is impressive, but not necessarily surprising, considering that its founder spent twenty years learning about the construction business prior to venturing out on his own. At the end of the Roaring Twenties, James Howell started his career working for the construction

Charles W. Fischer, James R. Howell and Carl Streufert (left to right) stand outside Lutheran Hospital nearing completion on July 20, 1961. Courtesy, Rocky Mountain News.

company C.E. Walker—where he quickly advanced. He worked as a carpenter and progressed to a superintendent, while working on what is now a Denver landmark: the Mountain Bell building, located on 14th Street next to the Performing Arts Complex.

In 1935, when C.E. Walker ceased doing business, James opened the doors

to his own firm: James R. Howell & Company (now Howell Construction) and continued working with his established clientele. During its first year of operation, James R. Howell employed a staff of six and saw a volume of approximately $50,000. Although it was difficult fostering a business during the Depression and World War II, James and his wife Hope continued to successfully build the company.

In 1946 their son Robert finished his wartime post in Oakridge, Tennessee— where he worked on the Manhattan project—and came home to join the family business.

The 1950s and 1960s saw an explosion of growth in the Denver area and Howell grew along with it. Although the number of employees increased, the company maintained its philosophy of not taking on more work than it could manage.

In 1973 James R. Howell retired and Robert Howell took over the firm and oversaw the company's operations for the next ten years. Jim, Robert's son, came on board after spending several years working for large international contractors where he managed offshore projects for the oil industry.

It was important for Jim to maintain the firm's philosophy of consistently focusing on building relationships rather than concentrating on a single project relationship with hard-bid work. The philosophy of building solid client relationships was the foundation of the seventy-year-legacy for which Howell Construction is known.

"We're not interested in just working on one job for a client. We're interested in building long-term relationships," Jim said. "We promote loyalty—the key to our success and longevity. Clients, subcontractors, and suppliers continue to work with us year after year. One of our longest-standing customers goes back seventy years." Unlike its competitors,

Steam crane performing earthwork so foundation can be poured at a downtown Denver project site

Howell's philosophy is, "Do not take on more work than you can manage." By following this concept, Howell consistently provides high-quality services to its clients and continues to build its repeat clientele. Jim Howell said, "A project that is too large can absorb a lot of your capacity and time which can be reflected negatively to your steady clientele. Howell Construction has maintained its place in the market by accepting projects they can dedicate their full attention to and successfully complete without impacting other projects. We work very hard to turn out a superior project. You can put money into marketing and bidding or you can put the same amount of money into improving relationships and processes with your clients. In one case you get to meet a lot of different people and in the other the same person a lot of times. We'd rather put the value into the job. You may not make much money in certain markets that way, but during down markets, you do much better because your existing clients have projects for you to build."

Mountain Bell Building.

In the late 1990s, after managing a major subcontracting company and working for a management consulting firm to the construction industry, Joe Slavik joined Howell Construction.

When Jim stepped down as president, it was not difficult for him to choose his successor. Although the transition meant that Howell would no longer be a "family business," Joe was the natural choice for president. Even though Jim still serves as chairman of the board, he has handed over the leadership and partial ownership of the company to Joe. "One of the reasons Joe is here is because he shares the same value systems that we have had for three generations," said Jim Howell.

The emphasis on strong relationships extends beyond Howell's clients to the people who work for the company. Howell's seventy-five employees average twelve years with the firm. Joe said, "We have very little turnover. We've been very picky about making sure there's a fit with the employee and the company's needs. Today, many firms will hire the best person available in the marketplace rather than waiting for the 'right fit.' We won't do that. It is too important for us to make sure our clients continue to enjoy working with our staff year after year." Joe added, "By demonstrating an incredible loyalty to our employees, we can be assured that when times get tough, the tough won't get going. Loyalty works both ways."

One of the biggest changes Howell has seen over the past seven decades is the price for materials and the cost of labor. Today a project is likely to have at least four times the overhead costs than a project would have in the 1930s, 1940s and 1950s. Back then materials were hard to come by—builders would save and re-use their materials. However, labor was inexpensive. Now, the opposite is true: materials are relatively inexpensive and labor is costly. In this sense, Howell's loyalty to and care for their quality employees has become increasingly important.

In another vein, the success of Howell Construction has depended increasingly on their ability to understand and accommodate the ever-changing needs of their client's industries. For example, in 1928

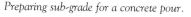
Preparing sub-grade for a concrete pour.

James R. Howell helped build the largest telephone building west of the Mississippi, when he worked for C.E. Walker. At that time, the structure was primarily a warehouse for equipment and people and its mechanical and electrical systems represented a mere 20 percent of the total cost of the project. Today, in the same kind of structures, the installation of mechanical and electrical systems can represent 80 percent of the cost of a job.

Howell is recognized in the industry as a leader in highly specialized markets, including telecom, data center, biotech, aerospace, high-tech, medical, and pharmaceutical.

The limitations of construction in medical and high tech are challenging. Not only are these projects driven by the processes of the client's company, from chemistry on a research scale to pharmaceutical production, but they are also driven by the utilities needed to

Howell Construction provided construction services for the Denver Country Club.

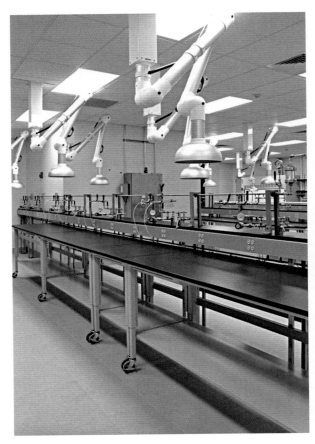

Dharmacon RNA Technologies Laboratory.

support these processes. Additionally, it is critical that construction in these technical environments does not interrupt a client's daily operations. In the high tech market, Howell is mindful that noise, dust, unexpected shutdowns, contamination and vibrations can affect research and development. Part of Howell's success lies in their understanding of how to work in an occupied facility without compromising client's production.

In order to stay at the forefront in its field, Howell Construction has learned to excel at collaborative project delivery. Its synergy with its subcontractors and clients has created a positive impact in the community. Giving back to the community has always been important to Howell Construction. Each year the company contributes more than 2 percent of its earnings to charities along with donating goods and services. For thirty years

Howell has completed a large amount of work for cost at Lutheran Hospital, formerly a nonprofit facility that primarily treated lung diseases like tuberculosis. Howell has also supported the Boys and Girls Club of America. James R. Howell was one of the founders of the Club in Denver and helped them build their first local facility. He also served on the organization's board for a number of years, as did Robert and Jim. Another Howell Construction veteran, Joe Slavik, followed suit by participating in the Boys and Girls Club's Associate Board.

As Howell has grown and prospered along with Denver, it has also evolved with the times. Jim Howell and Joe Slavik are proud of the projects they have worked on, their clientele, the dedicated staff they have retained and the fact that they have been in business for more than seventy years. The Howell family's values, high-quality service, and community involvement will keep the company prospering for many years to come.

IRON & METALS, INC.

Many Americans believe that recycling is a decidedly modern concept. In truth, the practice has been around for hundreds of years. Just look at the scrap metal industry. For centuries, scrap yards have been collecting and purchasing steel, aluminum, copper and other metals and selling them to steel mills, copper smelters and other entities that render the pieces into usable metals.

One Denver family has been involved in the scrap metal industry for more than ninety years. Robert "Bob" Cohen got an early introduction to metal recycling. His father-in-law had founded such a business in Nebraska before WWI, and Bob helped out in the scrap yard while growing up.

Bob was trained as a mechanical engineer, but decided that he wanted to follow in his father-in-law's footsteps with a scrap metal company of his own. The enterprising young man moved to California in 1961 to establish such an operation. The venture failed to get off the ground, but Bob was undeterred by the failure and remained determined to run his own business.

That same year Bob learned about a scrap metal business in Denver that was being forced to liquidate its assets due

Portable shear cutting a steel I-Beam, in front of the new 55,000 square-foot warehouse.

to legal problems. Bob jumped at the opportunity and convinced a couple of his former colleagues to provide financial backing for the acquisition. Although Bob purchased the assets of the liquidated scrap metal processor, he didn't inherit any employees or the name of the previous company. Only a single customer came with the deal: a manufacturer in Fort Collins, who is still a customer today. Basically, Bob had to start the company from scratch.

On December 10, 1961 Iron & Metals, Inc. (IMI) began operations at 585 Walnut Street, currently the site of the

viaduct between I-25 and the Auraria campus. Situated on six acres, the recycling operation included a warehouse building that measured approximately 10,000 square feet and included a small office. With ten employees, Bob got operations underway. Like other businesses of its kind, IMI purchased scrap metal, which it sorted by type and grade before cutting or baling it into compressed units to be sold to steel mills, copper smelters and other metal manufacturers. During the early days, the yard processed about 1,000 tons of scrap per month. As his employees strained to sort through what came in each day, Bob couldn't help but think that there ought to be a better way to get the job done.

Thanks, perhaps, to his education in mechanical engineering, Bob discovered a way to streamline the process for both his employees and customers—specialized containers. Manufacturing customers would benefit by placing scrap metal left over from their processes into specialized containers. This would help keep their plants cleaner and would allow them to receive more money for scrap because it was already separated by alloy. On IMI's end, the sorting process was simplified. Bob's creation cemented IMI's reputation as a service provider for its customers. It also made such an

A bale of old auto radiators is ready for shipment to a brass smelter, where they will be melted down to make new brass.

The new "centurion" high-speed baler.

promises and providing the highest quality service to customers was the top priority at IMI. That notion of fairness has remained as a cornerstone of the business, even as it has passed from one generation of Cohens to the next.

Bob's sons, Alan and Murray, both worked at the scrap yard as teens, performing a variety of tasks. Although both initially followed other career paths as adults, they eventually came to work with their father. Alan came on board full-time in 1978 as foreman of scrap steel, then became vice president, and eventually, CEO. When Murray joined the business in 1982, he took over the scrap steel department from Alan, and went on to become COO. By 1986 Bob and Alan had bought out the original financial backers, and IMI became a true family-owned and operated business.

An electromagnet on a crane loads cut steel on to a railcar for shipment to a steel mill.

impact on the scrap yard's operations and on its customers that other scrap metal businesses took note. Before long, specialized containers became the standard in the industry.

Although business picked up quickly, the early days at IMI weren't free of challenges. In 1965 the Platte River flooded, briefly leaving IMI under seven feet of water. Bob and his employees acted quickly and rescued the company's trucks from the rising waters. Because of their swift actions, IMI didn't lose a single day of service to its customers.

As the Denver area expanded during the 1960s and 1970s, so did IMI. By the early 1970s IMI had outgrown its original location. To meet increased demand, the company built a new, state-of-the-art facility on a twenty-acre lot that had once been a feed lot in the Stockyards area, north of downtown Denver.

Bob was determined to have the most advanced equipment available in the new facility. In addition, he wanted it to be the most service-oriented scrap yard in the Denver area. Bob succeeded on both these counts. When IMI moved into the new plant in 1975, it was equipped with the most modern piece of equipment in all of Denver: the area's first hydraulic shear for cutting steel. Customer convenience was vastly improved thanks to the new facility's 3,000 feet of rail tracks, a 55,000-square-foot warehouse, a vehicle repair shop and an office building.

From the beginning, Bob's business philosophy centered on fairness—to both customers and employees. Keeping

In the hands of the second generation, IMI continued to grow. Alan and Murray focused on serving manufacturers and demolition contractors—the key customers their father had cultivated from the start. Maintaining relationships with existing customers is one of the keys that helped IMI succeed for more than forty years.

In 1997 Alan's son Mike joined the family firm, marking the debut of the third generation at IMI. By 2004 Mike took on the role of president. With Alan, Murray and Mike on board, IMI continued to modernize. Just as Bob sought out the most technologically advanced equipment, so have IMI's current leaders. The hydraulic shears Bob introduced back in the 1970s have since been replaced by five portable shears. The firm also boasts a computerized high-speed baler for aluminum and copper.

The second and third generations of Cohens have also improved on the specialized containers Bob introduced. The containers, which revolutionized the industry, have become IMI's calling card. Today the firm specializes in container service for industrial customers of all sizes and provides more container

Cutting thick steel plate with the acetelyne torch.

sizes and styles than anyone in the Denver area.

As a testament to its commitment to service, IMI has also made improvements to its scrap yard. Customers who deliver scrap to IMI find twenty paved acres, two full-length truck scales, dedicated receiving docks and a crew that's dedicated to making the drop-off experience a pleasant one. An abundance of cranes, loaders and forklifts in the receiving area provide customers

with safe and hassle-free unloading. The modernization efforts have improved efficiency, allowing IMI to process about 8,000 tons of metal per month, including all grades of steel, cast iron, aluminum, copper, insulated wire, brass, stainless steel, titanium, high-temp alloys and more.

To keep all that metal moving and ensure that operations are running smoothly, takes the efforts of about sixty dedicated employees, one-fourth of whom have been with the company for more than two decades. Retaining employees and helping them grow as individuals has always been important at IMI. To help maintain employee loyalty, the family business leaders created a profit-sharing program. The generous bonus program puts one-third of the company's profits directly in the hands of its employees.

With both its employees and its customers, IMI has continually sought out long-term partnerships and relationships. Just as Bob Cohen focused on fairness and on delivering on promises to both customers and employees, the current leadership does the same. With this unparalleled commitment, it's no wonder that Iron & Metals, Inc. has been so successful for so many decades.

The original Iron & Metals, Inc. facility stood at 585 Walnut.

JOHNSON & WALES UNIVERSITY

Johnson & Wales University (J&W) was founded in 1914 in Providence, Rhode Island by Gertrude I. Johnson and Mary T. Wales. Through the years, the school has evolved from a business school to a dynamic, multi-campus nonprofit university. Though its roots lie on the east coast, the school's presence has blossomed in Colorado. Today, the uni-versity's twenty-six acre Denver campus serves as a preeminent choice for students interested in business, culinary arts and hospitality programs. Despite changing times and curriculum, Johnson & Wales University has always sought to serve its students first.

Johnson & Wales University counts over 16,000 students currently enrolled across four campuses. Nearly every state in the Union, and Washington DC, is represented. Close to 1,000 students hail from ninety-seven foreign countries. These students participate in fifty-eight different undergraduate programs.

These statistics are particularly amazing in light of the fact that the school could easily have closed its doors in the 1940s. At that point, the school had been in operation as a for-profit business for over thirty years. After so many years of dedicated service, Gertrude Johnson and Mary Wales wished to retire. However, they were torn about the fate of the school they had founded. Should they sell the

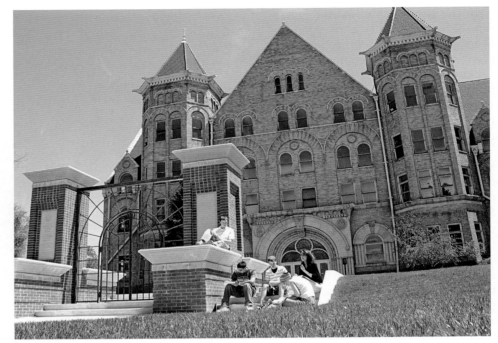

College of Business Graduate Melissa Fuller and her mother, Karen Fuller. Melissa is off to Nashville to launch a career in the music industry.

institution, or perhaps close its doors entirely?

Wilma Triangolo, an instructor at the school, urged the founders to speak with her husband, Ed. Ed and his Navy buddy, Morris Gaebe, offered to purchase the school and continue its legacy. Johnson & Wales University changed hands in 1947, and Ed Triangolo became the school's first president. Morris Gaebe remains the school's Chancellor and Chairman Emeritus to this day.

A landmark year for Johnson & Wales University was 1963. That year, the state of Rhode Island granted the school non-profit, degree-granting status. By 1970 this charter had expanded to include bachelor's degrees. In 1973 the university launched what is now known as the College of Culinary Arts and The Hospitality College. Many people find it surprising that the culinary and hospitality programs are relatively recent additions to the school, since the programs are now internationally renowned.

Johnson & Wales University not only expanded its curriculum and degree programs, but

New and old history converge. Students studying outside historic Treat Hall on the Coors Family Commons at the Taylor Gate, dedicated in May 2004.

its campuses as well. In the 1980s, campuses in Virginia and South Carolina were added to the J&W family. The campus in Norfolk, Virginia began as a training facility for culinary students through contracts with the U.S. military. From this small training area, a full-grown campus emerged, evolving even further in 2004 when it merged into the new Charlotte campus.

In the 1990s the school began looking toward the new millennium. A fully functioning western campus was a key target for the university. Many cities, including San Diego and Dallas, were considered. With the assistance of Pete Coors, the decision was finally made to call Denver, with its gorgeous mountain geography and ideal central location, home.

In 1999 a group of eleven faculty and administrators arrived in Denver full of pioneering spirit and ready to create a new campus. At the school's convocation on September 5, 2000, 325 students began as the inaugural class of Johnson & Wales University, Denver. J&W's small boutique campus in Vail, Colorado, which offered associate's degrees only, merged with the new

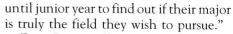

Denver campus when classes officially commenced in 2000.

In six short years, the Denver campus has experienced explosive growth. Fifty-two faculty and administrative staff members have expanded to 123 seemingly overnight. The student population has grown by nearly 500 percent.

Dean of University Relations Mike Pasquarella chalks this up to giving students what they want and need: practical skills that will help them attain meaningful employment after graduation. This includes a novel approach to undergraduate academics: students take classes aimed at their major in their first two years at school. This is contrary to traditional curriculum programming, which emphasizes core curriculum classes in the freshman and sophomore years.

The administration at J&W sees this approach as fundamentally important to the success of their students. When students arrive with some degree of focus, the university feels a responsibility to acknowledge and feed that drive. The university also employs a three term year, as opposed to the usual two. This system allows students to have a more concentrated schedule while still

Input from alumni in all industries contributes to what makes J&W America's Career University®.

Bette Matkowski, Johnson & Wales University Denver campus president.

accomplishing the same amount of work each school year.

The university believes that it makes good common sense to allow students to explore their interests right away. "It's probably motivating for students to follow their desires," explains Dean Pasquarella. "Best case scenario, it's what they came to school for. In another case, they don't have to wait

until junior year to find out if their major is truly the field they wish to pursue."

Dean Pasquarella recounts the famous portent given by numerous educators of yore: "Look to your left. Look to your right. Come graduation day, only one of you will remain." This is not the J&W philosophy. "There is no sifting out point," the Dean explains. "We want all three students to remain. And succeed."

The university measures its success by employment rates. Since 1977 Johnson & Wales University has had an astonishing 98 percent student employment rate within sixty days of graduation. As long as employers keep hiring Johnson & Wales University graduates, the formula must be right.

The university goes to great lengths to provide the best educational experience possible and to make the campus experience as rounded and balanced as any other undergraduate institution. Approximately 40 percent of J&W's Denver students live on campus. Most are traditional undergraduates, with a significant number of transfer students matriculating annually as well.

Johnson & Wales University also has a broad offering of co- and extracurricular activities. Several organizations are related to the main majors J&W offers and the industries students will be entering, such as Baking and Pastry Club and Chippers Ice Sculptors Club. Student government and academic organizations also abound on campus. Intramural and club sports and theatre groups also have a significant campus presence at Johnson & Wales University.

Historic Treat Hall, the original building on the campus of the now-closed Colorado Women's College, will be restored to create a hotel and restaurant. This will serve as the experiential learning facility for J&W business, hospitality and culinary arts students on the Denver campus. Thanks to corporate internship partners Sage Hospitality Resources and Myriad Restaurant Group, proceeds from the hotel will be used for scholarships.

Johnson & Wales University has other unique requirements for all

graduates. In addition to eleven weeks of experiential education, each student must fulfill a leadership concentration and a service learning requirement. Everything the university does is centered around leadership to ensure students are well-rounded professionals and life-long contributors to their communities. Students serve the community through twenty-five different service organizations, contributing over 65,000 hours of service since the Denver campus debuted. In dollars and cents, this effort has amounted to over $1.2 million in volunteer time.

Not only do students help in the community, they do so in ways that positively exploit their own talents. The culinary nutrition program blends the artistry of food with the science of nutrition. By lending their special skills to the Rocky Mountain Multiple Sclerosis Center, culinary nutrition students have helped those affected by MS live better lives through nutrition.

J&W culinary students have also made a remarkable difference in the lives of children living with PKU. PKU, or phenylketonuria, is charac-

Co-curricular programs like club sports, intramurals and campus activities complete the university experience.

terized by an inability to digest a particular essential amino acid. PKU can be controlled, but only through a highly restricted diet. J&W chefs and culinary students put their skills to the test and put together a menu that was not only safe, but enjoyable. The children and their parents were overwhelmed with gratitude.

While the school's expansion continues at a steady pace, the administration in Denver is careful to remain mindful of the university's first obligation to the

The College of Culinary Arts is market driven, providing bachelors degrees such as Culinary Nutrition to serve society's growing demands.

students it has currently enrolled. When asked if an extension or graduate program is imminent, the Dean explains that plans are definitely underway, but the school's first priority is to maintain the quality of its still relatively young program. Denver campus president Bette Matkowski came to the university in February 2005, and her vision has been to create the best university experience in Colorado. Though the growth of the school in Colorado has been explosive, the administration has resolved to maintain a strong foundation.

In all areas, Johnson & Wales University does its level best not to try to be everything for all people. Rather, the university prides itself on maximizing strong points. Whether this is in its students' service opportunities, or the school's own curriculum, J&W manages to be most balanced by setting priorities that serve its students and its Denver community. It is in this simple approach that the university is most innovative. It is also this positive approach that students carry away with them into highly promising and productive futures.

KIT CARSON COUNTY MEMORIAL HOSPITAL

Located in the rural farming community of Burlington—population 3,700—the Kit Carson County Memorial Hospital (KCCMH), part of the Kit Carson County Health Service District (KCCHSD), is a twenty-five-bed "Critical Access" hospital serving the Kit Carson County area.

Kit Carson County and its 793 farms ranks first in the state in wheat production (especially winter wheat), second in sunflower production, third in dry beans, fourth in the state in corn and third in the overall production of all crops, including barley. There are also four major feedlots in the Burlington area.

It is also home to the Kit Carson County Carousel. This hand-carved armored horse and forty-five other wooden animals were carved by the Philadelphia Toboggan Co. in 1905, and the Carousel is now registered as a National Historic Landmark. Much more than a children's amusement ride, the Carousel is a symbol of Burlington's powerful sense of community, which also imbues the Kit Carson County Health Service District.

KCCHSD states their mission is "to provide state-of-the-art, quality health services that will give the regional community both the opportunity and the

KCCMH's administrative team.

desire to receive care and treatment locally. It is our intent to deliver these services with utmost safety, honesty, and integrity." This mission is evident in the strong relationship and place of respect the hospital has enjoyed with the community since the medical facility's inception.

When the hospital was first established in 1948 as a replacement for the Hayes General Hospital, which had burned down, the new facility was known as "The Hospital that Wheat Helped to Build." The phrase reflects

Opening of Kit Carson Memorial Hospital in 1948.

the deep roots the hospital has in the local community.

Local wheat farmers pledged proceeds from crops, while other farmers hauled bricks, blocks and other supplies from as far away as Denver to assure that the hospital would be built. Women's groups, including the Modern Homemakers Club, the Happy Hours Home Demonstration Club and the Burlington Garden Club made drapes for the hospital sunroom and donated plants for the landscaping of the hospital. It was a community effort in every sense of the word.

Since the late 1940s many changes have taken place in medicine as well as the manner in which medical services are delivered to a rural community. Though hospitals like KCCMH may be small, they nonetheless must provide many of the same services offered by a hospital in a major city.

Jim Jordan has been with the hospital since 1975 and has served as CEO since 1998. Under his guidance, KCCMH has become a leader amoung the country's rural community hospitals. The hospital offers exceptional outpatient services, with its two Family Practice Clinics—the Parke Health and Stratton Medical Clinic and the Parke Wellness rehab facility.

KCCMH offers patients a full radiology and laboratory department and some

outpatient surgeries. Around thirty specialty clinic doctors regularly visit KCCMH from Denver, some three hours away. Visiting specialists offer services in the fields of: otolaryngology (ENT); urology; orthopedics; colorectal and laproscopic surgery; cardiology; gastroenterology; dermatology; neurology; oncology; hematology; pulmonary critical care; OB/GYN; CRNA-ARNP; general surgery; as well as pathology and radiology.

Providing rehab programs to eastern Colorado and western Kansas, the Parke Wellness Center (PWC) provides comprehensive physical and occupational therapies, and cardiac and pulmonary rehabilitation. PWC also offers therapy for orthopedic and sports injuries, developmental problems, faulty posture and arthritis. For a nominal monthly fee, the Center offers local residents an independent exercise program, as well as diabetic counseling, massage therapy, aquatic therapy and functional capacity testing for Workman's Compensation cases. PWC has licensed physical therapists, certified physical therapist assistants, cardiac rehab nurses and occupational therapist assistants.

The Stratton Medical Clinic (SMC)—located fifteen miles west of Burlington—is a satellite facility of KCCMH, serving the health care

The Parke Health and Wellness Center.

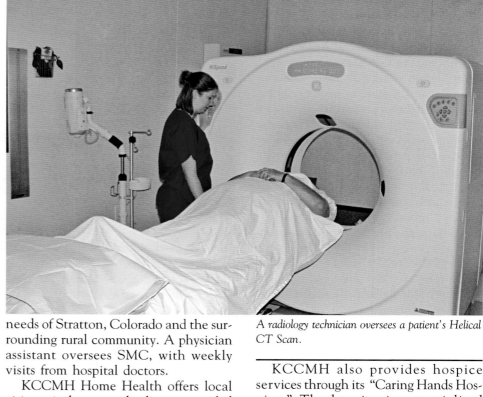

A radiology technician oversees a patient's Helical CT Scan.

needs of Stratton, Colorado and the surrounding rural community. A physician assistant oversees SMC, with weekly visits from hospital doctors.

KCCMH Home Health offers local citizens in-home medical care provided by licensed healthcare professionals (RN, LPN and CNA). Coordinated and supervised by a registered nurse, the services offered by Home Health include skilled nursing, home health aide, physical therapy, occupational therapy and speech therapy to Medicare, Medicaid, Workman's Compensation and private insurance clients.

KCCMH also provides hospice services through its "Caring Hands Hospice." The hospice is a specialized healthcare program, which emphasizes the management of pain and other symptoms associated with terminal illness. Through a ministry of care and love, the staff is dedicated to helping patients affirm the closing of one's life with dignity and integrity, as well as aiding the families and friends of hospice patients.

As part of its community outreach program, KCCMH offers $500 scholarships to five county high school students who will be continuing their educations in healthcare or medicine. In addition, there is a summer internship where students can learn about healthcare and how healthcare works. On average, the student interns work in about five or six different departments over the course of the summer including Parke Health, the Parke Wellness rehab clinic, the radiology department, and the lab, as well as possible visits to surgery or OB deliveries, where they can observe and/or facilitate.

Each year KCCMH staff members visit the five schools in the county and do a safety demonstration on bike helmets, instructing students to wear them while biking, inline skating, skateboarding or using a scooter. As part of this outreach program, bike helmets are donated each year to every first grader in the county.

Even with all the good work KCCMH does with the community and the excellent medical services they provide for Burlington residents, CEO Jim Jordan points out that there are still major challenges the medical facility faces on a regular basis. High on that list is the ability to recruit and maintain a professional medical staff. "Trying to get anyone, not just physicians, with advanced healthcare training, skills and degrees to move to rural America is tough," says Jordan. "We don't have the glamour and conveniences of a big city. We don't have doctors in the house twenty-four/seven to do ER. After our physicians have spent a full day in the clinic, they rotate in covering the ER. That's tough. They have evening and weekend calls. They work holidays. Typically, to overcome that, we have to give an above average wage. We probably offer $50,000 more than a similar

A patient shows off his work during the hospital's annual Christmas Door Decorating Contest.

family practice doctor working in downtown Denver just as an incentive to get them to come and work in rural America."

KCCMH also offers doctors partial loan repayment for medical school and a generous relocation package. In return a doctor, radiologist or other sought-after medical professional must commit

to working at the hospital for anywhere from five to eight years, depending on the recruitment package they have been offered.

Burlington residents have even chipped in to help with recruiting. A farmer promised to pay medical school tuition for two local young men as long as they agreed to come back and work at KCCMH for at least three years. Those two young men are now staff doctors at the hospital and have been for more than six years.

KCCMH has big plans for improving the quality of healthcare in Kit Crason County. A new 30,000 square foot expansion to the hospital is in the planning stages. KCCMH's Director of Growth and Development, Diane Mettling, says that with the new $10 million expansion, patients will experience more personalized hospital stays with private hospital rooms and baths and a more efficient ER. Currently the ER is located on the second floor and patients need to come up to the ER by elevator.

"As our mission statement affirms, our goal is to provide local access to quality healthcare," says Mettling. "It drives everything, and to that end we are in the process of getting an expansion approved so we can bring our patients a larger surgery area and a new and more efficient ground floor ER. We are always working to make sure that our hospital is big enough and modern enough so that our local community doesn't have to go elsewhere for medical treatment."

Mettling says that they will also be holding town meetings like in days past, with hopes of getting the community as involved with the building of the expansion as they were back in 1947.

Currently, there are three physicians, two physician assistants, one nurse practitioner and twelve RNs on staff. KCCHSD is the second largest employer in the area, just a few employees behind the local school district. KCCHSD employs 140 full and part-time staff.

To learn more about the Kit Carson County Memorial Hospital and the Kit Carson Health Services District, visit www.kccmh.org.

KCCMH's nursing staff celebrates Halloween.

LUCKY THREE RANCH

"You can catch more flies with honey than with vinegar."

We've all heard the saying, but for Meredith Hodges, it is a personal philosophy—a practice born of necessity. For the last twenty-five years Meredith has bred and trained some of the most accomplished sport mules in the country at her Lucky Three Ranch in Loveland, Colorado. Years of study and practice and scores of victories and failures have taught her that patience, kindness and consideration are prerequisite to winning the heart and mind of a mule.

As a top-notch trainer, competitor and educator, Meredith has played a crucial role in the effort to move mules into the equine mainstream and showcase their extraordinary athleticism and versatility. It has been a challenging, sometimes contentious, journey. She has generated curiosity, skepticism, even outrage; but the question observers have asked more than any other is, "Why mules?"

Meredith grew up in Minneapolis, where her father, *Peanuts* cartoonist

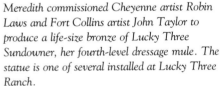

Meredith commissioned Cheyenne artist Robin Laws and Fort Collins artist John Taylor to produce a life-size bronze of Lucky Three Sundowner, her fourth-level dressage mule. The statue is one of several installed at Lucky Three Ranch.

Nestled near the foothills of the Rockies, Lucky Three Ranch has grown from 10 to 127 acres. The ranch is home to nineteen mules, two donkeys and eight horses.

Charles M. Schulz, and her mother, Joyce Doty, indulged her fondness for horses, particularly Arabians. After school, she pursued a career in the medical field, but her interest in equines never faded. In 1973 Meredith was employed as a psychiatric technician at Sonoma State Hospital when her mother Joyce Doty asked her to lend a hand on her 1,000-acre Windy Valley Ranch in Healdsburg, California. Joyce kept mules, and her stock was widely considered the best available. She traveled the country to find high-quality donkey jacks and mares and built a solid business breeding mules for clients such as Grand Canyon National Park.

Meredith agreed to come help, but not without some trepidation. After all, common knowledge held that while mules and donkeys may be tough, they are also stubborn, stupid, ornery creatures. She had heard all the myths: "If you want to get a mule's attention, you've got to hit him with a two-by-four," and "A mule never forgets. If you do him wrong, it might take a while, but some day, some way, he'll get you back."

As it turned out, Meredith had nothing to fear. Mules, she discovered, aren't stubborn—only cautious—and they certainly are not stupid. In fact, she was captivated by their intelligence and sensitivity. Within three months of signing on at the ranch, she had caught a case of "mule fever" so severe she never kicked it.

Meredith worked at Windy Valley for several years, halter-breaking the foals and serving as assistant trainer, groom and all-around helper. When her mother disbanded the ranch in 1979, Meredith moved to Loveland to pursue veterinary medicine at Colorado State University. She bought a ten-acre spread—an old, dilapidated sheep farm—and named it Lucky Three Ranch. She put her skills as a trainer to work and was soon training mules and horses full-time.

"Back then I still had so much to learn, but I was always looking for new ways to connect with the animals," she recalls.

Meredith understood the physical and psychological differences between mules and horses, and she knew that traditional techniques designed to "force" an animal into submission are ineffective with mules. From their donkey fathers, mules inherit a powerful instinct for self-preservation. Meredith had to gain not only the mule's respect but also his trust.

"A mule is an ideal reflection of the sort of person you are," she says. "He wants to please but won't if he's confused or fearful. It's simple, really. If he's not doing what you ask, then you're not asking the right way."

Meredith and her good friend Bonnie Shields both enjoy the company of mules. Bonnie, known as the Tennessee Mule Artist, illustrated all of the books in the Jasper the Mule *series.*

Jasper the Mule has become a popular celebrity. In 2005 he was Grand Marshall of the Bishop Mule Days Parade, and kids everywhere respond to his playful nature.

In her search for answers, Meredith recalled her work as a psychiatric technician. At the hospital, she had learned behavior-modification techniques based on positive rather than negative reinforcement—a reward for good behavior rather than punishment for bad. It was a slow process and at times, her frustration drove her to tears; but her diligence

paid off. The reward-based training techniques she developed produced reliable, versatile, happy animals.

Meredith also began her own breeding program with Little Jack Horner, the last donkey from Windy Valley and a direct descendant of George Washington's own breeding stock. In 1785 Washington received a prized Catalonian jack from the King of Spain. He named the donkey Royal Gift and used him to launch the country's first mule-breeding program. Within a century, mules in the U.S. numbered in the millions.

In the twenty years Meredith has bred mules, she has paired Little Jack Horner with Quarter Horses, Appaloosas, Arabians, Thoroughbreds, Paints and Trakehners. The mules inherit athletic ability and beauty from the mare and draw intelligence, strength and resilience from the donkey. Meredith's animals boast ample quantities of all of those attributes.

Both her mules and donkeys have excelled in competition. Many of their victories came at Bishop Mule Days, where Meredith has been a regular for two decades. Held annually in Bishop, California, Bishop Mule Days is the nation's largest mule show. Each Memorial Day weekend, more than 30,000 people gather to watch 700 mules compete in 150 events. In 1991 Little Jack Horner cleared a four-foot jump and still holds the record as the only formal jumping donkey in the world. In 2006 one of her star mules, Mae Bea C.T., was inducted into the Bishop Mule Days Hall of Fame.

Other achievements at Bishop include a Reining Championship, Donkey Driving Championships, Single-Hitch Driving Championships, the International Side Saddle Organization's International Championship for two years running, and two Third-Level Dressage World Championships. That's right, dressage.

Although many equestrians pick one event and stick with it, Meredith's curiosity and competitive spirit compelled her to try them all. As her animals became proficient in traditional Western events, she ventured into the English riding disciplines. Dressage is considered

both a path and a destination in competitive riding. Designed to develop the equine's natural athletic ability, the complex footwork requires suppleness, balance and obedience. Meredith was eager to give it a try, but first she had to convince the United States Dressage Federation to admit the mule. In 1986 she made a presentation to the organization and secured permission to enter the lower-level schooling shows. Meredith began training immediately.

"In some ways, it was like starting over," she says. "I was learning to ride in a whole new way."

Meredith and her mules made steady progress. Mae Bea C.T. advanced to third-level dressage, and Lucky Three Sundowner reached fourth level. Still it wasn't enough. Meredith and Mae Bea C.T. ventured into jumping, then into combined training, in which riders compete over two or three days in dressage, cross-country jumping and stadium jumping. Meredith raised more than a few eyebrows when she showed up at these events with a mule. Most who saw her were open-minded. Some, however, were insulted by the notion.

"No forty-dollar mule is going up against my hundred-thousand-dollar

Meredith's champion donkey, Little Jack Horner, still holds the record as the only formal jumping donkey, after his jump of nearly four feet at Bishop Mule Days in 1991.

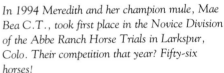

In 1994 Meredith and her champion mule, Mae Bea C.T., took first place in the Novice Division of the Abbe Ranch Horse Trials in Larkspur, Colo. Their competition that year? Fifty-six horses!

horse," was a common refrain. It was an insult to the sport, some said; others had concerns about safety, suggesting that mules and horses simply don't mix. But none could deny Meredith and Mae Bea C.T.'s skill demonstrated in competition.

Their crowning achievement came in 1994, when they took first place over fifty-six horses in the Novice Division of the Abbe Ranch Horse Trials in Larkspur, Colorado. Meredith considers it her proudest moment.

"We competed for three years and when we finally won, everyone was so

gracious," she says. "It was a wonderful moment for us and a great moment for mules."

Since then, others have followed in Meredith's footsteps, and recently the USDF changed its rules again to admit mules into all but the highest levels of competition.

Meredith has secured her reputation as a champion-level competitor and an expert within the industry, but she has also earned notice from the public at large, especially in Colorado. She has participated in countless parades and equine events in the state and received frequent coverage from local and regional media. At the Ride for the Cure fundraiser for breast cancer in 2003, she wowed the crowd by riding one mule while driving another in front, taking them through dressage patterns and over jumps. She has also been a guest speaker for the Loveland and Fort Collins Rotary Clubs, the Women's E-Network and schools throughout Larimer County. In 2005 even the Colorado State Senate acknowledged her work on behalf of mules with a Letter of Commendation.

During the years that Meredith has worked with these animals, mules and donkeys have enjoyed nothing short of a renaissance. By the early twentieth century, these once indispensable partners in the fields, mines, mountains and battlefields had largely been replaced by trucks, tractors and other vehicles. By the 1960s the number of mules in the U.S. had dwindled to fewer than 10,000. But in 1967 Texans Paul and Betsy Hutchins founded the American Donkey and Mule Society with the aim to register and promote longears. Other groups followed, and today no fewer than six magazines, more than 130 organizations and at least 300 shows exist to celebrate longears. As breeding standards improved and people like Meredith began to explore their potential, mules became increasingly versatile. Today they compete in an amazing variety of events, including dressage, jumping, hunter/jumper, endurance, Western events, English events, polo, racing, roping and driving. Mules even have their own holiday. National Mule Appreciation Day, established through an act of Congress, is celebrated on the twenty-sixth of October.

Meredith's role in this movement has become that of educator and advocate. In 1993 she published her first book, *Training Mules and Donkeys: A Logical Approach to Longears*. A series of ten videotapes on training and several more books followed, as well as an extensive Web site and a television series for RFD-TV.

"My training program is like grade school for mules," she says. "Each tape represents about a year of training, and the ten tapes are designed to be followed in sequence, regardless of the animal's age or ability."

Meredith's resistance-free training series, *Training Mules and Donkeys*, is the first correspondence equine training course. Meredith encourages her students to call or e-mail with questions and progress reports. If they are taking the time to do it right, she says, it is the least she can do.

This is typical of a woman raised in a down-to-earth Midwestern home, where the truth wasn't sugarcoated and one did not get lost in image and ego. Friends will say that despite abundant opportu-

Meredith trained her champion mule, Lucky Three Sundowner, to fourth-level dressage. They won the Third-Level Dressage World Championship at Bishop Mule Days, and Meredith helped pave the way for the United States Dressage Federation's recent decision to allow mules into most levels of competition.

nity, Meredith has never sought the limelight or put herself above pitching in to help. For her, the mules and donkeys are the real stars.

Meredith turned the spotlight on longears again in 2003, when, in honor of her father and inspired by her mother, she published her first children's book. The genesis of *Jasper: The Story of a Mule* was a letter she wrote to herself for her long-running magazine column "Mule Crossing." The missive from an imaginary young mule tells of his fears and frustration as he tries to please his human owner. From that piece, Meredith developed a series of holiday-themed books—including *Jasper: A Christmas Caper*, *Jasper: A Precious Valentine*, and *Jasper: A Fabulous Fourth*—and produced "Jasper: The Story of a Mule," an animated program based on the first book.

More than just a collection of entertaining stories, the Jasper the Mule series sparkles with wholesome values and a few lessons about life. Meredith continually strives to be of service to the community at large and promote her favorite cause. In this case, the Colorado Senate and Legislature marked her success with a Letter of Commendation for introducing mules to school children through her children's books.

Another example of Meredith's community-based efforts with mules in mind is her work with Hearts & Horses, a Loveland-based therapeutic riding cen-

ter. Meredith has provided significant financial support to the nonprofit organization, lobbied for the use of mules in the program and hopes to contribute some of her own someday.

Today, Lucky Three Ranch sprawls across 127 acres at the base of the Rocky Mountain foothills. The ranch is home to nineteen mules, two donkeys and eight horses, and Meredith frequently gives tours to visitors. In the last several years, she has amassed a respectable collection of longears-inspired art, including several life-size bronze sculptures. Her long-term plans include a longears sculpture park and museum open to the public—appropriate in a city known internationally for hosting the largest sculpture show in the world.

Meredith has plenty of new ventures in store. None, however, will take her far from home. Often enough, she is behind a podium making a speech or receiving an award, but she is just as likely to be found out back bathing and grooming half a dozen mules. Frankly, there is nowhere she would rather be. As for the question, "Why mules?" Meredith says it boils down to one simple truth: Because mules love you back.

MERRICK & COMPANY

Bridging the past with the future, Merrick & Company has more than half a century of experience building quality solutions that will last for years to come. The Aurora-based company has evolved into an employee-owned professional services firm specializing in engineering, architecture, design-build and geographic information services to improve daily living environments. Yet, the firm has never veered from its roots of integrity and quality. The company's foundation was firmly built upon the beliefs, desires and goals that Sears Merrick, its founder, envisioned in 1955.

Merrick was awarded a bachelor's degree in civil engineering from Syracuse University in 1940. He proudly served his country, beginning in 1941 as an instructor and professor at the United States Military Academy at West Point for the Army Corps of Engineers through World War II, and again during the Korean Conflict, ten years later. In 1955 Merrick, who had achieved the rank of major, was honorably discharged from the Army and relocated with his family to Colorado. With a successful military career behind him and an entrepreneurial spirit, Merrick, along with partner John Bugas, founded the engineering consulting firm of Bugas & Merrick.

As the country rebounded from the effects of war and military conflict, the operation saw a slow but steady beginning, offering structural engineering services. The first year's profits peaked at just $1,600, but Merrick believed that by producing quality work and exceeding his customers' expectations, the firm

Sears Merrick.

would not only sustain the test of time, but prosper.

The company had a year of milestones in 1959. Four years after opening, Bugas & Merrick moved to a two-room office located at 2700 West Evans in Denver. Bugas left the company soon after the move, but Merrick kept focused on the future, renaming the firm Merrick & Company. That same year, with the new name in place, the business officially became incorporated. Merrick served as president and H. Edward Lecuyer, who had joined the company four years prior as the first employee, became vice president and co-founder.

Over the next three years, Merrick & Company grew at a steady pace with numerous projects to its credit. The firm focused on surveying and design services for electrical transmission and distribution projects throughout the Rocky Mountain region. Most notably, Merrick & Company successfully completed a 150-mile 500KV line for the U.S. Department of Interior's Bureau of Reclamation.

The staff grew as the company's reputation for excellence expanded. In 1961 Merrick hired Bruce Walker, a young and eager engineer from Canada who had recently graduated from the University of Denver with a Bachelor of Science in Civil Engineering and a Master of Business Administration. Walker proved to be instrumental in the shaping of the relatively new company. Just five years after coming on board, Walker was promoted to chief of the civil engineering division, and by 1977, he was general manager of the company.

Merrick and Walker saw an opportunity for the company to both progress and maintain stability by providing employee ownership in the company. This approach enhanced recruitment possibilities and created a culture of personal investment by those who became a part of the team.

The rapid progression of construction technologies and the demand for more comprehensive services were all part of Merrick & Company's evolution. The firm, still strong in civil engineering and surveying, introduced all aspects of engineering as well as architectural services.

With additional staff and increased services, Merrick & Company was in need of its own facility. So in 1973 a new larger office was designed in the nearby city of Aurora. Eight years later expansion continued and an additional office was designed and built, giving the firm 40,000 square feet of operating space. The two facilities were a long way from Sears Merrick's home basement, but he had governed the growth and success of the company step by step.

In 1983 Merrick retired, as did Lecuyer in the '80s. Bruce Walker, who had been with the company for twenty-two years, assumed the role of president. Walker continued Sears Merrick's strong leadership, demonstrating that success was best gained by a team focused on offering the highest quality services. Under his direction, the company received the United States Small Business Administration's 1991 National Small Business Subcontractor of the Year award, personally presented to Walker by President George H.W. Bush.

Employees gather for the fiftieth anniversary in May 2005.

In 1997 the company incurred some trying times. Both Sears Merrick, 79, and Bruce Walker, 60, passed away. The company remained centered on the values instilled by both of these strong leaders as Ralph W. Christie Jr. was appointed president and CEO. Christie joined the company in 1992 as vice president of business development. He brought with him twenty-five years of experience in the fields of engineering, architecture and construction. He was recognized by *ColoradoBiz* Magazine as one of the state's top CEOs in 2001 and by the Aurora Chamber of Commerce as the organization's Man of the Year for 2002.

Through Christie's leadership, the firm has continued to grow. Merrick & Company now occupies a facility at 2450

President George H.W. Bush presents Bruce Walker with the SBA's National Small Business Subcontractor of the Year award in 1991.

South Peoria Street in Aurora, which serves as its headquarters. Today the company has more than 400 employees and satellite locations in Colorado Springs; Atlanta, Georgia; Los Alamos and Albuquerque, New Mexico; Guadalajara, Mexico; and Ottawa, Canada.

Since 1991 the company has consistently been ranked in the top 200 engineering design firms in the United States. It has also been recognized by *Engineering News Record* as one of the country's ten fastest growing design firms in 1995 and was selected as a finalist in the Malcom Baldrige National Quality Award in 1992. Other distinguishing

honors for the company include receiving the United States Postal Service Quality Supplier Award for an unprecedented three years in a row, from 2000 through 2002. This award was for demonstrating a commitment to customer service. Merrick & Company was also selected for several Engineering Excellence Awards from the American Council of Engineering Companies of Colorado from 2003 through 2006.

Merrick & Company's services have expanded to include work in architecture, engineering, design-build and construction management for special-use facilities. The company's specializations include design fabrication of equipment

Ralph Christie receivs the Man of the Year award.

for high containment, design services for biomass-to-energy conversion, Geographic Information Systems, mapping, land surveying and civil infrastructure projects for both civil and military contracts.

Merrick & Company's advancements were vast as the firm expanded, its leadership changed and technology evolved over the past fifty-plus years. However, the legacy of its founder, Sears Merrick, is honored every day as this comprehensive, employee-owned company moves forward, while upholding the goal to provide quality solutions to its clients worldwide.

Merrick & Company's Aurora offices, located at 2450 S. Peoria.

METROPOLITAN STATE COLLEGE OF DENVER

Metropolitan State College of Denver thrives in the center of the famed Mile High City. A heartbeat from Denver's financial, cultural and professional sports hot spots, Metro State is one of the largest public four-year colleges in the United States. An urban campus in the truest sense, Metro State shines as a community with a rich mixture of ethnicity, income and age.

Metro State celebrated forty years of service to Colorado in 2005 by appointing a new president and adopting a renewed vision, rooted not only in its passion for opportunity but also in the history of higher education in America. In doing so, the college took yet another stride in its all-inclusive quest to improve lives and enhance communities—locally, nationally, globally.

"I am excited for our future and here's why," Stephen Jordan, Ph.D., president, told the assembled students, faculty, staff and community members on September 7, 2005. "I believe that the 'metropolitan' student and faculty of the twenty-first century and in the future will be persons who do not merely reside in a geographical area designated as metropolitan Denver, or metropolitan Chicago, or any other metropolis. Indeed, the metropolitan student and faculty members will be engaged in a host

Metro State's students reflect a rich mixture of age groups, socioeconomic classes, ethnic backgrounds and lifestyles. Ethnic minorities make up 24 percent of the student population. The college ranks second in the state for graduating Hispanic students.

Metro State's main campus is located in downtown Denver at the Auraria Higher Education Center, a 175-acre site shared with the University of Colorado at Denver and Health Sciences Center and Community College of Denver. Right in the heart of the Mile High City, the campus is walking distance from the Denver Performing Arts Complex, the Colorado Convention Center, Invesco Field at Mile High, Coors Field, Pepsi Center and Six Flags Elitch Gardens Amusement Park.

of issues and problems, which cut across municipal and county boundaries, states and even nations. The problems and issues of a region will continue to be multi-dimensional and complex and those who are being educated will need to be able to live and work within increasingly interconnected and complex environments."

Flanked by the college's eleven-member Board of Trustees as well as Denver

Mayor John Hickenlooper and Rick O'Donnell, executive director of the Colorado Commission on Higher Education, Jordan explained his vision of making Metro State "the preeminent public urban baccalaureate college in the nation." He suggested borrowing the ideals of the 1862 Morrill Act, which President Abraham Lincoln signed into law on July second of that year. The historic legislation established land-grant institutions and changed the course of higher education in America. Jordan pointed out that the Act, "essentially provided for a working relationship between those who faced problems and those who were involved in finding solutions."

That same formula, Jordan explained, applies just as much today and not only improves the lives of individual students but entire communities. "Our faculty and students would be similar to [historical] county agents of extension units, but with a focus on business, schools, health care, social problems and the like, which are endemic to urban life," Jordan said. "We can build shared mission elements so that our teaching mission simultaneously promotes economic development, fosters social cohesion with individuals and groups and provides a locus for cultural vitality. However, in today's environment, students must be given not only the skills to live and work in the metropolitan life but they must also be educated in the arts and sciences, the utilization of technology, a sensitivity

to cultural and trans-cultural diversity, and an appreciation of 'civic-ness.'" Metro State turns toward the half-century mark with Jordan's ten-year, three-phase strategy well underway—continuing the legacy of Colorado's "College of Opportunity." As Jordan has said of Metro State's continuing mission, "We intend to be a place of hope, pride and accomplishment."

The idea of Metro State began in 1962, when Colorado's leaders saw the need for a new and different college in Denver. Other colleges in the area, they felt, only served the "privileged." Former Colorado Governor Roy Romer, who was a state representative at the time, "wanted to see a school that was for people who knew their futures would either rise or fall by their own wits." Betty Naugle, a Denver native from a pioneering family and a trustee of the State Colleges of Colorado, joined the cause. After what Romer calls "one hell of a fight," the 1965 state legislature appropriated funds for the creation of Metro State. The college opened October 4, 1965 as a two-year college. It became a four-year college in 1967.

Metro State's first president, Kenneth

The first four-year graduates, some seventy strong, received their diplomas at an event held at Phipps Auditorium in 1969. Another sixty-three students received their associate's degrees at that same commencement. Since then, Metro State has produced more than 57,000 graduates.

Phillips, Ph.D., challenged newcomers to higher education. "We have an open-door policy here at Metro State," he said. "We'll supply the teachers, the space, the resources, the programs—the open road to advanced knowledge . . . you supply the intellectual curiosity and the drive to succeed. . . . You are the one who must discover yourself."

With an initial enrollment of 1,189 students, administrators cobbled together rented space for offices and classrooms throughout the city. The Forum Building at West 14th Avenue and Cherokee Street, for example, housed registration. Frequent student visits to The While Mule on Colfax and Elati made it the de facto student union. The

Funded by a $1.9 million appropriation from the state legislature in 1970, the Auraria Higher Education Center houses Metro State's current campus. The campus features several historic buildings such as Denver's first church and a former brewery near the banks of the Platte River.

steady stream of students crossing heavy traffic on Speer Boulevard and Colfax Avenue in the heart of Denver resulted in the college switching mascots from mustangs to roadrunners in 1974.

Metro State grew and outgrew its rag-tag cluster of classroom spaces in buildings throughout Denver. In 1970 the state legislature approved $1.9 million for the creation of the Auraria Higher Education Center, where Metro State's campus now sits. The original land development plan called for a square design, with every wall, every column, every window divisible into five-foot units. Preservationists, however, won out. So, in addition to newer buildings, which indeed fit the five-by-five matrix, the campus includes Denver's oldest church (later a synagogue, now an art gallery), its first Hispanic church and a red-brick brewery, now the student union. The campus opened in 1977.

Over its first forty years, Metro State had seven presidents at the helm. From 1965 to 1971 Dr. Kenneth Phillips saw enrollment increase more than six fold, from just under 1,200 to more than 7,200. Between 1971 and 1978 Dr. James Palmer oversaw the monumental task of

moving onto the Auraria campus. During his presidency, from 1979 until 1981, Dr. Donald J. MacIntyre prevented a proposed merger with the University of Colorado-Denver. After joining the college in 1982, Dr. Richard M. Fontera brought back basketball before his untimely death from cancer in 1984. Between 1984 and 1987 Dr. Paul Magelli revived the Metro State Foundation and brought Metro State increased visibility through his business connections. Following in Dr. MacIntyre's footsteps, during his years as president, from 1988 until 1993, Dr. Thomas Brewer fought off another merger attempt and headed the successful drive to add "of Denver" to the college's name. Coming to Metro State in 1993, Dr. Sheila Kaplan helped the college gain independence with its own Board of Trustees in 2003.

Today nearly 21,000 students attend Metro State, making it Colorado's second-largest undergraduate student population and one of the largest public, four-year colleges in the United States. Students choose from 2,800 courses in fifty major fields of study and eighty minors. Coursework is divided into three schools: Business; Letters, Arts and Sciences; and Professional Studies.

Metro State offers day, night, weekend correspondence and online courses at the downtown campus and at its two suburban satellite campuses—Metro South and Metro North.

The Department of Aviation and Aerospace Science maintains a collection of twenty-two flight simulators and aviation software that is more comprehensive than at most flight schools, including those run by the airlines themselves.

In addition, the college offers certificate programs in thirty career fields, as well as teacher licensure programs in early childhood, elementary, secondary and special education. Academics run from the traditional—English, history, psychology—to business degrees in computer science, accounting and finance. Students also pursue professional programs in healthcare management, nursing and criminal justice, as well as pre-med, pre-law and pre-veterinary science.

Metro State offers day, night, weekend, correspondence and online courses at the downtown campus and at its two suburban satellite campuses—Metro South and Metro North. The college added its first-ever, all-online class in 1996—"Introduction to Technical Writing." In the 2005 fall term 3,600 students enrolled in one or more of 172 online courses, ranging from meteorology to auditing.

In 2004 Metro State received its largest-ever federal grant—$9.5 million from the Department of Education to create a model program with Denver Public Schools to increase the quality of teacher education. Metro State also is spearheading another $2 million, federally funded program that trains teachers to integrate digital technology and the Library of Congress online archives into classroom curricula. The college is one of only ten institutions nationwide—and the first one in Colorado—to receive this grant.

The Department of Aviation and Aerospace Science, the fifth largest in the country, sends countless graduates into high-profile roles with local aviation companies, national aerospace innovators and even NASA. The program's innovative World Indoor Airport boasts a collection of twenty-two flight simulators and aviation software that provides a deeper problem-solving curriculum than most flight schools, including some operated by the airlines themselves.

Two of Metro State's strategic partnerships include the Accelerated Nursing Program (ANP) and the College Assistance Migrant Program (CAMP). Designed to address a critical nursing shortage in the state, ANP was founded and funded by the college and four local healthcare organizations. ANP takes students who already hold bachelor's degrees in other areas through an intense thirteen-month nursing curriculum. The first class of thirty completed the program in March 2005. Another thirty-two students entered the program in April of that year. Funded for the second time by a $2.1 million

federal grant, CAMP provides assistance to students from Colorado migrant and seasonal farm worker families who are American citizens or legal residents. So far, nineteen CAMP students have earned their bachelor's degrees.

Real-world experience provides a solid stepping-stone to success. Each year, nearly 1,000 internships are available to students in a variety of fields. More than 600 businesses participate in internship programs. In 2003 and 2004 more than 500 students earned $2.7 million in salaries from internships. The college also offers internships through the Service Learning Program, where students volunteer in the community. Between 2003 and 2004 nearly 300 students contributed 41,595 hours of time and work worth $465,242.

Metro State reaches both into the halls of academe and into the business community to find faculty members, staff and administrators suited for the challenge of a modern, urban college. Metro State's 1,600 employees are among the most diverse in the state. Almost one-fifth of the college's tenure and tenure-track faculty are ethnic minorities.

Sylvia Dawson spent thirty years working as a journalist before joining Metro State's faculty. Her mother always told her she should be a teacher. Dawson says, "And she was right."

Students at Metro State learn from a broad mix of full and part-time faculty members, who bring an invaluable combination of scholarship and real-world experience into the classroom.

The faculty includes several Fulbright Scholars, including Psychology Professor Mary Ann Watson, who went to Kenya in 1998 and Egypt in 2004 to film case studies on topics of race, ethnicity, sexuality and gender. One of her productions, "Colorado to Cairo: Voices of Youth," a study in American and Egyp-

tian teenagers' perceptions about each other, won a Telly Award, a national honor for non-network-produced films.

Computer Information Systems Professor Stuart Monroe used his Fulbright opportunity to help improve a new entrepreneurship center in Malaysia. When he returned, Monroe took on a cross-disciplinary assignment to teach a class in entrepreneurship for the Business Management Department.

At the same time, a street-smart institution focused on solving problems needs an influx of constant energy from faculty members who've spent hard-earned time in the "real world" and who bring that experience into the classroom. Take Sylvia Dawson, for example. Back in 1974, her high school newspaper column attracted an editor at the local daily. He offered her a job as a reporter, and she's been a journalist ever since—working at many magazines over the past thirty years. Dawson came to Metro State in 2001 as an assistant professor of journalism, where she's

Stephen Jordan, Ph.D., Metro State's eighth president, began his appointment July 1, 2005, after a nationwide search of more than 200 applicants. Jordan, 57, came from his position as president of Eastern Washington University, where he had been since 1998. Jordan spent his childhood through the late 1980s in Colorado. He earned his doctorate and MPA from the University of Colorado-Denver and his bachelor's degree from the University of Northern Colorado. He spent fifteen years early in his career working in the Office of State Planning and Budgeting, the University of Colorado system and the CU Health Sciences Center. His strategic vision is to lead Metro State to become "the preeminent public urban baccalaureate college." He lives with his wife, Ruthie, near the Metro State campus. He considers her an equal partner in advocating for Metro State within the Colorado community.

Metro State's women's soccer (above, left) and men's basketball teams (above, right) have won a combined total of three national championships in recent years.

broadening the curriculum beyond traditional news and editorial emphases and into magazine feature writing and editing.

All told, Metro State's professors are master teachers, recruited for their desire and ability to teach. They average more courses and more time in the classroom than faculty at any other Colorado state college or university. Not content to rely on local resources alone, many academic departments tap into national wells of funding and ideas to bring the newest, best practices into the lives of Metro State students. By doing so, students can reach out into their own communities—and internationally—to improve the lives of others.

With an enrollment that tops 21,000, Metro State serves a diverse student body. Some come right from high school, but many are working adults, who attend classes nights and weekends, in addition to taking care of their families. While 60 percent of students enroll full time, a survey in 2002 showed that 87 percent of them work either full or part time. Nearly 94 percent of Metro State students come from Denver itself and the surrounding counties. Reflecting the diversity of a truly urban campus, classrooms at Metro

State fill with people from a rich mixture of ages, socioeconomic classes, ethnic backgrounds and lifestyles.

Unlike other colleges that may have suffered a spasm of self-reproach for lacking either women or ethnic minorities in the student body or faculty, Metro State got it right from the start.

Katherine Archuleta typifies the Metro State student. The first in her low-income family to go to college, Archuleta chose Metro State for its affordability, urban experience, excellent teacher training program and strong diversity. After graduation, she worked for eight years in the Denver Public Schools. Today, Archuleta serves as chief operating officer for the City and County of Denver. She once worked as chief of staff for former Denver Mayor Federico Peña, when he was Secretary of Transportation in President Bill Clinton's cabinet. Archuleta credits her education at Metro State with starting her on what Denver Mayor John Hickenlooper has described as a "thirty-year record of service to Denver and the nation." In addition, she co-founded the Center for Regional and Neighborhood Action and worked as executive director of the National Hispanic Cultural Center Foun-

Carlos Fresquez first came to Metro State as student. Now an art professor at the college, Fresquez says, "When I started back in 1974, it seemed as diverse then as it is now." He explains that he never felt disrespected because he's Chicano, adding "I always felt welcome." In fact, ethnic minorities make up 24 percent of the student body, and Metro State ranks second in the state for graduating Hispanic students.

Truly, all are welcome at the college. Karen Benson, the former director of Gay, Lesbian, Bisexual and Transgender Student Services, calls Metro State, "a bit of a haven within Colorado." Benson adds, "I know students who have transferred from other schools to here because they just couldn't handle the climate at schools they were going to."

Metro State students get involved in politics and other social causes. From the 1960s well into the twenty-first century, Metro State's students have protested against wars, Columbus Day and the World Trade Organization and for the freedom of Tibet and other oppressed people, to name just a few. Sometimes the problem is local, but with global ramifications. For example, in 2005 Metro State students boycotted a Denver-area restaurant because its name,

dation. Among her many civic contributions, Archuleta designed and led the Latina Initiative and helped found the Colorado Women's Foundation and Mi Casa Resource Center for Women.

along with some menu items, made light of exploitive sex tourism.

Thinking of an urban campus, it's easy to assume athletics might get small billing. But, in sports-crazy Denver, that is most definitely not the case. Roadrunners compete in seven intercollegiate sports, including men's baseball, women's volleyball, and men's and women's teams in basketball, cross country, soccer, swimming/diving and tennis. In March 2000 the men's basketball team earned the college's first-ever national title. They repeated the feat in 2002. Not to be outdone, the women's soccer team won the national championship in 2004.

Metro State produced more than 57,000 graduates in its first forty years. Each year, the college sees more graduates than the year before. As an affordable, modified open-enrollment institution of higher learning, Metro State attracts students of all kinds who

A lot has changed since the 1862 Morrill Act established land-grant colleges in America. According to Stephen Jordan, Ph.D., Metro State's president, that same formula applies just as much today, and not only improves the lives of individual students, but entire communities.

seek the opportunity a better education can provide. Metro State students, with an average age of twenty-six, are serious, working adults who balance demands at home with demands in the classroom. They have no time for nonsense. Many are the first in their families to attend college, leading the way for generations to come.

They strive to improve their own lives, certainly, but they also touch the city of Denver by their mere presence. More than 21,000 students regularly spend time on Metro State's main campus, right in the heart of Denver. They frequent local shops, share meals with friends at local restaurants and ride the Light Rail throughout town. It is urban living and urban learning at its best. When people live and work, study and grow, shop and relax together, they contribute more to a community than they receive. So the 41 percent of Metro State's annual budget, or just over $36 million, that comes from the state's

Metro State students flood Denver, the Mile High City, with their enthusiasm, vision and leadership. Since 90 percent of the college's graduates remain in Colorado, their cumulative contributions over a lifetime make the city better and stronger.

College Opportunity Fund is paid back in innumerable ways throughout the lives of Metro State students.

Some 90 percent of Metro State graduates remain in Colorado to live and work. They greatly influence the area—both in terms of economic impact and community involvement serving as the community's teachers, pilots, business owners and managers, nurses and more. From the legislature's halls to board room tables, from police cars to classrooms, Metro State graduates sway the city and state in new directions. They contribute time and energy to charities. They lead nonprofit or volunteer organizations that serve the underserved. They tell a new generation of educational leaders and legislatures, "Here's what's important today."

By being the largest college in Denver, arguably the most important modern city in the old West, Metro State provides hope, leadership and vision to those who are born in Colorado and those who continue to flock to the highest state in the union.

MONTROSE MEMORIAL HOSPITAL

A great hospital needs many things: a state-of-the-art facility, expert staff, outstanding physicians, advanced technology, helping hands in the form of volunteers, and a supportive community. Montrose Memorial Hospital is a regional medical center serving a diverse population spread over a large geographic area. The hospital has more than 550 employees and more than eighty physicians on staff, representing twenty-two medical specialties. It offers an extensive range of healthcare services including the San Juan Cancer Center, Cardiology Services, Rehabilitation Center, Family Birthing Center, Same Day Surgery, Complete Medical Imaging/ Radiology Facilities, Intensive Care Services, and satellite clinics in the tiny communities of Olathe and Naturita.

Justifiably proud of its reputation for providing up-to-date medical care, Montrose Memorial is also proud to be known for its personal service and its involvement in the community. While always striving to keep its technology on the cutting edge, the hospital has remained faithful to its small town roots, reflected in the hospital's description of the care it provides "as friends and family caring for friends and family," and "high-tech, high touch" referring to the

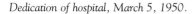

Dedication of hospital, March 5, 1950.

state-of-the-art care dispensed with an attentive and compassionate attitude.

In addition to providing high-tech medical care, the hospital strives to be an integral part of the community it serves, leading the way in improving and maintaining the health of the entire population. Hospital programs run the gamut from community health lectures to low income dental care to breast cancer support groups and migrant health programs to the annual health fair. The culture of community service is nurtured between and among the staff at Montrose Memorial. Hospital leadership is encouraged to exemplify the role

of a good citizen and to become involved in the workings of the community outside the hospital. Many employees are involved with local groups and activities and contribute countless hours of volunteer work. Numerous staff members have received awards for their community service efforts and the strong bond between the hospital and the communities it serves is continually renewed and strengthened, to the benefit of all.

Montrose Memorial Hospital was founded March 5, 1950 by the county of Montrose and has been providing high quality healthcare to residents of its service area for more than half a century. Originally a twenty-five-bed hospital, it has been remodeled, expanded, and upgraded several times notably in 1975, 1985, 1998 and 2005. The hospital campus has doubled in size and is now a seventy-five-bed facility. It offers complete and diverse specialty care and focuses a great deal of its education, marketing, and financial resources towards making its service area a healthier place. As a community grows, so must its delivery of healthcare. In this rapidly expanding part of southwestern Colorado, Montrose Memorial Hospital plays a vibrant and vital role in maintaining the health of the community it serves and attracting people to the area.

Montrose Memorial Hospital today.

THE SAN JUAN CANCER CENTER

Living in a remote rural area can be wonderful, but having access to cutting edge medical care can sometimes involve lengthy travel to an urban center. For residents of a huge six county area in southwestern Colorado, travel for complete cancer care got a lot easier in 2006 with the opening of the San Juan Cancer Center in Montrose. Residents of Montrose and many smaller towns were traveling a combined 500,000 miles a year for radiation therapy, formerly only available seventy miles away in Grand Junction. It's tough mentally and physically to not feel good and to have to endure the extra stress, fatigue, and expense of travel in addition to whatever therapy is needed.

The San Juan Cancer Center is a joint venture of Montrose Memorial Hospital, St. Mary's Hospital in Grand Junction, and Western Colorado Radiation Oncology, PC. The goal of this relationship was to bring the exemplary service already available at St. Mary's to the greater Montrose area. Historically, Montrose Memorial and St. Mary's have been competitors on some issues. Both organizations and the provider physicians saw

this joint endeavor as an opportunity to put that history behind them and work together for the benefit of the communities and patients they serve.

The emphasis at the San Juan Cancer Center is on treating the whole person and their family, not just the disease. The long awaited facility offers state-of-the-art equipment and technology combined with a renowned and experienced

Ribbon cutting ceremony.

oncology staff. Patients receive the most up-to-date cancer care available without having to travel long distances. The facility is warm and welcoming and offers a variety of resources to help people deal more effectively with all aspects of cancer. It provides patients with a full range of diverse treatment options including consultation and examination, chemotherapy, radiation therapy, cancer counseling, and coordination of care. A library and education kiosk offers patients and their families the latest information available on a variety of cancer related subjects.

Residents of Montrose and the surrounding communities raised nearly a million dollars through the fundraising efforts of the San Juan Healthcare Foundation to help make the dream of complete cancer care close to home a reality. Being diagnosed with cancer and choosing a course of therapy is stressful enough without having to travel for care. The new cancer center allows people from all over its expansive service area to complete their treatment without the added expense and discomfort of long car trips and time away from work and family.

The Linear Accelerator delivers radiation treatment.

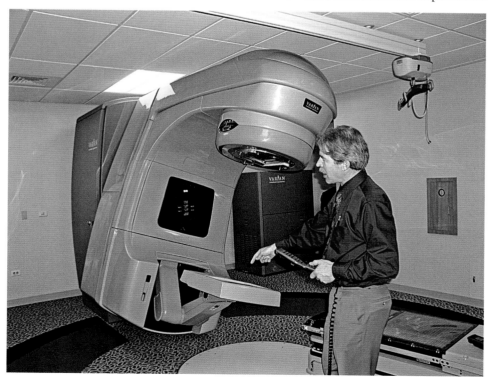

NEWMONT MINING COMPANY

Gold has been considered one of the most precious metals in the world for thousands of years. From wedding bands to the tombs of Egyptian kings to a standard for global currency, gold has played a unique role in human development.

Although some may be unaware of the many industrial uses of gold, it is an essential element in people's lives. Its high electrical conductivity, malleability and resistance to corrosion make it vital to the manufacturing of electrical components used in a range of products from computers and cellular phones to home appliances and vehicle airbags. Used on the exterior of satellites and spacecraft, the highly reflective property of gold creates a protective shield against the sun's radiation. Gold-coated reflectors are essential to focus light energy in industrial and medical lasers. Because it is biologically inactive, gold is a critical tool for medical research and treatment for conditions such as arthritis. Gold bars, coins and jewelry have been valued historically as a long-term, stable form of savings and investment.

Indeed, gold has a fascinating history —and so does one of the largest gold mining companies in the world: Newmont Mining Corporation.

Newmont's history goes back to 1921. That year Colonel William Boyce Thompson founded Newmont Mining Corporation as a holding company to invest in worldwide mineral, oil and gas companies. Thompson chose the name "Newmont" to pay homage to New York, the state in which he made his fortune, and Montana, the state in which he grew up.

Thompson hit the ground running with his venture. Newmont acquired interests in a Texas oil field in 1925, heralding the beginning of an oil empire that included more than seventy blocks in the Louisiana Gulf area and oil and gas production in the North Sea. Prior to the Great Depression in 1929 Newmont became a mining company with its first gold production by acquiring California's Empire Star Mine.

The discovery of gold in Nevada's Carlin Trend put Newmont on the gold mining map.

At the end of the Great Depression in 1939, while many American corporations failed in an uncertain economy, Newmont was operating twelve gold mines in North America. The following year, O'okiep Copper Company came into full production in South Africa. O'okiep formed the basis for Newmont to become the world's third largest copper producer with interests in eight copper operations worldwide.

Newmont's discovery of the Carlin Trend, however, put the company on the gold mining map. Newmont discovered disseminated gold in Carlin, Nevada in 1962 and began operating its first mill there in 1965 under the name Carlin Gold Mining Company. The Carlin Trend is this century's largest gold discovery in North America. In 1971 Newmont began using the heap leach technology on sub-mill grade ores at Carlin. The company was one of the first in the gold industry to use heap leaching, a process in which chemicals to remove the gold are sprayed on vast open-air piles of ore.

Newmont then ventured into coal mining. In 1977 Newmont was instrumental in organizing the consortium that purchased Peabody Holding Company, Inc., the largest coal producer in the nation. Newmont held a 50 percent interest in Peabody following the purchase. Another major milestone for Newmont came in the 1980s with the beginning of global exploration in Yanacocha, Peru, and Batu Hijau, Indonesia. Yanacocha is now the largest gold producer in South America.

Over the next several years, Newmont continued its rapid growth with additional mining interests in Australia, Bolivia, Canada, Mexico, New Zealand, the U.S. and Uzbekistan. In 1986 Carlin Gold Mining Company's name was changed to Newmont Gold Company, and five million shares were sold publicly for $47.5 million. Newmont Mining held a 90 percent interest. A decade later,

Newmont's assets were over $1.9 billion and income from continuing operations reached $338 million.

In August 1987 Newmont became the target of an unsolicited tender offer for control of the company. As a result, the company undertook a major restructuring. This included payment of a $33 per share dividend to all shareholders for a total of $2.2 billion, of which $1.75 billion was borrowed. To reduce this debt, the company undertook a divestment program involving all of its copper, oil, gas, and coal interests. In February 1989, as a further step in restructuring, the company moved its headquarters from New York City to Denver to be closer to its operations.

On the first of January 1994, Newmont Mining Corporation and Newmont Gold Company combined assets to form a unified worldwide gold company. Shareholders of both com-

Nevada's Carlin operations today.

panies had identical interests in the reserves, production and earnings of Newmont Gold's operations. Eventually, the two companies merged, with Newmont Mining Company as the successor. Shareholders of both companies had identical interests in the reserves, production, and earnings of Newmont Gold's operations.

Newmont merged with Santa Fe Pacific Gold Corporation to form North America's largest gold producer in May of 1997. The company merged with Battle Mountain Gold Company in 2001 and completed the acquisition of Normandy Mining Limited and Franco-Nevada Mining Corporation Limited of Canada in February 2002, making Newmont the world's largest gold producer.

Newmont Capital manages the company's merchant banking activities (which include the royalty, equity and asset portfolios) and provides in-house investment banking and advisory services. The Royalty Portfolio generates over $60 million in royalty and dividend income to Newmont annually. Since the 2002 merger, Newmont Capital has provided assistance in closing over 100 transactions worth over $2 billion.

Most recently, Newmont began exploration in Ghana in West Africa led by Chairman Wayne Murdy. Newmont

Newmont Mining Corporation is one of the largest gold mining operations in the world.

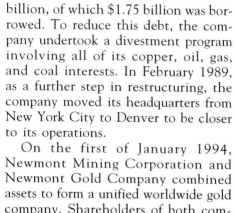

is particularly excited about the development of its Ahafo and Akyem projects in Ghana. These two projects were acquired as part of the Normandy transaction in 2002. Since then, Newmont has added more than 12 million ounces to reserves for a combined 16 million ounces at year-end 2004. Production began at Ahafo in the second half of 2006; the Akyem project is expected to commence in 2008.

Newmont has evolved over the years, both in size and in focus. While the early days of the company leveraged a diverse natural resource base, including oil, gas and coal, the company today is primarily focused on gold mining. Newmont mines small amounts of silver and copper in association with its gold mining and still holds investments in oil as a method to hedge against rising fuel prices. Newmont is unique among gold producers in that it is unhedged. That means its investors can realize full value price increases in gold.

In recent years, mining companies have come under public scrutiny in the wake of coal mining accidents and environmental concerns. Newmont has taken an active role in raising the bar for the mining industry for environmental and social responsibility. Murdy chairs the International Council on Metals and Mining (ICMM), an organization created to share best practices to improve sustainable development performance in the mining, minerals and metals industry.

Most gold mining is located in rural parts of the world and provides vital industrial activity in many developing countries. Mining operations create jobs in surrounding communities and can help to provide new or improved infrastructure, better healthcare and quality education. Supporting the communities in which they mine is very important to Newmont executives. Newmont's objective is to provide value with every ounce of gold it produces—to its stakeholders and to the communities where they operate.

Newmont's active communications program educates communities

Local children in New Zealand join in planting for the Waihi Bridge-to-Bridge project.

about mining issues and job opportunities. Also, the company makes investments in civic and charitable organizations within the local communities in which it does business. Focusing on contributing to organizations that can help sustain economic development beyond the life of the mine, Newmont works to offer economic opportunity in its operating communities.

The company has 15,000 employees and 18,000 contractors globally; roughly 300 employees are based in Denver. Beyond shareholder value and gold production, the company is first and foremost concerned about the safety of workers. To that end, Newmont has implemented a comprehensive set of environmental and safety management and performance standards through its Five Star Integrated Management System.

Newmont Capital is a product of the merger with Normandy Mining and Franco-Nevada. The three-way combination enabled Newmont to assemble an in-house merchant banking team that could not only manage a combined larger diversified set of portfolio assets, but also provide in-house investment banking, advisory, and transaction services. Mergers and acquisitions will play a key role in Newmont's growth, but these opportunities will also make sense for shareholders.

Exploration is a driver of Newmont's future. The company is dedicated to having the most effective gold exploration team in the world, based on consistent long-term performance, resulting in high-impact additions to Newmont's net asset value. Newmont's success depends both on a strong near-mine exploration emphasis and dedicated greenfield exploration in the world's most prospective gold belts. Technical ability, strong business skills, internal teamwork and the ability to work with junior and other major mining companies are keys to its success. Newmont's mission is to develop a long-term portfolio of quality exploration projects capable of delivering sustained reserve growth that maintains its leadership in gold production.

ST. MARY LAND & EXPLORATION COMPANY

Founded in 1908, St. Mary Land & Exploration Company is on a mission to build value for its shareholders through the exploration, exploitation, development, acquisition and production of natural gas and crude oil in five core areas in the United States. The Denver-based company does this by focusing on mature basins. It has developed leasehold positions and long-term relationships with some of the most recognized suppliers, prospect generators and operators in the industry.

St. Mary Land's story of building value by adding value began at the turn of the century with the purchase of a unique property in South Louisiana. Chester Congdon of Duluth had made a small fortune in the early 1900s from the development of iron mines in Minnesota and copper mines in Arizona. He believed in tangible investments only—the stock market was not for him. Congdon and many other financiers of the day

Chester Congdon, founder of St. Mary Land.

believed all true wealth flowed from the earth—food, fiber and minerals— and so invested their fortunes in lands that offered the promise of these natural resources.

Congdon did not attempt to build an oil and gas empire on his own. In fact, he didn't set out to build an oil and gas empire at all. Congdon partnered with four associates—Guilford Hartley, David Adams, A.L. Ordean and A.S. Chase—to pursue a land investment vision that saw agricultural interests as a profit center. In 1900 the five entrepreneurs bought land in St. Mary Parish, Louisiana. They intended to drain the marshlands to plant crops. Much of St. Mary Land's long-term success, however, can be attributed to their foresight to purchase both the surface rights and mineral rights to the lands. The latter would allow them to drill for oil.

Congdon and his comrades paid $11,000 for 17,700 acres of land and formed the St. Mary's Parish Land Company in 1908. St. Mary Land incorporated in 1915. Congdon and Adams also purchased 7,200 acres and formed Tidal Wave Land Company. The two companies merged in 1935. After completing the merger, a grand total of $68,000 of capital had been paid into the company. Not until 1992 was additional capital sought, reflecting the founders' convictions that "when seeking a profit, one doesn't share a good thing unnecessarily."

Explorers did not strike oil on the St. Mary Land properties for thirty years. The patience proved worthy of the discovery, however, when oil industry giants began exploring and leasing land from the company. Texaco's predecessor drilled the St. Mary No. 1 discovery well to the Horseshoe Bayou Field in 1938. Its depth was 9,910 feet for 335 barrels of oil a day, establishing Horseshoe as one of the "giants" in the United States. In 1941 St. Mary Land leased 4,000 acres to Atlantic Richfield, the forerunner of Vastar. On the eve of Japan's attack on Pearl Harbor, Atlantic Richfield drilled the discovery well to the Bayou Sale Field on St. Mary's land.

Oil development and production in both these fields were accelerated to

A 1938 Western Union Telegram regarding the well at Horseshoe Bayou Field.

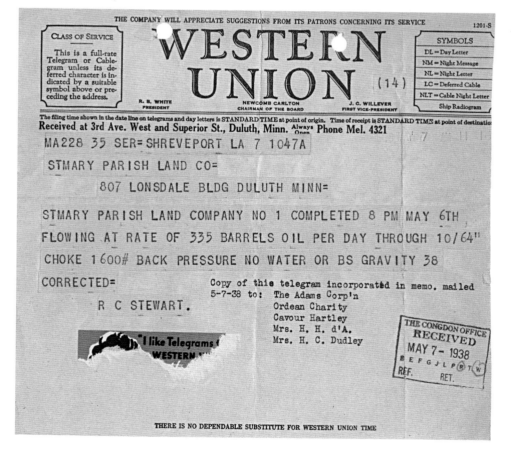

Tom Congdon, Chester Congdon's grandson.

serve the needs of World War II. But natural gas was deemed a worthless nuisance until after the war when oil pipelines were converted to the transport of gas and a fledgling market began to develop for this "orphan" commodity. Sun Oil Company, the predecessor of Oryx, discovered gas at Belle Isle in 1941 but did not lease the company's adjacent lands until 1950, completing its first St. Mary well in 1955 at the then extraordinary depth of 15,500 feet. Sun declared the Belle Isle Field in 1961 to be "one of the major hydrocarbon reserves in the Gulf Coast."

St. Mary Land began the payment of cash dividends in 1941 and continued to distribute almost all corporate income to its shareholders until the mid-1960s. In 1966 the directors astutely recognized the need to build assets to offset depletion of the Louisiana oil and gas reserves. Tom Congdon, Chester's grandson, would lead the company with this new strategy in relocated Denver headquarters. Until that time, St. Mary Land had been a conduit for royalty income from land leased to major oil and gas companies. When the grandson Congdon came aboard, he began taking a small portion of the royalty income and in-

vesting it with other oil and gas companies.

With only a handful of employees, St. Mary Land then began to explore for new reserves in the Rockies and the Mid-Continent by affiliating with experienced partners. Over the years, St. Mary Land built a strong relationship with George Anderman and eventually held joint ownership in Anderman Smith Operating Company. Production and reserves grew rapidly through the 1970s, particularly in the Anadarko Basin of Oklahoma. St. Mary Land continues to partner and form industry alliances to complement and leverage the company's portfolio of opportunities.

In the early 1990s the directors recognized that family management would not continue indefinitely, and a professional management team was recruited to direct the company's future growth. Mark Hellerstein, the company's current Chairman and Chief Executive Officer (CEO), joined St. Mary Land as executive vice president and Chief Financial Officer in 1991. In 1992 Hellerstein was promoted to president. That same year company executives decided to go public and issue common stock to raise needed capital and to provide liquidity for family shareholders. Hellerstein assumed the CEO position in 1994 and inherited the

Mark Hellerstein, CEO of St. Mary Land & Exploration Company.

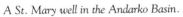

A St. Mary well in the Andarko Basin.

chairman position from Tom Congdon in 2002.

Hellerstein, together with Ron Boone, St. Mary Land's then Chief Operating Officer, were charged with expanding the company's technical and operating capabilities to become a full oil and gas operator. St. Mary Land gained this status, in part, through a series of strategic acquisitions. In order to expand its base of operations, the company established a partnership, Panterra Petroleum, with Nance Petroleum in 1991 to establish a foothold in the Rockies and acquired Nance Petroleum in 1999. Bob Nance continues to manage this wholly owned subsidiary and is a senior vice president of the company. In 1992 the company acquired the Oil and Gas division of TL James to establish a base of operations in the ArkLaTex region. St. Mary Land put its capital to good use, making several acquisitions in the Permian Basin in 1995 and 1996 and acquiring full ownership of the Anderman Smith Operating Company in 1996. In 1999 the company acquired King Ranch's Oil and Gas properties.

The acquisitions gave St. Mary Land initial positions in each of its core areas. These acquisitions, as well as others, gave the company a strategic acreage position and focus on establishing superior technical capabilities in its regions; its fiscal discipline and strong balance sheet and empowering its regional offices gave it competitive advantage in the industry, which led to widespread national and statewide recognition. *Fortune* magazine ranked St. Mary Land among the "100 Fastest Growing Companies of 2002." St. Mary Land has been on a growth streak ever since. Ernst & Young and the *Denver Business Journal* named the company the "Fastest Growing Colorado Public Company" in 2002. *Fortune* magazine ranked St. Mary Land among the "100 Fastest Growing Companies" again in 2004 and 2005. *Forbes* magazine ranked it among the "200 Best Small Companies" in 2004 and 2005. *BusinessWeek* included St. Mary Land in its list of "100 Best Small Hot Growth Companies" in 2005. *ColoradoBiz* magazine honored St.

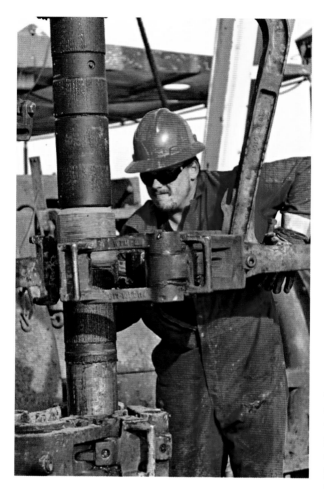

A St. Mary "roughneck" on site.

Mary Land as its "2005 Top Colorado Company" in the Energy and Natural Resources Category. Finally, in 2006, *BusinessWeek* once again ranked St. Mary Land among its "100 Hot Growth Companies."

St. Mary Land is now focused on technology resource plays, or unconventional plays, that involve shale, tight gas sands, coalbed and natural gas. These are resources that, fifteen years ago, were not considered economic. With the advent of new technology and oil prices rising, these types of resources are considered more viable.

St. Mary Land's strategies have changed over the years, but its value system remains the same as it was back in the early 1900s. The company strives to treat its people with the utmost respect. Executives maintain a high level of integrity. The Mid-Continent, Rocky Mountain, ArkLaTex, Gulf Coast and

Permian Basin regions are operated out of offices in Tulsa, Oklahoma; Billings, Montana; Shreveport, Louisiana and Houston, Texas. Executives in these regions are empowered to be entrepreneurial, which helps St. Mary Land stay on the cutting-edge of the industry.

St. Mary Land is committed to giving back to the community. The company, which employs 100 in Denver, contributes 1 percent of its pre-tax earnings to charities, including the United Way, Habitat for Humanity, rescue missions, arts interests, science and nature organizations and many others. Employees also volunteer their time to local charities. For all its success, company executives are most proud of the fact that it has provided strong returns to its shareholders consistently over a long period of time, while also giving back to the community and providing a superior work environment for its employees.

St. Mary Land is a financial success story. But company executives believe luck beats brains every time—and these shareholders have been lucky. The financial rewards of the last few years have obscured the high returns earned in years past. Private trades made in the stock in the 1930s were at less than one cent per share. The company received a purchase offer in the early 1960s at a price equivalent of $1 per share—a 200-fold return in less than thirty years. Since 1966 St. Mary Land shareholders have "beaten the market," but they are not likely again to see a "two hundred bagger" as their forefathers did. Still, since the company went public in 1992, and through the end of 2005, St. Mary Land has provided a 23 percent compounded return to shareholders. The company's goal is to continue this winning streak with integrity, charity, strategy and a little luck.

PINNACLE ARCHITECTURAL LIGHTING

Denver-based company Pinnacle Architectural Lighting opened in 2003 and is quickly making its mark on the lighting industry. Pinnacle may be the new kid on the block, but there is nothing new about its formula for success. With the experience of founder Michael Moore and the drive to be on the cutting edge of technology, Pinnacle is poised to continue its upward trajectory.

Pinnacle founder Michael Moore was born in Littleton, New Hampshire and lived in the northeastern United States during adolescence. Upon high school graduation, he was ready to venture out and explore the rest of the country. He took to the open highways with friends for a summer road trip. Along the way, Michael Moore found a treasure: Colorado.

"I instantly fell in love," Michael reminisced. At eighteen years-old, he knew that he would someday return to Colorado, the beauty and outdoor lifestyle of which had smitten him.

The summer came to an end and Michael Moore returned to Springfield, Massachusetts to begin college. After only three semesters, though, Michael knew that the chemical engineering degree he was pursuing was not right for him. He left school and traveled west again, this time to spend a winter in Vail, Colorado.

The 2005 Illuminating Engineering Society of North America progress report committee awarded Pinnacle Lighting recognition for a unique and significant advancement to the art and science in lighting for the Edge product line.

Michael Moore president and founder of Pinnacle Architectural Lighting.

The winter of 1979 stretched into a year, during which Michael was able to ski to his heart's content, supporting himself as a cook. After taking another travel jaunt to locales as far as tropical Hawaii, Michael was drawn back to Colorado. This time, he landed in Aspen. He spent four years there, working as a sous-chef at some of the city's toniest restaurants. His schedule making soups and sauces coincided perfectly with the schedules at the ski slopes, where he was a habitual visitor.

The well-traveled Michael Moore was on another, more personal, journey to find his calling. His most recent professional endeavor consisted of installing solar panels in Denver. But when the tax incentive that had been available for solar installations expired in 1985, the market, and Michael's career in solar paneling, dried up.

After much consideration, Michael Moore returned to college in 1986 as a student at the University of Colorado. He joined the architectural engineering depart-

ment as a solar engineering major. During his time there, he studied under David DiLaura, one of the most highly respected figures in the lighting field. Professor DiLaura's class and enthusiasm for his subject inspired Michael to change his major to illumination engineering.

After graduating from the prestigious program, which averages just ten graduates per year, Michael was on the road again. His first lighting job was in Wakefield, Massachusetts, where he designed a variety of lighting products. One particular fixture, known as the Imperial, is patented and remains in that company's catalog to this day.

From there, he traveled to a new work opportunity in Vancouver, B.C. LedaLite was a young company, and Michael saw it blossom into a large operation. The insight gained while working at Ledalite served Michael well later in his own professional journey.

Vancouver brought other joys. In 1993 Michael met Sheri, the woman who would become his wife after a whirlwind six-month courtship. After they married, it became clear to Sheri that Michael's heart was back in Colorado. By 1994 Colorado was home once again. Sheri not only helped inspire the move, she was also instrumental in motivating Michael to start his own business. Michael refers to her affectionately as "my muse."

Michael opened his first business in 1995. Along with two partners, he built a highly successful lighting business. Riding the wave of dot-com expansion, the company did breakneck business, hardly able to keep up with the orders it was shipping to Silicon Valley.

Within three years, the booming business was bought out by a multi-billion dollar conglomerate. Michael was pleased with the return on his investment but had other reasons for selling. He wanted the independence of having a business under his sole ownership someday. He stayed with the new company for two years, but found the corporate structure unsatisfying on many levels. He took a year sabbatical to help regroup and recharge before his next big adventure.

Pinnacle's people and headquarters in Denver.

Pinnacle Lighting opened in May of 2003 with only Michael and two engineers. Michael's many experiences in the industry had left a definite impression as to the directions he did, and didn't, want to go with Pinnacle. Topping the priority list was to shake up a staid industry with use of the latest in technology.

Pinnacle Lighting uses state-of-the-art technology and software to create its products. By using cutting-edge 3D software systems, it creates customized fixtures and lighting systems for all of its customers. Under traditional manufacturing systems, this would have been prohibitively expensive. By using the

Pinnacle Lightings staging and assembly area.

newest software, Pinnacle has effectively short-circuited the manufacturing process to its customers' benefit.

Elite software has also made it possible to "test drive" Pinnacle's proposed lighting systems. This software is only manufactured by two companies, one of which was founded by Michael Moore's professor and mentor, David DiLaura. Clients can see a simulation of their own buildings before any work has commenced. The computerized demo shows the look of the system and light output, allowing customers to assess the system's efficacy for their purposes from the outset.

Pinnacle Lighting has lighting agents in cities around the United States, Canada and Puerto Rico, ready to serve customer needs immediately. Pinnacle prides itself on streamlining the design and manufacturing process and bringing products to customers quickly. But Michael Moore feels that it is also Pinnacle Lighting's people that have distinguished the company in a highly competitive field.

With the success of the sale of his original company, Michael could have easily retired. Yet he had an undeniable affection for the industry and work. He also knew there was a gap in the field. Not only was the field ready for innovative design and products, but it was also ready for a company with a creative, open work environment. He wanted to create a workplace that people were excited to come to and products that were inspired.

As an industry veteran, he knows that the combination of the right product at the right price equals success. But the human element, the experience and enthusiasm cannot be underestimated. Nearly 90 percent of Pinnacle's now forty-strong workforce has worked with Michael Moore before, a true testament to his leadership and regard in the lighting field.

In only three years, Pinnacle has outgrown its 18,000 square-foot space and will be building a new 50,000 square-foot facility in 2007. Michael expects their employee roster to top 100 in another two years. Though still relatively new, Pinnacle has found a firm footing in the lighting industry. Through Michael Moore's commitment and leadership, Pinnacle Lighting is ready to continue its journey as a signature Colorado company.

PLANNED PARENTHOOD OF THE ROCKY MOUNTAINS

On May 27, 1916 Margaret Sanger made a historic visit to the city of Denver. It was one of many stops in major cities across the U.S. for the nurse, who was hoping to awaken interest in a controversial issue: birth control. In the early twentieth century birth control was a taboo subject, something that was only whispered about behind closed doors and rarely mentioned in public. There were women at the time who did practice some form of birth control, but they did so in secret. The vast majority of women, and especially the poor who had little access to medical care, knew nothing about the subject.

Sanger, who had opened a birth control clinic that year in New York City, had made it her mission to educate women about this important subject. Her message resonated loud and clear in Denver. That same year Ruth Cunningham, a Denver social worker and the wife of a prominent local physician, founded the Denver Birth Control League. The organization, which was dedicated to the sponsorship of birth control for the needy, would eventually become known as Planned Parenthood of the Rocky Mountains, an affiliate of the world's

Planned Parenthood Foundation of America founder Margaret Sanger said, "No woman can be free who does not own and control her own body." Margaret Sanger inspired ten Denver women to form Planned Parenthood of the Rocky Mountains, originally known as the Denver Birth Control League. Courtesy, Smith College.

largest and most trusted family planning organization.

Cunningham inspired several other influential and socially active women in the area to join the cause. Together, they raised $100 to fund a clinic. With those funds, the Denver Birth Control League opened its first birth control clinic in 1926. The clinic was housed in the base-

ment of the 17th Avenue Community Church, located at 1720 Emerson. The clinic's volunteers did much more than simply provide education about birth control. They offered transportation to and from the clinic and would even care for patients' children during their visits.

During the first year about 150 women received contraceptive services, which included education, examination and diaphragm fittings. That number may seem small when compared to Denver's population at the time, which was approximately 280,000. However, considering the dissemination of birth control information was illegal in Colorado in those days, the number was significant. At the time, distributing information about birth control was prohibited by the Comstock Laws that were intended to regulate obscenity.

The 1930s provided the backdrop for two great victories in the history of birth control. In 1937 the American Medical Association gave its first official recognition to birth control as a legitimate part of medical practice. In addition, a pair of landmark rulings by America's high courts legalized and protected the dissemination of contraceptives and contraceptive information provided by physicians.

Thanks to these victories, the 1930s proved to be a decade of growth for the distribution of birth control information in Colorado. Fundraising efforts were stepped up and additional birth control groups and clinics began in Boulder, Greeley, Pueblo and Colorado Springs. The Denver clinic, which had moved in 1928 to the obstetrical and gynecological outpatient clinic at Colorado General Hospital, moved again in 1935 to the Grace Community Church at 13th and Bannock, one of many moves to come.

By 1941 the growing number of birth control groups in the state had developed a statewide organization called the Colorado Committee for Planned Parenthood. During the 1940s the organization concentrated on expansion. Working together, the various groups focused on adding new services, strengthening relationships with other state and local agencies and increasing outreach

Volunteers selling Margaret Sanger's publication, The Birth Control Review. Margaret Sanger and activists across the nation risked jail time for dispensing information about birth control. Courtesy, Smith College.

Reverend David H. Fouse (on the right) made possible the first Planned Parenthood clinic in Denver by donating space in his church. Courtesy, Denver Public Library.

to minority communities. Their efforts paid off and, by 1943, the Denver group was seeing more than 900 patients every few months.

In 1949 the Denver chapter of Planned Parenthood incorporated as a nonprofit organization, and by the early 1950s, the clinic was making significant progress. A 1954 report boasted 1,684 total patient visits.

One decision made during the 1950s changed the course of Planned Parenthood forever. By making Pap smears a part of the regular clinic exam in 1959, the organization evolved from a purely social agency into a public health organization and provider of medical services for women. This helped establish Planned Parenthood as a resource for comprehensive care and set a precedent for further development along medical lines. That same decade witnessed another major shift within the organization when a policy was adopted to provide services to unmarried women.

Explosive changes lay ahead for the organization, which reincorporated as Rocky Mountain Planned Parenthood in 1972. The introduction of oral contraception—"the pill"—revolutionized birth control almost overnight. One Planned Parenthood board member

recalls that the availability of the pill was announced in a newspaper on a Monday and the following day, the clinic was flooded with calls. The number of patients at the clinic rose dramatically from 4,005 visits in 1960 to 12,833 in 1962. In 1964 another new birth control device, the Intra-Uterine Device (IUD), began to be prescribed at Planned Parenthood clinics but it never matched the popularity of the pill.

Throughout the 1960s birth control grew in acceptance within society. Along with this acceptance came the understanding that minors could benefit from birth control education and services. During this decade, Planned Parenthood began offering services to minors and in 1969, it opened a teen

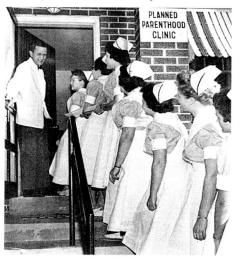

Planned Parenthood welcomes nurses to work in its clinics. In its early history, Planned Parenthood of the Rocky Mountains focused solely on providing birth control to married women, relying on the skills of nurses and nurse practitioners. Courtesy, Denver Public Library.

clinic designed to provide contraceptive advice and testing for venereal disease.

During the 1970s Planned Parenthood was faced with potentially devastating cutbacks in federal funding. To continue to provide its family planning services, the organization was forced to find new sources of funding. This need ushered in a new era of fundraising focusing on private individuals and foundations that has continued to the

The 17th Avenue Community Church, seen here in 1926 at 1720 Emerson Street in Denver, was the site of the first Planned Parenthood of the Rocky Mountains clinic. Courtesy, Denver Public Library.

present day. On top of that, the organization opened a clinic based on a self-sustaining model in which all expenses were met solely through patient fees. For only $2 a month, a woman could pay for all services, supplies, lab tests and educational materials. The concept worked, and the clinic was able to meet its expenses and actually make a small surplus. Based on this success, more self-sustaining clinics opened.

Perhaps the most controversial change at Planned Parenthood came in 1973. The Supreme Court's decision that year, in the case of Roe v. Wade, legalized abortion with virtually no restrictions, as long as the procedure was performed within the first twelve weeks of pregnancy. The new law gave Planned Parenthood the option of providing abortion services, which it chose to do, in keeping with its mission to provide comprehensive family planning services. This action thrust the organization involuntarily into the political arena and forced its leaders to learn the ins and outs of politics and activism.

Throughout the late twentieth century the organization, which became

Sylvia M. Clark, President and CEO of Planned Parenthood of the Rocky Mountains from 1986 to 2003. Sylvia, a certified OB/GYN nurse practitioner, brought her background to PPRM's leadership during a time of serious threats to reproductive rights and choices.

Sheri Eberhart Tepper was the Executive Director of Rocky Mountain Planned Parenthood from 1963 to 1986. Sheri presided over Planned Parenthood during a period of extensive geographic expansion, and in the expansion of PPRM's health, education and advocacy services.

known as Planned Parenthood of the Rocky Mountains (PPRM) in 1986, continued broadening its services and widening its reach. Today the ninety-year-old organization ranks as the fifth largest of 121 Planned Parenthood affiliates in the nation with thirty-one health centers in five states, including Colorado, Nevada, New Mexico, Wyoming and Missouri.

The once-tiny organization that began in a church basement is currently located at 950 Broadway, where it moved in 1996. PPRM has made tremendous progress since the early days and has evolved into a dynamic community resource that offers a wide range of affordable medical services, sexuality education and advocacy programs. Its thirty-one health centers currently provide services for more than 100,000 clients and education programs for more than 20,000 participants. The organization also boasts more than 27,000 activists in the area.

The number of services offered at PPRM continues to increase and cur-

rently includes birth control, emergency contraception, pregnancy testing, STD testing and treatment, HIV testing and referral, annual exams, screening for breast and cervical cancer, menopause/mid-life services, prenatal counseling, adoption referrals and surgical and medical abortion. The cornerstone of Planned Parenthood's work remains prevention, and the organization does more to reduce the need for abortion than any other health care provider or advocacy group. Thousands of women continue to rely on PPRM as a primary resource for obtaining contraceptives. PPRM's current contraceptive options include birth control pills, Depo-Provera, the birth control patch, Nuvaring, IUDs, diaphragms and cervical caps.

Empowering people to make responsible choices about health and sexuality, PPRM offers a growing number of education programs that provide medically accurate sexuality information. PPRM collaborates with more than 200 agencies to provide a wide range of culturally sensitive, age-appropriate programs. These programs focus on the prevention of STDs and unintended pregnancies, comprehensive sex education, family planning, sexual health and positive parenting. In 2005 PPRM's Education Department reached over 18,000 individuals with its comprehensive sex education.

After a decade of government promoted and funded Abstinence Only programs for youth, a growing number of young adults lack basic information about sexual and reproductive health. These programs teach abstinence as the only method for avoiding unitended pregnancies and STDs, but do not discuss contraceptives or condoms. Therefore, reaching youth with medically accurate sex education has become more important than ever to PPRM in maintaining a focus on prevention and sexual health.

PPRM is addressing the educational needs of young people with a variety of programs. One of PPRM's oldest and most successful programs is the the Dollar-A-Day (DAD) program, which was launched in the 1980s. It has proven to be so successful that it serves as a

The esteemed "condom ladies" Jennie Shank (left) and Mary Silverstein (right). Longtime Planned Parenthood supporters, these multi-talented women volunteered every Thursday morning to affix labels to condoms. Photo by Havey Productions.

national model for other programs. DAD aims to help at-risk teenage girls avoid unintended pregnancy by empowering them to take personal responsibility for their sexual health and by providing an atmosphere for peer support.

In an effort to promote healthy lifestyles from an early age, PPRM created the Growing Up Smart (GUS) program. Geared to young people between the ages of ten and fourteen, GUS is designed to help youngsters make healthy life choices and develop healthy interpersonal relationships. Armed with

these tools, young people are more likely to delay the onset of sexual activity and practice behaviors that prevent pregnancy and STDs, including HIV/AIDS.

Meeting the needs of teens between the ages of fourteen and eighteen is the Personal Responsibility Education Program (PREP). Taught by a trained facilitator, PREP provides comprehensive sex education in a supportive, safe environment. Other programs include the Experiential Wilderness Program, launched in 1997 in collaboration with Colorado Outward Bound. This challenging adventure program allows young people to practice and reinforce their ability to make healthy, responsible choices.

In addition to its youth development education programs, PPRM provides education programs for the community at large. In keeping with its tradition as an organization that reaches out to

Young Teens for Tomorrow participants are honored at the Grant-Humphreys Mansion in Denver for their contribution to the Growing Up Smart program, which works with youth, ages ten to fourteen, in conjunction with other agencies like the Boys and Girls Clubs of Metro Denver.

people with few rescources, PPRM created Project Prevention, which serves high-risk youth between the ages of twelve and twenty-one. Most of these youth are homeless or runaways, and some already have children, but none of them have insurance or health care resources. The program's education focuses on risky behaviors that are connected to unplanned pregancies and STDs.

For each person who participates in one of PPRM's education programs or receives services in one of its thirty-one health centers, there are thousands more who have questions about their sexual and reproductive health. To address the concerns of the community at large, PPRM has a centralized call center and a comprehensive Web site (www.pprm.org). The site provides detailed information on sexual and reproductive health topics. In addition, it outlines the various health and education services offered by PPRM and allows visitors to locate a health center in their area and to make appointments online.

Vicki J. Cowart has servd as president and CEO of PPRM from 2003 to the present.

Making all of this happen are more than 300 staff members and about 500 volunteers. That's a far cry from the handful of women who launched the organization in 1916. And although the organization has changed dramatically over the past nine decades, the hundreds of people currently involved are determined to carry on the legacy of Margaret Sanger, Ruth Cunningham and other early supporters.

ROCKY MOUNTAIN FIBER PLUS, INC.

In the summer of 1982 a loan representative from Denver, Colorado, stood in the middle of a grassy field in Kiowa, about fifty miles southeast of the city, and looked around him. As far as he could see, not a single structure rose above the level of the plain. "I have to tell you," he said, "this is the first time in my life that I have stood in a field where everywhere I look I see nothing, and somebody's trying to get a loan for a commercial building."

Denise Serres, founder of Rocky Mountain Fiber Plus (RMFP), stood next to him and laughed. Her company had grown considerably over the past few years, and they had already been obliged to move the operation from a motor home in Price City, Utah, to a home office in Salt Lake City, to a rented space in Parker, Colorado. This time, Serres was determined to create a permanent office space. An abundance of land in Kiowa, coupled with its proximity to Denver—which was already becoming the United States' telecommunications Mecca—gave her just the place to do it.

By now, Serres was used to having to search for a place for herself. When she founded RMFP in 1978, the women's liberation movement had been progressing

Denise Serres, founder of Rocky Mountain Fiber Plus.

for over a decade, yet many opportunities—particularly in the world of business—remained open only to men. Serres, as one of the only women working in cable construction and one of a small number who owned her own business, frequently encountered problems that arose because of her gender.

"When we went to sign the loan," she relates, "the president of the bank said, 'There's no doubt in my mind you can do it. But it's going to get turned down because the name on the line is a woman's.'" Nevertheless, determined to get the money she needed, Serres went to her friend Gene Cabral of Telecommunications, Inc. (TCI) for help. He co-signed on the loan and passed the money on to RMFP. That money, coupled with a small loan from Denise's

in-laws, M.E. and Lois Robinson, made it possible to break ground for the 11,000-square-foot building that would become their permanent offices.

For RMFP, the issue of discrimination was sadly familiar. Serres was denied funds or credit several times throughout the company's history simply because she was a woman. But familiar, too, was their means of overcoming it. What allowed the company to expand in 1982 were precisely the qualities that have enabled them to succeed over time: determination, ingenuity and—most of all—friendship.

Rocky Mountain Fiber Plus is a cable construction company based out of Kiowa with branches in several cities throughout the U.S. and Santo Domingo. Now employing between fifty and seventy-five workers, in addition to numerous independent sub-contractors, the company began in response to a necessity. In the late 1970s the cable industry was growing at an incredible rate. Every major multiple-system operator (MSO)—a company that operates more than one cable system, such as Comcast—was building, expanding, and getting franchises across the country. And the faster they grew, the harder they searched for people who could build and upgrade their systems.

TCI found Denise Serres. She had over a decade of experience in the cable business and was, in addition, their former employee. Having worked with pioneer cable engineer Richard Rexroat and been mentored by Gene Cabral, Serres had accumulated the knowledge and experience TCI was looking for. First to call was Cabral. He was followed by Dave Willis and J.C. Sparkman—the COO of the company in those days. They talked logistics; they talked finance. Eventually, Serres agreed to start Rocky Mountain Communications, as it was then called, to help TCI move forward.

The largest MSO in the country at that time, TCI initially hired the company to do "walk-out," a process which is almost as simple as it sounds. Telecommunications companies need to know the distance between telephone poles and the distance from the ground to the first cable, power, or phone line to

Rocky Mountain Fiber Plus had its first office in in Salt Lake City.

The company had a shire hitch for many years and was asked to represent Colorado in the 1998 Washington, D.C. Fourth of July parade.

determine if there is enough room to build the necessary equipment. Doing walk-out means walking into the field and taking measurements, which are then used to create maps.

TCI was remarkably supportive of their new contractors. Because Serres didn't have enough money to start a business in the beginning, she was assured of timely payments to ensure that she would be able to cover her expenses. About a year later, when RMFP began to need additional trucks to handle their workload, Gene Cabral stepped in once again to guarantee that the payments would be made. Working for people they could count on allowed the company to expand from doing walk-out to building entire cable systems.

Work began to pour in—not just from TCI, but from other major MSOs as well, many of which were located in Denver. Soon to be the nation's telecommunications capital, Denver was home to the majority of companies with which RMFP did business, and Serres and her associates spent much of their time flying to and from the city to bid on and negotiate contracts. Eventually, the company

decided to relocate to Kiowa to be closer to the industry's center. There they began to hire more employees to help handle the ever-increasing workload.

One of those who answered the newspaper ad was Jesse Hill. Though he walked in with no knowledge of the industry, he seemed to have an insatiable desire to learn. The company hired him for the latter quality, and their belief

Laying out design maps so construction could start in Santo Domingo. Denise Serres (standing left) and Gene Cabral to her right.

in him paid off. Eventually, he became Serres' front-man, standing in when a woman was not welcome in negotiations. And after years of dedication, he became the company's president, a title which he still holds today.

Over the next decade, RMFP designed and built cable television systems in most major cities in the nation, including Pittsburg, Chicago, Miami, St. Louis, Kansas City, Dallas, Fort Worth, Houston, Little Rock, Denver, Salt Lake City, Phoenix, San Francisco and many more. Although one might think that workflow would dwindle after a while, it actually increased with the demand for updated technology. RMFP expanded across the nation, not only with the support of TCI and other MSOs, but by aggressively promoting employees, such as Jesse Hill and Dave Knepp, from within the corporation.

Through everyone's hard work, enterprising ideas and a greater-than-usual dose of ingenuity, RMFP made it through this period with their feet on the ground and their eyes looking straight ahead. By 1990 some of their major obstacles had nearly dissolved. And, with the technology boom of the 1990s pend-

ing, it didn't happen a moment too soon.

From 1990 to 1996 the cable industry was popping with interest in fiber optics. Although the telephone industry had already been using fiber optics for some time, the technology was just beginning to be applied to cable, and it therefore required new techniques and new equipment. Once again, RMFP was called upon to be a leader in the field, to do something they had never done before.

An optical fiber is a transparent fiber made of glass or plastic which is smaller than a human hair. Like electrical wire, these fibers can be used to transmit information; however, unlike electrical wire, they can be packed into large bundles and use light waves to send huge amounts of information very quickly. A fiber optics system takes up less space and is faster and more accurate than an electrical system, but it also requires entirely different techniques to install.

A new company building in Kiowa, Colorado.

Many of the techniques in current use were designed by RMFP. The company developed winching methods, including ball-bearing rollers to support fiber optics cables at the poles, to pull in cables of up to seven and a half miles without exceeding a maximum pulling pressure of 600 pounds. In effect, this new method enabled them to build fiber optics networks more quickly and over greater distances without fear of damaging them.

As their list of contracts lengthened, RMFP became a widely recognized leader in fiber optic installation. The company was asked not only to install the fiber cable networks, but to teach local operators how to use and repair the new technology. In addition, they helped write the fiber optic installation manual for the Society of Cable Engineers.

According to Serres, one of the highest honors RMFP ever received was when the company was asked to rewrite TCI's construction manuals. Though it subsequently sold to AT&T, TCI was the largest MSO in the world at the time, and therefore their construction manuals contained the most widely used methods of building and installation in the industry. Those methods originated with RMFP.

In 1993 the company appeared in an article in *USA Today* entitled "Fiber Optics Frenzy Taxes Contractors" as one of the major players in the telecommunications industry. The article was a confirmation of the company's reputation and its place as one of the largest and most advanced cable television construction contractors in the United States—perhaps even in the world. To Serres, this was the company's crowning achievement.

The last half of the 1990s brought about several developments that would change the cable television industry forever. With the information superhighway well underway, telephone companies were starting to look at cable

Some of Rocky Mountain Fiber Plus' semis and bucket trucks.

television providers as methods for alternative revenue. At the same time, cable TV providers were venturing into and providing Internet and phone services. The three industries' methods of operation were growing more and more similar; the push was on for them to join forces, to provide phone, cable and Internet services with a single company.

Big minds in the industry continued to think along this line for several years. When AT&T purchased TCI in 1999, it became obvious that the phone service and cable TV providers were no longer separate entities. To keep up with the changing times, companies began to integrate and evolve.

The mindset to merge did not only exist between service providers, however. Perhaps inevitably, it spilled over into the construction world, causing a change to take place in construction philosophy. Historically, contractors had been small companies, often owned by individuals who could maintain high standards of quality control. However, there was a movement in the late 1990s for public holding companies to purchase private companies in an effort to obtain

Rocky Mountain Fiber Plus holds Pioneer dinners where employees are presented with a ten year ring.

Rocky Mountain Fiber Plus holds a turket shoot on trap range property for charity.

the huge contracts being generated by the merging industries.

In a surprisingly short time, RMFP's status changed from that of preferred contractor to that of a much smaller contractor. Many thought the company too small to handle their modern needs and preferred to give projects to the large conglomerations of formerly private contractors. RMFP was approached time and time again by the holding companies, but they refused to sell.

Their refusal was not just a matter of pride. It was based on the conviction that if the company was sold, it would lose

much of what had originally made it great: the people. "These people built the company," Serres says. "I could not have done it without the belief, enthusiasm, and support of Gene Cabral, Jesse Hill, Dave Knepp, Kurt Breuchman, and a lot of people who've stuck with me a long time." Then, with a laugh, she adds, "Besides that, we knew it wouldn't work."

As it turned out, they made the right decision. Although Serres concedes that they had some rough times, they survived—which is more than one can say of many of the public companies. Financially unstable, unable to complete their projects and meet the demands of the industry that created them, most of the conglomerates that sprouted up in the late 1990s failed. RMFP, however, is still going strong, as are many of the employees that started with the company over two decades ago.

Rocky Mountain Fiber Plus reflects the hometown spirit of rural Colorado through its dedication to friendship, honesty and excellence. But the company also demonstrates the urban spirit of cities like Denver, where technological advancement and business techniques are continually pushing ahead. For almost thirty years, it has grown to represent the best of Colorado, both at home and around the world.

ROCKY MOUNTAIN LAW ENFORCEMENT FEDERAL CREDIT UNION

For the men and women dedicated to protecting the people and places of the Denver area, Rocky Mountain Law Enforcement Federal Credit Union has proudly provided the opportunity for financial stability and security since 1938.

Like many longstanding credit unions, Rocky Mountain Law Enforcement Federal Credit Union was founded to fill a very specific and vital need within its community. As the United States was recovering from the devastating toll of the Great Depression in the late 1930s, many of the country's law enforcement workers were seeking financial assistance. Their options, however, were severely limited. Banks, still unstable from the nation's economic collapse, often denied loans to police officers, leaving one of the most important community service sectors without the means to live well or provide for their families.

One group of law enforcers, who dedicated their lives daily to serving others, found a way to help one another. On August 2, 1938 three Denver police officers—Harold Dill, Ivan Elder

The current main office was purchased in 1999.

and Roy Floyd—chartered the Denver Police Federal Credit Union. With the blessing of Mayor George Bagold, the credit union opened for business out of a single desk drawer within the Denver Police personnel bureau.

The new credit union, which paid $1 per month to maintain its charter, was founded by these officers not only to provide financial opportunities to law enforcement employees, but more importantly, to do so at a low rate. The primary offerings were savings accounts

and small loans, with a maximum savings deposit of $25 and a maximum loan of $200.

Ivan Elder, one of the founders, ran the growing organization in addition to attending to his law enforcement responsibilities. Although he was a volunteer, Elder helped shape a strong culture, based on solid customer service and trust, which continues today. In fact, it is said that on more than one occasion, Elder pulled money from the drawer and replaced it with a simple slip of paper in the form of an IOU.

As time passed, the specific needs of the Denver Police Federal Credit Union members changed and, as all successful organizations do, the credit union adapted accordingly by offering expanded services. In 1987 membership doubled when members of the Aurora Police Association were allowed to join. The scope of membership continued to evolve, as the credit union opened up services to active and retired police officers from multiple agencies within the Denver metropolitan area. They also welcomed other members of law enforcement, including employees of the sheriff's department and district attorney's office and their families. In 2001 membership eligibility was broadened again as the credit union began to accept civilians employed with accepted law enforcement groups.

Left to right: Tom Tedesco, Bill Threlkeld, Christine Wiley, Steve Allison and Lyle Hesalrand.

Although its core principles remained the same, the Denver Police Federal Credit Union had grown beyond its original name. In 2003 the board of directors voted to change the organization's name to Rocky Mountain Law Enforcement Federal Credit Union (RMLEFCU), in order to better reflect a diverse membership and increased geographical reach. Far from the days when the organization operated out of a desk drawer, RMLEFCU now has approximately 8,600 members, assets in excess of $125 million and more than thirty-eight employees.

One of those staff members, Christine Wiley, has been an integral part of the credit union's evolution for more than twenty years. Wiley, who joined the organization in 1986 as a teller, worked her way up to Chief Executive Officer in just ten years. While working full-time, Wiley earned a Bachelor of Science in Management from Metropolitan State College and a Master of Business Administration in Accounting from Regis University in 1997. She has been instrumental in growing the organization from under $35 million in assets to over $125 million today.

Wiley's longstanding and successful career with RMLEFCU reflects not only the culture of the credit union, but her personal belief in its future. "I am so proud to be a part of an organization with such integrity. In today's environment, 'integrity' seems to be an over-used and self-defined term. However, for Rocky Mountain Law Enforcement Federal Credit Union it is how we operate in every way. Rather than talk about integrity, we demonstrate it by the way we manage our credit union and serve the membership," Wiley said.

That same dedication to serving its membership is reflected in the credit union's efforts to support its community. The staff is encouraged to share their time and talents with nonprofit and charitable organizations including the Police Athletic League, Cops Fighting Cancer and The Denver Police Foundation. RMLEFCU is also a constant presence at several fundraisers each year that benefit a variety of local causes.

The outreach efforts by the credit

union are numerous; however, one event rises above the rest. Since a large number Denver-area law enforcers also serve in the armed forces—many in the reserves—the horrific events of September 11, 2001 had a significant impact on RMLEFCU's membership. In just one week, the credit union raised more than $550,000 to help victims and their families.

The credit union's original safe.

Christine Wiley oversees the badge award ceremony, with presenter Denver Police Chief Gerald Whitman.

Being a true community partner for the RMLEFCU is part of operating on a day-to-day basis. A clear focus is set on delivering exceptional service to each member. Solid membership relations have proven to be a key to success; RMLEFCU has almost double the assets of credit unions with comparable membership numbers.

The organization continues to be a top performer among Colorado credit unions, despite—or perhaps, partially because of—the acquisitions and mergers embarked upon by peer organizations. As other credit unions have pursued growth and altered their charters to become community financial institutions, RMLEFCU has remained focused on its core membership and mission.

Guided by a volunteer board of directors and a management team that believes in the organization's mission, Rocky Mountain Law Enforcement Federal Credit Union is a financial institution with a solid past, present and future of service to the local law enforcement heroes of the Metro Denver area.

ST. MARY'S ACADEMY

When three Sisters of Loretto boarded the crowded mail coach in Santa Fe, New Mexico on a June day in 1864, they bravely set aside any apprehension and focused on the mission at hand. A Catholic priest in Denver had invited the women to come to Colorado to start a school for girls in hopes of countering the "Wild West" atmosphere of the booming city. With all of their possessions in one trunk, Sisters Johanna Walsh, Beatriz Maes and Ignatia Mora made the exhausting five-day journey to Denver. Five weeks later, St. Mary's Academy opened its doors to twenty students.

The first classes were held in a spacious frame house on the corner of 14th and California streets in Denver. A three-story brick building was constructed five years later, and by 1884, the school had 100 boarders, 125 day students and twenty-five teachers. In 1911 a new school was built at the corner of 14th and Pennsylvania streets, neighboring the home of the legendary Molly Brown.

After eighty-eight years in the downtown area, St. Mary's Academy relocated as a day school to University Blvd. on the former estate of businessman A. R. Hickerson in 1952. The twenty-acre campus includes the lower school, built

The Sanders House is the focal point of the St. Mary's Academy campus. Built in the 1930s, the white-columned Georgian Colonial house serves as the school's administrative center.

Graduates and students gather on the front steps of the St. Mary's Academy building, located at 14th and Pennsylvania Streets in Denver, on graduation day in 1890. Over 130 classes of young women have graduated from the school since the school's first graduate, Jessie Forshee, was awarded her diploma in 1875.

in 1952; the Hickerson home (now known as the Sanders House), which was constructed in 1938, and now houses the administrative offices; Bonfils Hall, built in 1964, which houses the high school; the Bishop Evans Sports Center, built in 1985; and a middle school constructed in 2001. The athletic facilities include a softball diamond and a large field for soccer, lacrosse and field hockey.

A pioneering spirit and willingness to serve—just as the Sisters of Loretto had shown—remain the hallmarks of St. Mary's Academy, more than 140 years after its founding. Today the Catholic independent school has an enrollment of 800 students representing a variety of religious, ethnic, and socioeconomic backgrounds. St. Mary's Academy takes great pride in its diversity. Half of the students are Catholic, and the remainder includes Protestants, Hindus, Muslims and Jews. Students of color make up 22 percent of the student body. "We provide a nurturing atmosphere and show respect for all of our students," said Judith Baenen, president of St. Mary's Academy. "Faith, justice, community, and respect—these are all Loretto values that we try to instill in every aspect of what we do."

Classes are offered to both boys and girls in kindergarten through grade eight. At the high school level, the Academy provides Colorado's oldest and largest all-girls program, which enables young women to learn in an environment that bolsters their self-confidence and leadership skills. The academic success of the Academy's students is evidenced by the fact that 100 percent of the graduates continue their educations at four-year colleges. In addition, the overwhelming majority go to the school of their first choice.

St. Mary's Academy has a challenging curriculum that includes programs in religion and values, language arts, social studies, science, mathematics, foreign language, fine and performing arts and physical education. Public speaking and creativity are an integral part of the classroom experience. From as early as kindergarten, children learn to speak and perform with poise in front of an audience. Students in all grades are encouraged to take advantage of leadership opportunities.

Each year, St. Mary's Academy hosts a leadership conference for girls in grades seven through twelve, which is

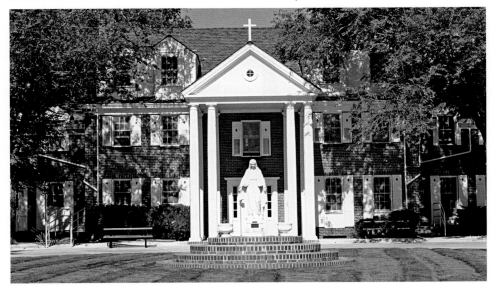

open to students from other school systems. Keynote speakers have included a female astronaut, as well as entrepreneurs and entertainers. The 2006 speaker was Emmy-winning actress Nancy Cartwright, the voice of Bart in the animated television show *The Simpsons*. Attendees also participate in seminars led by prominent women from the Denver community, enabling girls to learn about practical leadership topics such as building coalitions, negotiating and handling stress.

In keeping with the Loretto tradition, every student from kindergarten through twelfth grade is challenged to participate in community service projects. Throughout the year, students donate their time to help those often neglected by society: the disabled, the poor, the homeless, the elderly, abused women, troubled teens and the sick. "We have a coordinator of community service who assists students in finding an appropriate service opportunity. We also encourage our students to stretch themselves, to discover they can do things that they didn't think they could," said President Judith Baenen.

In the elementary grades, children take part in a monthly project called "Helping Hands," in which they collect mittens, school supplies, coats and other items for less fortunate children. Students in the middle school volun-

St. Mary's Academy brings together education and technology in a variety of ways, including use of an ACTIVBoard in Advanced Placement Biology. ACTIVBoard is an interactive "whiteboard" that utilizes graphics, animation and the Internet to help students learn. A dedication to integrating technology into everyday student learning is encompassed in all grades.

Students in the kindergarten class at St. Mary's Academy listen as teacher Kathy Jordan reads a story to them. The school's commitments to low student-to-teacher ratio and multiple teaching styles challenges and inspires students to become their best selves.

teer at clothing centers and prepare and serve food at soup kitchens. In the ninth grade, students must complete twenty hours of community service. At the end of the year, they give a twenty-minute presentation entitled "What It Means to Be Human" to a panel composed of St. Mary's Academy alumnae, parents and other adults from outside the school. The presentation is comprised of all the students have learned during their ninth grade year, both inside and outside of the classroom. Tenth graders prepare a similar presentation focusing on their service experiences. Students must complete thirty hours of service in grade eleven and forty hours of service in grade twelve. For their final project, they participate in a service seminar that allows each student to explore sociological issues and discuss what circumstances brought the people they have helped to their point of need. "What the students discover is that the people they serve are not that much different from themselves," said Baenen. "They see that they have been given privileges of

birth or successful parents and they are in a different place, but they are not different people from those they help."

With its strong sense of spirituality and excellent academic programs, St. Mary's Academy has educated thousands of women who are now making a difference in their communities and around the world. Notable alumnae include U.S. Secretary of State Condoleezza Rice; MacArthur Fellow Jane Lubchenco, a Distinguished Professor of Zoology at Oregon State University; and Fulbright Scholars Kamleh Shaban and Donna Haraway, an author and professor at the University of California, Santa Cruz. While their graduates' achievements are impressive, the school's present success would not have been possible without the three Sisters of Loretto, whose convictions and compassion motivated them to follow through on a divine calling that remains intact to this day.

UNITED STATES AIR FORCE ACADEMY

Built high up on the side of the majestic Rocky Mountains just above Colorado Springs, at an altitude of 7,200 feet, is the campus of the United States Air Force Academy (USAFA). Since its inception, the Academy has been known for its high standards of academics. However, producing cadets with exceptional qualities of character, personal integrity and leadership has been the Academy's true hallmark.

The youngest of the U.S. service academies, the formation of the USAFA did not come about easily. In fact, the Academy was in the planning stages for nearly half a century before it came into existence. The Wright Brothers made their historic flight on December 17, 1903, giving rise to the possibilities of an air force and its potential role in national security. Creating an air arm of the military became a growing topic among the existing branches of the armed services. By 1919 air service men were growing in number and operating with some autonomy, but the idea of forming a separate air corps did not have enough government support. Training for military flying was done independently or at academies such as West

Aerial view of the Academy's Cadet Area.

Point. Many attended flight school after they were already admitted into the Army or Navy, but there was no specific training program or location for this evolving branch.

Airpower's pivotal role in WWII made it clear that a separate air arm of the military was justified. In 1947 the National Security Act was passed and the Air Force was officially created. One year later, in 1948, a Service Academy

Board was formed by the Secretary of Defense, James Forrestal, to determine the need for an academy specifically designed for airmen. The Board reviewed the existing military academies to determine if a separate training program was necessary. They recommended "that the Air Force Academy should be established without delay and the appropriate legislation to accomplish this purpose, including the authorization of interim plans, should be obtained." The practical need for an Air Force Academy finally had the political support needed in order to become a reality. It was agreed that the institution would be known as the United States Air Force Academy. However, it would still be another five years before the Academy would open.

Initially, progress was made quickly; in 1949 a site selection committee was chosen. The committee collectively traveled 21,000 miles and considered 580 proposed sites in forty-five states. Criteria for the Academy's new location included "...natural beauty, a variety of local educational, religious, cultural and recreational facilities, as well as proximity to large cities," states Dr. Elizabeth Muenger, historian/librarian

Cadet Chapel.

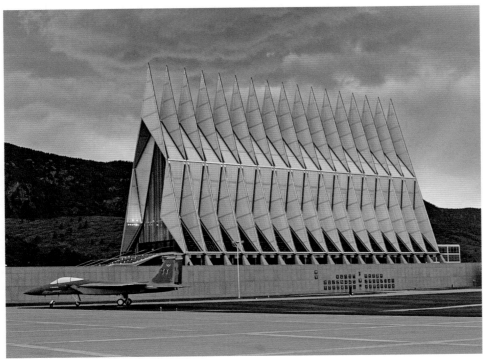

of the Academy. The committee was led by former Air Force Chief of Staff, Gen. Carl Spaatz and included Lt. Gen. Hubert R. Harmon, who was later designated the "Father of the Air Force Academy" for his vision, passion and leadership in heralding the formation of the school.

Unfortunately, the Korean War began and all efforts to establish the Academy were put on hold due to financing and war-related issues. Staunch advocate for the Academy, Dwight D. Eisenhower, was elected president in 1952 and the issue of starting the Academy resurfaced. In May of 1953 House Armed Services Committee Chairman Dewey Short of Missouri introduced House Resolution 5337, a bill "To Provide for the Establishment of the United States Air Force Academy." Finally, on March 29, 1954, the bill was passed. President Eisenhower signed the legislation on April 1.

In June 1954 a new site selection committee, known as the Air Force Selection Commission, was chartered by Air Force Secretary, Harold E. Talbott. This new panel included Generals Spaatz and Harmon, who were joined by Brig. Gen Charles A. Lindbergh, Dr. Virgil M. Hanche and Merrill C. Meigs. This group also considered 580 sites in forty-five

Core values.

states; however, only one site made both committees' lists: Colorado Springs.

On July 11, 1955 the temporary site of the Academy, a corner of Lowry Air Force Base, near Denver, was dedicated. The first class of 306 cadets was sworn in there by Gen. Harmon. Meanwhile, the creation of the permanent site was underway. Leading design firms and various artistic talents were commissioned to make the permanent site of the Academy a landmark just as notable as West Point and Annapolis. Design talents included photographer Ansel Adams, architectural firm Skidmore, Owings and Merrill, industrial designer Walter Dorwin Teague, landscape architect Dan Kiley and graphic designer Herbert Bayer. The effort was incredibly

successful and the result—a National Historic Landmark.

In keeping with the distinctive modern design of the Academy's architecture, The seventeen-spired Cadet Chapel was built in 1961 and is the most distinctive building in the Cadet Area. Nearly half a million visitors each year visit the Cadet Chapel, which is considered one of the most distinctive and beautiful examples of academic architecture in America. On April 1, 2004, fifty years after the bill signing to establish the Academy, the Cadet Area of the Academy was designated as a National Historic Landmark.

The Academy's degree program was accredited in the early part of 1959—which was unusual, considering the first class did not graduate until June of that year! In addition to exceeding standards of excellence in its academic and military development programs, the Academy set new standards in creating curriculum for character and leadership development. The Academy's Character and Leadership Education Division was developed to provide classroom, seminar, workshop and experiential-based learning programs. The Academy's Honor Code states, "We will not lie, steal, or cheat, nor tolerate among us anyone who does."

In addition to their academic and military studies, cadets annually dedicate more than 20,000 hours to community service. "Our core values are Integrity, Service before Self, and Excellence," states Johnny Whitaker, Director of Communications. "The wording may have changed over the years, but our mission has basically remained the same—to produce young officer-leaders of character . . . for the security of our country and for the civililan sector."

Each graduate exits the Academy and enters the military with a superior education and a strong character—the institution's hallmark. During the Academy's half century of existence, more than 38,000 have graduated, and 51 percent of those are still on active duty today.

Cadets marching in their parade uniforms.

UNIVERSITY OF COLORADO

The dream of a world-class university in Colorado began in 1874 with the passion of two legislators and a group of committed citizens from the then small hamlet of Boulder, Colorado. The bill to construct a university was first introduced to the Colorado Territorial Legislature by Boulder's representative in the House, James P. Maxwell. Passage of the bill faced many hurdles, not least of which was that many other Colorado communities, such as Denver and Burlington (now Longmont), wanted the first state university to be established in their city. One of the main obstacles Boulder faced was the final version of the bill, which cut the capital appropriation from $30,000 to $15,000 and required that an additional $15,000 be raised by the people of Boulder before the bill could be enacted. Opponents of a Boulder location included the stipulation assuming that the people of Boulder would not be able to meet the requirement and thus lose the university.

Captain David H. Nichols, later elected speaker of the House, knew that this intense rivalry could prevent Boulder from being the home of the new university. So he left his seat in the assembly one evening about 6 p.m.,

In 1861 a bill passed by Colorado's Territorial Legislature established the University of Colorado. Several cities received votes for a new university. Boulder's mountain backdrop makes CU-Boulder one of the most beautiful campuses in the U.S.

Old Main, completed April 18, 1876, housed the entire university. One early grad noted it was surrounded "by nearly a mile of mud."

mounted his horse and sped toward Boulder, thirty miles away.

Nichols went to every prominent citizen he knew in Boulder, including the local members of the board of trustees to consult their support. His efforts garnered sufficient pledges to meet the $15,000 matching requirements of the Legislature. By 10 a.m. the next day, Nichols was back in his seat before the delegates from other localities could take advantage of his absence.

Though Nichols' ride is not documented, it lives in folklore as the "midnight ride" of Captain David Nichols. He has been compared to Paul Revere, riding through the dark night, spurring his tired horse on through a drizzling winter rain and returning early the next morning, winning for Boulder the "crowning jewel" of the state educational system.

Ground was broken on July 27, 1875 for the university's first building, which would be called "Old Main." On September 5, 1877 the University of Colorado (CU) officially opened with an inaugural address by the its first president, Joseph Sewall. Two courses of study were offered—the Classical Course, requiring two years of Greek, three years of Latin and two years of mathematics; and the Scientific Course, which included botany and chemistry, both taught by President Sewall.

During the first year, President Sewall hired Mary Rippon, who became head of the Department of German Language and Literature and taught at the university for the next twenty-eight years. Rippon was one of the first women in the United States to teach at a state university.

By 1879 the school had seventy-eight students and tuition was free to any state citizen. But the university had few books. Local Boulderite and school supporter, Charles Buckingham, donated $2,000 to start a library, which was established in Old Main. University students served as the first librarians. Furniture was purchased from the proceeds of lectures, concerts and other cultural events.

The university matured and extended its reach under the guidance of strong leaders. Extension offices were established in Denver (1912) and Colorado Springs (1920).

One of the longest serving presidents of the Boulder campus was George Norlin(1919-1939), professor of Greek studies. Over his twenty-year tenure, Norlin oversaw Charles Klauder's redesign of the campus, stood up to the Ku Klux Klan (then a powerful influence in Colorado politics) and successfully led the university through the difficult Depression years.

By 1939 Norlin had elevated CU to rank among the best "medium-sized" higher education institutions in the country. He did so by expanding offerings, such as establishing the Mountain Research Station in 1921, a field education and research station that has become a preeminent world center for the study of the environment.

Mackey Auditorium was completed in 1922 as a memorial to Andrew J. Mackey, president of the First National Bank of Boulder. Upon his death, Mackey left the university $300,000 for its construction. The venue still hosts performances for the university community and Coloradans.

Norlin's legacy also includes building a new 26,000-seat stadium and gymnasium, which were dedicated in 1924. First known as the Colorado Stadium, then Norlin Stadium it hosted CU's first football games. In 1955 the stadium was expanded to 44,000 seats. Now it seats 51,000 and is now known as Folsom Stadium.

In 1945 CU and Harvard jointly managed an observatory in Colorado. CU gained full control later, which created the High Altitude Observatory. In 1960 Boulder was home for the National Center for Atmospheric Research (NCAR) largely due to the observatory.

The flatirons, the foothills and unique architecture provide spectacular settings for CU-Boulder, which is at 5,400 feet above sea-level.

Today, 130 years later, the University of Colorado, the state's flagship institution, has students from all over the world. The university educates more than 50,000 students annually, 28,000 of those being undergraduate and graduate students attending classes on the 700-acre Boulder campus.

The Boulder campus is an acclaimed research institution with particular strengths in environmental studies, law, aerospace, engineering, bioscience, music, journalism and business. The campus, known for its beauty, is nestled amid the inspiring Rocky Mountains.

It offers more than 2,500 courses in over 150 areas of study through its nine colleges and schools. Four faculty have earned Nobel Prizes: John Hall won the 2005 Nobel Prize in physics; Carl Wieman and Eric Cornell also won the 2001 Nobel Prize in physics; and Thomas Cech won the 1989 Nobel Prize in chemistry.

The university has one of the oldest and most prestigious space programs in the country. It began with the launching of suborbital sounding rockets in the late 1940s and early 1950s. Today, the Boulder campus ranks number one in space. CU receives more NASA funding than any other public university in the United States.

CU faculty and students continue to be among the world's leaders in observations and new findings in space. CU-Boulder scientists annually are among the top users of the Hubble Space Telescope. With it they took the first images of Venus, the first look at dust storms on Mars and examined exploding supernovas. CU-Boulder is the only research institution in the world to design and build space instruments for NASA that have gone to every planet in the solar system.

CU-Boulder has controlled satellites from campus, that were designed,

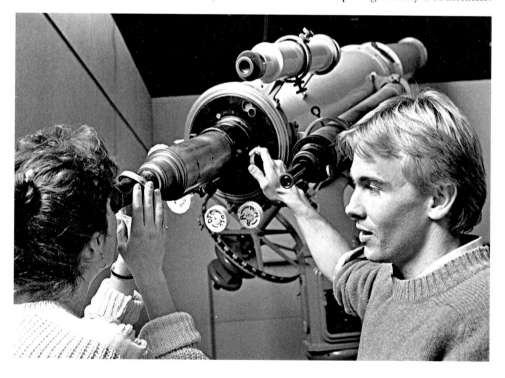

COLORADO

built and tested primarily by under-graduates. Seventeen CU alumni have flown in space, beginning with Boulder native Scott Carpenter, one of the original Mercury 7 astronauts in the 1960s.

The univesity's research also addresses more technological matters. In 2001 the University of Colorado garnered world-wide attention when it received $250 million, the largest gift ever given to an American university, to establish the

The university created an extension division in Denver in 1912, which accommodated the growing needs of Denver area students.

In 1962 the Colorado Springs (left) and the Denver Extension centers earned full-degree granting status, expanding CU's ability to serve the educational needs of Coloradans.

Coleman Institute for Cognitive Dis-abilities. National in scope, it supports research that tailors technology to help those with cognitive disabilities, such as Alzheimer's disease, brain trauma and Down Syndrome, live a more in-dependent and participatory life.

The university is also at the forefront of national efforts to discover alterna-tive energy solutions, CU's renewable energy and environmental work has

garnered international honors with its zero-energy solar home. CU won the first and second international Solar Decathlon in Washington, D.C.

In addition to the vibrant Boulder campus, CU continues its contributions to the state and nation at its other cam-puses. In 1911 the Denver and Gross College of Medicine in Denver merged with CU's School of Medicine, paving

In 1951 cancer research took on a renewed focus at the Medical School with the dedication of a new research wing. Today, CU's Cancer Center is the only National Cancer Institute designated comprehensive cancer center in the Rocky Mountain region.

the way for the school's move to Denver. The city turned over the Denver City and County Hospital to CU, making it the largest hospital for clinical instruction in the Rocky Mountain region. In 1925 the medical school moved to new facilities at Ninth Avenue and Colorado Boulevard. The facilities were described as "the greatest medical center between the Missouri River and the Pacific Coast."

In addition to its medical school in Denver, the university created an extension division in Denver in 1912 to accommodate students in the metro area. After moving from building to building for nearly twenty-six years the extension center found a permanent location in 1938 in the C.A. Johnson Building on 17th Street. Several hundred students were expected to enroll at the new center in 1940; instead more than 1,500 showed up to register. By the 1950s student enrollment had grown into the thousands.

To meet the growing demand for areas of study and classroom space, between 1973 and 1976 CU's Denver campus partnered with Metropolitan State College of Denver and the Community College of Denver to create one physical downtown campus for all three educational institutions. The new campus was named "Auraria," which means gold in Latin.

In 2004 the Denver campus and the Health Sciences Center consolidated to form the University of Colorado at Denver and Health Sciences Center (UCDHSC). The merger placed it in a more prestigious group of comprehensive major teaching and research universities. UCDHSC attracted more research awards than any institution in the Rocky Mountain Region. It educates more than 27,000 students, half of whom are pursuing graduate degrees.

UCDHSC College of Architecture and Planning addresses the challenges and opportunities of Colorado's dynamic setting. More than 80 percent of the population lives along the Front Range where a thousand miles of the semi-arid Great Plains meet the Rocky Mountains. Many of the school's fac-

A 1972 state constitutional amendment guaranteed full university status for the Denver and Colorado Springs campuses. Between 1973 and 1976 Colorado built the Auraria Higher Education Center on a 127-acre downtown campus shared by CU-Denver.

ulty are drawn from the major professional design and planning offices in the region.

There is perhaps no other field that has been so significantly affected by the intersection of past and future than the arts. The College of Arts & Media at UCDHSC focuses on visual arts. The College is also the first in the Rocky Mountain Region dedicated exclusively to the arts and entertainment.

UCDHSC has worked with the community to create the most extensive and dynamic film/video program in the Rocky Mountain region—the Colorado Film School.

CU's College of Arts & Media, the Denver Film Society and the Starz Encore Group bring the best of film to Denver through events such as the annual Denver International Film Festival. The Starz Film Center is Denver's only true cinematheque, committed to presenting the best in films with an eye toward titles not readily available on the big screen.

Colorado's emergence as a bioscience hub has created exciting opportunities for the CU-Denver Bard Center for Entrepreneurship. A bioscience intern-

ship program at the Bard Center focuses on developing business people to provide expertise to new bioscience businesses.

One of the premier health sciences institutions in the nation, CU's Health Sciences Center is home to five schools—medicine, nursing, dentistry, pharmacy and graduate; three hospitals—University of Colorado Hospital, Children's Hospital of Denver, and Colorado Psychiatric Health and forty-two research and health centers. School of Medicine faculty members provide services at University of Colorado Hospital, The Children's Hospital, Denver Health, National Jewish Medical and Research Center and the Veterans Administration Medical Center.

In 1995, when Fitzsimons Army Base was placed on the Base Realignment and Closure list, officials from Health Sciences Center, University of Colorado Hospital and the City of Aurora presented an innovative proposal to the Department of Defense in Washington, D.C. It emphasized the full benefits of transforming the decommissioned base into a world-class, academic health center, including state-of-the-art healthcare facilities. The U.S. Army considers the redevelopment of Fitzsimons a model base closure.

The 227-acre Fitzsimons redevelopment project allows CU to create a new model for twenty-first century academic health care. One of its distinct characteristics is that Fitzsimons gives CU an opportunity to create a new medical center directly connected to a major research and development park. Its proximity to private biotechnology firms will foster the synergy for discovery and new partnerships that should lead to medical breakthroughs from the laboratory to the patient's bedside. The park is the first of its kind west of the Mississippi River.

The director of the National Institutes of Health, Elias Zerhouni, said that "no one has put together the firepower, intellectual and physical, that I see here [at Fitzsimons] today."

Fitzsimons will also be a major driver of Colorado's economy. By 2010

The CU-Denver and Health Sciences Center's move to Fitzsimons will be on 227 acres with an additional 1.5 million gross square feet of research space.

Fitzsimons will directly and indirectly be responsible for more than 34,800 jobs. At development, the campus will drive an estimated 67,000 Colorado jobs.

CU faculty provides healthcare services to thousands of patients from across the state and region. The Anschutz Centers for Advanced Medicine provide health care, diagnostics and cancer treatment. The Anschutz Outpatient Pavilion offers dental, medical, nursing and pharmacy services; outpatient surgery and complete diagnostic testing.

The Anschutz Cancer Pavilion provides a breadth of services for cancer patients. The Lions Clubs of Colorado and Wyoming helped fund the Rocky Mountain Lions Eye Institute at Fitzsimons, providing the latest in eye treatments and diagnostics.

In the early 1960s Colorado Springs became the home to CU's third campus. David Packard of Hewlett-Packard was the catalyst for developing a campus when he agreed to bring his company to Colorado Springs if a university could be built to support his employees. In 1964 local businessman George T. Dwire offered the University the Cragmor Sanatorium and its surrounding eighty acres for the sum of one dollar. The University of Colorado at Colorado Springs (UCCS) was created by an act of the Colorado Legislature in 1965.

UCCS, located on 514 acres, is one of the fastest-growing universities in Colorado and the nation. It emphasizes a broad range of degree programs in the liberal arts and sciences and professional programs in business, engineering, nursing, education and public affairs. UCCS enrolls about 7,600 undergraduate and graduate students and is growing rapidly. It offers twenty-five bachelors degrees, seventeen masters degrees, and two doctoral degree programs through six colleges.

In recent years, *U.S. News and World Report* named UCCS a top Western public university. The American Association of State Colleges and Universities named the

In 1997 CU-Colorado Springs dramatically changed the landscape of its campus when it constructed a Housing Village to accommodate 600 residential students. Formerly, it was a commuter campus.

university one of two national leaders in community engagement efforts.

The UCCS Beth-El College of Nursing started in 1905. Its key contribution to Colorado is to train nurses through accelerated programs to help people in other careers transition into healthcare. It also offers online master's programs in nursing to reach people in rural communities.

Another field the campus is taking a lead on is Geropsychology. The exemplary program helps the state meet the needs of the growing over-sixty-five population. Colorado has one of the fastest growing aging populations in the nation, with some counties expected to have 600 percent increases in population over age eighty-five. Three of the ten geropsychologists in Colorado are on the UCCS faculty.

The University of Colorado is home to an array of research and education activities focused on cutting edge science and training. The more than 50,000 students and 2,600 full-time faculty members in the CU system make it the largest institution of higher learning in the state. In 2005 CU was awarded $630 million for sponsored projects. The National Science Foundation consistently ranks CU among the top ten public research universities.

For more information about the University of Colorado please visit www.cu.edu.

Before 1900 Colorado ran on horse power and, as this scene in the mining town of Alma documents, burro power. The Colorado livestock industry not only fed, but also transported Coloradans. Business in horses, mules, oxen and burros was as brisk then as it is today in motor vehicles. Courtesy, Colorado Historical Society

VALLEY BANK & TRUST

Even though Valley Bank & Trust has a network of thirteen branches, there is no mistaking that this Colorado institution still has a small business philosophy: provide excellent service and customer satisfaction. This commitment is punctuated with Valley Bank & Trust's genuine interest in its internal staff of "team members" and the surrounding community. Valley Bank & Trust stands out as a distinctly friendly face in a sea of modern corporate banking.

James "Jim" O'Dell, the bank's founder, didn't mean to become a banker. He grew up in western Kansas, the son of a farmer. He left the farm to pursue a degree in economics at Ottawa University and had no plans of going back home. However, his father's encouragement brought young Jim back to the farm after he graduated from college. Within the next five years, Jim got married and enjoyed a wonderful working relationship with his father. When an opportunity to become an agricultural representative at Hoxie State Bank, in Hoxie, Kansas, arose in 1963, Jim thought it over carefully.

Valley Bank & Trust corporate headquarters at 4900 E. Bromley Lane, Brighton, Colorado, also houses the Bromley Park branch.

While Jim was mulling over his options, the banker who originally offered him the job suffered serious health problems. The job never materialized, but the offer set Jim off in a completely new direction. Eager to see what other opportunities might exist in the local banking field, he promptly marched into the nearest bank and asked for a job. Explaining that he was just a farmer looking for a banking job must have shown a sufficient amount of moxie. A new position was created just for Jim at Consolidated State Bank in Hill City, Kansas. Banking agreed with him; he worked diligently at that institution for the next year and a half.

Though Jim enjoyed his new profession, he did not enjoy the service his new bank was giving its customers. "I didn't feel they were fair with people," Jim explained. "The bank president would make a farmer wait for an hour while he pretended to be busy." Growing frustration with his boss inspired bigger dreams in Jim, and he was soon fishing around to purchase his own bank. The only problem, at that point, was financing. "I had dreams, but no money," Jim O'Dell remembered.

Two other gentlemen did have the

necessary financing. After finding an ideal bank in Eastern Colorado, they approached Jim to partner with them. By September of 1965 the bank was purchased, and Jim, who had little management experience, was in charge. Jim was undaunted: he was young, optimistic and ready for a challenge. Soon enough, he was ready to take on even more responsibility. His bank was located in a tiny town of only five hundred residents, and he was ready to stretch his wings farther. He and his business partners began looking for more populous county seat towns with only one bank in the community. With a larger surrounding population, the partners felt they could offer county residents another banking choice. They soon found what they felt was an ideal location in Brighton, Colorado.

The partners applied for the necessary banking charter in 1969. This required them to show that there was a public need for a bank in that area and that the bank would create an advantage for the community. Because the city of Brighton already had a bank, their request was summarily rejected. The decision spurred Jim and his partners to do something radical: sue the state bank-

Built in 1972, the Main branch housed corporate headquarters and the Main branch until third quarter 2003, when the Bromley Park facilitiy opened.

ing commission to win the hard way—through the very same courts that had denied their charter.

Emerging from the lawsuit victorious, Jim and his partners were finally able to open Platte Valley Bank in September of 1971. The bank employed only five people when it opened. Services were standard for the time: checking and savings accounts, loans and CDs. Between 1975 and 1982 three more banks were added to the Valley Bank family across the state of Colorado. By the late 1970s Jim O'Dell, the farmer's son from Kansas, was president of the Colorado Bankers Association and was on the board of directors of the American Bankers Association.

In 1993 Colorado began to allow branching of banks. Valley Bank, First National Bank of Brighton, Valley Bank

of Frederick and Centennial State Bank were all merged into one bank with four branches. Nine more branches would be added over time, with the most recent addition occurring in 2005. The bank's services would expand over the years as well. In addition to mortgage services and online banking, Valley Bank & Trust is unique in that it is one of the few smaller banking institutions to have a fully operational trust department. The bank has team members, including attorneys, on hand to handle any trust account for its customers.

Valley Bank & Trust has also made it a priority to always offer business loans to organizations large and small. Other banks tended to stop lending within particular industries if some loans went into default or were otherwise not profitable. Throughout his banking career, Jim has remained committed to staying consistent with his customers, and not pulling loan opportunities because of a small

number of defaults. Jim O'Dell believes in the practice for consistency's sake and because there is a genuine need— especially in industries that are affected by peaks and valleys inherent to the economy. Since Valley Bank & Trust extends agricultural loans, droughts can be difficult on both customers and the bank itself. Construction lending can also be drastically affected by local and national economic conditions. When booming, the economy supports growth and expansion within the state. When in decline, the effects on the construction industry are felt at the bank.

Despite this, Jim has always maintained lending opportunities for these industries. He has an innate sense about the balance of the bank's interaction with its customers. "Yes, there is some risk involved," he acknowledged. But despite this, Jim asserts that keeping lending options open for customers "can be positive as well." It is this give-and-

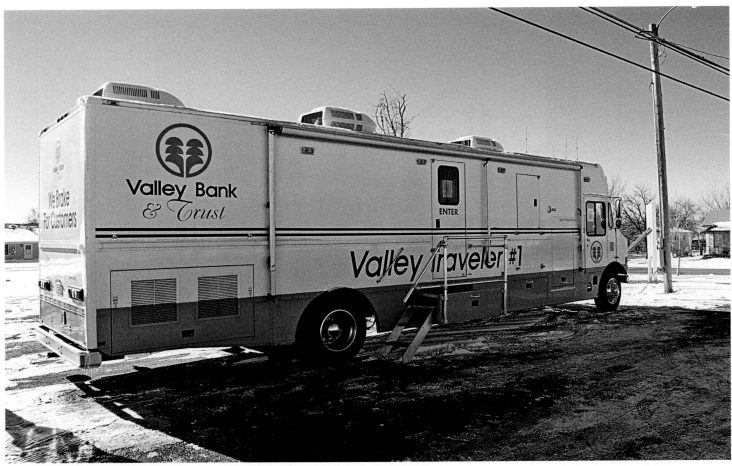

take attitude that sets Valley Bank & Trust apart not only from other Colorado banks, but within the American banking industry as a whole. Jim O'Dell still has the heart of a farmer, with the understanding that life is not all dollars and cents. He also knows better than most that sometimes factors outside human control come into play.

Over the years other changes in the United States have affected the bank. In the early 1980s nearly all banks had serious difficulty when the major oil companies pulled out. Though this was before Valley Bank & Trust had been permitted to have branches, Jim's foresight helped pull the bank through this time. In 1976 he and his partners had formed a bank holding company for the four banks they owned. Though some of the individual banks were hit hard, the holding company held strong and weathered this challenging time.

Fire has also played an interesting part in the bank's history. In 1999 Jim received call in the middle of the night

from the fire department informing him of a fire in the bank's data processing building—just next to the bank building. Fortunately, none of his team members were in the building at the time and the bank was spared from any serious damage. The equipment in the department, however—which had just been upgraded in anticipation of Y2K—was lost. The culprit: a table that had rubbed an electrical cord one time too many.

All equipment was moved out of the building to facilitate repairs, which lasted nine long months. Three team members relocated to Monet, Missouri, for a few weeks to continue with the bank's data processing. By the end of the refurbishing, the data processing department was back to its pre-fire condition. Though it was quite an ordeal for the bank, Jim is sure that customers had no idea there was even a problem. Thanks to daily data back-ups, nearly all customer information, including all account information and check records, was recovered without missing a beat.

Traveler 1, a temporary mobile branch for Denovo branches while permanent facilities are under construction.

Team members are a vital component to Valley Bank & Trust's ongoing success. It is the human element that grounds the company. Six team members have been with Valley Bank & Trust for over twenty years. The bank's most dedicated staff member has been with the company for thirty-three years. Even though over the past fifteen years she has fought cancer, she has continued to come in to work, if only for a few hours, each day. Not only has she continued to serve the bank, but has found comfort in her extended family at Valley Bank & Trust. At one point, a couch was brought into her office to give her a place to rest at lunch time. In a world of downsizing, Jim O'Dell has never considered extending her anything other than full support. "She has been a wonderful team member," he said, "and it's important to maintain these relationships."

In fact, in over forty years in a profession known for its bottom-line attitude, Jim is most pleased with the 401K program in place for his eighty-five team members. Of those eligible to participate, 90 percent make 401K contributions. Initially, team members could participate in an employee stock ownership program (ESOP). However, Jim felt uncomfortable leaving this benefit on the rolling tide of the bank's stock. The retirement fund would be contingent on the bank's financial health. The ESOP funds were eventually rolled over into the 401K, ensuring these dollars would still grow, regardless of the bank's well being. Though many large companies were incorporating ESOP plans during the early 1980s, Valley Bank & Trust was one of the first smaller companies to adopt this type of plan.

Team member scholarship and tuition reimbursement programs are in place as well. The bank currently employs many high school students and has committed to assist them meet their financial needs for their college journey. A helping hand is extended to all bank team members that are graduating from high school and are college-bound. College scholarships are also extended to the community. Valley Bank & Trust does not have stringent criteria on basic qualification; unlike other institutions, there is no requirement for study in a banking or economics field. Instead, the scholarships are made available to anyone seeking higher education.

Valley Bank & Trust makes a significant effort to be actively involved in the community it calls home. Grade 13 & Beyond is a scholarship program for elementary school children in grades three through five. Its purpose is to teach children about money and financial responsibility from a young age. In-school presentations are made to children, teachers and parents. Ongoing meetings also occur during the school year to help students understand the function of banks and how to carry this knowledge into young adulthood.

At sevety-one years of age, Jim O'Dell is optimistic the bank will remain a family business. His daughter, Donna Petrocco, is now the bank's president.

The temporary building that housed Valley Bank & Trust when it opened in September 1971 as Platte Valley Bank.

She is a widely respected banker, businesswoman and mother of two. His son, Richard, spends part of his time participating in the bank as well. His younger daughter lives in western Kansas with her two young children. Two of his grandchildren, both college-aged, have worked in the bank in various capacities. "As long as Donna and Richard, or other family members are willing," Jim forecasts, "the bank will stay in the family."

Valley Bank & Trust has contributed to the fabric of Colorado—and the banking industry at large—as a result of Jim O'Dell's sensible and personal approach. This has been encompassed by remembering the Golden Rule: to treat others as you yourself would want to be treated. It also demanded offering personal value in an industry that tends to forget people and look only at bottom lines and balances. Valley Bank & Trust has always remembered to be the one serving its team members and customers, not the other way around.

WORLD CONSTITUTION AND PARLIAMENT ASSOCIATION

The World Constitution and Parliament Association might seem to be ahead of its time. Founded in response to the proliferation of weapons of mass destruction and global warfare, the organization seeks to create a non-military world government under a unified world constitution. However, founder and Secretary General Philip Isely notes that the idea is neither new nor revolutionary. "Proposals for world government have been around a long time," he explained.

Indeed, Greek and Roman philosophers of yore put forth the idea long ago. More recently, Dante, Grotius and Kant contributed to the world government discussion in their works. Writer H.G. Wells, also known to have been a man well ahead of his time, posed the idea of a world-state consistently throughout his literary career. Some of the greatest thinkers ever to have lived have believed that not only was world government possible, but very probably necessary, for the survival of the species.

To understand the World Constitution and Parliament Association, one

Founder and Secretary General Philip Isely circa 1950.

must become acquainted with Philip Isely. Thinking outside of the box is Mr. Isely's business. He and his late wife, Margaret, started a business in an innovative new field over fifty years ago. Vitamin Cottage Natural Grocers began modestly in the 1950s. The Iselys started out small by selling whole grain bread door to door in Colorado. They would return later to take vitamin sub-

Philip (far left) and Margaret Isely (to his right) at the Provisional World Parliament, New Delhi, India, 1971.

scriptions. This was a radical concept at the time. Organic and whole foods were hardly in vogue yet, but the Iselys had a firm belief that once educated as to the benefits, people would begin to understand, and buy, organic.

The Iselys' door-to-door success was so great that they were able to open an actual retail store within six months. At the time, there were few businesses like Vitamin Cottage. The company was built on personal ideals and passion. Large-scale profit was not really fathomable at that point, let alone a motivating factor. The Iselys merely believed in what they were doing, believed that it would help those around them and therefore pursued it vigorously.

In the last fifty years, Americans have come to embrace the idea of organic growing and have become more health conscious than ever. Health and fitness is now a booming industry, poised to continue expanding. Today, Vitamin Cottage Natural Grocers is a chain of twenty-three stores throughout Colorado and New Mexico. Though it started out small, Vitamin Cottage Natural Grocers forged ahead. The truth about the benefits of healthy and responsible living was undeniable. Once the public was willing to hear this message, they embraced the idea of eating organic and taking better care of themselves. Vitamin Cottage started out as an ideal and is now a successful family business committed to continuing to educate people on healthy food options.

This seems a fitting business for the man who founded the World Constitution and Parliament Association. Philip Isely, at ninety, has had an illustrious life as a Renaissance man. He was born in Montezuma, Kansas, and is the father of five grown children. He is an accomplished writer and the designer of a prefab modular system of construction. He was even a candidate for the United States Congress. Straightforward and wry, thoughtful and committed, Isely has retained hopeful ideals without being overly idealistic. Philip Isely is a practical man who believes in making a difference.

Philip Isely meets with the Secretary General of the leading political party in India.

After World War II ended, the global mood was grim. Some estimates put the worldwide toll of the war at 62 million, including those who died as a result of disease and starvation. The majority of the war casualties were civilians. The country of Poland alone lost approximately 16 percent of its entire population between 1939 and 1945. The devastation was catastrophic.

This state of affairs compelled Philip Isely to get involved. Not satisfied to sit on the sidelines, Mr. Isely carefully considered what actions may be most useful in preventing such global destruction again. He became involved with Campaign for World Government (CWG), the first world federalist organization. CWG was founded in 1937 and based out of Chicago.

The motivation of many world government organizations was, and is, to amend the charter of the United Nations. However, to do so would require the unanimous agreement of the five permanent members of the UN Security Council. These members comprise the most powerful nations on the planet: the United States, Russia, the United Kingdom, France and the People's Republic of China. The problem lies in the very nature of the international power struggle. Each nation would likely be loath to approve any amendment which might dilute its own power or global position. The practicality of this endeavor, achieving unanimous support to alter the charter, therefore appears futile to Mr. Isely.

Additionally, the charter of the United Nations is based on continuing national sovereignty. To achieve the kind of world government, which could effectively operate under the proposed constitution, would require more international cooperation than this concept would provide. Therefore, the process of overhauling the charter would be a colossal, if not impossible, feat altogether.

After joining CWG, Philip Isely quickly surmised that the most practical course of action would be to work outside of any existing governmental structure. The best method would be to pursue a world constitution, written from scratch. A world government would be impossible without a ratified agreement as to the form and function of a governing body. Many other world government organizations had their hearts in the right places, but sought unity without form. Once a uniform agreement could be proposed, debated, and voted on, then the world government movement would really be going somewhere.

Philip Isely branched off to begin his own quest for world government. In 1958 a call was put out to national governments, as well as individual citizens, to send delegates for a World Constitutional Convention. It was with this call that the work of the World Constitution and Parliament Association truly began. The organization was based

Philip and Jelica Isely's wedding at Mount Vernon Country Club, May 6, 2001.

in Colorado and even had the ardent support of Colorado State Senator Neil Bishop since its inception.

Over the next ten years, the organization worked tirelessly to rally support and disseminate the idea of a world constitution. Delegates were summoned and Preparatory Congresses were held. In 1968 the actual drafting of the World Constitution began. By this point, 200 delegates from twenty-seven countries were participating, spurred by the continuing threat of the destruction of mankind. The organization never held a doomsday philosophy; it merely carried on aware of the potential harm that could be inflicted by the weapons that were accumulating across the globe. Inspired and motivated, the movement was well under way.

The first draft of the World Constitution was finished in 1974 and circulated worldwide. Commentary was requested. By 1976 comments had been compiled and integrated into a second draft. This amended version was circulated around the globe as well. By 1977 the World Constitution was debated and parsed, section by section, paragraph by paragraph. The amended document was approved by 138 signers from twenty-five nations spanning

Meeting at the second International Conference of Chief Justices of the World, 2001.

Visiting Republic of Kiribeti, January 2006.

six continents. A call for ratification was put out. The proposed constitution was sent to every nation, as well as the United Nations, in the hopes that some members of national and/or international government would boldly support the movement.

Throughout the 1980s support for the World Constitution and Parliament Association grew exponentially. Meetings continued. The first Provisional World Parliament session convened, adopting five world legislative acts covering issues from world disarmament to world graduate school. The first Provisional District World Court met in Los Angeles, California and began work on the case to outlaw nuclear weapons worldwide.

In the next decade the fourth and fifth sessions of the Provisional World Parliament were held in Portugal and Malta. A Global Ratification and Election Network (GREN) was developed to continue efforts at ratification and the election of delegates from around the globe.

Though the draft of the world constitution has been submitted to all countries, it has been ratified by none. Philip Isely remains steadfast and undaunted. He believes that it will take time for

countries to take the leap. It may very well be lesser developed nations that take the initiative to make the first, crucial steps. Poorer nations seem to have the most to gain. By opening the door to a world government, these nations would be opening the door to greater economic opportunities. From their disadvantaged point of view, any collective government would certainly help improve their condition.

However, there is a real possibility that an open show of support could have a drastically different effect. Sometimes actions have unintended consequences. To step out of conventional bounds of foreign policy could invoke the wrath of the economic super powers and result in economic retribution. It isn't a matter of lack of support or bravery, but the black cloud of dismal fiscal consequences that keep some nations in their place.

Philip Isely sees the whole picture very differently. By creating an entity that could begin to make a significant impact on diminishing violence and propagating disarmament, every nation on the planet has everything to gain. There is resignation, but understanding, in his voice when he remarks that sometimes people elect not to think about dire possibilities because it is easier that way. It is difficult to see danger ahead when your current outlook is rosy.

Philip Isely also notes that a world parliament may be difficult for wealthier nations to warm up to. Any watering down of their autonomy isn't likely to be easily accepted. As one of the most technologically advanced in the field of warfare, the United States is unlikely to embrace disarmament for reasons of retaining military might. This might has kept the United States on its upward trajectory for over 230 years. What would possess the U.S. government to abandon it now, especially with the whole world on high alert from the terrorist threats that have abounded in recent years? This self-perpetuating cycle of fear and violence frustrates Isely.

"The main outlook of the United States is to defend profit-making," said Isely, "not the welfare of people all over the world." This is the natural priority of a capitalistic society. In order for all people of the world to be

After WCPA meeting in Malta, October 2003.

looked after "requires a world government," Philip Isely concludes.

"Maybe it's presumptuous," Philip Isely says. "But what future is there for the world unless our organization succeeds? Our objectives are vital for the survival of the world."

Nonetheless, Philip Isely and his second wife, Jelica, from Macedonia (former Yugoslavia), continue to move forward. There is growing support in India. Libya is set to host a session of the Constitutional Convention. Countries all over the world have hosted

events: Germany, Italy, Malta, United Arab Emirates and Portugal. What started with a few dozen committed individuals has now grown, in various incarnations and through NGOs (non-governmental organizations) to thousands of active participants in about 150 countries.

Philip Isely is a man ahead of his time in many respects, yet he moves forward in his endeavors unfazed. He has a much broader viewpoint than most, seeing not the small picture, but a global scene. In this technologically advanced age, the world is beginning to seem like a smaller place. It is also technical advances in weaponry that shrink our planet further, and put all citizens on equally unstable footing. Philip Isely seeks not to foist his ideals upon anyone, but to educate and encourage responsibility. He merely believes in what he is doing, believes that it will help those around him, and therefore pursues it vigorously. He is hopeful that the message will spread and people will come to see the merits of his arguments. Mr. Isely may be ahead of his time, but his call for humanity and peace should be seen as perfect timing.

The third International Conference of Chief Justices of the World, 2002.

YMCA OF THE ROCKIES

The YMCA of the Rockies is proud to have served families and conferences for 100 years. As a nonprofit religious organization, governed by a volunteer Board of Directors, it is one of more than 2,500 independent Ys that fall under the YMCA of the USA. However, unlike most other facilities, the YMCA of the Rockies' Estes Park Center has cabins and hotel-style lodges, where families and other groups can stay while they experience the wholesome and versatile programming and activities the center has to offer. Caring, honesty, respect, responsibility and faith are the guiding principles by which all programs are designed. With these values as their core, YMCA of the Rockies changes and enhances the lives of nearly 250,000 visitors each year.

Two Colorado YMCA leaders, William E. Sweet and Bruno Hobbs,

The chapel, at sunset.

envisioned establishing a permanent summer encampment in Colorado where YMCA workers could receive training in their profession and be renewed in spirit. In July, 1907 twenty-two YMCA leaders, clergy, laymen and their families gathered in Grand Lake, Colorado to bring the vision to fruition. During five days of Bible study, prayer, discussion of YMCA affairs and recreation, the foundation was laid for the Western Conference of the YMCA. After adjournment, six men and two dogs hiked over the Continental Divide, where they met the other founders in Estes Park to inspect various properties. They decided to rent the Wind River Lodge for the 1908 summer.

With its tranquil setting on the slopes of Emerald Mountain, Wind River Lodge was the perfect location. It was so popular, in fact, that ninety-three men and their families attended the first YMCA training encampment in 1908. Before adjourning, the Board of Directors decided to purchase suitable land in Estes Park before the next

A view of Estes Park Center YMCA.

summer—in spite of the fact that the YMCA's bank balance was $0.45. In April 1909 the group purchased the Wind River Lodge, its outbuildings and 334 acres for $8,500. Building began the next year—on what would become the Estes Park Center campus—with the construction of the Administration Building and a water system as well the relocation of the Wind River Lodge buildings.

In 1912 the corporate name was changed to the "Estes Park Conference of the YMCA." Over the next decade, the Y experienced tremendous growth as the summer training school prospered. It was during these formative years that the foundation was laid for the present mission of serving families, conferences and youth. The YMCA began accommodating the family members of its students as well as other families who were interested in taking advantage of the camp's Christian atmosphere and beautiful natural surroundings. To serve them, the Y initiated recreational programming. As the reputation of the Estes Park Conference spread, national YMCA, YWCA and religious groups asked to hold their conferences on site. These visiting groups availed themselves of the resources offered by the training school and recreational programs. The Estes Park Conference began formally serving youth in 1924 with a kindergarten program—effectively founding the oldest day camping program in the YMCA.

Prosperity continued for the YMCA until the mid-1920s, when the national YMCA deemphasized summer training programs, such as those in Estes Park. After the collapse of the summer school, the Estes Park Conference neared bankruptcy during the Great Depression. Longtime friend and benefactor of the organization, A.A. Hyde, purchased the mortgages, thus saving the Estes Park Conference.

Set adrift without a national YMCA training program, the Estes Park Conference realized that its Christian environment could be shared and expanded with a variety of other conferences: religious, educational and recreational. Finding renewed strength in serving families in need of renewal, peace and recreation, the Y continued on, despite the shortages of World War II. However, it was the baby boom, coupled with post-war prosperity, that truly awakened the Conference. Long-neglected facilities were rehabilitated and new ones constructed. In the early 1950s Walter Ruesch and the Board of Directors transformed the Y from a summer only camp to a year-round facility. As the Estes Park Conference began

The friendly faces of YMCA of the Rockies.

expanding the number and types of conferences it served, new cabins were constructed and family programming was expanded.

In 1965 three men of vision—Dwight Dannen, Wendel Ley and Walter Ruesch—took the Y back to Grand County to establish Snow Mountain Ranch, which opened in 1969. The purchase and development of an additional camp prompted the Y to change its corporate name to the "YMCA of the Rockies." A third site was opened in 1980, when Camp Chief Ouray was acquired from the Denver YMCA. The new camp's multi-generational affiliation with many Colorado families created a rich legacy. Camp Chief Ouray offered youth a traditional YMCA resident camping experience, where teens could participate in a variety of character building and leadership training programs. Today the YMCA of the Rockies owns almost 6,000 acres and operates the two largest YMCA family vacation

and conference centers in the world, with combined guest capacities of 7,700.

The YMCA of the Rockies expends $28 million annually, serving 220,000 guests and 1,800 resident youth campers from all fifty states and many foreign nations. It hosts 2,250 conferences of a spiritual, educational or recreational nature. In addition, more than 25,000 people attend over 800 family reunions. To serve its guests during peak season, the YMCA employees fifty-five volunteers, forty part-time workers and a seasonal staff of 800—from thirty states and forty foreign nations. They are supported by a full-time staff of 170.

For the past century, the YMCA of the Rockies' mission of Christian service has been a guiding light for its members. The organization is truly driven by its mission. By putting "Christian principles into practice through programs, staff and facilities in an environment that builds healthy spirit, mind and body for all," it is eager to continue to serve others for the next 100 years.

Campers gather at the Park in the winter of 2005.

A TIMELINE OF COLORADO'S HISTORY

10500–9000 B.C.
Clovis peoples inhabit Colorado. Their distinctive projectile points are first found at Clovis, New Mexico, then at Dent, Colorado.

9000–8000 B.C.
Folsom peoples inhabit Colorado. Their fluted projectile points are found at Folsom, New Mexico, then at Lindenmeier and Zapata Ranch, Colorado.

A.D. 1–1300
Ancient Puebloans inhabit Mesa Verde area, but move to New Mexico and Arizona during the great drought of 1275-1300.

A.D. 1100–1500
Utes move into Colorado, where many still reside. They are the oldest continuous occupants of the state, where they have two reservations to this day.

1500s–1700s
Apaches occupy southeastern Colorado before being displaced by Utes and Comanches.

1682
Robert de La Salle explores the Mississippi River and claims its drainage for France, including eastern Colorado.

The Ancient Puebloan village at Chimney Rock near Pagosa Springs has been excavated and preserved as the northernmost outpost of the Proto-Puebloan people. Today the National Forest Service offers guided tours of the site, which also features occasional dances by modern day Taos Indians, who claim the site as an ancestral home. Photo by Tom Noel

Whites quickly disposed Colorado's Indians, sometimes building towns before the Indians had left. The elegant Strater Hotel, left, opened in Durango while some Utes were still camped in this southwestern Colorado railroad town. Courtesy, Tom Noel Collection

1700–1860
Comanches occupy southeastern Colorado.

1694
Don Diego de Vargas explores the Upper Rio Grande in Colorado.

1706
Juan de Ulibarrí claims Arkansas River Valley for Spain.

1720
Pedro de Villasur explores Platte River Valley.

1739
Frenchmen Paul and Pierre Mallet, traveling from Illinois to Santa Fe, explore and name the Platte River.

1765–1775
Juan Maria de Rivera explores San Juan Mountains, La Plata Mountains and Gunnison River, prospecting for gold and silver.

1776
Padres Francisco Atanasio Domínguez and Silvestre Vélez de Escalante explore, map and report on southwestern Colorado.

1800
Cheyenne and Arapaho enter Colorado, displacing the Utes and the Comanches on the eastern plains.

1803
President Thomas Jefferson buys Louisiana Territory from Napoleon, Emperor of France, for $15 million, thus doubling the size of the United States. The new territory includes present-day Colorado south of the Arkansas River and east of the mountains.

1806–1807
Zebulon M. Pike explores southeastern Colorado. "The Lost Pathfinder" confuses the headwaters of the South Platte, Red, Arkansas and Rio Grande, but publishes an important report on southeastern Colorado.

1811
The Missouri Fur Company sends trappers to the upper Arkansas River.

1819
The Adams-Onis Treaty sets boundary between New Spain and the United States along the upper Arkansas River.

1820
Major Stephen H. Long explores part of eastern Colorado and concludes that it is the "Great American Desert" and unsuitable for settlement.

1821
Mexico gains its independence from Spain and opens up the Santa Fe Trail to Yankee traders.

1828
Antoine Robidoux establishes Fort Uncompahgre near the junction of the Uncompahgre and Gunnison Rivers (present-day Delta).

1833

William and Charles Bent establish Bent's Fort on the Arkansas River and make it a major commercial hub on the Santa Fe Trail. Anglos, French, Spanish and Native Americans meet at this adobe fort for peaceful trading purposes.

Mexico grants the Conejos Land Grant on the west side of the San Luis Valley to settlers from New Mexico.

1834

Mexico give the *Sangre de Cristo* Grant on the east side of the San Luis Valley to settlers from New Mexico.

1835

Louis Vasquez and Andrew Sublette build Fort Vasquez on the South Platte River as a trading post. It has since been restored as a fur trade museum by the Colorado Historical Society.

1836

Lancaster P. Lupton builds Fort Lupton as a trading post on the South Platte.

1842

El Pueblo, a trading post, is established at the junction of the Arkansas River and Fountain Creek on the current site of Pueblo.

1843

Mexico transfers the Vigil and St. Vrain

Dr. Edwin James, the Long Expedition botanist, admired Colorado wildflowers such as the pin cushion cactus. Courtesy, Tom Noel Collection

Grant of four million acres (present-day Las Animas and Huerfano Counties), where both Hispanics and Anglos settle on this parcel between the Arkansas and the Purgatorie Rivers.

1848

Treaty of Guadalupe Hidalgo transfers southern and western Colorado from Mexico to the United States.

1851

First permanent Hispanic town in Colorado is established at San Luis.

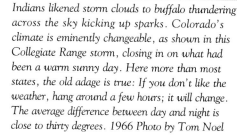

Indians likened storm clouds to buffalo thundering across the sky kicking up sparks. Colorado's climate is eminently changeable, as shown in this Collegiate Range storm, closing in on what had been a warm sunny day. Here more than most states, the old adage is true: If you don't like the weather, hang around a few hours; it will change. The average difference between day and night is close to thirty degrees. 1966 Photo by Tom Noel

1852

Fort Garland (originally Fort Massachusetts) is founded as a U.S. Army base in the San Luis Valley. Once commanded by Kit Carson, it is now restored as a Colorado Historical Society museum.

1853

Captain John W. Gunnison leads a U.S. Army exploring party through central Colorado, along what is now the Gunnison River, before he is killed by Utes.

1857

Our Lady of Guadalupe, the oldest continually operating church in Colorado, is built in Conejos.

1858

The William G. Russell party from Auraria, Georgia find gold in the South Platte near its confluence with Cherry Creek, triggering the great Colorado gold rush. Auraria City is founded on October 30 and, across Cherry Creek, Den-

ver City is founded on November 22.

1859

John H. Gregory finds gold in Gregory Gulch, a mother lode that gives birth to Central City and Black Hawk at either end of this gulch flowing into Clear Creek.

George A. Jackson discovers gold at present day Idaho Springs.

William N. Byers publishes the first issue of the *Rocky Mountain News*, Colorado's first newspaper, on April 23.

1861

Colorado Territory is established, and President Abraham Lincoln appoints William Gilpin the first governor.

1862

Colorado volunteers help defeat a Confederate army invading Colorado at Gloriéta Pass in New Mexico on March 28.

1864

Colonel John M. Chivington's Colorado Volunteer Cavalry massacres an estimated 163 Cheyenne and Arapaho, mostly children, women and old men at Sand Creek on November 29.

Georgetown becomes Colorado's first major silver mining town.

1866

Charles Goodnight pioneers first major Texas cattle drive to Colorado on the Goodnight-Loving Trail.

Miners at the Gold Standard Mine near Cripple Creek. Photo by Harry Buckwalter, courtesy, Colorado Historical Society

Buffalo thrived on the plains and in the mountain valleys of Colorado. Photo by Tom Noel

1867

The Medicine Lodge Treaty removes Cheyenne and Arapahoe from Colorado to Oklahoma and Wyoming reservations.

1868

Nathaniel Hill opens Colorado's first major smelter at Black Hawk to process gold ores.

1869

At the Battle of Summit Springs, the U.S. Army, with scout William F. Cody, defeats the Cheyenne and kills Chief Tall Bull in the last battle on the Colorado plains.

Deer Trail cowboys stage Colorado's first rodeo.

1870

Denver Pacific and Kansas Pacific railroads connect Denver to the national rail network. Railroads give birth to many towns, including Greeley, founded this year by New York City colonists who had been organized by Horace "Go West" Greeley.

1871

William J. Palmer builds the Denver & Rio Grande Railroad and founds Colorado Springs.

1873

Utes sign Brunot Agreement, ceding the San Juan mining region to whites.

1876

Colorado becomes the thirty-eighth state on August 1.

The Atchison, Topeka and Santa Fe Railroad reaches Pueblo.

1877

First students enter University of Colorado.

1878

Leadville, the largest silver city of all, is founded.

1879
Utes at the White River Agency kill Nathan Meeker and others, and attack troops led by Major Thomas Thornburgh.

1882
Ute lands in western Colorado open to white settlement after Ute bands are moved to the Southern Ute and Ute Mountain reservations in the southwest corner of Colorado or to Utah.

1890
Gold discovered at Cripple Creek is the last and greatest of the Colorado gold rushes.

1891
President Benjamin Harrison sets aside the first federal forest reserves (national forests).

Pikes Peak Cog Railway begins operation.

1892
Davis H. Waite, a Populist, governs for two turbulent years of unsuccessful efforts at radical reform.

1893
Women gain the right to vote in Colorado elections.

A depression, triggered by decline in the price of silver, grips much of the state.

1899
Colorado's first sugar beet factory opens in Grand Junction.

American Smelting and Refining Company formed to ultimately monopolize many Colorado—and international—ore processing plants.

1902
Congress passes Newlands Act, signaling the start of federal water projects.

1903–1904
Miners strike at Cripple Creek and elsewhere around Colorado for a minimum wage of three dollars a day and an eight-hour day. Management fights back in violent confrontations that lead to the crushing of the Western Federation of Miners by mine owners and the state militia.

1905
Epitomizing political corruption and chaos, Colorado has three governors in one day.

1906
Mesa Verde National Park is created to preserve and celebrate the culture of pre-

historic Colorado Native Americans, displaying pit house, pueblos and cliff dwellings.

Denver hosts its first National Western Stock Show, celebrating the city and state's emergence as a major ranching hub.

1907
Reformer, Judge Ben Lindsey, establishes America's first Juvenile Courts, aimed at rehabilitating—rather than punishing—youths.

1908
Democratic National Convention meets at Denver's new City Auditorium to nominate William Jennings Bryan for president (July 8–10).

1909
Colorado Highway Commission is established and undertakes to pave and expand the road system for motor vehicles.

1910
Voters approve state constitutional amendment giving citizens power to initiate laws and to amend the constitution by majority vote.

Black agricultural colony of Dearfield founded east of Greeley.

1912
Grand Valley Canal transforms Palisade, Grand Junction and Fruita area with apple, cherry and peach orchards.

1913
The big snow, burying much of Colorado in three to five feet, sets all time record.

1914
State militia intervention in coal miners' strike in southern Colorado triggers Ludlow Massacre (April 20), killing women and children.

The Colorado State Fair, held in Pueblo every summer since 1887, treats visitors to prize-winning specimens of livestock and, as show here, the people who handle them. Attractions include rodeo acts, such as calf roping and trick riding. Courtesy, Denver Public Library

1915
Rocky Mountain National Park is created, straddling the Continental Divide in Boulder, Larimer and Grand Counties.

1916
Colorado begins statewide prohibition of alcohol, which continues until the federal government repeals prohibition in 1933.

Emily Griffith founds Denver's Opportunity School "For All Who Wish to Learn."

Spencer Penrose, owner of Colorado's Spring's Broadmoor Hotel, builds an automobile road to the top of Pikes Peak and sponsors an auto race, the Pikes Peak Hill Climb, which is still held every summer.

1917
William F. "Buffalo Bill" Cody dies in Denver and is buried atop Lookout Mountain.

1918
Influenza epidemic kills nearly 8,000 in Colorado.

Climax Mine north of Leadville begins producing commercial quantities of molybdenum.

1921
Arkansas River flood kills at least 100 people in Pueblo.

1922

Colorado River Compact allocates use of Colorado River water among seven southwestern states.

KLZ in Denver begins broadcasting with the first Colorado commercial radio license.

1924

Clarence Morley, a Klansman, is elected governor as the Ku Klux Klan comes to power in Colorado.

1928

Moffat Railroad Tunnel opens, at a cost of $18 million and twenty-nine fatalities, to give Denver a direct all-weather route under the Continental Divide.

1929

Denver Municipal (later Stapleton) airport opens.

1932

Drought and dust storms began to ravage eastern Colorado.

Central City Opera House reopens with Lillian Gish starring in *Camille*.

1934

Taylor Grazing Act regulates ranchers' use of public lands.

1936

Voters approve state income tax.

1937

Congress authorizes Colorado–Big Thompson water project, which begins bringing Colorado River Water to northeastern Colorado.

1941–1942

World War II facilities established in Colorado include Rocky Mountain Arsenal northeast of Denver, Camp (later Fort) Carson southwest of Colorado Springs, Pueblo Ordnance Depot east of Pueblo, Camp Hale training center for ski troops north of Leadville and Amache internment camp for U.S. citizens of Japanese descent.

1945

Mary Coyle Chase becomes the first Coloradan to win a Pulitzer Prize for her best-selling, long-running play *Harvey* about an amiable alcoholic and his drinking companion, a six-foot-tall rabbit.

1947

Aspen opens Colorado's first commercial ski area.

1948

Uranium prospectors rush to western

Colorado.

1949

The Aspen Music Festival is started, helping to inspire a revival of the old silver mining city.

1952

Colorado's first TV station, KFEL (Channel 7), begins broadcasting in Denver.

1953

Rocky Flats, a facility to make plutonium "triggers" for hydrogen bombs, opens northwest of Denver.

1956

Glenn L. Martin (later Lockheed-Martin) Company constructs factory south of Denver to produce Titan intercontinental ballistic missiles.

1958

U.S. Air Force Academy opens in Colorado Springs.

1960

The Denver Broncos, the state's first major-league sports team, begin playing football.

1962

President John F. Kennedy signs Fryingpan-Arkansas water bill, increasing Colorado water storage and additional diversion of Western Slope water to the east.

Vail ski area opens and later becomes the largest snowboarding and skiing resort in North America.

Hewlett-Packard begins operations in Colorado Springs, helping launch the city as a center for high technology.

Women's Clubs founded libraries in many communities. Among these is the Sarah Platte Decker Branch Library, named for one of Colorado's most active club women. This romantic, cottage-style landmark in South Denver features a cozy fireplace inside as well as literary murals, such as the Pied Piper of Hamlin. Courtesy, Denver Public Library

1965

Rodolfo "Corky" Gonzales founds Crusade for Justice, an aggressive, vocal organization crusading for Hispanic rights.

South Platte River floods on June 16, causing more than $300 million in damage.

Reacting to Urban Renewal Authority demolition of old downtown, Dana Crawford and other pioneer preservationists found Larimer Square, Denver's first historic district

1967

August 1, the day Colorado became a state in 1876, is declared Colorado Day

1972

Coloradans reject the 1976 Winter Olympics in a pioneer pro-environmental, anti-growth election.

1973

Eisenhower Johnson Tunnel is opened underneath the Continental Divide on Interstate 70.

1973–1974

OPEC embargo raises oil prices and causes energy boom in Colorado, lead-

ing to oil shale development in the West and Denver office-building frenzy.
1976
Busing begins in Denver in an attempt to achieve racial desegregation in the public schools.

Big Thompson River floods, killing 145. Auraria Higher Education Center opens in downtown Denver. The campus, shared by the Community College of Denver, Metropolitan State College of Denver and the University of Colorado at Denver, soon becomes the state's largest higher education center with more than 36,000 students.
1977
Denver Broncos reach Super Bowl for the first time.
1978
Denver Center of the Performing Arts opens.
1980
Voters approve a state lottery, which begins operating in 1983 with proceeds to fund open space and parks.
1982
Exxon shuts down its Western Slope oil shale project, triggering a statewide economic downturn and loss of population. Colorado Fuel and Iron shuts down last of its large blast furnaces in Pueblo.
1990
Voters approve casino gambling in Black Hawk, Central City and Cripple Creek. Legal gambling begins in 1991 with taxes on it to support historic preservation statewide.
1992
Voters approve Amendment 2, which bans local laws protecting gays. Colorado faces national protests and boycotts. U.S. Supreme Court rules Amendment 2 unconstitutional in 1996.

Climax Molybdenum Mine north of Leadville closes after having processed 470 million tons of ore, destroying Bartlett Mountain in the process.

Voters approve Taxpayer's Bill of Rights (TABOR) amendment to the state constitution, limiting state and local revenue, leading to heavy cuts in state funding for education, healthcare and transportation.
1993
Colorado Rockies, the state's first major-league baseball team, plays its first home

The awesome foothills campus of the Air Force Academy north of Colorado Springs includes the neo-Gothic metallic spires of the campus chapel. Courtesy, Tom Noel Collection

game in Denver on April 9 and moves into new Coors Field in 1995.

World Youth Day (August 11–16) and Pope John Paul II attract 186,000 to Colorado.
1994
Fourteen firefighters die battling fire on Storm King Mountain near Glenwood Springs.

The Regional Transportation District opens its first electric light rail line, connecting South Broadway, Auraria and Five Points
1995
Denver International Airport opens on the country's largest airport site (55 square miles).

Denver's greatly expanded Central Public Library opens in a spectacular building designed by leading post-modernist architect Michael Graves. The library boasts an especially strong Western History Department.
1996
Colorado Avalanche hockey team wins its first Stanley Cup.

1997
Summit of Eight world leaders meets in Denver June 19–June 22.
1998–1999
Denver Broncos win two consecutive Super Bowl championships.
1999
On April 20, two students murder twelve other students and one teacher at Columbine High School in Jefferson County.

Black Canyon of the Gunnison National Monument becomes Colorado's third national park.
2000
Great Sand Dunes National Park is upgraded to become Colorado's fourth national park. The site is expanded to include the adjacent Baca and Zapata Ranches.

The Regional Transportation District opens its southwest corridor line serving Englewood, Littleton and Highlands Ranch.
2001
Colorado's sixty-fourth county, the City and County of Broomfield, begins operating.
2002
The 137,000-acre Hayman fire, southwest of Denver, and other wildfires destroy hundreds of thousands of acres and kill nine people during a year of severe drought.
2005
Metro Denver voters approve $5 billion expansion of the Regional Transportation District's Light and Commuter Rail lines, adding six new lines to DIA: Louisville and Longmont, Arvada and Wheat Ridge, Lakewood and Golden, Thornton and Northglenn and Westminster and Boulder. Funded by a 1 percent sales tax, this comprehensive scheme is scheduled for completion in 2016.

Brothers John and Ken Salazar become the first Hispanic Coloradans elected to, respectively, the U.S. House and U.S. Senate.
2006
I-25 widening is completed between Denver and Douglas County, along with the Regional Transportation District southeast corridor light rail line to the Denver Tech Center and Park Meadows Shopping Mall.

101 BEST BOOKS ABOUT COLORADO

Abbott, Carl, Stephen J. Leonard & Thomas J. Noel. *Colorado: A History of the Centennial State.* Niwot: University Press of Colorado, 2005 fourth heavily revised edition. xvi + 553p. index. bibliography. endnotes. 125 photos, maps, drawings. biographies. Officials. Statistics and symbols. 6" x 9 1/4" hardback & paperback. $29.95.

This thorough survey offers stimulating interpretations and emphasis on the state's 20th century urbanization, multiculturalism and boosterism.

Afton, Jean, David F. Halaas & Andrew E. Masich. *Cheyenne Dog Soldiers A Ledgerbook History of Coups and Combat.* Introduction by Richard N. Ellis. Niwot: University Press of Colorado and Colorado Historical Society, 1997. xxxii + 400p. index. endnotes. bibliography. 124 color photos. maps. glossary. 3 appendices. $49.95. 11" x 8 1/2" hardback & softback.

Cheyenne warriors painted their military exploits on this captured ledger-book, providing a rare and compelling look at Colorado history from the Indian perspective.

Arps, Louisa Ward, 1901-1986. *Denver in Slices.* Denver, CO: Sage Books, 1959/ 1998 reprint by Ohio Univ. Press, Athens with new Introduction by Thomas J. Noel. xii + 263p. index. endnotes. photos. maps. 6" x 9" $4.50 original hardback, $16.95 paperback reprint.

Delicious slices of Denver's past including the mint, drinking water, City Ditch, Cherry Creek, the South Platte, Tabor ghosts, the Windsor Hotel, the Baron of Montclair, Overland Park, Buffalo Bill, Elitch Gardens and Eugene Field. A delightfully written and diligently researched appetizer.

Babb, Sanora. *An Owl on Every Post: A Personal Recollection of Life on the Plains.* NY: The McCall Pub. Co., 1970/1994 reprint Albuquerque: University of New Mexico Press. 217p. 6" x 8 3/4" hardback/softback reprint.

A lively account of the author's girlhood in early 1900s in a sodhouse, homesteading the "grey desert" of eastern Colorado.

Baca, Vincent C. de, editor. *La Gente: Hispano History and Life in Colorado.* Niwot, CO: University Press of Colorado and the Colorado Historical Society, 1999. xix + 294p. index. bibliography. endnotes. photos. $21.95. 6" x 9" paperback.

Thirteen authors chronicle Hispanic women, art, labor, rug-making, militants, cultural landscapes and other topics. Backus, Harriet Fish. *Tomboy Bride.* Boulder, CO: Pruett Pub. Co., 1969. 273p. Photos. $6.50. 6" x 9" hardback.

The wife of a mining engineer chronicles their cold, lonely, isolated life with warm memories and rich description of the Silvery San Juan.

James H. Baker, ed. LeRoy R. Hafen, associate ed. *History of Colorado.* Denver, CO: State Historical and Natural History Society of Colorado and Linderman Co., 1927. 5 vols. index. footnotes. photos. maps, Vols I, II & III are a topical history, Vols. IV & V are biographical sketches. 6 1/2" x 9 3/4" hardback.

Topically arranged, this magnum opus features fine overview essays on major subjects by leading authorities. Hafen, the first official state historian, complains about co-authoring with the dictatorial and dying Baker, an East High principal who became president of CU in his autobiography, *The Joyous Journey,* which was not always so joyous.

Bauer, William H., James L. Ozment, John H. Willard. *Colorado Post Offices, 1859-1989: A Comprehensive Listing of Post Offices, Stations and Branches.* Golden, CO: Colorado Railroad Museum, 1971; 1990 2nd revised edition. vi + 280p. bibliography. 40 b & w photos. $39.95. 9" x 11 ½" hardback.

Valuable reference guide listing each post office (and its name changes) with its county, dates of establishment and abandonment and very brief remarks. This is a most useful place name aid and best indication of a town's birth and death.

Beebe, Lucius Morris. *Narrow Gauge in the Rockies.* By Lucius Beebe and Charles Clegg. Berkeley, CA: Howell-North, 1958. 224p. b & w and color photos, paintings. maps. 8" x 11 ½ hardback.

This duo steamed around the country tracking down railroadiana in their own private palace car, writing extravagant and colorful rail history full of flair.

Benson, Maxine. *Martha Maxwell: Rocky Mountain Naturalist.* Lincoln: University of Nebraska Press, 1986. xix + 335 p. index. bibliography. notes. appendices. photos. 9" x 5 1/2" hardback.

——. *1001 Colorado Place Names.* Drawings by Robin Richards. Lawrence: University Press of Kansas, 1994. xvii + 237p. index. drawings. 5" x 8 1/2" $25 hardback, $11.95 paperback.

Colorado's former state historian has compiled the best place name guide.

Bird, Isabella Lucy, 1831-1904. *A Lady's Life in the Rocky Mountains.* NY: G.P. Putnam's Sons, 1879-80. xii + 269p. drawings. New ed. pub. by University of Oklahoma Press, Norman, 1960, 1969 with introduction by Daniel Boorstin. (Western Frontier Library, 14). 7 1/4 x 5 3/4" hardback and paperback.

This tiny, eccentric English world traveler left a memorable picture of 1870s Colorado but not a flattering one. "The great braggart city spread out brown and treeless upon a brown and treeless plain," she calls Denver, and the South Platte she found "shriveled into a narrow stream with a shingly bed six times too large for it, and fringed by shriveled cottonwoods."

Bolton, Herbert E. *Pageant in the Wilderness: The Story of the Escalante Expedition to the Interior Basin, 1776 including the Diary and Itinerary of Father Escalante Translated and Annotated.* Salt Lake: Utah Historical Society, 1951. 265p. index. bibliography. footnotes. photos. maps. 8 1/2" x 6" paperback.

Padre Escalante, a Franciscan missionary, produced this first written report on Colorado.

Borland, Harold Glen "Hal", 1900-1978. *Country Editor's Boy.* Philadelphia, PA: J.B. Lippincott Company, 1970, 313p. $5.95. 6" x 8 3/4" hardback.

The Seventh Winter. Philadelphia, PA: J.B. Lippincott & Co., 1960. 256 p. $3.95. 6" x 8 3/4" hardback. *High, Wide and Lonesome.* Philadelphia, PA: J.B. Lippincott & Co., 1956. 251 p. 6" x 8 3/4" hardback.

In this trilogy, a distinguished and prolific writer recalls his boyhood on the plains of Colorado during the early 1900s. Borland, who became a nature writer and editorialist for the *New York Times,* has written two dozen other works, fiction and non fiction, capturing the strange, lonesome beauty of the high plains.

Brettell, Richard B. *Historic Denver: The Architects and the Architecture, 1858-1893.* Denver: Historic Denver, Inc., 1973. xii + 240p. index. bibliography. endnotes. b & w photos. drawings. 9 1/2" x 12 1/2" hardback.

A gorgeously-illustrated, smartly written tribute to the brick and brownstone city now bowing to glass, steel, cement and asphalt. The fine, brief overview of 19th century Denver is followed by a critical look at its leading architects, Frank E. Edbrooke, William Lang, and Robert Roeschlaub.

Brigham, Lillian Rice. *Colorado Travelore, a Pocket Guide: Romance of Its Trails, Railroads, Highways, and Airways*. Denver, CO: Peerless Printing Co., 1938, 1943. xxxii + 447p. index. photos. maps, including foldout and endpaper maps. 5 1/2" x 8" hardback.

Cassells, E. Steve. *The Archaeology of Colorado*. Boulder, CO: Johnson Books, 1983, 1997 revised edition. vi + 325p. bibliography. photos. index.

The best overview and introduction to prehistoric Coloradans.

Caughey, Bruce & Dean Wainstanley. *The Colorado Guide*. Golden, CO: Fulcrum Publishing., 1989; 1997 rev. ed. xxvi + 575p. index. photos. $19.95. 6" x 9" paperback.

The best guide since the 1930s WPA guide provides not only eating, drinking, sleeping, and playing tips but also historical perspective.

Coel, Margaret Speas. *Chief Left Hand: Southern Arapaho*. Norman: University of Oklahoma Press, 1981. xiv + 338 p. index. bibliography. endnotes. photos. maps. notes.

A fascinating, sad look at the Arapaho chief who welcomed palefaces and paid the price at Sand Creek.

————. *Goin' Railroading: A Century on the Colorado High Iron* as told by Sam Speas to Margaret Coel. Niwot: Pruett Pub. Co., 1985, 1998 Niwot: University Press of Colorado paperback reprint, 1998. xiii + 180p. index. bibliography. endnotes. photos. map. 10 ½" x 9 ½" hardback.

Superb railroadiana based on interviews with her father by one of Colorado's rising literary lights.

Coleman, Annie Gilbert. *Ski Style: Sport and Culture in the Rockies*. Lawrence, KS: University Press of Kansas, 2004. Photos, maps, endnotes, bibliography, index. 299 pages. 6" x 9-1/2". $29.95 hardcover.

Colorado: A Guide to the Highest State. Comp. by Colorado workers of the Writers' Program of the Work Projects Administration. NY: Hastings House & Colorado State Planning Commission 1941, 1973/ 1987 paperback reprint by University Press of Kansas, Lawrence

with new introduction by Thomas J. Noel. xxxiii + 511p. index. bibliography. photos. maps. chronology. (American Guide Series).
6" x 9" hardback.

Colorado Atlas & Gazetteer. Yarmouth, ME: Delorme, Inc., 4th edition 1998. 104p. Color maps. $16.95. 16" x 11" paperback.

Colorado, 1870-2000: Historical Landscape Photography by William Henry Jackson, Contemporary Photography by John Fielder, Text by Ed Marston. Foreword by Eric Paddock. Afterword by Roderick Frazier Nash. Englewood, CO: Westcliffe Publishers, Inc., 1999. 224p. b & w and color photos. 12 ½" x 16 ¼" hardback. 2005 sequel.

The best-selling photo book compares Jackson's 19th century Colorado with Fielder's 2000 shots of the same scenes a century later. See also the sequel and full explanation of the photos, Thomas J. Noel & John Fielder, *Colorado, 1870-2000 Revisited*. Englewood, CO: Westcliffe Publishers, Inc., 2001. 319p. photos. index.

Dallas, Sandra. *The Diary of Mattie Spenser*. NY: St. Martin's Press, 1997. 229p. novel. $21.95. 6" x 8 1/2" hardback.

This novel from one of Colorado's literary lights focuses sharply on the lives of frontier women, including domestic violence, adultery and other topics that historians usually avoid.

————. *No More Than Five in a Bed: Colorado Hotels in the Old Days*. Norman, OK: Univ. of Oklahoma Press, 1967. xiv + 208p. index. bibliography. photos. drawings. 6 1/4" x 9 1/4" hardback.

Well illustrated descriptions of 37 early Colorado hotels, resorts, spas and watering spots, many of which are still around.

Danilov, Victor J. *Colorado Museums and Historic Sites: A Colorado Guide Book*. Niwot, CO: University Press of Colorado, 2000. x + 445 p. index. bibliography. photos. appendices. 6" x 9" paperback.

A remarkably comprehensive and useful work.

Dodds, Joanne West. *They All Came To Pueblo: A Social History*. Virginia Beach, VA: The Donning Co., 1994. 216p. index. bibliography. 300 b & w photos. drawings. $34.95. 9" x 11 1/2" hardback.

Dunning, John. *Denver*. N.Y.: Times Books, 1980. 407p.

A lusty historical novel that vividly portrays Denver journalism, politics and

the Ku Klux Klan in the 1920s.

Dyer, John Lewis. *The SnowShoe Itinerant: An Autobiography…*. Drawings by Mrs. Helen H. Chain. Cincinnati, OH: Cranston & Stowe, 1890/ various reprints. 362 pp.

Autobiography of the last and best known of the circuit riders of the Methodist Episcopal Church.

Ellis, Anne. *The Life of an Ordinary Woman*. With an introduction by Lucy Fitch Perkins. Boston: Houghton Mifflin Co., 1929/ 1981 reprint by Univ. of Nebraska Press, Lincoln, NE with introduction by Elliott West. xiii + 301p. photos. 8 1/2" x 5 1/2" hardback.

A lively, candid account of everyday lower class life in mining towns by an extraordinary woman.

Faulkner, Debra Benson. *Touching Tomorrow: The Emily Griffith Story*. Palmer Lake, CO: Filter Press, 2005.. x + 150 pages. Photos, timeline, end-notes, bibliography, index, 9" x 6". $12.95 paperback.

The inspirational story of Colorado's great teacher with a murder mystery surprise ending.

Fay, Abbott. *Ski Tracks in the Rockies: A Century of Colorado Skiing*. Evergreen, CO: Cordillera Press, 1984. 93p. index. bibliography. photos. 10 ½" x 8 ½" paperback.

One of many well written, lively, well researched works by a premier Western Slope historian.

Fell, James Edward, Jr. *Ores to Metals: The Rocky Mountain Smelting Industry*. Lincoln, NE: Univ. of Nebraska Press, 1979. xiii + 341p. index. bibliography. endnotes. photos. figures. maps. $21.50. 6" x 9" hardback.

An important, readable book on the neglected, unromantic, but crucial subject of ore processing, which made paydirt pay off.

Ferril, Thomas Hornsby. *Thomas Hornsby Ferril and the American West*. ed. by Robert C. Baron, Stephen J. Leonard & Thomas J. Noel. Golden, CO: Fulcrum Pub. Co. & Center for the American West, University of Colorado, 1996). x + 166p. bibliography of all Ferril's poetry and prose. photos. 6" x 9" $19.95 paperback & $50 hardback.

Colorado's greatest poet, in nationally acclaimed work, often focused on change in Denver and Colorado. This anthology pulls together his best poetry and prose with commentary from admirers.

Fowler, Gene. *Timber Line: A Story of*

Bonfils and Tammen. N.Y.: Covici, Friede, 1933, many reprints. 480 pp. 6" x 9" hardback.

A gossipy, not always true, account of the adolescence of *The Denver Post,* written with as much zest and a shade more accuracy than the former conman Bonfils and former bartender Tammmen ever mustered for their outrageously sensational (and profitable) newspaper. One of the funniest and best-selling books ever written about Denver.

French, Emily. *Emily: The Diary of A HardWorked Woman.* ed. by Janet Lecompte. Lincoln: Univ. of Nebraska Press, 1987. viii + 199 p. index. endnotes. epilogue. 6 1/4" x 9 1/4" hardback and paperback.

A painfully detailed look at a year in the life of a washerwoman with insight on the life of an ordinary woman, bearing the stigma of a divorce and "working out."

Gehres, Eleanor Mount, Sandra Dallas, Maxine Benson & Stanley Cuba. *The Colorado Book.* Golden, CO: Fulcrum Publishing, 1993. xvii + 414 p. index. bibliography. illus. map. 6 3/4" x 8 3/4" hardback.

The best anthology of the best that has been written about Colorado with brief excerpts from the writings of some 150 explorers, historians, journalists, novelists, poets, and scientists.

Goldberg, Robert Alan. *Hooded Empire: The Ku Klux Klan in Colorado.* Urbana: Univ. of Illinois Press, 1981. xv + 255p. index. bibliography. endnotes. maps. tables. figures. Glossary of Klan Titles and Terms. $14.95.6 1/4" x 9 1/4" hardback.

The best study of the 1920s KKK nightmare comes to some surprising conclusions.

Grinstead, Steve and Ben Fogelberg, ed. *Western Voices: 125 Years of Colorado Writing.* Golden, CO: Fulcrum Publishing, 2004. Photos, endnotes. 396 pages. 6" x 9". $19.95 paperback.

Griswold, Donald L. & Jean Harvey. *History of Leadville & Lake County.* Denver: Colorado Historical Society & University Press of Colorado, 1996. 2 vols. LII + 2374p. index. endnotes. b & w photos. endpaper maps. 11 1/2" x 9" boxed set. See how exhaustive local history can be.

Gulliford, Andrew. *Boomtown Blues: Colorado Oil Shale, 18851985.* Foreword by Richard D. Lamm. Niwot: Univ. Press

of Colorado, 1989. xviii + 302p. index. bibliography. endnotes. photos. drawings. maps. $19.95. 9 1/4" x 6 1/2" hardback.

A good updating of Colorado's boom and bust story making admirable use of oral history.

Hafen, LeRoy Reuben. *Colorado and Its People: A Narrative and Topical History of the Centennial State.* NY: Lewis Historical Pub. Co., 1948. 4 vols. index. footnotes. photos. drawings. charts. endpaper maps. 8" x 11" hardback.

With topical essays by noted authorities, this is still the most detailed and documented state history.

Halaas, David Fridtjof. *Fairmount & Historic Colorado.* With an introduction by Robert G. Athearn. Denver, CO: Fairmount Cemetery Association, 1976. 104p. bibliography. photos. appendices of selected pioneers & public officials buried at Fairmount or Riverside. 9" x 11 1/2" paperback and hardback.

Dr. Halaas, the former Colorado State Historian, has made this potentially morbid tale an engrossing history not only of Fairmount, but of other early Denver boneyards.

———. and Andrew E. Masich. *Halfbreed: The Remarkable True Story of George Bent: Caught Between the Worlds of the Indian and the White Man.* Cambridge, MA: Da Capo Press, 2004. Photos, maps, endnotes, bibliography, index. xv + 458 pages. 6" x 9". $30 hardcover.

Hall, Frank, 1836-1917. *History of the State of Colorado, Embracing Accounts of the Pre-Historic Races and Their Remains; the Earliest Spanish, French and American Exploration...the Development of Cities and Towns, with the Various Phases of Industrial and Political Transition, from 1858 to 1890.* Chicago, IL: Blakely Print. Co., 1889-1895. 4 vols. index. drawings. Vol. 4 pub. in a 2nd ed. by Blakely Print., Co., 1897? 2nd ed. of vol. 4 includes 13 new chapters by J.G. Brown, covering Colorado history from 1890 to 1987. 8" x 10 1/2" hardback.

Near-definitive early history by Judge Hall, an active participant.

Haruf, Kent. *Plainsong.* New York: Alfred A. Knopf, 1999. 301 p. $24. novel. 6 1/2" x 9 3/4" hardback.

One of the best-selling and best novels of life on the Colorado high plains.

Haywood, William Dudley, 1869-1928. *Bill Haywood's Book: The Autobiography of William D. Haywood.* NY: International

Publishers, 1929, 1969. 368 p. appendices. photos. 9" x 6" hardback and softback.

Uproarious autobiography of the one-eyed, heavy drinking socialist union organizer who used to terrorize the Oxford Hotel bar and the Mining Exchange Building before he was deported to the Soviet Union in 1919. Big Bill was the star promoter of The Western Federation of Miners and the Industrial Workers of the World (the IWW or Wobblies).

Hoig, Stanley Warlick. *The Sand Creek Massacre.* Norman: University of Oklahoma Press, 1958, 1961. xiii + 217p. index. bibliography. appendix. footnotes. photos. drawings. maps. 7 1/2" x 4 3/4" paperback.

Perhaps the best book so far of two dozen works on this controversial tragedy.

Hosokawa, William. *Thunder in the Rockies: The Incredible Denver Post.* NY: William Morrow and Co., 1976. 447p. index. sources. photos. $12.95. 7" x 9 3/4" hardback.

A candid, insider's story of the paper that has done so much to shape 20th century Denver. A sequel and reliable antidote to Gene Fowler's *Timber Line.*

Hughes, Johnson Donald. *American Indians in Colorado.* Boulder, CO: Pruett Pub. Co., 1977. viii + 143p. index. bibliography. endnotes. photos. maps. (Colorado Ethnic History Series; no. 1). 5 1/2" x 8 1/2" paperback.

Hyde, George E. *Life of George Bent: Written from His letters by George E. Hyde.* Ed. by Savoie Lottinville, Norman: University of Oklahoma Press, 1968. xxv + 389p. index. bibliography. footnotes. photos. drawings. maps. 6 1/2" x 9 1/4" hardback.

Indian history by the sons of William Bent and Owl Women, who chose to live—and fight—with his mother's folk, the Southern Cheyenne.

Iversen, Kristen. Foreword by Muffet Laurie Brown. *Molly Brown: Unraveling the Myth.* Boulder: Johnson Books, 1999. xxv + 294 p. index. bibliography. endnotes. photos. $18 paperback 6 x 9."

A spirited attempt to replace the comical social climber with a mythical lioness with charitable and feminist inclinations.

Jameson, Elizabeth. *All that Glitters: Class, Conflict and Community in Cripple Creek.* Urbana: Univ. of Illinois Press, 1998. xii + 367p. index. bibliography.

endnotes. photos. maps. charts. $23.95. 6" x 9" paperback.

A good example of the new western history written from the bottom up.

Kelsey, Harry E., Jr., 1929- . *Frontier Capitalist: The Life of John Evans.* Boulder, CO: Colorado Historical Society & Pruett Pub. Co., 1969. xiv + 371 p. index. bibliography. endnotes. photos. 9 1/4" x 6 1/4" hardback.

The best biography of the key man in 19th-century Colorado.

Langdon, Emma Florence, 1874-19??. *The Cripple Creek Strike: A History of Industrial Wars in Colorado, 1903-4-5: Being a Complete and Concise History of the Efforts of Organized Capital to Crush Unionism.* Denver, CO: Great Western Pub. Co., 1903-4-5. 596p. photos. cartoons. drawings. appendices. 6" x 8" hardback.

First hand account from the young journalist who dared defy the state militia and stick up for striking miners.

Lavender, David Sievert, 1910- . *Bent's Fort.* Garden City, NY: Doubleday, 1954, 1961/ 1968 reprint by P. Smith, Gloucester, MA. 450p. index. endnotes. endpaper maps. $5.50. 8 1/2" x 6" hardback.

Lecompte, Janet. *Pueblo, Hardscrabble, Greenhorn: The Upper Arkansas, 1832-1856.* Norman: University of Oklahoma Press, 1978. 320p. illus. maps, signed, 6" x 9 1/4" hardback.

Some of the earliest white/Hispanic communities explored by one of the most through and graceful historians.

Leonard, Stephen John, 1941- .*Trials and Triumphs: A Colorado Portrait of the Great Depression, with FSA Photographs.* Niwot: University Press of Colorado, 1993. xi + 313p. index. bibliography. photos by Russell Lee, Beaumont Newhall, Marion Post, Harry Rhodes, Arthur Rothstein, John Vachon and others. 8 3/4" x 11 1/2" hardback. hardback. With

With telling anecdotes and fine wit, Prof. Leonard recaptures the defining decade in 20th-century Colorado.

————. 1941- & Thomas J. Noel, 1945- . *Denver: From Mining Camp to Metropolis.* Niwot: University Press of Colorado, 1990/ 1994 paperback edition. xiv + 544 pp. index. bibliography. endnotes. photos. drawings. maps. appendices.

The most comprehensive history with separate chapters on the suburban counties, automobilization and aviation. Over two-thirds of the book is devoted

to the 20th century metropolis.

Lindsey, Benjamin Barr, 1869-1943, and Harvey J. O'Higgins. *The Beast.* NY: Doubleday, Page & Co., 1910. 1970 edition by University of Washington Press. xxvi + 340 p. photos. 8" x 5 1/2" hardback.

Chilling exposé by the celebrated Juvenile Court judge and muckraking reformer who blackens Denver's power elite: Evans, Moffat, Hughes, Cheesman, and sparing not even the clergy—Buchtel. The trail of the Beast in Denver led, according to the Judge, "step by step, from the dives to the police board, from the police board to the lower courts, from the courts to the political leaders to the corporation magnates who ruled all. The trail leads from the offices of the corporations to the doors of the Capitol, it ascends the steps of the State House; it enters the sacred precinct of the Supreme Court itself." A fast cure for any nostalgic soul hungry for the good old days when politicians were supposedly honest and democracy supposedly pure.

Mangan, Terry William. *Colorado on Glass: Colorado's First Half Century as Seen by the Camera.* With a Directory of Early Colorado Photographers by Opal Murray Harber. Denver, CO: Sundance Ltd, 1975. x + 406 p. index. bibliography. Directory of photographers. b & w photos. drawings. 9" x 11" hardback.

A crackerjack collection of photographs with biographical sketches of the men and women who took them.

Michener, James A., 1907-1997. *Centennial.* N.Y.: Random House, 1974. many editions. x + 909p. endpaper maps. 6" x 8 1/2" hardback.

This historical novel provides a lively overview of Colorado prehistory and history. A broad survey of Colorado from prehistoric times to 1976, it is the all time best-selling book on Colorado, a fairly comprehensive, well researched history of the South Platte Valley of northeastern Colorado in the guise of a novel. Michener has chapters on Indians, trappers, miners, cowboys, sugar beets and Hispanos.

McGovern, George S., 1922- & Leonard F. Guttridge. *The Great Coalfield War.* Boston, MA: Houghton Mifflin, 1972/ 1996 paperback reprint by Univ. Press of Colorado, Boulder. xii + 383p. index. bibliography. photos. maps. endpaper maps. $8.95. 6 1/2" x 9 1/2" hardback.

The 1914 Ludlow Massacre in South-

ern Colorado was the deadliest confrontation in the history of the American labor movement. Based on Senator McGovern's Ph.D. dissertation at Northwestern University, this is the best overview of a still controversial, much written about conflict.

McManus, Carol Crawford. *Ida: Her Labor of Love.* Ouray, CO: Western Reflections, 1999. 283p. photos. 6" x 8 1/4" paperback.

One of the best accounts from a pioneer woman of early day life on the western slope. Ida spent her life consoling the sick, tending the poor, comforting the dying and trying to get her husband to settle down.

Mills, Enos A., 1870-1922. *In Beaver World.* Boston, MA: Houghton Mifflin, 1913, 1917, 1924. 228 p. bibliography. index. b & w photos by the author. 5 1/2 x 8" hardback; 1990 reprint by Univ. of Nebraska Press, Lincoln, with introduction and notes by James H. Pickering, xxxvii + 233 p. index. bibliography.

————. *The Grizzly: Our Greatest Wild Animal.* Boston, MA: Houghton Mifflin, 1919. 288p. index. b & w photos. drawings. 5 1/2" x 8" hardback.

————. *Bird Memories of the Rockies.* Boston, MA: Houghton Mifflin, 1931. 288p. index. b & w photos. 5 1/2" x 8" hardback

————. *The Rocky Mountain National Park.* Boston, MA: Houghton Mifflin, 1917, 1924 memorial edition. 239 p., photos, 5 1/2 x 8 1/2 hardback

————. *The Rocky Mountain Wonderland.* Boston: Houghton Mifflin, 1915. xiii + 363p. index. map. photos. 5 1/2 x 8 1/2 hardback; 1991 reprint Univ. of Nebraska Press, Lincoln, with introduction and notes by James H. Pickering, iii + 386 p. bibliography.

This is a sampling of the two dozen books by Enos Mills (18701922), the pioneer—and still the most important—conservationist of Colorado. He settled near Longs Peak as a boy, climbed it hundreds of times, rode avalanches, fathered Rocky Mountain National Park, and instigated and led the crusade to preserve the Colorado wilderness. Mills spent weeks at a time even in winter roaming the Colorado high country alone, then recording his experiences in his numerous articles and books. For an objective biography of this difficult and controversial hero,see Alexander Drummond, *Enos Mills: Citi-*

zen of Nature (Niwot: Univ. Press of Colorado, 1995) 431 p., index endnotes, illus).

Moody, Ralph. *Little Britches: Father and I Were Ranchers*. NY: W. W. Norton & Company Inc. 1950. 260p. drawings by Edward Shenton. 9" x 6" hardbound.

Classic account of growing up on a Colorado ranch.

Noel, Thomas J. *Buildings of Colorado*. NY: Oxford University Press, 1997. xvii + 669p. index. bibliography. photos. drawings. maps. (Society of Architectural Historians Buildings of the United States) 5" x 9" hardback.

The first detailed survey of the notable prehistoric, historic and contemporary structures in each of Colorado's 63 counties.

———. Colorado: *A Liquid History & Tavern Guide to the Highest State*. Golden, CO: Fulcrum Pub. Co., 1999. xviii + 254p. index. bibliography. photos. drawings. map. $18.95. 7" x 9" paperback.

———. Paul F. Mahoney, & Richard E. Stevens. *Historical Atlas of Colorado*. Norman: University of Oklahoma Press, 1993, 2000 revised paperback edition. ix + 160p. index. bibliography. maps. 11" x 14" hardback & paperback.

Surveys in maps and one-page chapters major developments in Colorado, from Indian battlegrounds to historic hospitable landmarks, from transportation systems to literary landmarks.

———. *Riding High: Colorado Ranchers & The First 100 Years of the National Western Stock Show*. Golden: Fulcrum Publishing Co, 2005. xxi + 318 p. index. bibliography. appendices. maps. 350 photos and drawings. 9 x 12 hardback $50. paperback $32.

Norgren, Barbara S. & Thomas J. Noel, Thomas. *Denver: The City Beautiful & Its Architects, 1893-1941*. Denver, CO: Historic Denver, Inc., 1987, 1993 paperback reprint. vii + 248 p. index. bibliography. photos. drawings. maps. glossary of architectural terms. Biographical sketches of architects. 12 1/2" x 9 3/4" hardback and paperback.

Includes discussions of styles common in Colorado, building types and biographical sketches of leading Colorado architects.

Nossaman, Allen. *Many More Mountains: Volume 1: Silverton's Roots*. Denver: Sundance Books, 1989. 352 p. index. footnotes. bibliography. color and b & w photos. maps. tables. signed. 9" x 11" hardback.

———. *Many More Mountains: Volume 2: Ruts into Silverton*. Denver: Sundance Books, 1993. 352 p. index. footnotes. bibliography. color and b & w photos. maps. tables. signed. 9" x 11" hardback.

———. *Many More Mountains: Volume 3: Rails into Silverton*. Denver: Sundance Books, 1998. 352 p. index. footnotes. bib. color and b & w photos. maps. tables. 9" x 11" hardback.

Nossaman, a CU-Boulder grad and editor of the *Colorado Daily*, resembles Horace Greeley in several ways, including the wire rim spectacles and beard long enough to hide mice in. As long-time editor of the *Silverton Standard and Miner*, he championed historic preservation and heritage tourism as a tonic Colorado's least populous, most isolated county. His eloquence and fairness led townsfolk to select him as the only non-lawyer municipal judge in the state. This is an exhaustive history of Silverton and San Juan County, once mineral rich but now so small and poor it can't sustain a single attorney.

Osterwald, Doris B., 1921- .*Cinders & Smoke: A Mile by Mile Guide for the Durango and Silverton Narrow Gauge Trip*. Lakewood, CO: Western Guideways, 1965. 2001 8th edition, 24th printing. 102 p. photos. maps. drawings. signed. 6" x 9" paperback.

This best-seller is a model guide, complete with history, archaeology, geology and botany as well as railroadiana galore.

Papanikolas, Zeese. *Buried Unsung: Louis Tikas and the Ludlow Massacre*. Foreword by Wallace Stegner. Salt Lake City, UT: Univ. of Utah Press, 1982. xix + 331p. index. bibliography. endnotes. photos. maps. 6 1/2" x 9 1/2" hardback.

A beautifully written attempt to reconstruct the life of the Greek labor organizer murdered by Colorado authorities at Ludlow.

Pyle, Robert Michael. *The Thunder Tree: Lessons from an Urban Wildlife*. N.Y.: Houghton Mifflin Co, 1993. xix + 220p. sources. map. $19.95. 5 3/4" x 8 1/2" hardback.

Eloquent reminiscences of an ecologist who found the High Line Canal a great escape from the proliferating suburbs of Aurora, Colorado's largest city in terms of square miles and third largest in terms of population.

Perkin, Robert L., 1914-1978. *The First Years: An Informal History of Denver and the Rocky Mountain News, 1859–1959*.

Foreword by Gene Fowler. N.Y.: Doubleday, 1959. 624 p. index. bibliography. footnotes. photos. $5.95. 6 1/2" x 9 1/2" hardback.

This witty, highly readable account of the *Rocky Mountain Snooze* and Denver is a splendid complement to the less reliable *Timber Line* by Gene Fowler, who wrote the introduction for this treasure chest of knowledge and trivia.

Robertson, Janet. *The Magnificent Mountain Women: Adventures in the Colorado Rockies*. Lincoln, NE: Univ. of Nebraska Press, 1990. xxi + 220p. index. endnotes. sources. chronology. glossary. map. photos. $21.95. 9 1/4" x 6 1/4" hardback.

Rockwell, Wilson. *The Utes: A Forgotten People*. Denver, CO: Sage Books, 1956; reprint Ouray, CO: Western Reflections, 1998. 307p. index. bibliography. appendix. footnotes. 53 photos. drawings. $19.95. 9" x 6" paperback.

Rockwell, a western slope rancher and legislator, writes well of a land and a tribe he knows well.

Secrest, Luther Clark, 1937- . *Hell's Belles: Denver's Brides of the Multitudes with attention to Various Gamblers, Scoundrels, and Mountebanks and a Biography of Sam Howe, Frontier Lawman*. Aurora, CO: Hindsight Historical Publications, 1996. xx + 348p. index. bibliography. photos. drawings. maps. appendices. $80 limited hardcover edition of 200. $32.95 8 1/2" x 11" softcover.

Secrest, a former Channel Nine anchorman, *Denver Post* media columnist, and longtime editor of *Colorado Heritage*, offers the most tenacious and titillating examination of Colorado's Sisters of Perpetual Indulgence.

Shikes, Robert H., M.D., *Rocky Mountain Medicine: Doctors, Drugs and Disease in Early Colorado*. Boulder, CO: Johnson Pub. Co., 1986. x + 261p. index. bibliography. endnotes. photos. $34.95. 9 1/2" x 12 1/2" hardback.

Simmons, Virginia McConnell. *The San Luis Valley: Land of the Six-Armed Cross*. Boulder, CO: Pruett Pub. Co., 1979. 2nd ed., 1999. 6" x 9" paperback reprint by Niwot: University Press of Colorado, 366 p. index. bibliography. endnotes. photos. 9" x 11 1/2" hardback.

Best account of the south central Colorado Valley where Spanish surnamed people first settled along the Rio Grande.

Simonin, Louis L., 1830-1886. *The Rocky Mountain West in 1867*. Translated and annotated from the French by Wilson O. Clough from *Le grand-oeust des Etats-Unis*. Lincoln: University of Nebraska, 1966. xiv + 170p. index. footnotes. $5.50. 6 1/4" x 9 1/4" hardback.

A look at early Colorado through the letters of a young, witty French mining engineer who was as fascinated by pioneer society as he was by the minerals.

Smiley, Jerome Constant, 1852-1924. *History of Denver, with Outlines of the Earlier History of the Rocky Mountain Country*. Denver, CO: Denver Times, Times-Sun Pub. Co., 1901. 978p. photos. drawings. maps. Limited edition of 850 copies published by J.H. Williamson, Denver, 1903; reprint by Unigraphic, Evansville, IN, 1971 with index by Robert L. Perkin.

Centuries from now Smiley will probably still be the definitive and the longestwinded biographer of 19th century Denver. A booster history written with amazing grace, wit, and insight.

Smith, Duane Allan, 1937- . *Horace Tabor: His Life and the Legend*. Boulder, CO: Colorado Associated University Press, 1973/1990 reprint by Univ. Press of Colorado, Boulder. xiv + 396 p. index. bibliography. endnotes. map. photos. 8 3/4 x 5 3/4" hardback.

Tabor's top biographer makes a heroic effort to unravel the mythical silver tycoon.

Sprague, Marshall, 1909-1994. *Money Mountain: The Story of Cripple Creek Gold*. Boston, MA: Little, Brown and Co., 1953, numerous editions. xx + 342p. index. chapter notes. bibliography. photos. maps. 6" x 9" hardback.

Liveliest account so far of "the World's Greatest Gold Camp."

——. 1909-1994. *Newport in the Rockies: The Life and Good Times of Colorado Springs*. Denver, CO: Sage Books, 1961, 1971/1987 revised edition by Swallow Press/University of Oklahoma Press?, 1987. xix + 370p. index. endnotes. bibliography. photos. endpaper maps. $5.75. 6" x 9" hardback.

An insider's witty, well-written account of the personalities and institutions that shaped Colorado's second largest city.

Stegner, Wallace. *Angle of Repose*. Garden City, NY: Doubleday & Co., 1971. 569p. 6 1/2" x 8 1/2" hardback.

This 1971 Pulitzer-Prize winning novel explores America's mining frontiers from one family's perspective, setting one man's obsession with mining against his wife's yearnings for the cultural opportunities she left in the East.

Steinel, Alvin T., 1878-19?? *History of Agriculture in Colorado, 1858-1926*. Fort Collins, CO: The State Agricultural College, 1926. 659 p. index. photos. charts. 9 1/2 x 6 /2 hardback.

This plodding but definitive work awaits an update.

Suggs, George G., Jr. *Colorado's War on Militant Unionism: James H. Peabody and the Western Federation of Miners*. Detroit, MI: Wayne State Univ. Press, 1972. 242p. index. bibliography. endnotes. 11 photos. $14.95. 6 1/2" x 9 1/2" hardback.

Taylor, Bayard, 1825-1878. *Colorado: A Summer Trip*. NY: G. P. Putnam & Son, 1867/ 1989 reprint Univ. Press of Colorado. 185 p.

A leading travel writer of the 1860s produced a positive, detailed look at Colorado, discrediting "The Great American Desert" in the process.

Ubbelohde, Carl W., Maxine Benson and Duane A. Smith. *A Colorado History*. Boulder, CO: Pruett Press, 1965. First edition by Ubbelohde, frequent revised editions with Benson & Smith. xiii + 421p. index. suggested reading. photos. maps. appendices. chronology. 5 1/2" x 8 1/2" hardback and paperback.

Varnell, Jeanne. *Women of Consequence: The Colorado Women's Hall of Fame*. Boulder, CO: Johnson Books, 1999. 321 p. index. bibliography. photos. 6" x 9" paperback.

West, Elliott, 1945-.*The Contested Plains: Indians, Goldseekers and the Rush to Colorado*. Topeka: University Press of Kansas, 1998, 2000 paperback reprint. xxiv + 442 p. index. bibliography. endnotes. photos. drawings. maps. $34.95. 6 1/2" x 9 1/2" hardback.

A major re-interpretation, eloquently written by one of the best and brightest Western historians.

Whiteside, James. *Colorado: A Sports History*. Niwot: Univ. Press of Colorado, 1999. xvi + 494p. index. endnotes. bib. photos. 6 1/4" x 9" hardback.

Wilkins, Tivis E. *Colorado Railroads: Chronological Development*. Boulder, CO: Pruett Pub. Co., 1974. 309p. photos. maps. 9" x 11½" hardback.

A most useful reference guide to the building and abandonments of some 100 Colorado railroads arranged by year. List the miles of track involved, and brief, basic information.

Wolle, Muriel Sibell, 1898-1977. *Stampede to Timberline: The Ghost Towns and Mining Camps of Colorado*. Boulder, CO: 1949. 1st ed., Rev. ed. pub. by Sage Books, Denver, 1962, many more editions. 337p. index. glossary of mining terms. drawings and maps by the author. 8" x 10 1/2" hardback.

The first and still the best of Colorado mining ghost town guides is enriched by the author's paintings of ramshackle ruins. A professor of art at the University of Colorado, she began painting and writing up ghost towns in the 1920s when many of them were still lively.

Wyckoff, William. *Creating Colorado: The Making of a Western American Landscape, 1860-1940*. New Haven, CN: Yale University Press, 1999. xiv + 336p. index. endnotes. bibliography. photos. maps. 6 1/2" x 10" hardback.

Wynar, Bohdan S. *Colorado Bibliography*. Littleton, CO: Libraries Unlimited, 1980. 565p. index. 7 1/4" x 10 1/4" hardback.

Chapters on history, Indians, geography, natural resources, flora and fauna, economic conditions, mining, agriculture, transportation, communication, social environment, politics, government, education, literature, the arts, health, medicine, recreation, sports, and religion listing 9,182 books and booklets "of permanent and scholarly value."

INDEX